Lecture Notes in Computer Science 2823

Edited by G. Goos, J. Hartmanis, and J. van Leeuwen

Springer

Berlin
Heidelberg
New York
Hong Kong
London
Milan
Paris
Tokyo

Amos Omondi   Stanislav Sedukhin (Eds.)

Advances in Computer Systems Architecture

8th Asia-Pacific Conference, ACSAC 2003
Aizu-Wakamatsu, Japan, September 23-26, 2003
Proceedings

Springer

Series Editors

Gerhard Goos, Karlsruhe University, Germany
Juris Hartmanis, Cornell University, NY, USA
Jan van Leeuwen, Utrecht University, The Netherlands

Volume Editors

Amos Omondi
Flinders University
School of Informatics and Engineering
Bedford Park, SA 5042, Australia
E-mail: amos@infoeng.flinders.edu.au

Stanislav Sedukhin
The University of Aizu
Aizu-Wakamatsu City, Fukushima 965-8580, Japan
E-mail: sedukhin@u-aizu.ac.jp

Cataloging-in-Publication Data applied for

A catalog record for this book is available from the Library of Congress

Bibliographic information published by Die Deutsche Bibliothek
Die Deutsche Bibliothek lists this publication in the Deutsche Nationalbibliografie;
detailed bibliographic data is available in the Internet at <http://dnb.ddb.de>.

CR Subject Classification (1998): B.2, B.4, B.5, C.2, C.1, D.4

ISSN 0302-9743
ISBN 3-540-20122-X Springer-Verlag Berlin Heidelberg New York

Springer-Verlag Berlin Heidelberg New York
a member of BertelsmannSpringer Science+Business Media GmbH

http://www.springer.de

© Springer-Verlag Berlin Heidelberg 2003
Printed in Germany

Typesetting: Camera-ready by author, data conversion by Steingräber Satztechnik GmbH
Printed on acid-free paper   SPIN 10953617   06/3142   5 4 3 2 1 0

Preface

This conference marked the first time that the Asia-Pacific Computer Systems Architecture Conference was held outside Australasia (i.e. Australia and New Zealand), and was, we hope, the start of what will be a regular event. The conference started in 1992 as a workshop for computer architects in Australia and subsequently developed into a full-fledged conference covering Australasia. Two additional major changes led to the present conference. The first was a change from "computer architecture" to "computer systems architecture", a change that recognized the importance and close relationship to computer architecture of certain levels of software (e.g. operating systems and compilers) and of other areas (e.g. computer networks). The second change, which reflected the increasing number of papers being submitted from Asia, was the replacement of "Australasia" with "Asia-Pacific". This year's event was therefore particularly significant, in that it marked the beginning of a truly "Asia-Pacific" conference. It is intended that in the future the conference venue will alternate between Asia and Australia/New Zealand and, although still small, we hope that in time the conference will develop into a major one that represents Asia to the same extent as existing major computer-architecture conferences in North America and Europe represent those regions.

This year's conference attracted 39 submissions from all over the world – Japan, Australia, the United Kingdom, Germany, South Africa, Egypt, Canada, China, Russia, Czech Republic, India, The Netherlands, Sweden, the USA, and Taiwan – some of these countries were new to the conference. Most of the submissions were of a high quality, but various constraints limited the number that could be accepted for presentation. After a review process, in which each paper was refereed by at least 3 people (including many outside the program committee), we finally selected the 23 papers that are included in this volume. In addition to these "regular submissions", there are a further eight papers that cover "invited talks"; these contributions also represent a new aspect of the conference.

Past Asia-Pacific Computer Systems Architecture Conferences have always been part of the Australasia Computer Science Week, a group of conferences held at the same time and at the same place, and this has always kept the financial and organizational burden low. This year therefore presented new challenges, and we are very grateful to our sponsors, the University of Aizu and the Kayamori Foundation of Information Science, whose generous support made it possible for us to successfully meet these challenges. We also acknowledge our debt to the authors who submitted papers, the referees, the members of the program committee, and the others members of the executive committee.

September 2003   Amos Omondi
                                                             Stanislav Sedukhin

Organization

The 8th ACSAC 2003 international conference was organized by the University of Aizu, Aizu-Wakamatsu City, Fukushima, 965-8580, Japan.

Executive Committee

Honorary Chair: Tetsuhiko Ikegami (University of Aizu, Japan)
Program Chairs: Amos Omondi (Flinders University, Australia)
                                Stanislav G. Sedukhin (University of Aizu, Japan)
Publication Coordinator: Subhash Bhalla (University of Aizu, Japan)
Local Organization: Stanislav G. Sedukhin (University of Aizu, Japan)
                                Kenichi Kuroda (University of Aizu, Japan)
                                Miho Nanaumi

Program Committee

David Abramson	Monash University, Australia
Lars Bengtsson	Chalmers University, Sweden
R. Govindarajan	Indian Institute of Science, India
Ian Gibson	Canon Research, Australia
Bernard Gunther	Motorola Australia Software Centre, Australia
Gernot Heiser	University of New South Wales, Australia
Chris Jesshope	University of Hull, UK
David Koch	University of Newcastle, Australia
Kenichi Kuroda	University of Aizu, Japan
Feipei Lai	National Taiwan University, Taiwan
Robert Lang	Intensys, USA
John Morris	University of Western Australia, Australia
Tadao Nakamura	Tohoku University, Japan
Yukihiro Nakamura	Kyoto University, Japan
Ronald Pose	Monash University, Australia
A.P. Preethy	Georgia State University, USA
Benjamin Premkumar	Nanyang Technological University, Singapore
Masatoshi Shima	University of Aizu, Japan
Naofumi Takagi	Nagoya University, Japan
Tay Teng Tiow	National University of Singapore, Singapore
Theo Ungerer	Ulm University, Germany
Jingling Xue	University of New South Wales, Australia
Rumi Zahir	Intel, USA

List of Reviewers

Ben Abderazek	The University of Electro-Communications, Japan
Lars Bengtsson	Chalmers University of Technology, Sweden

Annamalai Benjamin P.	Nanyang Technological University, Singapore
Jayanta Biswas	Indian Institute of Science, Bangalor, India
Anu G. Bourgeois	Georgia State University, USA
Doug Burger	University of Texas, Austin, USA
Manuel Chakravarty	University of New South Wales, Australia
Kevin Elphinstone	University of New South Wales, Australia
Peter Folkesson	Chalmers University of Technology, Sweden
Bernard K. Gunther	Motorola Australia Pty. Ltd.
Yuanqing Guo	University of Twente, The Netherlands
Gernot Heiser	University of New South Wales, Australia
Shyh-Ming Huang	National Sun Yat-Sen University, Taiwan
Koji Inoue	Fukuoka University, Japan
Jonas Jalminger	Chalmers University of Technology, Sweden
Chris Jesshope	University of Hull, UK
Junji Kitamichi	University of Aizu, Japan
Victor V. Korneev	Research and Development Institute "Kvant", Russia
Edmund Lai	Nanyang Technological University, Singapore
Feipei Lai	National Taiwan University, Taiwan
Thomas Lundqvist	Chalmers University of Technology, Sweden
Nagi Mekhiel	Ryerson University, Canada
John Morris	University of Western Australia, Australia
Vasily Moshnyaga	Fukuoka University, Japan
Tadao Nakamura	Tohoku University, Japan
Kiyoshi Oguri	Nagasaki University, Japan
Amos Omondi	Flinders University, Australia
Ronald Pose	Monash University, Australia
Daniel Potts	University of New South Wales, Australia
Vinod Prasad	Nanyang Technological University, Singapore
Damu Radhakrishnan	State University of New York, New Paltz, USA
Govindarajan Ramasswamy	Indian Institute of Science, India
Pradeep Rao H.	Indian Institute of Science, Bangalor, India
Emmanuel Sabu	Nanyang Technological University, Singapore
Mostafa I. Soliman	University of Aizu, Japan
Chris Szmajda	University of New South Wales, Australia
Naofumi Takagi	Nagoya University, Japan
Shigeyuki Takano	University of Aizu , Japan
Matthew Taylor	Motorola Australia Pty. Ltd.
Georgios Theodoropoulos	University of Birmingham, UK
Tay Teng Tiow	National University of Singapore, Singapore
Kun-Lin Tsai	National Taiwan University, Taiwan
Harvey Tuch	University of New South Wales, Australia
Pavel Tvrdik	Czech Technical University, Czech Republic
Fredrik Warg	Chalmers University of Technology, Sweden
Adam Wiggins	University of New South Wales, Australia
Vera Xavier	Malardalens University, Sweden
Andre Yakovleff	Motorola, Inc.
Edmund Yuen	Motorola Australia Pty. Ltd., Australia

Sponsoring Institutions

The University of Aizu, Japan
The Kayamori Foundation of Informational Science Advancement, Japan

Table of Contents

How Can the Earth Simulator Impact on Human Activities

Tetsuya Sato, Hitoshi Murai, and Shigemune Kitawaki

Earth Simulator Center, Japan Marine Science and Technology Center,
3173-25 Showa-machi, Kanazawa-ku, Yokohama, 236-0001, Japan,
{satot,murai,kitawaki}@es.jamstec.go.jp

Abstract. The Earth Simulator (ES) is a vector-parallel supercomputer, consisting of 5120 vector processors. The peak performance of each vector processor is 8Gflops. Eight processors make one node with 16GB shared-memory and 64Gflops peak performance. The total system thus consists of 640 nodes that are connected by a single stage full crossbar network. The development project started in April, 1997 and was completed in February, 2002. In May, 2002 remarkable sustained performance of 35.86Tflops in the Linpack benchmark was achieved, which is a surprising result for a distributed memory parallel system. More Surprisingly, the ES has achieved 26.58Tflops for an application program, specifically, an optimized atmospheric global circulation simulation code. This striking performance assures that the ES can bring humans crucial impacts on many fields, such as environmental preservation, human life, manufacturing process, and scientific methodology.

1   Introduction

One hopes eagerly that natural and environmental changes such as typhoons, El Niño, earthquakes, global warming, etc. be predicted accurately well in advance. Current computer capabilities are insufficient to carry out trustable simulations for global changes in climate and generation of earthquakes.

The Earth Simulator (ES) project was planned with aiming at elucidation and prediction of global environmental changes as precisely as possible. The ES is now in operation at the Earth Simulator Center (ESC), Japan Marine Science and Technology Center (JAMSTEC).

2   Overview of the Earth Simulator

2.1   Hardware System

The Earth Simulator is a distributed memory parallel system which consists of 640 processor nodes connected by a 640 × 640 single-stage crossbar switch (Figure 1). Each node is a shared memory system which is composed of eight arithmetic vector processors (AP), a shared memory system of 16GB, a remote access control unit (RCU), and an I/O processor (IOP). The peak performance

A. Omondi and S. Sedukhin (Eds.): ACSAC 2003, LNCS 2823, pp. 1–7, 2003.

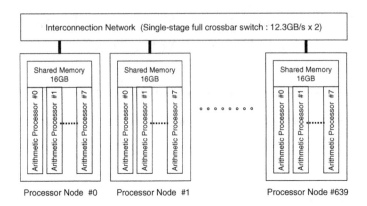

Fig. 1. Configuration of the Earth Simulator

of each AP is 8Gflops. Therefore, the total number of processors is 5120 and the total peak performance and the main memory capacity are 40Tflops and 10TB, respectively. A 0.15 micron CMOS technology with Cu interconnection is used for LSIs[1, 2].

The AP contains a vector unit (VU), a 4-way super-scalar unit (SU), and a main memory access control unit which are mounted on a one-chip LSI. The chip size is about 2cm × 2cm and it operates at clock frequency of 500MHz, partially 1GHz. The VU consists of 8 sets of vector pipelines, vector registers, and some mask registers. Vector pipelines have six types of operation pipeline which are add/shift, multiply, divide, logical, mask, and load/store pipelines. Eight operation pipelines of the same kind work together by a single vector instruction and different type of the pipelines can operate concurrently. There are 72 vector registers of 256 vector elements. The SU is a super-scale processor with a 64KB instruction cache, a 64KB data cache, and 128 general-purpose scalar registers. Branch prediction, data prefetching and out-of-order instruction execution are employed. The VU and SU support the IEEE 754 floating point data format.

The memory system (MS) in the node is equally shared by 8 APs and is configured by 32 main memory package units (MMU) with 2048 banks. A 128 mega-bits high speed DRAM operating at 24 nsec bank cycle time is used for the memory chip. The memory capacity of each node is 16GB. Each AP has a 32 GB/s memory bandwidth and 256 GB/s in total. The RCU in the node is directly connected to the crossbar switch by two ways of sending and receiving, and controls inter-node data communications. Several data transfer modes such as three-dimensional sub-array accesses and indirect accesses are supported.

The single-stage crossbar network (IN) consists of two units; One is the inter-node crossbar control unit (XCT) which is in charge of coordination of switching operations. The other is the inter-node crossbar switch (XSW) which is an actual data path. XSW is composed of 128 separated switches, each of which has 1Gbits/s bandwidth operating independently. All the pairs of nodes and switches are connected by electric cables. The theoretical data transfer rate between every two nodes is 12.3 GB/s × 2 ways.

Two nodes are placed in a node cabinet, the size of which is 140cm(W) × 100cm(D) × 200cm(H), and 320 node cabinets in total were installed in the building. Two XCTs are placed in an IN cabinet, so are two XSWs. The size of the IN cabinet is 120cm(W) × 130cm(D) × 200cm(H) and there are 65 IN cabinets in total.

2.2 Software System

The basic software such as operating system, programming tools, and operation supporting software of the ES should have large scalability and should be a readily usable system by researchers in different application fields. Then, a hierarchical management system is introduced to control the ES. Every 16 nodes are collected as a cluster system and therefore there are 40 sets of cluster in total. A set of cluster is called an "S-cluster" which is dedicated for interactive processing and small-scale batch jobs. A job within the node can be processed on the S-cluster. Other sets of cluster but the S cluster is called "L-cluster" which are for medium-scale and large-scale batch jobs. Parallel processing jobs on several nodes are executed on some sets of cluster. Each cluster has a cluster control station (CCS) which monitors the state of nodes and controls electricity of the nodes inside the cluster. A super cluster control station (SCCS) plays an important role in integration and coordination of all CCS operations.

An operating system running on the node of the ES is basically a UNIX-based system and provides execution environments as conventional UNIX systems. It also provides parallel execution environments to the distributed memory system of the Earth Simulator. In addition to the usual UNIX system, a high-speed file system and a parallel file system for large-scale scientific computations are supported. Principal style of job processing on the Earth Simulator is a batch job processing, and a job scheduler plays an important role for smooth operation. We have developed a flexible job scheduler which assigns batch jobs to the nodes independent to L-cluster.

The ES provides three-level parallel processing environments: vector processing in an AP, parallel processing with shared memory in a node, and parallel processing among distributed nodes via the IN. An automatic vectorization and automatic parallelization in a node are supported by the compilers for programs written in conventional Fortran 90 and C languages. Shared memory parallel programming are supported for microtasking and OpenMP. The microtasking is a sort of multitasking provided for the Cray's supercomputer at the first time and the same function is realized for ES. There are two methods for using microtasking. One is automatic parallelization by the compilers and the other is manual insertion of the parallel directive line before the target do loop. The OpenMP is the standard shared memory programming API. A message passing programming model by MPI2 libraries both within a node and between nodes is prepared as a base programming environment so that the three-level parallel processing environment can be used efficiently.

Principal users of the ES are thought to be natural scientists who are not necessarily familiar with the parallel programming environment or rather dislike it. Accordingly, it is strongly invoked to provide a higher level parallel interface language. The HPF/ES is provided with HPF2 approved extensions, HPF/JA extensions, and some extensions for the ES. The extensions include features for irregular grids problems, user controllable shadow, and so on[3]. We adapted the HPF/ES compiler to a plasma simulation code IMPACT-3D with 512 nodes of the ES and 12.5 Tflops performance is obtained, which is 39% of the peak performance. This result shows us that the HPF/ES has a high scalability and can be used readily in developing an actual simulation program.

2.3   Earth Simulator Building

The ES is installed in the building at the Earth Simulator Center of the Yokohama Institute for Earth Sciences, JAMSTEC located at 40km south of Tokyo. The building has two stories with seismic isolation system, the size of which is 50m × 65m × 17m. The ES is protected against electromagnetic wave coming from outside the building by covering with steel plates.

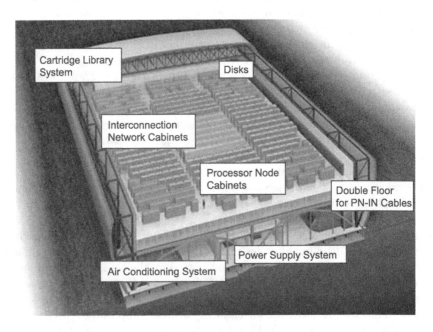

Fig. 2. Earth Simulator installed in the building

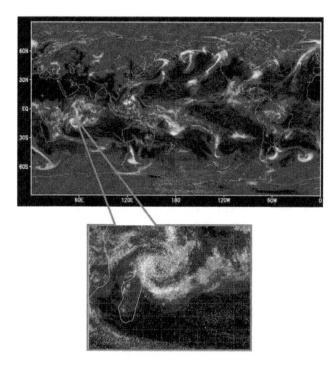

Fig. 3. A snapshot of the precipitation obtained by an atmospheric global circulation code

3   Applications

Several application programs have been carried out so far (three months) on the ES in order to acquire the real performance data of the ES. In this paper two examples are introduced.

The first one is an optimized code for the atmospheric general circulation. The dynamical equations are the global three-dimensioned hydrostatic primitive equations. This code employs a spectral transformation in horizontal dimensions and a finite element method on a sigma coordinate (vertical). Horizontal wind, temperature, surface pressure, specific humanity, cloud water and others on every grid point are calculated stepwise in time. Figure 3 is one snapshot of the precipitation. The resolution corresponds to the case with about 10km in horizontal dimensions and 96 vertical layers. Meso-scale phenomena, such as a cyclone appearing near the Madagascar Island and T-bone shape fronts appearing around 50N and 50S, are clearly and vividly observed. This indicate that the ES can definitely describe meso-scale phenomena by a global simulation.

Regarding this particular program we would like to particularly emphasize that the performance of 26.58Tflops was achieved. This corresponds to about 65% of the peak performance, which is an extraordinary value.

The second example is an optimized oceanic global circulation simulation. The horizontal resolution is also 10km in this example. Figure 4 shows a snapshot of the global sea surface temperature. It is to be noted that the Kuroshio current on the pacific side of Japan is clearly generated and also the Mexican Gulf Stream alongside the east coast of Northern America. This result also ensures that the ES can be an excellent prediction tool of the global climate change.

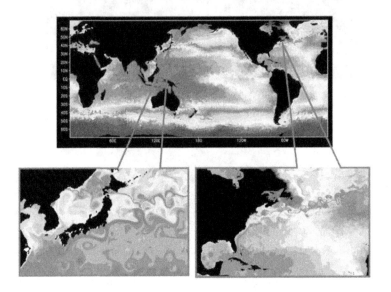

Fig. 4. A snapshot of the sea surface temperature obtained by an oceanic global circulation code

4   Summary

The development of the Earth Simulator was successfully completed at the end of February, 2002. Outstanding performance of 35.86Tflops was achieved in the Linpack Benchmark, which is 87% of the peak value. More interestingly, the performance of 26.58Tflops, which is about 65% of the peak value, was obtained by an atmospheric global circulation code. This undoubtedly ensures that the Earth Simulator could strongly contribute to the security and welfare of the humankind by providing trustable predictions on short-term, medium-term and long-term climate changes. Not only this, but the Earth Simulator could also contribute to opening-up a new science field, namely, the Complexity Science that deals with far-from-equilibrium, nonlinear open systems, to changing the manufacturing process that requires frequent costly model changes such as the automobile engine, and to drastic reduction of the developing cost of an innovative gigantic devise such as a fusion reactor and a rocket engine.

Acknowledgement

The authors would like to thank all members of the Earth Simulator Center and the Earth Simulator Research and Development Center which was closed at the end of February, 2002 when the Earth Simulator was completed.

References

1. M. Yokokawa, S. Shingu, S. Kawai, K. Tani and H. Miyoshi, "Performance Estimation of the Earth Simulator," Towards Teracomputing, Proc. of 8th ECMWF Workshop, pp.34-53, World Scientific (1998).
2. K. Yoshida and S. Shingu, "Research and development of the Earth Simulator," Proc. of 9th ECMWF Workshop, pp.1-13, World Scientific (2000).
3. High Performance Fortran Language Specification Version 2, High Performance Fortran Forum, January (1997).

Toward Architecting
and Designing Novel Computers

Tadao Nakamura

Tohoku University, Graduate School of Information Sciences,
Computer Architecture Laboratory
Aramaki Aza Aoba 01, Aoba-ku, Sendai, 980-8579, Japan
nakamura@archi.is.tohoku.ac.jp

Abstract. Recent CMOS technology faces challenging difficulties toward architecting and designing new computers. In the near future, chips will form a
logic-sea, consisting of an immense number of gates and a very large amount of
wires. This outstanding increase in chip density will require a drastic change in
the building of computers, requiring novel microprocessors to be architected
and designed. This paper introduces a novel architecture that considers the
structural and behavioral constraints toward the implementation of future computers. A computation model that is strongly associated with this architecture is
described with emphasis on the scheme of data processing. Finally, simple
benchmarking illustrates the correctness of this architectural approach.

1 Introduction

VLSI systems are growing up to one-ten billion transistors systems that are too complicated to imagine in terms of functionality. Naturally, commercial needs will continue driving and motivating computer architects to challenge the design of new computer systems using such complex and high density chip environments. However, to
simplify the design, architects mainly rely on the MIMD (Multiple Instruction
streams, Multiple Data streams) architectural model. The MIMD model utilizes the
available chip area to integrate multiple processors, at a system processor architecture
level. To exemplify, we could imagine such a system would be similar to a cluster of
PCs put together on a single chip. Obviously, gathering a number of processors into
one chip is expected to achieve performance higher than that offered by a uniprocessors chip. However, such performance is likely be limited by physical limitations
related to wire delays [2], [3]. Such wire limitations are expected to increase as transistor technology improves, requiring architects to come up with novel architectural
models other than the MIMD, in order to hide, reduce or even eliminate wire delay
problems.

This paper gives a brief direction toward architecting and designing novel computers. First, fundamentals of computers' structure and behavior are reviewed based
upon the data processing concept of a computer, that is, its datapath. Then, a novel
architecture targeting the design of billion-transistor-chips including wire-delays is

A. Omondi and S. Sedukhin (Eds.): ACSAC 2003, LNCS 2823, pp. 8–13, 2003.
© Springer-Verlag Berlin Heidelberg 2003

proposed. The proposal is expected to have a very efficient datapath to be a suitable architectural model for the next generation of computers.

2 Fundamentals for a Novel Architecture

A computer consists of a datapath and a control unit. The datapath contains one or more ALUs, a register file and buses for operating microinstructions. The functions of a datapath include: 1) to execute microoperations for arithmetic, logic and shift computation, using operands stored within registers and 2) to transfer data from one register to another by using buses. A microoperation is the most important function in the behavior of computers. Usually, a microoperation is performed by a microinstruction that is a piece of a microprogram. A microinstruction can consist of a few microoperations. However, today's RISC architecture mostly utilizes microinstructions consisting of a single microoperation. In this case, we can say that microinstructions were elevated to the category of machine instructions.

2.1 How to Architect a Novel Computer

As mentioned in the previous section, most computer architects rely on the MIMD model to develop an architecture. This paper however considers the MISD (Multiple Instructions streams, Single Data stream) model. Both MIMD and MISD are part of the so-called Flynn's taxonomy. Although considered a technically possible classification, MISD has not so far realized except for arithmetic pipelines whose stages functions are constant. One reason why we could not architect the MISD was because the transistor density on a chip was not so high, making impossible to manage multiple instruction streams. However, the high transistor density feature of today's VLSI technologies enables us to introduce the MISD paradigm. Advances in VLSI lead to smaller transistors, and therefore more transistors can be integrated on a chip. With more transistors available, larger and more complex hardware resources can be implemented. Also, smaller transistors have a shorter feature size, and consequently a shorter switching time. These faster transistors make it possible to implement faster logic gates, and consequently obtain faster microprocessor clock speeds.

However, in order for wires to connect to smaller transistors, their cross-section must shrink, resulting in higher wire resistance per unit of length. The spacing between wires, called wire pitch, also shrinks, and consequently the capacitance per unit of area increases. Since the delay of a wire is proportional to the product of its resistance by its capacitance, wire delays tend to become paramount in comparison with logic gate delays. This discrepancy between the gate and the wire performance will limit the fraction of a chip that can be reachable in a single clock cycle. In other words, a future microprocessor is likely to be a collection of logic islands, which are not able to communicate with distant islands within a single clock cycle. A high transistor density chip have logic islands on a logic sea, where a logic island is a distance of signal transmission during one clock cycle, and a logic sea is the whole transistor environment. Fig.1 shows the number of clock cycles that are necessary to traverse a chip for several VLSI technologies. As shown in the figure, at 0.1 μm technology there are eight logic islands from one edge to the other edge of the chip. In other words, it will be hard to transmit a signal trough the chip within one or a small number of clock cycles, and therefore the large number of transistors on the chip will be under-utilized.

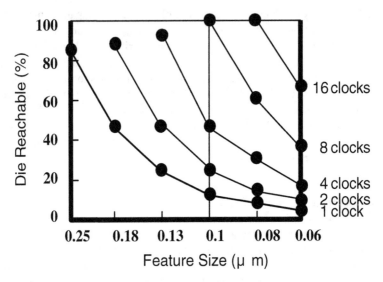

Fig. 1. The clock locality metric.

3   The SHIFT Machine: A Novel MISD Computer

From the above phenomena, we have naturally created a novel architecture called the SHIFT architecture [1]. The model of this architecture is shown in Fig. 2. A single data stream goes through the array of ALUs with shift registers. The execution is done in a pipeline fashion. A unit of a CPU and registers is called a stage of the pipeline. The register files are connected forming a moving memory. Data produced in one stage is shifted (moved) from one register file to another, so that it can be used by the next stage. This efficiently improves on the functions of the datapath: the transfer of data between registers. Since the data is transferred between contiguous registers, a very short-size bus (or even no bus!) would be necessary. In other words, only short wires would be necessary for data transfer.

As instructions are fetched from multiple ALUs and data is transferred in one direction as a single stream, this computing model can be regarding as an MISD model.

In order to represent mathematically the computation model of this MISD structure, we introduce the SHIFT grammar, as follows

$$P_{i+1} = D_i(P_i). \tag{1}$$

$$D_{i+1} = P_i(D_i) \cdot \tag{2}$$

where P_i is either algorithms and data structures or algorithms in the i-th stage. D_i is either data or data structures and data in the i-th stage. Equations (1) and (2) indicate that a program which processes data in a step is changed into the next program to process the data in the next step.

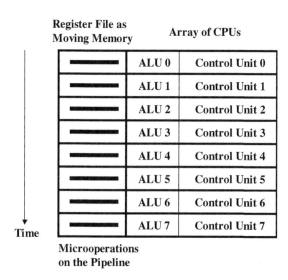

Fig. 2. The SHIFT architecture.

4   Evaluation

In order to evaluate the efficiency of the model described above we have performed software simulations that faithfully represent the model described by Equations (1) and (2).

As a benchmark, we utilized a threadlized program for the transform

$$F(u,v) = \frac{1}{4} c_u c_v \sum_{x=0}^{7} \sum_{y=0}^{7} f(x,y) \cos\frac{(2x+1)u\pi}{16} \cos\frac{(2y+1)v\pi}{16},$$

$$0 \le u, v \le 7 , \ 0 \le x, y \le 7 \tag{3}$$

The example is evaluated in two scheduling policies: not-optimized and optimized ways, as shown in Fig. 3. In a general not-optimized way, the order of the threads follows the sequential order of the code, and requires communication between threads.

On the other hand, we say that the thread schedule is optimized if we arrange the computation order as a pair of u and v along outer loops. Details of the parallelization of the code can be found in [4].

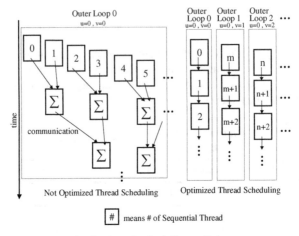

Fig. 3. Thread scheduling policies.

Evaluation results are shown in Fig. 4. The performance is shown in terms of execution time (clock cycles) for different configurations ranging from 2 to 16 processing stages.

In this machine implementation, a processing element (PE) corresponds to one stage, as introduced in Equations (1) and (2). As can be observed in the figure, the performance considerably increases with the number of PEs. In other words, the larger the number of transistors available in the chip is, the higher the performance obtained becomes.

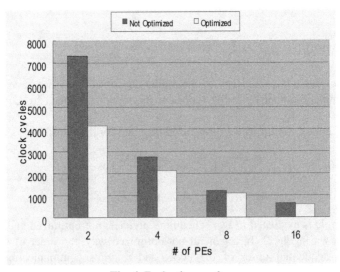

Fig. 4. Evaluation results.

5 Conclusions

Through the analysis of the current limitations of current VLSI technology, this paper has indicated the direction of how to architect and design novel computers in one to ten billion transistors era. We have proposed a new architecture based on the MISD model, which is able to reduce the influence of wire delays by using a moving memory structure, formed by register files. Our preliminary evaluations show that scheduling is possible and that considerable performance can be obtained in this proposal.

In addition, the reduction in the impact of wire delays is expected to translate into computers with very high clock speeds. Also, we understand that wire delays shorter than a logic island delay are acceptable because data transmission can be done simultaneously to data processing within a stage. Therefore, not only reducing wire delays but also tuning these delays at the circuit level to fit in a pipeline stage is important. One of our future works is to tune wire delays to have the same delay of a logic islands.

References

1. Clecio D. Lima, Kentaro Sano, Hiroaki Kobayashi, Tadao Nakamura, and Michael J. Flynn, "A technology-scalable multithreaded architecture," *Proc. of the 13th Symp. on Computer Architecture and High Performance Computing*, pp.82-89, 2001.
2. Doug Matzke, "Will physical scalability sabotage performance gains?," *IEEE Computer*, pp.37-39, September 1997.
3. Michael J. Flynn, Patrick Hung, and Kevin W. Rudd, "Deep-submicron microprocessor design issues," *IEEE MICRO*, pp.11-22, July/August 1999.
4. Tadao Nakamura, "Architecting the SHIFT Machine," *Proc. of the 5th International Conference on Computer and Information Technology*, pp.600-603, Dhaka, Bangladesh, December 2002.

Designing Ultra-large Instruction Issue Windows

Doug Burger

Department of Computer Sciences, The University of Texas at Austin,
Austin, TX 78712 USA,
dburger@cs.utexas.edu

Abstract. To continue historical rates of improvement, future high-performance processors are likely to exploit more instruction-level parallelism. The best way to find much of that parallelism is by implementing an out-of-order issue core with an ultra-large issue window. However, there are serious challenges in building large issue windows that can hold hundreds or thousands of instructions, including how to build them, how to fill them, and how to empty them efficiently. In this paper, we describe some of the solutions proposed by other researchers that address the limitations currently constraining issue window sizes. We also describe the solutions being incorporated into the University of Texas TRIPS processor, which will contain a 1024-instruction window in each processor core.

1   Introduction

Commodity microprocessors have shown enormous performance gains over the past three decades, typically cited at 55% per year. Over the past 15 years, the bulk of those performance improvements have come from faster clock rates, improving at 40% per year, and even faster recently. This rate of growth is unsustainable, however, as pipelines are nearing their optimal depths [6]. Once clock rates reach that point in the next few years, the most promising source of continued performance improvements is increased parallelism, whether it be coarse-grained parallelism on a multiprocessor, or increased exploitation of instruction-level parallelism (ILP). Given the difficulties inherent in parallelizing irregular codes, and the lack of success in doing so over the past decades, we believe that striving for increased ILP is a more promising approach.

In this short paper, we discuss how out-of-order issue cores can exploit large windows of instructions to achieve higher ILP. These windows, which may eventually hold thousands of instructions, have enormous implementation challenges, particularly in the face of emerging technology constraints such as power ceilings and multi-cycle wire delays.

The major challenges associated with these kilo-windows of instructions (KWIs), are four-fold:

1. Implementing a kilo-instruction window
2. Filling a kilo-instruction window
3. Flushing a kilo-instruction window
4. Emptying a kilo-instruction window

A. Omondi and S. Sedukhin (Eds.): ACSAC 2003, LNCS 2823, pp. 14–20, 2003.

Each of these challenges will require new techniques to solve effectively. We describe both the issues for conventional processors as well as the solutions being incorporated into the TRIPS processor prototype being designed at the University of Texas at Austin. The TRIPS processor will be the first example of a KWI; the each of the four processor cores on the prototype chip will issue instructions out of order from a window of at least one thousand instructions.

In the rest of this paper, we describe the challenges and current solutions to the four challenges described above. If solved, these challenges will provide significant performance increases, since past studies have shown that ILP is available out to thousands of instructions [2]. Recent studies have also shown that long-latency operations, such as cache misses to main memory, can be tolerated with ILP so long as the instruction window is sufficiently large and branch mispredictions do not invalidate a significant fraction of the window [8].

2   Implementing a KWI

Building large conventional, centralized issue windows is infeasible given four issues: growing on-chip wire delays [1], the quadratic growth of window complexity with issue width [20], long latencies for large windows, which must match broadcast register tags against every entry associatively, and the power limitations of building large associative structures.

Researchers have proposed techniques for building large but scalable windows. These approaches include building hierarchical windows, where a small, fast one backs up a larger, slower one [5, 11], clustered processors [9], or dependence-based queues [10, 13].

The TRIPS processor, conversely, implements a physically partitioned window [12, 17] that distributes an issue window among multiple execution units, treating them jointly as reservation stations, an issue window, operand buffers, and a distributed reservation station. These functionalities were originally merged into one structure in the Register Update Unit (RUU) [19]. The TRIPS window organization has two major differences from the RUU. First, the TRIPS window is a highly partitioned structure, with a partition at each execution unit (which number from 8 to 64, depending on the issue width of the processor core). Second, the mapping of instructions to slots in the window is performed partially by the compiler, since the TRIPS processor employs a Static-Placement, Dynamic Issue (SPDI) execution model.

This compiler mapping enables dependent instructions to be placed close together, and it also permits each partition of the window to be constructed with non-associative logic. Since the instruction set specifies that each instruction contain the physical locations of its consumers, an instruction can send its operand directly to the exact window slot where a consuming instruction is guaranteed to be buffered. Thus, while the TRIPS approach requires a change in instruction set and execution model, it supports out-of-order execution with a scalable issue window, which can grow linearly with the number of execution units. There are also power advantages to this approach, as the issues window is both partitioned and avoids the need for power-hungry, high-latency CAMs to implement associative lookups for waking up instructions.

3   Filling a KWI

The second major challenge for building feasible KWIs, aside from building scalable and practical physical structures, is filling them with useful instructions. The two challenges for filling KWIs is high-bandwidth fetch and effective prediction. We discuss each below.

3.1   High-Bandwidth Fetch

Much research has focused on increasing the bandwidth of the front end instruction fetch unit. There are several challenges to sustaining the levels of bandwidth required to keep large windows full at high rates of ILP, including fetching past multiple branches per cycle, renaming many instructions per cycle, and dispatching many instructions per cycle to the issue window.

Techniques to improve instruction fetch bandwidth include trace caches [16], fetch target buffers (FTB) [15], and many more. Trace caches are an example of a technique that deals with branches by crafting a linear sequence of instructions dynamically, whereas the fetch target buffer exploits idle time to run ahead of the actual front end fetch rate. By running ahead, the FTB prevents performance loss when the program enters brief periods when the front end cannot sustain enough bandwidth for the machine (e.g., too many predicted taken branches).

The solution that we employ in the TRIPS processor is to use large hyperblocks as the unit of fetch and map. Hyperblocks are predicated regions of code that have only one entry point, but which may have multiple exits. We couple these hyperblocks with an exit predictor that chooses the first taken exit branch in a hyperblock [14]. By making only one prediction per hyperblock (and implicitly predicting all the branches before the predicted exit in that hyperblock), a large number of instructions–80 on average–can be fetched with each prediction.

Due to the SPDI execution model, in which the compiler places instructions in a fixed-format block, the instruction caches can be distributed to rows of ALUs, columns of ALUs, or individual ALUs. When a prediction is made, the global controller looks up the address produced by the branch target buffer in the instruction cache tags. If an I-cache hit occurs, the controller broadcasts the correct index to all distributed I-cache banks, which proceed to fetch their portion of the statically mapped block in parallel. The exit predictor, coupled with a BTB and the distributed I-cache banks, can run ahead with its predictions, similar to an FTB, but with many more instructions per prediction and a much higher sustainable bandwidth from the distributed I-cache array.

3.2   Prediction

For most irregular codes without regular, predictable loops, mispredictions will result in a small fraction of a KWI being utilized. Currently, integer codes (such as SPECINT2000) demonstrate a rate of two to ten Mispredictions per Thousand (kilo) Instructions (MPKI), with an average of roughly 5 [18]. By dividing 1000 by the average MPKI for a benchmark, the average number of useful instructions fetched before a misprediction can be obtained. Even the most accurate predictors currently proposed in the literature, such as the perceptron predictor [7], cannot achieve under 1 MPKI for most benchmarks, indicating that if straight branch prediction is to be used, considerably more accurate predictors will need to be developed. Predication of branches has been proposed to reduce the rate of branches that must be predicted, but it does not typically improve the predicatility. when an unpredictable branch is removed, the removal often pushes the poor predictability onto other branches [3].

Simulation results show that the TRIPS processor currently loses 33-50% of its potential performance to branch mispredictions. The approach that we are taking is to be more aggressive with if-conversion and loop unrolling, forming larger hyperblock regions for fetching that contain multiple paths, thus trading useless instruction overhead for better predictability. Predictability is improved, however, only when basic blocks that reside on multiple control paths are added to a hyperblock until they re-join in the control flow graph. If-converting to control flow merges allows the processor to exploit control independence in a clean manner, since the successor block is predictable. The challenges to this approach are (1) providing enough buffering and execution resources that the overhead (non-taken path) instructions do not impede performance, and (2) ensuring that the non-taken paths included in the mapped blocks do not have critical paths significantly longer than the taken paths. The balancing of these path lengths and the decisions about which paths to include is made at compile time, and is an active area of research.

4   Flushing a KWI

When a control misprediction occurs in a large window, an enormous number of in-flight instructions may be invalid. Future systems will benefit from keeping the flushing and recovery costs as low as possible. This problem is fairly simple to solve in a conventional processor, which typically defers handling of the misprediction (or synchronous exception) until the faulting instruction reaches the head of the reorder buffer, at which point the entire pipeline is flushed.

That solution is considerably less attractive in a distributed, large-window microarchitecture with high communication delays, since it may take many cycles for the faulting instruction to become the oldest instruction. We are investigating two techniques to reduce the performance losses due to flushes, the first of which reduces the overhead of the flush, and the second of which reduces the frequency of flushes.

Tag-Based Flushing: An alternative to waiting for the faulting instruction to complete is to actively squash only the mis-speculated instructions in flight. Explicit squashing of all in-flight, mis-speculated instructions is particularly difficult in a distributed microarchitecture. The approach that we are exploring involves tagging each block that is mapped to the execution substrate and updating and broadcasting a tag that indicates that all operations past a mapped block are now invalid. This approach is similar to how conventional microarchitectures handle mis-speculated loads that return from memory after a pipeline has been flushed and re-filled with correct work. Even more efficient would be simply injecting new blocks with updated tags when a misprediction was detected, requiring little waiting time at all. This scheme adds both the complexity of tag management and a verification challenge–since old and new operations may be in flight together–but permits lower-latency flushes.

Distributed Selective Re-execution: The other approach that we are currently exploring is to minimize the frequency of complete flushes. The pipeline is flushed on control mispredictions, but for other kinds of speculative violations, such as a load/store ordering–or any violation that involves the right instructions computing with the wrong data–we perform selective re-execution, re-firing only the instructions that depended on the faulting instruction. With this approach, when the right kind of misprediction occurs, the pipeline does not need to be flushed, no useful work is thrown out, and no instructions need to be re-fetched. We describe a protocol for achieving selective re-execution in a distributed microarchitecture elsewhere [4].

5   Emptying a KWI

In conventional architectures that commit one instruction per cycle, on average, draining the instruction window of completed instructions is relatively straightforward. The Alpha 21264 [9] is able to commit up to 11 instructions per cycle, but can only commit one branch per cycle.

In a distributed microarchitecture, however, commit is significantly more difficult. Determining the correct order to remove the instructions from the partitions is both necessary and challenging, particularly in a multiprocessor where ordering must be maintained to satisfy memory consistency models. Stores are typically written back to the memory system at commit, and register values to the architectural register file.

A centralized structure to track orderings of written stores, pipelining permissions across multicycle communication delays, is one feasible approach. One drawback of this approach is that a cache miss on a store could quickly make the commit stage a bottleneck. The store issue argues for write-back, write-noallocate level-one caches. It is not clear that commit will be a bottleneck for KIW machines, but it is certainly possible that new approaches will need to be devised to permit these machines to get instructions *out* of the pipeline sufficiently fast.

6   Summary

Future performance gains for uniprocessors, above and beyond those afforded by faster transistors, will have to come from either instruction or thread-level parallelism. Many (if not most) workloads still do not lend themselves to easy parallelization or multithreading. Consequently, instruction-level parallelism will likely grow significantly in importance in the coming decade.

However, to maintain greater ILP, it is likely that the research community will need to develop wide-issue out-of-order cores that can sift through many more instructions than today to find enough ready-to-issue instructions each cycle. These large windows have a number of daunting implementation challenges, including filling the window, designing a practical window, deallocating instructions for commit, and efficient flushing of the window upon a misprediction.

The TRIPS processor prototype being designed at the University of Texas will have 1024-entry, distributed instruction issue windows in each processor core (with four processors on each chip). We have solved several of the challenges of designing a practical kilo-window, and have shown how to fill it quickly with a high-bandwidth front end. We are working on the compiler technology to permit predication to control-flow merge points in an attempt to improve the predictability of the instruction stream and thus fill the window for irregular benchmarks. If this effort fails, alternative methods to improve the predictability must be found. Currently, we are still in the process of designing our commit and flush logic, which may employ some of the principles described in this paper. We hope to have a working prototype by the end of 2005, successfully demonstrating solutions to the problems enumerated in this paper.

References

1. V. Agarwal, M. S. Hrishikesh, S. W. Keckler, and D. Burger. Clock rate versus IPC: The end of the road for conventional microarchitectures. In *Proceedings of the 27th Annual International Symposium on Computer Architecture*, pages 248–259, June 2000.
2. T. M. Austin and G. S. Sohi. Dynamic dependency analysis of ordinary programs. In *Nineteenth International Symposium on Computer Architecture*, pages 342–351, Gold Coast, Australia, 1992. ACM and IEEE Computer Society.
3. Y. Choi, A. Knies, L. Gerke, and T.-F. Ngai. The impact of if-conversion and branch prediction on program execution on the intel itanium processor. In *Proceedings of the 34th International Symposium on Microarchitecture*, pages 182–191, Dec. 2001.
4. R. Desikan, S. Sethumadhavan, R. NAgarajan, D. Burger, and S. L. keckler. Lightweight distributed selective re-execution and its implications for value speculation. In *Proceedings of the First Value Speculation Workshop, Associated with ISCA-30*, June 2003.
5. D. Ernst and T. Austin. Efficient dynamic scheduling through tag elimination. In *Proceedings of the 29th International Symposium on Computer Architecture*, May 2002.

6. M. Hrishikesh, N. Jouppi, K. Farkas, D. Burger, S. Keckler, and P. Shivakumar. The optimal logic depth per pipeline stage is 6 to 8 FO4 inverter delays. In *Proceedings of the 29th International Symposium on Computer Architecture*, pages 14–24, May 2002.

7. D. Jimenez and C. Lin. Dynamic branch prediction with perceptrons. In *Proceedings of the 7th International Symposium on High-Performance Computer Architecture*, pages 197–206, Jan. 2001.

8. T. Karkhanis and J. Smith. A day in the life of a cache miss. In *Proceedings of the 2nd Annual Workshop on Memory Performance Issues (WMPI02)*, 2002.

9. R. Kessler. The alpha 21264 microprocessor. *IEEE Micro*, 19(2):24–36, March/April 1999.

10. H. Kim and J. Smith. An instruction set and microarchitecture for instruction level distributed processing. In *Proceedings of the 29th International Symposium on Computer Architecture*, pages 71–81, 2002.

11. A. R. Lebeck, J. Koppanalil, T. Li, J. Patwardhan, and E. Rotenberg. A large, fast instruction window for tolerating cache misses. In *Proceedings of the 29th International Symposium on Computer Architecture*, May 2002.

12. R. Nagarajan, K. Sankaralingam, D. Burger, and S. W. Keckler. A design space evaluation of grid processor architectures. In *Proceedings of the 34th Annual International Symposium on Microarchitecture*, pages 40–51, December 2001. Submitted by: Ramadass Nagarajan.

13. S. E. Raasch, N. L. Binkert, and S. K. Reinhardt. A scalable instruction queue design using dependence chains. In *Proceedings of the 29th International Symposium on Computer Architecture*, pages 318–329, May 2002.

14. N. Ranganathan, R. Nagarajan, D. Burger, and S. Keckler. Combining hyperblocks and exit prediction to increase front-end bandwidth and performance. Technical Report TR2002-41, Department of Computer Sciences, The University of Texas at Austin, Austin, TX, September 2002.

15. G. Reinman, B. Calder, and T. Austin. A scalable front-end architecture for fast instruction delivery. In *Proceedings of the 26th International Symposium on Computer Architecture*, June 1999.

16. E. Rotenberg, S. Bennett, and J. Smith. Trace cache: a low latency approach to high bandwidth instruction fetching. In *Proceedings of the 29th Annual International Symposium on Microarchitecture*. ACM, 1996. Submited by: simha.

17. K. Sankaralingam, R. Nagarajan, H. Liu, C. Kim, J. Huh, D. Burger, S. Keckler, and C. Moore. Exploiting ilp,tlp, and dlp with the polymorphous trips architecture. In *Proceedings of the 30th Annual International Symposium on Computer Architecture*, May 2003.

18. A. Seznec, S. Felix, V. Krishnan, and Y. Sazeides. Design tradeoffs for the alpha ev8 conditional branch predictor. In *Proceedings of the 29th International Symposium on Computer Architecture*, June 2002.

19. G. S. Sohi. Instruction issue logic for high-performance, interruptible, multiple functional unit, pipelined computers. *IEEE Trans. Comput.*, 39(3):349–359, March 1990.

20. J. S. Subbarao Palacharla, Norman Jouppi. Complexity-effective superscalar processors. In *Proceedings of the 24th International Symposium on Computer Architecture*, 1997. Submitted by: Hrishi.

Multi-threaded Microprocessors –
Evolution or Revolution

Chris Jesshope

Department of Computer Science, University of Hull, HU6 7RX, UK
{c.r.Jesshope@dec.hull.ac.uk}

Abstract. Threading in microprocessors is not new, the earliest threaded processor design was implemented in the late 1970s and yet only now is it being used in mainstream microprocessor architecture. This paper reviews threaded microprocessors and explains why the more popular option of out-of-order execution has a poor future and is not likely to provide a pathway for future microprocessor scalability. The first mainstream threaded architectures are beginning to emerge but unfortunately based on out-of-order execution. This paper will review the relevant trends in multi-threaded microprocessor design and look at one approach in detail, showing how wide instruction issue can be achieved and how it can provide excellent performance, latency tolerance and above all scalability with issue width. This model exploits ILP and loop level parallelism using a vector-like instruction set in a chip multiprocessor.

1 The Forces at Play in ISA Design

There are two forces that determine the form and function of microprocessor architecture today. The first is the technology and the second is the market. These forces are quite at odds with each other. On the one hand, technology is all about change. In 1965, Intel's founder Gordon Moore predicted that the number of transistors on a chip would double every 2 years. His prediction of exponential growth has not only been achieved but in some cases exceeded. On the other hand, the market is all about inertia or lack of change. At ACAC 2000, the invited speaker Rumi Zahir, who led the team responsible for the instruction set architecture of IA-64, told us an anecdotal story about the briefing his team had been given by Andy Grove. They were given a clean sheet to do whatever they wanted, but with one exception... the resulting microprocessor should be able to boot up a binary of DOS from floppy disc! In the event, Moore's law solved their problem and the Itanium core processor is not binary compatible with X86 processors, instead it has a separate compatibility unit in hardware to provide IA32 compatibility.

There are two routes to ISA development, evolutionary or revolutionary and it appears that the evolutionary route always relies on technological improvements and results in ever increasing complexity in design. We have good examples of this in current out-of-order issue superscalar microprocessors. Intel has demonstrated this

A. Omondi and S. Sedukhin (Eds.): ACSAC 2003, LNCS 2823, pp. 21–45, 2003.

approach, requiring each new ISA to be backward compatible with the previous one. On the other hand revolutionary change has been made, for example Motorola and IBM moved away from their respective CISC ISAs to the RISC-based Power PC architecture, first introduced in 1993. Such a major divergence in machine code forced Apple, a major user of the 68000 processor, to emulate the 68000 ISA on the Power PC for backward compatibility. Emulation has been used by a number of other microprocessor designs, including the Transmeta Crusoe, which was targeted at high performance but low-power applications. The benefits of speed and power savings made software emulation a practical alternative to hardware compatibility.

Perhaps we should first ask what the issues are that require changes to an ISA design as we follow the inevitable trends of Moore's law? In fact there is just one issue and that is in providing support for concurrency within the ISA. More and more gates mean increased on-chip concurrency, first in word width, now in instruction issue width. The move to a RISC ISA was revolutionary, it did not introduce concurrency explicitly, rather it introduced a simple, regular instruction set that facilitated efficient instruction execution using pipelines. In fact many people forget that the simplicity of RISC was first adopted in order to squeeze a full 32-bit microprocessor onto a single chip for the first time. RISC has also been introduced as an evolutionary development, for example, Intel's IA32 CISC ISA, which has a very small set of addressable registers, is implemented by a RISC engine with a much larger actual register file. This is achieved by dynamically translating its externally visible CISC ISA into a lower-level RISC ISA. Of course this is only possible due to the inexorable results of Moore's law. Intel was able to maintain backward compatibility in the IA32 from the 8086 in 1978 through to the Pentium 4 first introduced in 2000 but have now moved to a new ISA, which introduces a regular and explicit concurrent instruction set.

2 Concurrency in ISAs

Concurrency can be introduced into a computer's operation via the data that one instruction processes or by issuing instructions concurrently. In this paper we do not consider the data parallelism found in SIMD or vector computers, although we do look at a vector model of programming that is supported by wide instruction issue. Neither do we consider the data flow approach. This leaves just two ways in which concurrency can be introduced explicitly into conventional ISAs, through VLIW or through multi-threading. There is a third way, which is that currently used by most commercial microprocessors. This is to extract the concurrency from a sequential instruction stream dynamically in hardware. We will look at each of these in turn beginning with the excesses of the latter in terms of consuming silicon real-estate.

2.1 Out-of-Order Instruction Execution

Out-of-order instruction execution can be seen as a theoretically optimal solution for exploiting ILP concurrency, because instructions are interleaved in the wide-issue pipelines in close to programmed order, whilst honouring any data and control dependencies or indeed any storage conflicts introduced by the out-of-order instruction execution. The major benefit is that it is achieved using the existing sequential instruction stream and therefore maintains code-base compatibility. In effect, the instruction stream is dynamically decomposed into micro-threads, which are scheduled and synchronised at no cost in terms of executing additional instructions. Although this may be desirable, speedups using out-of-order execution on superscalar pipelines not so impressive and it is difficult to obtain a speedup of greater than 2, even on regular code and using 4- or 8-way superscalar issue, e.g. [1]. Moreover, they scale rather badly as issue widths are increased.

To understand why this is, let us first look at how a typical superscalar pipeline works. Instructions are prefetched, sometimes along more than one potential execution path. Instructions are then partially decoded and issued to an instruction window, which holds instruction waiting to be executed. Instructions can be issued from this window in any order, providing resource constraints can be met by register renaming. Instructions are then issued to reservation stations, which are buffers associated with each of the execution units. Here a combination of register reads and bypassing, using tagged data, matches each instruction to its data. When all data dependencies have been satisfied, the instructions can be executed. Eventually an instruction will be retired in program order by writing data into the ISA visible registers to ensure sequential execution machine state.

The first and most significant problem with this approach is that execution must proceed speculatively and even though there is a high probability of control hazards being correctly predicted [2], this must but put into context. As a rule of thumb, a basic blocks is often no longer than 6 instructions [3] and if we assume a 6-way instruction issue superscalar microprocessor with 6 pipeline stages before the branch condition is resolved [4], we are likely to have of the order of 6 branches unresolved at any time. Even with a 95% successful prediction rate for each branch, there is a 1 in 4 chance of failure in any cycle. With unpredictable branching, the situation is much worse and branch prediction failure is almost guaranteed in any cycle (98% chance of failure). These parameters will also limit multi-path prefetching, as instruction fetch and decode bandwidth is exponential in the number of unresolved brunches. In other words we could be fetching and decoding up to 64 different instruction paths in a multi path approach. A second problem is that of sequential-order or deterministic machine state, which lags significantly behind instruction fetch due to the many pipeline stages used in out-of-order execution. This means there are significant delays on non-deterministic events, such as on an interrupt or an error, caused by the miss prediction of a branch condition for example. Recovery for miss prediction therefore can have a very high latency. The final problem is one of diminishing returns for available resources [5], which we will look at in more detail below.

Out-of-order executions requires large register files, large instruction issue windows and large caches. As the issue width increases, both the number of register ports and hence the size of the register file must both increase. The physical size of the register file increases more than quadratically with instruction issue width [1] and this is largely due to the size of the register cell, which requires both horizontal and vertical busses for each port. The proposed Alpha 21464 illustrates this problem very well [6], its register file comprises 512 64 bit registers and occupies an area over four times the size of the L1 D-caches of 64KB. The area of the instruction window also grows with issue width. It can be thought of as a sliding window over the code stream within which concurrency can be extracted, it grows with the square of the number of entries due to the scoreboard logic that that controls instruction issue. The 21464 has 128 entries. It must be large so as to not unduly limit the potential ILP that may be exploited in an out-of-order issue. The problem is compounded because out-of-order execution introduces additional dependencies (WAR and WAW), which are resolved by register renaming and drive up the size of the register file. These are not real dependencies but simply resource conflicts. Again the proposed 21464 illustrates the problem well, the 128 entry out-of-order issue queue + renaming logic is approximately ten times the size of the L1 I-cache, also 64KB. Finally, out-of-order issue increases the complexity of the memory hierarchy, both in levels of cache implemented and in prefetching and cache management techniques. It is well known that caching produces only diminishing returns in terms of performance for chip area occupied and current L2 cache arrays will typically occupy between 1/3 and 1/2 of the total chip area [6].

Clearly something is very wrong with the out-of-order approach to concurrency if this extravagant consumption of on-chip resources is only providing a practical limit on IPC of about 2. Having said that further improvements in IPC have been observed in Simultaneous Multi-Threaded (SMT) architectures, which are based on the superscalar approach. However we have to consider whether this is the most appropriate solution, adding yet further hardware resources to an already non-scalable approach to increase instruction issue width still further. Note that the 21464 [6] is an SMT supported out-of-order issue architecture.

2.2 VLIW ISAs

Let us now consider explicit concurrency in an ISA using VLIW, which is both synchronous and static. VLIW encodes a number of operations into one long instruction word and these operations are executed in lock step on parallel functional units. The approach was originally called horizontal microcode as early designs used microcoded pipelines to execute the operations simultaneously. Later the name very long instruction word (VLIW) was coined. The origins of this approach can be traced back to signal processing solutions of the late 1970s and the Floating Point Systems AP120B [7] is a good early example. Although called an array processor the instruction set is wide and it executes several operations simultaneously. Array processing applies to the mode of programming, which used libraries of array-based operations. True VLIW computers were built without cache and exploited loop-intensive code. A fixed memory latency and branch behaviour that was predictable at compile-time enabled these devices to function effectively in their domain. They were not however general purpose computers. Moreover the limitation of cacheless architecture is a significant problem with modern technology, where processor speeds are significantly higher than memory speeds.

The most notable recent adoption of VLIW is Intel's new IA-64 ISA [8], renamed again to EPIC. This is a generalisation of VLIW and differs from it in a number of ways. Firstly the instruction set is designed to be future compatible. It does not describe explicit hardware resources but the extent of software concurrency. Thus each instruction packet can contain an arbitrary number of operations that are executed concurrently or sequentially depending on the extent of the instruction issue width. Secondly it provides greater flexibility than earlier VLIW ISAs by providing support for the two key problems in VLIW, namely, keeping the processor running in the presence of non-determinism in both data and control. The use of predicated instruction execution overcomes many control hazards and an explicit prefetch instruction, followed by a check when the data is required is used to avoid non-deterministic latency in memory loads.

These problems are universal but the adverse results are particularly severe in VLIW architectures, as any failure in these mechanisms can kill the schedule and force all units to wait for one hazard to be resolved. This is as a result of the lockstep nature of the ISA. This solution also comes at a cost, which is redundant computation. Predication is a form of multiple-path execution, where the compiler determines the extent of redundant computation in order to maintain the static schedule in the presence of what would normally be considered branches. Clearly any form of multi-path execution is a form of speculation, which consumes hardware resources and perhaps more importantly, energy. There are also limitations on what Intel calls data speculation, i.e. hoisting speculative loads high enough in the instruction stream to overcome potential memory latency problems, which include memory aliasing problems. Prefetches can be hoisted above conditional branches but if each branch path requires different data, speculative memory bandwidth requirements would increase exponentially with the number of branches over which the prefetch was hoisted.

2.3 Multi-threaded ISAs

We have seen that both VLIW and out-of-order issue require some form of speculation in order to operate effectively. Multi-threading on the other hand makes any form of speculation unnecessary, although some multi-threaded approaches do rely on speculation [9]. Multi-threaded instruction execution need not suffer from the problems encountered using speculative execution, with one exception and that is fundamental, it is synchronising across many concurrently issued instructions and requires a large register file. In a threaded microprocessor, it is not necessary to issue instructions in a thread out-of-order and hence we need only deal with true data dependencies. This can simplify processor design considerably, see [11], which considers a range of processor designs in developing chip multi-processors, it suggests a packing density difference of a factor of 8 between in-order issue and out-of-order issue processors. However a chip multiprocessor based on a threaded scheduling will also require additional hardware to support context stores and mechanisms for scheduling and synchronising inter-thread dependencies.

The major benefit of multi-threading is tolerance to latency in memory accesses, true concurrency and other non-deterministic events. It can even be used to avoid speculation on conditional branches [12], thus making branch prediction unnecessary, in all but single-threaded code.

In Multi-threaded code, even if a compiler decides where context switches occur, the instruction schedule is dynamic, as ready threads depend on non-deterministic events and then can be scheduled in any order. High-latency memory events, such as cache misses, true data dependencies and conditional branches are triggers which can be used to determine when to context switch, which provides a new source of instructions to be executed while the event is resolved and data produced. There is some cost for this but the cost can be made small. The result is, that instructions from more than one thread can be executed in one or more pipelines. But what impact will this have on the ISA design?

The most flexible approach is to have dynamic thread management, where instructions are added to some base ISA to provide for some or all of the following actions:

• thread creation
• thread termination
• thread synchronisation and related initialisation

Initially, this approach seem to have only an incremental impact on the ISA, leaving it backward compatible with the base ISA on single-threaded application code. We will see later however, that this is not necessarily true and in the example below we see that instruction tagging for context switches and register specifiers are also likely to change in the Multi-threaded ISA.

Multi-threading has been applied in a variety of different ways and for a variety of applications and programming paradigms. These include multiprocessor supercomputers, such as the HEP [12], Horizon [13] and Cray MTA [14], an alternative approach to the implementation of data flow computers (see [10] for the rationale) and more recently for Java byte-code engines in micro controllers [15] and streaming applications [16]. One of the more interesting recent developments is the use of threading in order to develop so called network processors [17]. This approach has been adopted by both Intel [18] and IBM [19]. It is clearly a well suited application as the low context-switching overhead of a thread microprocessor can be used meet the real-time demands of network switching.

The extent of any taxonomy in multi-threaded architecture is also dependent on the base micro architecture, instruction issue, e.g. out-of-order issue or in-order, number of instructions issued simultaneously, the extent of sharing of various resources, e.g. superscalar or multi-processor approaches, programming model, etc. Suffice it to say that most combinations have been explored. An excellent survey of processors with explicit multi-threading can be found in [20], which covers most, if not all, different approaches to multi-threading. This survey provides a number of taxonomic distinctions in Multi-threaded architectures:

Blocking and non-blocking - typically non-blocking threads are used in data flow architectures (but not exclusively so), a non-blocking thread will resolve all dependencies prior to launching the thread by decoupling the memory accesses from the computation, e.g. [21].

Explicit and implicit - implicit approaches attempt to increase performance of sequential code by thread-level speculation, e.g. [22]

Block-threading, interleaved multi-threading and simultaneous multi-threading - in block multi-threading instructions are executed until some event causes a context switch. Typically there will be support for a small, usually fixed number of threads, each of which has its own register set and stack pointers to maintain its context without spilling to memory. Interleaved threading is where a context switch takes place on every cycle, as instructions are interleaved from multiple threads into a pipeline that assumes no structural hazards. Finally when instructions are issued simultaneously from multiple threads to a superscalar pipeline, this is called simultaneous multi-threading. This should not be confused with multi-thread support for chip multiprocessing, where many processors without shared resources may use multiple threads to support concurrency. For many examples of each approach see [20].

3   Micro-threaded Execution Model

In this section we take a look at one particular model in detail, that based on [12]. This approach uses a block-threaded approach with a blocking model for threads. Unusually however for a block-threaded approach, it is possible to interleave threads on a cycle-by-cycle basis, as its context switching overhead is zero cycles. It is based on a simple in-order issue pipeline and is designed to support wide instruction issue using a chip-multiprocessor approach. Before we look at the model in detail and evaluate its costs, we give some results of recent simulations. More detail of simulation conditions are given in previous papers presented at this conference [24, 25].

3.1 Simulation Results

The first results show vertical threading, on one single-issue pipeline and illustrate the tolerance to latency that can be achieved. The comparisons are between the base architecture and the same architecture augmented with a micro-threaded scheduler. This simulations use a level-1, cache-miss latency of 5 processor cycles and a level-2 cache-miss latency of between 10 and 1000 processor cycles, representing a range of memory architectures from tightly coupled through to distributed. First we show the performance of micro-threading on the K3 Livermore loop, which is an inner product calculation. The thread is a loop body comprising just 4 instruction, i.e. not much opportunity for parallelism, as each thread is dependent on the previous one. The 4 instructions are two load words, which will usually miss cache as no prefetching is assumed, a multiply requiring both loads which are independent in each thread and an add instruction which is dependent on the result of the multiply and the result of the add from the previous iteration. This is in executed with a thread-based vector instruction, which generates a family of threads for the entire recurrence loop. The conventional code would have two more instructions to control the loop, one to increment the index and a conditional branch to terminate the loop. These functions are performed in hardware in the micro-threaded pipeline using its vector thread create instruction.

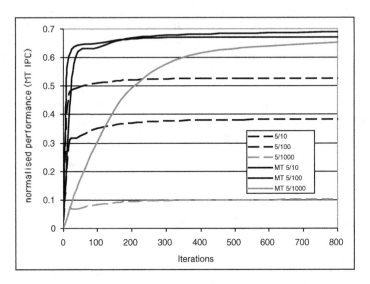

Fig. 1. Relative performance of micro-threaded (solid lines) vs conventional pipeline (dashed lines) on Livermore K3 loop. Each line shows a different cache delay e.g. L1/L2.

Figure 1 shows the performance of the micro-threaded pipeline for the Livermore K3 loop kernel. This shows that a micro-threaded pipeline achieves the same asymptotic performance (IPC = 0.7) regardless of the cache delay but requires more iterations to achieve it. For a 1000 cycle L2 cache miss penalty, the half performance vector length is 120 iterations. What is significant is that for 240 plus iterations, the micro-threaded pipeline has a better performance with a 1000 cycle penalty, than the conventional pipeline has with a miss penalty that is 2 orders of magnitude smaller!

This result assumes unlimited registers, which is an unreasonable assumption, the simulation was repeated with a fixed number of registers (128) and the results are shown in figure 2. For the 1000 cycle L2 miss penalty, performance is register limited and it is only marginally better than the conventional pipeline. Less than 32 iterations can run in parallel in this configuration, which is insufficient to tolerate cache misses of 1000 cycles and also has an impact on the 100 cycle L2 miss performance as well.

The final simulation we present here shows the scalability of the model as a chip multi-processor (CMP) with multiple instruction issue per cycle, based on a 1- 2- and 16-way CMP, each with a cache delay of 5 and 10 cycles respectively for L1 and L2 cache. This is shown in figure 3. In these results, 1 and 2-pipe simulations use 128 registers and the 16 pipe simulation uses 4096. The results show normalised performance, which is the IPC per pipe and this is plotted against iterations per pipeline, giving a normal form for each result. Ideally, with perfect scaling, all results should be coincident, which is just about what is observed. Admittedly the results are based on the K7 Livermoore loop, which is a parallel loop with no dependencies. However, peak performance has an IPC of just below 1 instruction per cycle per pipeline and the half performance vector length is about 5 iterations per pipeline, showing that at least a 95% utilisation can be achieved with this model even on issue widths of 16.

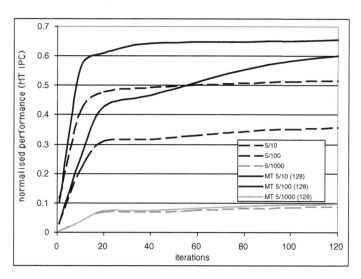

Fig. 2. Relative performance of micro-threaded (solid lines) vs conventional pipeline (dashed lines) on Livermore K3 loop with 128 registers.

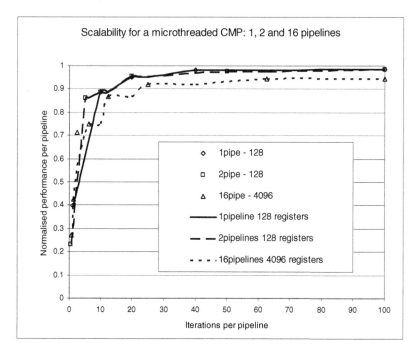

Fig. 3. Performance of a micro-threaded CMP of 1, 2 and 16 processors on Livermore K7 loop.

3.2 Micro-threaded Model

Now let us look at the model these results are based on in more detail in order to understand how and why these results are possible. Figure 4 shows a modified pipeline, with shared and duplicated parts indicated by shading. This is a very conventional in-order issue pipeline with micro-threading components added. These will be described as we outline the micro-threaded abstract model and its implementation.

The model supports a number of concurrent threads all drawn from the same context, these were called micro-threads to distinguish them from other multi-threaded techniques. The term micro-thread captures the notion of this approach, that of creating, interleaving and terminating very many small sequences of instructions efficiently, perhaps just a few machine instructions each. One disadvantage of micro-threading as proposed in [12] and shared in nano-threading [23] is that they both require the allocation of registers to threads at compile time. This is a major disadvantage for micro-threading where the aim is for general computation using ILP and data parallelism. Dansoft's nano-threaded approach has just two nano threads and allocation of registers is trivial, a subordinate thread would typically be used to preload values from memory into a registers for later use by the main thread.

The solution to this problem in micro-threading was reported in [24 and 25], which describe a dynamic register allocation scheme combined with a thread creation mechanism that produces families of threads, based on the same fragment of code. Without this solution, threading a number of iterations from a loop would require different instances of code with unique registers allocated to each instance. Using this approach, one thread-create instruction generates a family of threads across a loop-like triple that defines the start step and limit of the index value for each thread created. This is very similar to a vector instruction set. Each family of threads can iterate a loop concurrently to the maximum extent of resources available. Thread creation thus becomes a two-stage process:

- *stage one* creates a descriptor for a family threads, which waits until resources are available, and
- *stage two* allocates each thread in the family to a set of resources as they become available. The thread is now able to execute.

The resources required are a continuation queue slot and a contiguous set of registers defined by the thread header.

A major benefit of this dynamic allocation is that it supports a model that can trivially schedule work on multiple processors in a CMP. A potential problem is that the compiler must be aware of resource deadlock issues, for example an inter-thread dependency that spans more than the available chip resources.

A secondary problem introduced by dynamic allocation of registers is that of binding between allocated registers in dependent threads. In an inter-thread synchronisation, one thread will produce a value and another will consume it. In the micro-threading micro-archtecture, synchronisation is performed using full/empty bits on registers and the problem of binding between dynamically allocated registers is solved by allocating threads in strict sequence and by providing an offset in the thread header between producer and consumer within that sequence. This allows runtime

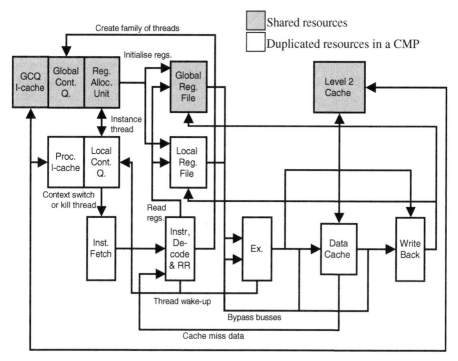

Fig. 4. CMP showing shared and duplicated resources for a wide-issue Multi-threaded architecture

structures to be maintained that allow the sharing of registers between threads, even if allocated to different processors. More detail on this is given in section 4.3.

3.3   Context-Switching Model

In [20], our micro-threaded model is classified as static, block-threaded and with explicit switching. This is because the compiler explicitly tags instruction where a context switch should take place. The context switching overhead is zero cycles, as the tagged instructions trigger an exchange of PC at the instruction fetch stage of the pipeline and then continue to execute. The next cycle sees the first instruction executed from the new context. Context switching can occur on every cycle if so tagged. Tagged instructions include conditional branches and any instruction that reads a register, where the compiler cannot guarantee that the data will be available. Deterministic delays can be compiled into sequences of instructions in the normal manner but for non-deterministic delays a context switch is signaled. There are two kinds of synchronisations, where a context switch is required. The first is intra-thread synchronisations where the result of an earlier load word is required and where there is no guarantee that the load hit the cache. The second is an explicit synchronisation between instructions in different threads, where one thread produces data and another consumes it.

A context switch will only occur when there is at least one other thread ready to run. In the case of single threaded code, or where all other threads are suspended or otherwise unable to run, the current thread will continue to issue instructions as there is a chance that the synchronisation will succeed. If it does, then we avoid a bubble in the pipeline while the thread is suspended passed down the pipeline and cycled back to the continuation queue on a successful synchronisation. If it does not succeed, the thread will suspend on the empty register and await its data and any subsequent instructions issued will be aborted. In this case, the instruction issue stage will have to wait for a thread to be made active before continuing. In the case of a branch instruction, it is possible to add branch predictors but on such a simple pipeline, this is probably not an optimal solution and we use branch delay slots in single threaded code.

Instructions are also terminated for thread termination by the compiler. This means that any instruction can be tagged as being the last in its thread. Both context switch and kill therefore are implemented at zero overhead as both overload otherwise useful instructions. A thread kill tag is similar to a context switch in that it forces a context switch as well as signaling the LCQ that this is the end of the current thread.

3.4 Synchronisation Model

Synchronisation between threads occurs on registers using a three-state model (full/empty/waiting). In the waiting state, the thread reference is stored in a previously empty register and awaits data before being rescheduled. Synchronisation between registers and memory can be added using full/empty states and this may be required in a massively parallel system. Memory synchronisation will cause the consumer thread to wait in the register while the memory system awaits synchronisation with another context. Of course higher levels of concurrency may require software scheduling mechanisms and the full state of the registers must be saved in this situation. The LCQ state can also be used to trigger software context switches, instead of having the pipeline idle.

The justification for using registers as synchronisers for micro threads is to provide a very low-latency synchronisation mechanism within a single context and this model requires that all registers in the micro-architecture implement a modified i-structure [26]. A successful synchronisation incurs zero overhead and recycles the suspended thread to a runnable state within just a few cycles (e.g. the number of cycles to the register read stage in the pipeline + 1, assuming an I-cache hit on rescheduling). Thread suspension occurs at the register read stage when a read is attempted on an empty register. In this case the instruction reading the register is transformed into an instruction that writes the thread reference into the empty register. To do this, the thread's reference travels down the pipeline with each instruction executed. A subsequent write to that register will extract and reschedule the thread whose reference is waiting there. In this way, neither suspend or wakeup require any additional pipeline stages and only a failed synchronisation will require an additional cycle to re-launch the incomplete instruction. The instruction that writes to a waiting register first reads and reschedules the waiting thread before writing to the register. An extra cycle is also required when a deferred memory access is made, as this must insert a new write back instruction into the pipeline, or when all both read ports are used in the instruction that writes the waiting register (e.g. and R op R -> R instruction). In this case a one cycle stall is required to extract the waiting thread reference or an additional register port is required.

Each register implements a modified i-structure that is allocated in the empty state on resource allocation. It has two operations i-store and i-read. I-store updates a specified register with a value and sets the register to the full state. Normally only a single i-store operation is allowed on a given i-structure but this single write is not enforced, to allow the registers to be used in a conventional manner if required. The i-read operation either suspends the thread containing it, if the register is empty, or it returns the value stored. Note that no further i-read instructions can take place on a register that contains a suspended thread. The compiler must therefore enforce binary synchronisations. If there is a requirement for multi-way synchronisation, i.e. many threads suspended on one event, the solution is to create a single guard thread that performs the synchronisation and then creates any number of other continuations. Note that the guard thread's only actions are to await synchronisation, to create a number of other threads and to terminate. This could require just two instructions with a vector create.

3.5 Subroutine Linkages

Micro-threading draws its concurrency only from within a single context and it relies on this fact to provide low-overhead concurrency controls for threads. Thus there must only be a single thread of control when performing subroutine linkages. The single persistent thread is called the main thread for identification purposes only. There are two general solutions to achieving this restriction in multiplicity of threads across subroutine linkages. The first is to make the concurrency user controlled, i.e. the compiler must generate instructions to synchronise to the main thread and to kill all other threads prior to a subroutine call or return. This can lead to large overheads in some programming paradigms, such as "winner-takes-all." Many synchronisations may be required to determine the winner and to signal this to all the other threads. The alternative solution, which is the one we prefer, is to provide a hardware imposed sequentiality across subroutine boundaries. This allows any thread to call or return and hardware cleans up any active threads and allocated resources as a part of the linkage.

As an illustration, assume that we link to a subroutine and the main thread creates a number of threads to search some space, each exploring a small part of that space. In our model any thread on gaining a solution can execute a return, which would kill all other active threads, relinquishing their resources in the process. It does not matter that we have redefined the main thread in this process, as a thread will use global state to communicate results.

3.6 Summary of ISA Requirements

In order to implement a micro-threaded ISA we have to add only four instructions to the base ISA. However, in order to make code more readable, we also add a number of pseudo instructions. The instructions added are:

- *Cre ref* - create a thread unconditionally where the long literal "ref" is a pointer or handle to the thread code;
- *Creq $a $b ref* - create a thread if the registers $a and $b are equal "ref" here is short and PC relative literal;
- *Crne $a $b* - create a thread if the registers $a and $b are not equal;
- *BSync* - suspends the current thread and awaits termination of all other threads before this thread continues.

In addition to the instructions above, three pseudo instructions are defined, which translate into executable instructions.

- *Wait $a* - waits for data in register $a and continues;
- *Setf $a* - signals register as full (n.b. the value in $a is undefined);
- *Sete $a* - signals register as empty.

Finally the compiler tagging of instructions for context switching is translated into pseudo instructions. Three distinct actions are encoded on any instruction requiring a two-bit extension field.

- i.   the next instruction comes from the same thread (*normal execution*);
- ii.   the next instruction comes from another thread, if one exists, otherwise from the same thread (*context switch*);
- iii. the current thread is killed and the next instruction comes from another thread (*kill thread*).

In the original micro-threading paper these were called horizontal transfer, vertical transfer and kill respectively. Here we define them by pseudo instructions, which follow the instruction that they encode:

- *Swch* - switch context if any threads are waiting execution;
- *Kill* - kills the current thread.

Note that these instructions are not translated into executable instructions but simply encode the previous instruction with the additional action. For example:

    add $a $b $c
    kill

Generates one instruction, which performs a add operation and which is tagged to signal the IF stage to terminate this thread. The next instruction comes from another thread. Similarly:

    mul $a $b $c
    swch

Generates one instruction in the pipeline, which performs a multiply operation and is tagged to signal the IF stage to context switch. The next instruction comes from another thread but only if one is available.

4   Implementation Issues and Chip-Area Overheads

In this section we look at more details of implementation and compare the overheads of this model to the Alpha 21464 described in Section 2.1. Clearly the simulation results given above look very promising but what are the consequences on silicon real-estate and scalability in the micro-threaded model. In this comparison, we have adopted a MIPs-like ISA as a base architecture, implemented with a simple 5-stage pipeline, namely {Instruction fetch, Register read, ALU, Memory, Writeback}. A 5 stage pipeline is very simple by current microprocessor implementations. However, it illustrates the fact that much of the complexity of current microprocessors derives from the out-of-order issue and are simply not required by a micro-threaded pipeline, thus reducing its latency.

It is difficult to compare a micro-threaded pipeline to current practice in detail as that requires a detailed implementation of both. In this paper we look only at the instruction issue and register files and compare these to the out-of-order issue pipeline. Note that execution may not be optimal on the micro-threaded pipeline but optimisations, such as allowing 2-way (integer and floating point) in-order VLIW issue, would resolve any redundancy in execution units at a small additional cost. In both superscalar and micro-threaded architecture we are comparing wide instruction issue. In the case of the micro-threaded pipeline this is as an 8-way CMP. In the case of the 21464 it is an 8-way issue superscalar SMT extracting instructions from up to 4 threads.

4.1   Thread State and Register Allocation

In order to understand the implementation issues we must look at the state model of micro threads in some more detail. Table 1 shows the various states, events and representation of threads in the micro-threaded model.

The literal in the create instructions provides a pointer to the thread description block, which contains all of the parameters that define a family of micro threads. Figure 5 shows this data structure and also a schematic representation of the three major state changes from executing a create instruction to running the thread. The parameters are:

- the number of local and shared registers required by each instance of the thread {*local, shared*}
- a triple {*start, step, limit*}, which defines the number of instances of the thread and an index value for each
- the dependency distance {*dep*}, which links the consumer to the producer thread in the sequence of threads
- a pointer to the code for the body of the thread {*tp*}.

When a thread is created, the parameter block is copied into the GCQ, which is shared between all processors on a chip, see figure 4. The GCQ holds the abstract descriptions of all families of threads that have been created but not yet allocated to a proces-

Table 1. State transition table showing detailed state changes in the micro-threaded model.

Old state	Event causing transition	New state	Thread state stored in
Not-defined	Execution of: Cre	Creq	Crne	Created	Global continuation queue (GCQ)
Created	Resource availability on any processor	Active	Local continuation queue (LCQ)
Active	Thread is at head of LCQ and IF signals a context switch or kill	Running	LCQ + PC + LCQ slot no. in pipeline
Running	IF signals context switch	Suspended	LCQ + LCQ slot number in pipeline
Running	IF signals kill	Killed	LCQ
Suspended	Register read succeeds and instruction isn't a conditional branch	Active	LCQ
Suspended	Instruction at ALU stage is a conditional branch	Active	LCQ
Suspended	Register read finds one or more operands empty	Waiting	LCQ + LCQ slot no. in register
Waiting	Register written	Active	LCQ
Killed	Dependent thread is killed	not defined	All state is relinquished

sor. In each machine cycle an allocation will be attempted on each processor from one family of threads. Allocation requires a free LCQ slot on that processor and the required number of locals registers. In addition, for P processors, P times the number of globals must be allocated from the global register file. The result of the allocation is a set of base addresses, detailed below, the initialisation of the registers to empty, with the exception of the first local register, which is initialised to the loop count for that thread. Each allocated thread is uniquely identified during its lifetime by the tuple comprising its processor number and LCQ slot number.

4.2 Registers and Register Addressing

Register addressing uses a simple base + offset mechanism, where the base address is a part of a micro-thread's state and the offset is defined by the register specifier in the instruction executed. The ISA identifies four different types of register and a base address is required for each. Two bits of each register specifier define the register type, the remaining bits the offset. The register types are:
- *Global registers* - are allocated statically, stored in the global register file and read by any processor;

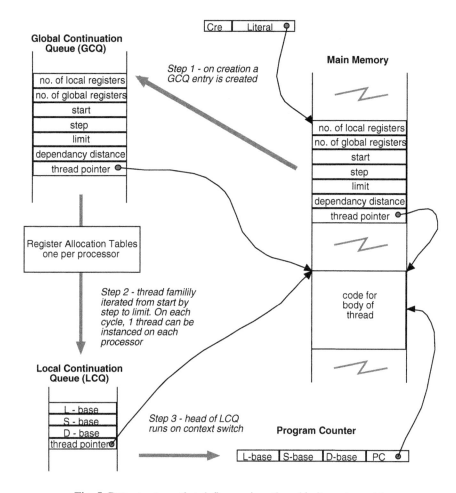

Fig. 5. Data structures that define a micro-thread in its various states.

- *Shared registers* - allocated dynamically for each thread and stored in the global register file;
- *Dependent registers* - not allocated but refer to the shared registers of the thread this one is dependent on;
- *Local registers* - allocated dynamically for each thread in a processor's local register file.

The four different kinds of register in the ISA are identified in the assembly language by adopting a register specifier that uses $ followed by the first letter of the register type {G,S,D or L}, followed by the register number, e.g. $L0, is local register 0 and this is always initialised to the loop number.

We can immediately see some benefits of the micro-threaded approach over an out-of-order issue architecture. The micro-threaded ISA separates local and global registers. Each processor has its own local register file and these will only require 3 register ports in the implementation and hence the chip area required for local register files will be negligible compared to that the 21464 described in Section 2.1. Remember the 21464 has a single 512 register register file with 24 ports in total. It occupies an area some 5 times the size of the L1 D-cache, which is 64KB [6], a packing density hit of two orders of magnitude over the cache memory cell!

If we assume the same number of registers in the micro-threaded CMP as in the 21464, we would have 8 local register files of 32 registers each and a global register file of 256 registers. The issue we must resolve in order to compare the two is how many ports we require for the CMP's global register file. In our simulations [24, 25] we observed that on average, only two instructions in three read the global register file and only one in three write to it, even in threads which have a loop dependencies. Thus we can assume that the register file will require 9 ports, which more than matches the average number of hits required per cycle from 8 processors. We use this figure but note that it may result in some stalls due to conflict due to uneven load distribution and this is an issue we have yet to quantify in our simulation and one of the tradeoffs in any design.

If we assume the area of the 21464 is 1 and we assume a square law increase in register file area with number of ports and a linear increase one in number of registers, then the combined local register files of the CMP would require an area of only 0.8% of the 21464's register file and the CMP global register file would requires an area of 7% of the 21464's register file. There would also be a linear reduction in the area required for bussing data to and from the register files based on number of ports. So in the CMP we can reduce the area required for register file size by an order of magnitude in an 8-way issue processor but what of overheads for dynamic allocation of the registers.

4.3 Dynamic Register Allocation

The register allocation cycle is shown in figure 6. The Register Allocation Units (RAUs) maintain the allocation state of all register files. In each cycle registers are allocated on each processor's local register file and for each processor in the global register file. This is equivalent to 2 allocation units per processor, each maintaining 32 registers, where one allocates locals and one globals. In practice the global allocator will share some resources, so this is an upper bound.

Registers must be allocated in a contiguous block as we are using base + displacement addressing. If we assume a 3-bit displacement field, giving a 5 bit register specifier (i.e. 2 bits to select register type), then the maximum number of registers of one type that could be allocated to a thread is 8. The logic to implement an allocator is not complex. Even allocating to an arbitrary boundary in the register file would require little more than 1 bit of storage as an allocated flag, a 3-bit counter and a 3-bit comparator for each register. However, the area cost of the RAUs is linear in the number of registers with the constant being proportional to the displacement field, and moreover, it is small compared to the register file itself. There is an added complication, as we have to keep track of dependencies.

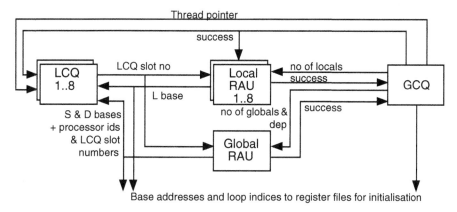

Fig. 6. Register allocation cycle showing the major components and interactions between them.

Synchronisation between two threads uses a shared register on which i-read and i-store operations can take place. If we call the thread performing the i-store the producer and that performing the i-read the consumer, then the shared register is allocated to the producer from the global register file and it is accessed using the shared base address, e.g. $S1. The consumer references the same register using the same offset but with the dependent base address, e.g. register specifier $D1, i.e. register $D1 in the consumer thread is the same register as $S1 in the producer thread. To achieve this dependency tracking we use the *dep* field from the thread header, which specifies the dependency distance between producer and consumer in terms of the thread issue sequence. The D-base of the consumer thread must be set to the same value as the S-base of the consumer thread. In order to locate and bind the producer and consumer threads in this way on a multi-processor chip, a number of rules must be followed in creating threads.

i.   all thread families in the GCQ must be iterated in order of creation to various processors;

ii.   the loop iterator must be defined such that the producer thread is allocated before the consumer thread;

iii. shared registers are allocated to all threads and a table of S-base, LCQ slot number and processor id are stored against the thread's sequence number modulo the maximum number of threads in the global RAU;

iv.   the S-base, LCQ slot number and processor id of the producer thread are then determined from this table for each consumer thread using its sequence number minus dep, and the producer's S-base is copied and becomes the consumer's D-base.

Note that the processor id and LCQ slot number of the producer thread are required by the consumer thread's LCQ to signal the producer's LCQ when it has been killed, as only then can the producer thread's shared resources be released. If we assume that each LCQ has 64 slots, enough to have one thread waiting in each of the CMP's 512 registers, then keeping track of dependencies requires another 13 bits of storage per register and again is linear in the number registers in the CMP.

We have seen therefore that register allocation, including keeping track of dependencies has a chip area, which is linear in the number of registers in the CMP and which has a small constant. The area of this is negligible compared to global register file, which is dependent on both number of registers and number of ports squared.

4.4 LCQ, Thread State and I-Cache Prefetching

The LCQ is perhaps the major overhead associated with the micro-threading model in terms of chip area. We have already assumed that the number of threads in the CMP is equal to the total number of registers available. It cannot reasonably be more, as blocked threads wait in registers but it might be less. So we are looking at an upper bound here.

The LCQ is a linked memory structure and associated logic that implements a given thread priority, probably a FIFO, as our simulations have shown that scheduling priority has little bearing on the efficiency of execution [25]. This is hardly surprising due to the fine-grain nature of the threads involved. The LCQ is implemented as a store addressed by thread reference or slot number, which has two 6-bit fields for creating various priority queues. It requires a 3-bit field for thread state and a field, which points to the producer thread of any dependency, which may be on any processor and hence requires 9 bits. Finally it requires a thread pointer (PC), which we assume is 40 bits, giving a total of 64 bits per register in the CMP. The memory is likely to be multi ported but with a small number of ports, we estimate 4 read and 4 write ports as the LCQ interacts with RAU, pipeline, I-cache. This would mean the combined LCQ structures in the CMP are approximately equal to its global register file size, which we know is approximately 7% of the area required by the 21464's register file. What is important however is that it scales linearly with the issue width. The number of ports required is a structural and implementation issue and is independent of the issue width.

We estimate therefore, that the combined LCQs in an 8-way issue micro-threaded CMP would be about 3% of the size of the 21464's instruction issue logic.

There are more benefits and area savings in a micro-threaded model if we consider the LCQ's interaction with the I-cache in more detail. This can be used to avoid stalls in the pipeline due to I-cache misses. The state of a micro thread can be used to determine a prefetch and replacement strategy and conversely the state of I-cache lines can be used to set the thread state so that pipeline stalls on I-cache fetch can be avoided completely. The prefetch/replacement strategy is deterministic and very simple, each I-cache line only requires a counter of the number of active threads using that cache line. When a thread is allocated to a processor, a prefetch will be made to its thread pointer. If the prefetch hits, the line counter is incremented and the thread becomes active. If it misses, the memory block will eventually be fetched into any line with a zero counter. Until this happens the thread remains in a suspended state. When a thread enters the running state additional blocks may also be fetched to avoid I-cache stalls. Remember however, that any conditional branch will normally suspend the thread and we can ensure that the thread is not made active until the I-cache block along the new path has been fetched. A running thread either runs until it is killed or is suspended and in either case its code is no longer required in the I-cache and the I-cache line counter is decremented. Cache replacement therefore, is based on thread counters. Any line with a counter of 0 can safely be swapped and the cache will wait until this condition is eventually reached, as earlier threads suspend or are killed. When a thread is rescheduled after being suspended, the same process is followed as when it was created, i.e. it remains in the suspended state until the code in the cache. The overhead for this strategy is trivial, just a 6-bit counter and some associated logic per cache line.

5 Programming Model

Before we draw conclusions from the above analysis let us consider the programming model that might be used with a micro-threaded microprocessor. There are three issues here, binary code compatibility, sequential language compilation techniques and finally a concurrent programming models. These are each briefly discussed.

Concerning binary code compatibility, we have already said that only a small number of additions need be made to a base ISA in order to support the micro-threading model. We have also said that register specifiers and instruction tagging must be supported. It would be possible to use binary code translation to support backward compatibility by not using any of the additional instruction and by tagging everything to not context switch. This would leave us with single threaded code, which would not exploit the wide issue of a CMP. It is possible to develop techniques to do binary code analysis and create threaded code from sequential code by analysing dependencies in the instruction stream. This approach has not yet been studied in any depth.

If binary code compatibility is discarded it is possible to compile existing sequential source code to generate very efficient micro-threaded code. This is because the compilation can extract concurrency across loops, even in the presence of inter-loop dependencies. These techniques have been used in order to hand compile the code used in our simulations [24,25]. There are limitations on the complexity of loops that can be supported by a family of micro threads, because the synchronisation in this model requires a single constant dependency distance between loop iterations. For example, the two code fragments below could both be compiled in a single family of threads (vector instruction):

> For i = 1 to n do
> > x[i] = x[i] + x[i+j]
> For i = 1 to n do
> > x[i] = x[i] + x[i+j]
> > y[i] = y[i] + y[i+j]

If j is a constant then the thread header is static, if j is a variable, the thread header would need to be constructed dynamically.

The following fragments however, could not be compiled to a single family of threads (unless k = j).

For i = 1 to n do
    x[i] = x[i] + x[i+j]
    y[i] = y[i] + y[i+k]

It could however be translated into two families of threads, with a global synchronisation before the creation of the second family, where each family performs just one assignment from all loop iterations. The overhead for this would not be large, just a few cycles amortised across n iterations.

New techniques need to be developed to fully understand the code generation issues but the basic code analysis is well understood and it comes from dependency analysis found in standard optimising compilers and vectorisation techniques used in compilers for vector supercomputers.

The final method of programming we consider is that for which this execution model was originally designed for [27], namely an explicit data-parallel model [28]. Such languages provide a simpler analysis and more information for optimisation in terms of the symmetries that they possess [29] and hence give us an easier route to generating efficient code, than in compiling sequential languages.

Note that loop parallelism other than indexed loops can be compiled with the micro-threaded model, including speculative techniques but these techniques tend to be marginally less efficient as they typically require one create instruction for every thread created rather than one instruction per family. Obviously the extent of the inefficiency is smaller for longer micro threads. These are all issues that are being considered in our current work but we have already simulated a pointer chasing loop based on a while loop and even with sequential order termination it provides better performance than a conventional single-issue pipeline.

6   Conclusions

It appears that Moore's law is a two-edged sword. The exponential growth of on-chip resources for storage and processing has tended to mask creeping inefficiencies in current microprocessor designs, such as out-of-order issue microprocessors, including those with multi-threaded instruction issue units. An exponential increase in gates with a short time constant can easily hide the underlying lack of scalability in any given approach. The problem is, that there are strong commercial pressures for an evolutionary development in microprocessor design. However, the fundamental scaling issues that have been highlighted are always going to be an issue at some stage, unless no other approach can be found with better scaling properties, and then a revolutionary change will be required. This has already happened with both radical and conservative microprocessor vendors but on different time scales (note for conservative read market leader).

The fundamental issues in out-of-order issue microprocessors are in the complexity of two main components in this design, namely the instruction issue logic, which grows as the square of the instruction window size (proportional to the issue width) and the register file, which is used for global communication and synchronisation between the concurrently issued instructions, and which grows with the square of the number of register ports (proportional to issue width). What is required to alleviate these problems is an instruction issue strategy that is linear in the issue width and a register file that is partitioned between local and remote synchronisations. Note that the global nature of communications is always going to grow with a square law if we want constant delay, as this is a connectivity problem. Thus the only option we have open to us here is to partition the register file into local and global parts, thus mitigating the square law scaling. Micro-threading does exactly this in a CMP.

This paper has therefore looked at multi-threading as an alternative approach to out-of-order issue. It investigates the diversity of multi-threaded design in achieving large instruction issue widths. Among these options we have shown micro-threading to be a particularly efficient form of multi-threading. We show this technique to be very effective in tolerating latency and in the avoidance of speculative execution. Moreover, it can extract concurrency from both ILP and loop-level parallelism by supporting a vector like instruction to generate families of threads for executing loops. Thus micro-threading can be used as the basis for wide instruction issue in a chip multi-processor.

The instruction issue mechanism distributes work between processors in the form of micro-threads that execute just a few instructions. This fine grain distribution enables a very even distribution of load, one of the factors, which determines the efficiency of a parallel system. The example simulated here on a micro-threaded CMP uses the Livermoore K7 loop and our compilation generates a family of threads, each of which comprises just a few instructions, all of them performing useful, rather than bookkeeping work. The second factor, which determines the efficiency of a parallel system is the overhead incurred in scheduling and synchronisation the threads. It is clear from this simulation that the multi-issue, micro-threaded CMP has negligible overheads. It achieves an asymptotic IPC of between 95 and 100 percent per pipeline, for up to 16 pipelines, demonstrating what has been said in previous papers [12,24,25], namely that the model has very small overheads for scheduling threads both on single and multiple issue pipelines. The half-performance vector length for achieving this is also just 3 iterations per pipeline but that would be expected for a highly parallel loop with no dependencies.

Finally we have considered the overheads of implementing the instruction issue logic and register files for a CMP, both are components that we know in an out-of-order issue pipelines are not scalable. In the CMP, we have shown that instruction issue scales linearly with the number of pipelines and we compared this with out-of-order instruction issue, which is responsible for the single largest component on the 21464 (with the exception of the L2 cache). We have also shown that the register file can be partially distributed to individual pipelines, again giving linear scaling, for the local parts. However, micro-threading also requires low-latency, inter-processor synchronisation and this is achieved in the model using a global register file. In the CMP however, many register references will be routed to the local register files and the number of concurrent accesses to the global register file will reduced. Hence we can reduce the number of ports in the global register file, which is the root cause of the bad scaling. This component is not scalable in the CMP but it is more scalable than in an out-of-order issue microprocessor. We estimate that a reduction in chip area for the global register file in a micro-threaded, 8-way CMP of 93% compared to an out-of-order issue pipeline of the same width. This is based on one micro-threaded instruction in three writing a word to the global register file and two in three reading a word from it.

References

1. Jessica Tseng and Krste Asanovic (2003) Banked multiported register files for high-frequency superscalar microprocessors, To appear, 30th International Symposium on Computer Architecture (ISCA-30), San Diego, CA, June 2003,
   http://www.cag.lcs.mit.edu/scale/papers/bankedreg-isca2003.pdf
2. K Skadron, P S Ahuja, M Martonosi and D W Clark (1999) Branch prediction, instruction-window size and simulation techniques, IEEE Trans. Comput., 48(11) pp 1260-81
3. D. W. Wall. Limits of Instruction-Level Parallelism. Technical Report 93/6, Digital Western Research Laboratory, November 1993.
4. R. E. Kessler, E. J. McLellan, and D. A. Webb. The Alpha 21264 Microprocessor Architecture. 1998 International Conference on Computer Design, pages 24–36, October 1998.
5. V Agarwal, H S Murukkathampoondi, S W Keckler, and D C Burger (2000) Clock rate versus IPC: The end of the road for conventional microarchictectures, Proc 27th International Symposium on Computer Architecture (ISCA), June, 2000.
6. R P Peterson et. al. (2002) Design of an 8-wide superscalar RISC microprocessor with simultaneous multithreading,ISSCDigest and Visuals supplement.
7. W R Wittamayar (1978) Array processor provides high throughput rates, Comput. Design, 17 (3), pp93-100
8. Intel, (2000) Intel IA64 Architecture Software Developer's Manual, Volume 1-4.
9. D M Tullsen, S J Eggers and H M Levy (1995) Simultaneous Multithreading: Maximizing On-Chip Parallelism. ISCA 1995: 392-403.
10. G M Papadopoulos and K R Traub (1991) Multi-threading: a revisionist view of dataflow architecture, Computations Structures Group memo 330, March 1991, MIT.
11. K Sankaralingam, R Nagarajan, H Liu, C. Kim, J Huh, D Burger, S W. Keckler, C R Moore (2003) Exploiting ILP, TLP, and DLP with the Polymorphous TRIPS Architecture, to appear Proc ISCA 2003, San Diago, June 2003.
12. A Bolychevsky, C R Jesshope and V B Muchnick, (1996) Dynamic scheduling in RISC architectures, IEE Trans. E, Computers and Digital Techniques ,143, pp309-317.
12. B J Smith (1978) A pipelined shared-resource MIMD computer, IEEE Proc. 1978 Intl. Conf. on Parallel processing, pp6-8.
13. M Thistle and B J Smith(1988) A processor architecturefor Horizon. In Proceedings of the Supercomputing Conference (Orlando, FL). 35–41.
14. R Alverson, D Callahan, D Cummings, B Koblenz, A Porterfield AND B J Smith (1990) The Tera computer system. In Proceedings of the 4th International Conference on Supercomputing (Amsterdam, The Netherlands). 1–6.
15. R German, M GIiampapa, D Gresh, M GUupta, R Haring, H Ho, P Hochschild, S Hummel, T JOnas, D Lieber, G Martyna, U Brinkschulte, C Krakowski, J Kreuzinger and T Ungerer (1999) A multithreaded Java microcontroller for thread-oriented realtime event-handling. In Proceedings of the International Conference on Parallel Architectures and Compilation Techniques (Newport Beach, CA). 34–39.

16. M Tremblay J Chan S Chaudhry A W Conigliaro and S S Tse (2000) The MAJC architecture: a synthesis of parallelism and scalability, IEEE Micro 20, 6, 12–25.
17. P N Glaskowsky (2002) Network processors mature in 2001 Microproc. Report. February 19, (online journal).
18. Intel Corporation (2002) Intel Internet exchange architecture network processors: flexible, wirespeed processing from the customer premises to the network core. White paper. Intel, Santa Clara, CA.
19. IBM Corporation (1999) IBM network processor, Product overview. IBM, Yorktown Heights, NY.
20. T Ungerer, B Robic and J Silc (2003) A survey of processors with explicit multithreading, ACM Computing Surveys (CSUR) March 2003 35(1), pp29-63.
21. K M Kavi, D L Levene and A R Hurson (1997) A non-blocking multithreaded architecture. In Proceedings of the 5th International Conference on Advanced Computing (Madras, India). pp171–177.
22. P Marcuello, A Gonzales and J Tubella (1998) Speculative multithreaded processors. In Proceedings of the 12th International Conference on Supercomputing (Melbourne, Australia) pp77–84.
23. L Gwennap (1997) DanSoft develops VLIW design, Microproc. Report 11, 2 (Feb. 17), 18–22.
24. C R Jesshope (2001) Implementing an efficient vector instruction set in a chip multiprocessor using micro-threaded pipelines, Proc. ACSAC 2001, Australia Computer Science Communications, 23, No 4., pp80-88, IEEE Computer Society (Los Alimitos, CA, USA), ISBN 0-7695-0954-1.
25. B Luo and C R Jesshope (2002) Performance of a Micro-threaded Pipeline, in Proc. 7th Asia-Pacific conference on Computer systems architecture, 6, (Feipei Lai and John Morris Eds.) Australian Computer Society, Inc. Darlinghurst, Australia, ISBN ~ ISSN:1445-1336 , 0-909925-84-4 , pp83-90.
26. Arvind and Thomas, R.E.,"I-Structure: An Effective Data Structure for Functional Languages" MIT,LCS- TM178, Lab. for Computer Science, MIT, 1978.
27. A Bolychevsky (1994) The fundamental Issues and Construction of a Data-parallel Dataflow computer, Technical Report. Computer Systems Research Group, University of Surrey.
28. C R Jesshope (1982) Programming with a high degree of parallelism in FORTRAN, Comp. Phys. Comm., 26, pp237-246.
29. A V Shafarenko (1995) Symmetries in data parallelism Computer Journal, 38, pp365-378.

The Development of System Software
for Parallel Supercomputers

Victor Korneev

Research & Development Institute "Kvant", 15, 4th Likhachevsky Lane, Moscow, Russia
korv@a5.kiam.ru

Abstract. Presented is the architecture and software for the supercomputer MVS-1000M. Given is the analysis of causes for another, unlike MVS-1000M, approach to the creation of system software for parallel supercomputers, namely: the implementation of joint use of resources of many, in the general case, various computer systems within the network environment of distributed high-performance computations, e.g. on the basis of the Grid technology. Presented is the variant of implementation of system software for parallel supercomputers on the basis of Globus, the original proprietary systems of monitoring, resources and tasks management being built in the Globus.

1 The Statement of the Problem

The parallelism and programmability of the computer system's structure as the ways to achieve high performance, specialization of the problem being solved, fault-tolerance and availability make up the basis of the concept (proposed rather a long time ago [1]) of constructing parallel computer systems.

In the course of implementation of this concept a number of parallel supercomputers have been created, MVS-1000M being the most high-performance one [2, 3]. As computer modules (CM) we use commercial motherboards UP2000 with two microprocessors Alpha 21264, the clock frequency 667 MHz, with the second-level cache memory of 4 Mbytes, the main memory of 2 GBytes and disk memory of 20 GBytes.

The supercomputer has the 768-processor array made up by 6 basic blocks, containing 64 two-processor CMs apiece. The structure of the supercomputer MVS-1000M is given in Fig. 1.

Two-processor CMs are connected via the PCI buses to the communication fabric Myrinet 2000 and to the Fast Ethernet.

The communication fabric Myrinet 2000 is intended for the high-rate exchange between CMs during parallel computations. The Myrinet 2000 fabric consists of six 128-port switches each of them located in every basic block. 64 CMs of the corresponding block are connected to each of the switches. The remaining 64 ports of each switch of a block are used to connect the switches of different blocks. While exchanging "point-to-point" data (i.e. between any couple of two-processor CMs) the throughout capacity of 110-150 Mbytes/sec is achieved.

A. Omondi and S. Sedukhin (Eds.): ACSAC 2003, LNCS 2823, pp. 46–53, 2003.

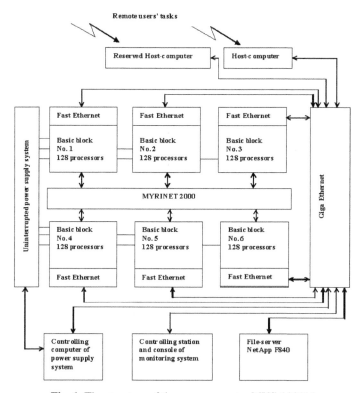

Fig. 1. The structure of the supercomputer MVS-1000M

The Fast Ethernet contains six switches, each of them being located in the corresponding computer block and connected to the CMs of this block. The switch of every block is connected via Gigabit port to the Gigabit Ethernet switch. CMs reach the host computer and the file-server via this Gigabit Ethernet switch. The Fast Ethernet is used to perform the initial loading of programs and data into a CM, to provide the access of CMs to outside facilities and file-server, and to control and monitor hardware and software during the computer process.

The supercomputer MVS-1000M is provided with the system of uninterrupted power supply accompanied by monitoring the parameters of hardware and the software environment. The supply of CMs and other hardware, the units of uninterrupted supply among them, is automatically power off in marginal states.

In general, the software of the supercomputer MVS-1000M keeps the succession with MVS-1000/200 and MVS-100 [2]. The evolution of software tends to the extension of parallel programming resources, parallel program debugging, securing the remote program run, and enhancing the efficiency of the supercomputer's resources and its availability.

In the course of transition from MVS-100 to MVS-1000/200, the systems of planning the loading of tasks [6, 7], of providing safe remote access [8] were added to the means of parallel programming on the basis of communications exchange [4, 5] and manual initiation of programs on the entire chosen resource (sections, the totality of sections, the whole supercomputer). This made it possible to provide a number of users with resources of a CM discreteness. In this case a user does not know on which particular CMs his or her parallel program is being executed.

In MVS-1000M, as compared to MVS-1000/200, developed are the system of continuous monitoring of hardware-software resources [9, 10] and that of power supply control [11].

If the monitoring system detects any faulty (inoperative) CM, the system of task loading is informed about it and it excludes these CMs from the resources and completes the parallel program using the faulty CMs.

For all the instructions on the access to the supercomputer MVS-1000M and on the preparation of parallel programs see the sites www.jscc.ru and www.kiam.ru.

The design of the next-generation supercomputers requires the critical analysis of problems arising in the creation of parallel supercomputers and the experience of applying MVS-1000M:

1. The supercomputer MVS-1000M is considered to be the single resource and is loaded from one host computer. Here, the assigned by the administrator policy of resources allocation is uniformly applied to all the tasks coming to the host computer.

The problem is that more than 50% of the total number of tasks to be performed requires the number of CMs not exceeding the resources of a basic block. Moreover, the tasks form checkpoints on the local disks of CMs, to transfer them throughout the Fast Ethernet to the file-server would require unacceptably much time. Therefore, the following run of the task from the checkpoint of the same CMs is desirable.

An alternative to the decision taken in MVS-1000M may be the construction of every basic block as an independent supercomputer with its own system of loading the parallel tasks and with the introduction of one or more additional (extra) control levels. These levels make it possible to consistently allocate resources of several basic blocks to perform tasks requiring their total resources.

2. It is typical for the use of computer systems when several generations of computer devices coexist simultaneously in an arrangement of a few generations of computer means:

- out-of-date but still used computer means,
- up-to-date and mastered ones,
- being installed and still in the process of mastering computer means.

Moreover, the resources of a computer system may be accumulated step-by-step due to various reasons, the stage-by-stage allocation of finance among them. Equipment bought with the intervals of a few (4-6) months differs in parameters. In such cases it is preferable to create separate CSs rather than combine dissimilar components within a CS.

3. The evolution of integral circuits enables the creation of one-chip computer systems. The BlueGene project of IBM is the example of it. In this case we originally have the problem of combining individual CSs into a system.

4. Computer systems may have specific architecture-structural implementations making them to be oriented to certain classes of problems to be solved and to modes of application. For instance, the performance to solve some problems may be significantly enhanced due to the use of a programmable coprocessor for the basic node processor. Another example is the use of computer systems with low-cost communication environment to debug parallel programs. At the same time, it is necessary that all these computer systems with their specific architecture-structural implementations be presented to a user within one CS. For the transition from one CS to another, as a rule, it is necessary for serious tasks to transfer large data arrays

which is hardly realizable (one could hardly reconnect the file-server from one station to another).

The above arguments and a number of other considerations make up the basis for another, unlike MVS-1000M, approach to the creation of system software for parallel supercomputers, namely: the joint use of many, in the general case, various computer systems within the network environment of distributed high-performance computations, e.g. on the basis of the Grid technology [12].

The network environment for distributed computations should be a totality of computer systems whose host computers and, perhaps, computer modules are connected via one or many communication fabric. The possibility of performing parallel programs should be provided, both on the computers of one CS and using the resources of several CSs. The migration of tasks to balance the load and fault tolerance should be guaranteed.

2   Network Environment for Distributed Computations

2.1   The Foundations of Construction

The proposed variant of system software for the next-generation parallel supercomputers is realized via the totality of interacting decentralized systems of monitoring, resource management and tasks control.

The monitoring system (MS) should control the state of resources and the required composition of resources and modes of their operation.

The system of resource management (SRM) should keep the resources efficient by inputting and outputting them from the procession, providing their maintenance and repair.

The system of tasks control (STC) should allocate efficient resources to tasks and redistribute the tasks if in the course of their execution the availability of resources changes.

Naturally, the system software should first solve the problems of safe use of resources by many users. Therefore it was decided to take, as the basis of the system software being created, Globus, the free-distributed software product [13] with its security system. Globus is the infrastructure of services and a toolkit for developing distributed applications rather than a complete system for users.

The creation of the required system software on the basis of Globus implies the building into it original proprietary systems of monitoring, resource management and tasks control.

The functions of the management system are implemented by the corresponding managers: MS manager, RMS manager and TCS manager. Hereinafter, manager (M) stands for the totality of these managers.

The management system is realized as a tree-like hierarchical structure comprising various-level resource managers. The nodes of the tree-like structure are assigned to subnets due to architecture-structural peculiarities of computer systems, territorial and administrative division principles or according to another approach.

For each component of the management system, be it the system of monitoring, resource management or task control, we distinguish three types of managers making up the hierarchical structure: M0, M1, M2 and of higher levels:

- the M0 manager is a node manager (is executed on a node);
- the M1 manager is a computer system manager (is executed on the host computer of a CS);
- the M2, M3, ... managers are the managers of subnets (are executed on host computers of computer systems in a subnet, or on special computers connected to a network of these CSs).

The structure of managers' hierarchy is given in Fig. 2.

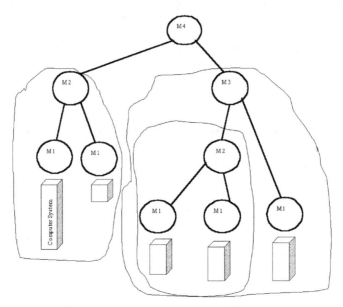

Fig. 2. The structure of managers' hierarchy

Managers keep the fault-tolerant (reconfigurable and self-repairing after faults) logical tree-like structure of connections.

The acyclic hierarchy of resource managers makes it possible to avoid deadlocks when implementing the protocol of managers' interaction during dynamic resource allocation to tasks with asynchronous parallel distribution of resources among tasks.

2.2 The Monitoring System

The system of resource monitoring is created on the basis of Meta Directory Service (contained in the Globus Toolkit) on the LDAP protocol and the package Flame [9, 10] which realizes the monitoring of resources. Data storage of the monitoring system FLAME on the state of facilities is performed on the LDAP-server. Such presentation of information about available computer resources is used in the Globus system. The extension of functionality in this direction enables us to build the FLAME system as the monitoring component into distributed computer systems on the basis of Globus.

Such systems as HP OpenView, Sun Net Manager, etc., created for the active monitoring of computer nets, are being applied nowadays to mass parallel systems and metacomputer structures. Such an approach has a number of disadvantages due to insufficient consideration of parallel computations, the impossibility to make changes in monitoring systems in the course of computer system (CS) advancement due to the absence of source code. FLAME is realized on the basis of open source software and is the product with full source code.

The active monitoring system FLAME consists of a manager, dynamic database, a console, SNMP-demons and HTTP-agents.

The role of the device being monitored in the FLAME system may be performed by a software or hardware module with an activated SNMP-demon or HTTP-agent, the latter receiving the required data directly from the operational system and hardware.

The dynamic database with assigned parameters and holding the data about the actual state of software/hardware being monitored is located in the host computer monitoring the parameters of devices.

The manager of the FLAME is activated in the host computer and has the description of the CS configuration consisting of two components. The first component consists of the list of all the monitored devices for which MIBs are read at the initialization stage. The second component is the list of couples (URI, time interval) determining the set of functions to be monitored. These functions will be (with certain intervals) calculated by the manager irrespective of requests from the consoles. To determine the value of the function, the data should be taken from the dynamic base if they are considered "fresh" enough. In case of "old" data a request of the data on the state of devices is formed. On arrival of such data to the dynamic base the calculation of function resumes.

The consoles, according to the configuration of the visualizing part assigned by operators, address the intermediate HTTP-server which is a gate between them and the manager of the FLAME. HTTP-server does all the necessary work to support HTTP-connections, to analyze requests, and passes these requests to the manager of the FLAME.

Alterations in the description of the CS configuration, the totality of periodically calculated functions among them, is performed by programming the description of the configuration in the interpreted language built in the FLAME. The language of configuration description is, in terms of algorithms, a complete declarative language based on the XML metalanguage.

The use of the existing script languages to describe the configuration was said to be unsuitable since it is difficult to guarantee safety when running a program swapped from the net (which is necessary in case of the configuration import). Below are the reasons to use the XML language as the basis:

- the XML language is the natural modern representation of hierarchical structures, computer systems being one of them;
- the possibility to modify the monitored configuration within the operation of the monitoring system and, in sight, to dynamically reconfigure by means of the net;
- the possibility to directly assign the structure of the obtained XML which is consumed by visualization subsystem so that in the vast majority of cases one could do without programming additional primitives in C++ (for instance, the present solution enables us to generate HTML and to use the usual HTML-browser as visualizer).

For the description of the FLAME, the system of functional active monitoring, the software documentation and the source code see the Web-site: http//flame.s2s.msu.ru.

The system of active monitoring FLAME proved its efficiency on the supercomputer MVS-1000M, it is installed and operated on the clusters in the Research & Development Institute "Kvant" and the Institute of Program Systems of the Russian Academy of Sciences in Pereslavl'-Zalesskii.

2.3 The System of Tasks Control

The managers of TCS are realized by adding the functions necessary for task managing and by the corresponding modification of the Jobmanager service of the GASS service (contained in the Globus Toolkit).

Each manager "knows" its position in the hierarchy relative to the upper and lower levels to provide the transmission of requests to a higher manager or to lower managers. The requests of managers to each other are realized in the Resource Specification Language (RSL) which provides uniform interaction of a user and resource manager, and of different managers. In terms of Globus this architecture level of resource management is called the Resource Broker.

Manager of the 1st-level (M1) of a computer system realizing the allocation of a task (or its fragment) plays the part of the gate to the tasks control system of the corresponding CS.

Each manager keeps its own queue of tasks. According to a planning algorithm a manager selects a task from the queue and determines the route of this task. The travel of a task up the managers' hierarchy may be realized due to the initiative of both a lower and an upper manager.

When taking a decision about task mapping a manager may leave the task in its queue, send it to an upper manager, send it to one or several lower managers. The range of possible algorithms varies from the user's direct instruction about computers and CSs he needs to the solution of optimization problems and application of methods of intelligent data analysis.

If a task is sent to a few managers (a distributed task) then the coordination of the 1st-level managers' operation occurs (i.e. the managers of computer systems on which the fragments of a user's task are planned). These managers determine which communication fabrics (communication environment) may be used to perform exchanges in a parallel program. After that network addresses of resources are allocated to the task they are used to create the communicator of MPI of a parallel program to be run on allocated resources. The 1st-level managers provide synchronous initiation of the task's fragments allocated for different computer systems.

References

1. E.V. Evreinov, J.G. Kosarev. Homogeneous universal high-performance computer systems. Novosibirsk, Science. 1966. 308 p.
2. A.V. Zabrodin, V.K. Levin, V.V. Korneev. The massively parallel computer system MVS-100. - Lecture Notes in Computer Science, N 964. Parallel Computing Technologies. Third International Conference, PaCT-95, St. Petersburg, Russia, Sept. 1995, Springer. pp.341-355

3. V.E. Fortov, V.K. Levin, G.I. Savin, A.V. Zabrodin, V.V.Karatanov, G.S. Elizarov, V.V. Korneev, B.M. Shabanov. Supercomputer MVS-1000M and perspectives of its use. "Science and Industry of Russia". № 11 (55), 2001, p. 49-52

4. A.O. Lacis. A Multy-Process Virtual Channel Network Technical note. Institute of Applied Mathematic of Academy of Science of Russia, 1995

5. A.O. Lacis. Application Programmer's Manual for MVS-1000 Communication Library Router+. www.kiam.ru

6. A.O. Lacis. Operating System of Supercomputer MVS-1000. Main ideas. Annotated List of manuals. www.kiam.ru

7. A.V. Baranov, A.O. Lacis, M.J. Khramtsov. Implementation of Multi-users' Mode Operation of Multiprocessor Computer Systems. Proceedings of Russian Science Conference "High-Performance Computing and its Applications". Chernogolovka City. 2000, pp. 67-69. Publ. Moscow State University

8. A.V. Baranov, A.O. Lacis, S.V. Sagin, M.J. Khramtsov. MVS-1000 User's Manual. www.kiam.ru

9. V.A. Vasenin, V.V. Korneev, M.J. Landina, V.A. Roganov. Functional Active Monitoring Environment FLAME. Journal of Programming. No. 3. 2003.

10. D. Zelting, E. Golovin, I. Shagurin, S. Rotnov, V. Soloviev. Peculiarities of MVS-1000M Power Supply System. Journal of Open Systems. No. 12. 2000

11. Ian Foster, Carl Kesselman, Steven Tuecke. The Anatomy of the Grid. Enabling Scalable Virtual Organizatons, http://www.globus.org

12. Globus Toolkit 1.1.3. System Administration Guide, December 2000.

Asynchronous Bit-Serial Datapath for Object-Oriented Reconfigurable Architecture PCA

Kiyoshi Oguri[1], Yuichiro Shibata[1], and Akira Nagoya[2]

[1] Department of Computer and Information Sciences, Nagasaki University,
Nagasaki, 852–8521 Japan,
{oguri,shibata}@cis.nagasaki-u.ac.jp,
http://www.cis.nagasaki-u.ac.jp/labs/oguri/
[2] NTT Network Innovation Laboratories,
Yokosuka-shi, 239-0847 Japan,
nagoya.akira@lab.ntt.co.jp

Abstract. In this paper, design and organization of bit-serial asynchronous arithmetic circuits on PCA (Plastic Cell Architecture) which is reconfigurable architecture consisting of communicating, memorizing and processing facilities is discussed. Based on the evaluation results of the implementation, a novel architecture of a configurable part of PCA is also proposed. The implementation of bit-serial asynchronous arithmetic circuits does not depend on PCA. Since asynchronous circuits operate with handshaking not with clock signals, different design techniques are required from those adopted in synchronous circuit design. We propose such a new technique for design of multiplier circuit. Furthermore, novel structure for an FIR (Finite Impulse Response) filter, which can also be applied to synchronous implementation, is proposed.

1 Introduction

A characteristic of computers that are now used widely lies in its distinctive *generality*. After appreciating and investigating the sense of the generality, we have concluded that the essence of general purpose computers is incarnated in the *double dual-structure* described as follows;

The first dual-structure: Any functions are carried out by a combination of dual components — software and hardware.

The second dual-structure: Actual operations of functions are performed by hardware. To make it perform any functions, the hardware must have a variable part in it. However, if the hardware were composed only of variable parts, it could not be configured or given a sense. In order to make this possible, hardware must also have a fixed part. Namely, hardware is composed of dual components — a variable part and a fixed part.

A. Omondi and S. Sedukhin (Eds.): ACSAC 2003, LNCS 2823, pp. 54–68, 2003.

Based on this consideration we have proposed a novel architecture called PCA (Plastic Cell Architecture) that is different in a way of realization of the double dual-structure from the conventional computers [1],[2],[3]. In the structure of PCA, SRAM type FPGAs (Field Programmable Gate Arrays) are scattered over fine grain networks spanned all over the chip. By writing appropriate configuration data to SRAM of the FPGAs, desired circuits can be configured. The SRAM can be also used as the storage of information. By making the best use of this structure, the essence of computation, which are memory, processing and transfer of information, can be directly operated in parallel. In addition, by transferring configuration information of FPGAs, the structure and scale of the configured circuits can be adapted to the behavior of applications. In PCA, a unit of configuration of the circuits is called an *object*. Circuits are configured separately for each object and are added into the system on-the-fly. The objects in the system that become unused are stopped and detached. To make it easy to add and remove objects on-the-fly, PCA has taken an approach of asynchronous circuits that has been widely noticed as technique for designing low power consumption circuits and for alleviating the performance degradation caused by global clock skew [4],[5],[6]. In asynchronous circuit desgin, it is not necessary to make clock periods of various size objects even. Moreover, an object can be easily connected or detached since all the interface signals stay '0' unless the object receives a request.

The first LSI of PCA [7],[8],[9] was designed and fabricated by NTT, and it was verified to operate according to the theory. The interest has been shifted to making it clear how applications should be implemented on PCA and to the refinement of the architecture. As the architecture of CPU has been improved in various ways, the architecture of PCA will be increasingly improved. Then, what is the real nature of PCA? The answer is the double dual-structure in which a fixed part of hardware (including the configuration mechanism for the variable part) is realized by communication facilities and a variable part corresponds to memory and processing facilities of information.

The most basic element for application processing is arithmetic. Basic implementation strategies of the arithmetic functions can be classified to a bit-parallel approach and a bit-serial approach. Although bit-parallel systems are widely used now, the bit-serial approach will be more advantageous when the skew problems spread to data signals in the bit-parallel systems. Therefore, we investigate implementation of bit-serial arithmetic operations that are likely to be more relevant to asynchronous circuits on PCA.

The rest of the paper is organized as follows. In Sect. 2, design methodologies of asynchronous circuits are summarized as the premise of the discussion. In Sect. 3, the structure of PCA is presented which is the premise of the implementation. In Sect. 4, design, analysis and evaluation of bit-serial datapath on PCA are described. Then in Sect. 5, based on the evaluation and analysis of the design, we propose novel architecture of PCA. Finally, the paper is concluded in Sect. 6.

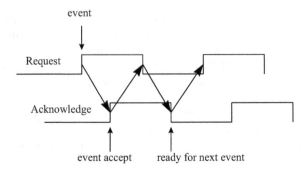

Fig. 1. 4-cycle asynchronous signaling protocol

2 Asynchronous Circuit

There are two major signaling protocols for asynchronous circuits; a 4-cycle signaling protocol (RZ: return to zero) and a 2-cycle signaling protocol (NRZ: non-return to zero) [10],[11], [12]. In this paper, we deal the 4-cycle signaling protocol that was adopted in PCA-1 (Fig. 1).

2.1 Petri Net

The behavior shown in Fig. 1 can be expressed by Petri nets with two color tokens as shown in Fig. 2 [13]. Now, let a black token, which represents a rising edge of a signal, be sent into *placeA* in Fig. 2 (1) from the left. This passage of the black token makes *Request* signal '1', which corresponds to the edge labeled as "event" in Fig. 1. Then *transition1* fires since there is a token in each input place, and thus black tokens are sent to all of the output places. This results in the assignment of tokens shown in Fig. 2 (2), and *Acknowledge* signal goes '1' since the black token passes. This corresponds to "event accept" in Fig. 1. Since *placeB, transition1, placeC* and *transition2* form a loop, one of *placeB* or *placeC* has a token exclusively. Therefore, the token in *placeB* in Fig. 2 (1) represents the vacancy of *placeC* that means the place is acceptable. In the transition from Fig. 2 (2) to Fig. 2 (3), the inverter changes the black token that passed through *transition2* into a white token which represents a falling edge of the signal, and the white token is sent to *placeB*. As far as digital circuits are concerned, a rising edge of a signal must be followed by an falling edge. This is why we have introduced black and white tokens that correspond to rising and falling edges, respectively. When neither token exists, there is no change in the signal. In this way, the 4-cycle signaling protocol can be related to the behavior of Petri nets.

2.2 Muller's C Element

An output of Muller's C element [10],[11], [12], which is indispensable to implementation of asynchronous circuits, goes '1' when the two inputs are both '1' and goes '0' when both inputs become '0'. While the two inputs have different

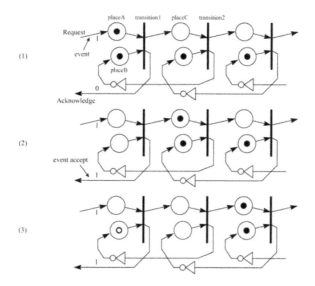

Fig. 2. Modeling by Petri net

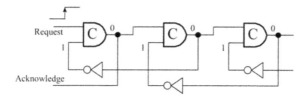

Fig. 3. Corresponding logic circuit using C-elements

values each other, the C element keeps the output value unchanged. Here, we describe the action in which a C element turns over its output value as the C element *fires*. Note that once a C element fires, the input values that made the C element fire are not able to make it fire any more. For example, let an output of a C element be '0'. Thus the input value that can make the C element fire is '1'. When both the inputs go '1', the C element fires and the output goes '1'. At the same time, the input value that can make the C element fire becomes '0' (not '1'). This mechanism is exactly fit for the relationship between fire of a transition and tokens in the input places of a Petri net. Therefore we can relate a C element, fire of the C element, input signals, and the value that can make the C element fire to a transition, fire of the transition, input places, and tokens, respectively. The circuit with C elements corresponding to Fig. 2 is shown in Fig. 3.

2.3   Simplified Petri Net

Since *placeB* in Fig. 2 just represents the vacancy of *placeC*, by making an additional transition firing condition that the output places of the transition should empty, the notation can be much simplified. For instance, Fig. 2 can be expressed as Fig. 4. This simplified notation is used in the rest of the paper.

2.4   Including Datapath

There are two implementation methodologies of asynchronous datapath [14]. One is a dual-rail protocol in which timing information is included in data, and the other is a bundled protocol in which data and timing information is separated.

In this paper, the bundled protocol is discussed, which was adopted in PCA-1 (Fig. 5). The structure of a latch used between combinational circuits is shown in Fig. 6.

3   PCA-1 Architecture

PCA-1 is the first architecture that actualizes the concept of PCA and consists of a 2-dimensional mesh of *PCA cells* each composed of a *built-in part* and a *plastic part*. A built-in part and a plastic part in each PCA cell are connected to buit-in parts and plastic parts in adjacent PCA cells [7],[8],[9]. A plastic part has the structure called sea-of-LUTs in which 4-input 1-output LUTs (look-up tables) are spread over. Circuits including registers are configured on these plastic parts. Between a built-in part and a plastic part, two kinds of connection are provided; one is for read/write operations of LUT memory in plastic parts and the other

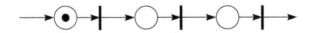

Fig. 4. Simplified notation of Petri net

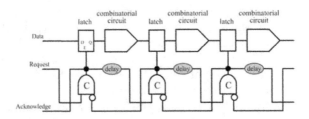

Fig. 5. Asynchronous pipeline with bundled datapath

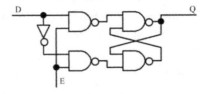

Fig. 6. Latch used in bundled datapath

is for communication with circuits configured on plastic parts. To make this possible, each built-in part has 5 input ports each has the same structure and recieves requests from the plastic part in addition to adjucent 4 built-in parts. The input port is controled by 11 kinds of commands. By routing commands, which are "east", "west", "north", "south" and "pp", an input port is set up to form a shift register. Once the shift register is formed, the input port transfers all data and commands to the specified dirction until it recives "clear" command. In order to access to LUT memory in the plastic part, "config_in", "config_out" and "coci", are provided. The plastic parts are treated as circuits namely objects and connected to the built-in parts when "open" command is asserted. To detach objects from the built-in parts, "close" command is used. Since asynchronous circuits configured on the plastic part can not resolve the meta-stable situation, the asynchronous arbiters provided for arbitrating conflicts between the input ports are indirectly used to form large scale asynchronous systems.

4 Asynchronous Bit-Serial Datapath

4.1 Asynchronous Bit-Serial Pipeline Multiplier

Although the method of constructing the parallel multiplication circuit of asynchronous operation [15],[16] or the bit serial pipeline multiplication circuit of synchronous operation [17] is known well, the method of constructing the bit serial pipeline multiplier by the asynchronous circuit is hardly reported until now. A method of constructing a digit (4-bit) serial pipeline multiplier of asynchronous operation has been proposed [18]. However, the flow of control of the opposite direction is needed with the data flow on a pipeline. That is, both of handshakes for telling information leftward and for telling information rightward need to be performed between adjacent modules. In this paper, the construction method of the bit serial pipeline multiplier by the asynchronous circuit that operation data can be calculated only by passing in the single direction is proposed.

Bit-serial pipeline multiplier. The principle of a bit serial pipeline multiplier is first explained along with Fig. 7 [19]. Figure 7 shows the case where 4bit × 4bit = 8bit multiplication is performed. In advance, the multiplicand is stored in b0, b1, b2, b3, where b0 is LSB, and b3 is MSB. Multiplier a3a2a1a0 flows from the left to the right, and makes LSB a head. A, B, C and D express the partial products. A serves as the partial product of b0, B as the partial product of b1, C as the partial product of b2, and D as the partial product of b3.

It is shown in Fig. 8 from which timing a partial product is made. In Fig. 8, t1 corresponds to the time of Fig. 7. At t2, although partial product a0b0 reaches the input of FA2, partial product B is '0' since the multiplier has not arrived, and the output of FA2 serves as a0b0. Similarly, a0b0 reaches FA4 at t4, and a0b0 is outputted as LSB of a product. Partial product a1b0 made from A at t2 reaches the input of FA2 at t3, and partial product a0b1 is made by B at this time. This is because a0 that was found at the input of partial product A at t1 has reached the input of partial product B at t3, 2-unit times after t1. Thus, if

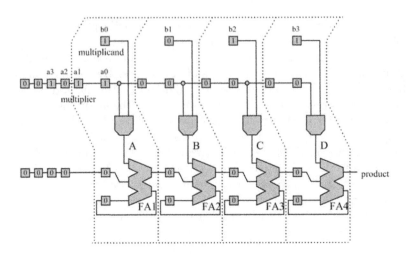

Fig. 7. Bit-serial pipeline multiplier

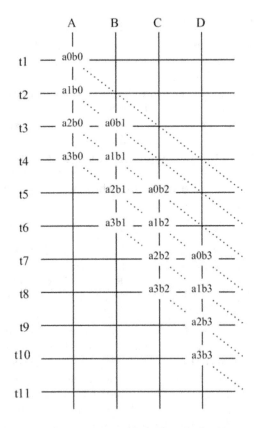

Fig. 8. Time chart of pipeline multiplier

the partial sum is passed by one twice the speed of a multiplier on a pipeline, a certain bit of the product can be obtained by adding the partial product on the dashed line of the slant drawn on Fig. 8. A carry generated by addition of partial products is added to addition of the higher bit in the product. Thus, MSB of the product is obtained at t11.

Asynchronous implementation. A speed difference can be produced by the number of register stages passed in a synchronous circuit. The method of producing a speed difference in an asynchronous circuit is proposed below. A multiplication pipeline's stage for 1 bit enclosed with the dashed line of Fig. 7 is constructed by the asynchronous circuit, as shown in Fig. 9, and initial tokens are arranged as shown in Fig. 10.

The pipeline stages of Fig. 10 are connected directly or connected by the asynchronous pipeline with arbitrary number of stages that contain no token, as shown in Fig. 11. If a token is not sent from the left, the token in a multiplication pipeline is unmovable. Only the number with same the token (upper row) of a multiplier and the token of the partial sum (middle) shall be sent from the left.

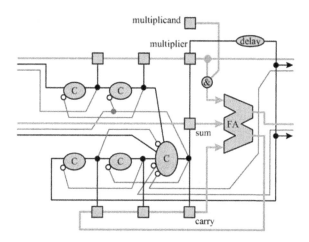

Fig. 9. Asynchronous implementation of pipeline stage

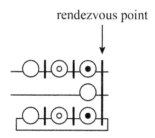

Fig. 10. Corresponding Petri net expression

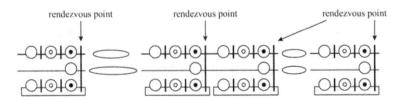

Fig. 11. Interconnection between asynchronous pipeline stages

If the token of the partial sum goes into a stage, it will go to the next stage together with the token of the multiplier for which it was already waiting on the stage. The token of a multiplier cannot go on, if the token of the following partial sum does not reach. Therefore, the speed to pass will be different by 2 times. Thus, if the numbers of the initial black tokens at the waiting point are 0 and 1, then a twice as many speed difference as this arises. When they are 0 and n, then the speed difference of $(n + 1)$ times arises.The numbers of the initial black tokens at the waiting point cannot be such as 2 and 3. It is because waiting conditions are met and the tokens flow to the right.

Incidentally, the lower row of Fig. 10 is a loop for returning the carry produced by a certain addition to the following input of addition. Now, like the case of a synchronous circuit, these n pipeline stages are connected and suppose that n bits of multiplicand were set. Here, if m bits of multiplier and m bits of the partial sums '0' are supplied, the lower m bits of the product will be outputted from the pipeline. Furthermore, if n bits of multiplier and n bits of the partial sums '0' are supplied, while the higher n bits of the product will be outputted and multiplication will complete. At the same time, the multiplier of '0' can remain into the pipeline and the following multiplication can be equipped.

Mapping to Object-Oriented Reconfigurable Architecture PCA If the pipeline stage of Fig. 9 is implemented as an object of PCA, a bit-serial pipeline multiplier of some bits width can be constructed by allocating same number of the objects, and connecting them with built-in parts between them. With this construction, since objects on plastic parts forms the multiplier circuit together with built-in parts, these built-in parts cannot be used for other message passing any more. Although the built-in part of PCA was introduced to perform dynamic message passing between processing circuits on plastic parts, in this paper we demonstrate that built-in parts can be used for static connections as parts of circuits. By this method, as well as the number of object kinds will be reduced, it becomes easy to adapt the bits width of operation to the application requirement. For the PCA-1, total procedure from initial configuration to multiplication is as follows.

(1) Configuration of objects
(2) Initialization of objects and connecting them to built-in parts
(3) Making route onto built-in parts
(4) Setup of multiplicand

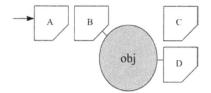

Fig. 12. Routing among built-in parts and PCA object

(5) Injection of multiplier and partial sum, i.e., execution of multiplication

"Config_in" command can perform (1), and "open" command can perform (2). Since an object is connected with the built-in part at two points, input and output, "open" command is required twice.

If the object is designed so that route setup commands may only be passed, (3) is done like next example(Fig. 12). Let all built-in parts: A, B, C and D are in initial state at first. As built-in part in initial state is only affect by command, the first command: "east" makes easterly route in A, the next command: "pp" is passed through A, and reach B, and makes route toward the object in B, the next command: "north" is passed through A, B and the object, and reach D, and makes northern route in D, and so on. The command codes for setting up a multiplicand and for multiplication must be differ from routing commands. If the object is designed so that it accept a bit of multiplicand as far as not having the bit, bits of multiplicand can be set one bye one along the bit-serial pipeline of them by just pushing bits onto pipeline. If multiplication clears the object's condition having a bit of multiplicand, we can set the different multiplicand after multiplication any times we wish. Adding these functions to multiplication function, the total circuit of the object becomes as Fig. 13.

This circuit was manually mapped to the sea of LUTs of plastic parts using a NTT's layout editor PCASE for PCA-1 (Schematic Editor for PCA). In this design, 16 PCA cells which contain 4096 LUTs of 4-input 1-output were used for the object, and the operation cycle was estimated to be 240ns. That is, one object will occupy half area of PCA-1 chip mostly. For comparison, a synchronous circuit of the almost same function was designed where a request signal was treated as a clock signal. When 0.8 micron CMOS technology for ASIC was used, it required 53 gates (4 transistors were counted as 1 gate) and the cycle of the operation was estimated to be 4.2ns. When this was mapped to FPGA (ALTERA company's EPF10K20RC 240-4), the cycle of the operation was estimated to be 21.8ns. Since the object mapped on the sea of LUTs was not a design that aimed to minimize area for PCA-1, and there are differences such as the advantage of asynchronous circuit and dynamic reconfigurability for various bit width operation etc., the simple comparison with other implementation should not be carried out. However, it can be said that such a design of a bit serial operation circuit is not necessarily efficient in occupancy area to PCA-1 that adopted sea of LUTs as plastic part of PCA. Since PCA-1 is a prototype LSI designed aiming stable operation rather than performance, and the design

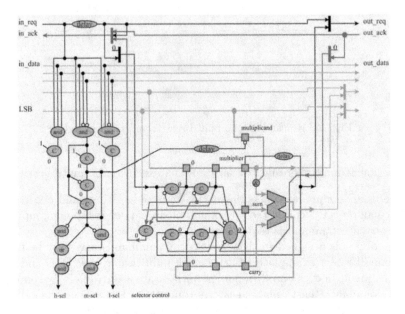

Fig. 13. Pipeline multiplier stage as PCA object

of this object also aims stable operation, simple comparison among speeds of the operation should not be performed. Still, much more improvement in performance is desired too. Although it is an advantage that circuits can be considered in the completely free way of thinking because of its highly symmetric structure, if certain structure is enough for application, Sea of LUTs should be replaced bye it. In Sect. 5, we will discuss about this.

4.2 Bit-Serial Divider

While bit-serial divider for finite GF (Galois Field) is investigated [20], we cannot find any articles describing elementary bit-serial divider for integer. But, it is easy to come up with the following structure. Figure 14 demonstrates how we construct a nonrestoring bit-serial divider. Dividend and divisor are put in

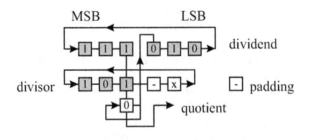

Fig. 14. Nonrestoring bit-serial divider

two looped sift registers respectively. The divisor register must be enlarged by padding as the dividend register is larger than divisor register bye one. Operation is done at central portion of the figure. When the special padding x reaches the operating portion, quotient becomes available. What is important is that the divider consists of only sift register and simple operation circuit.

4.3   Bit-Serial Pipeline FIR Filter

In pipeline structured FIR filter, a signal length width shift registers is used for setting up sampling delays, and adders are placed between registers which are parts of the shift registers. Each adder's remained input is connected to a multiplier which outputs the product of the input signal and some coefficient. When we apply bit-serial manner to the shift registers with adders, noting that an integer multiplication can be decomposed into addition operation and shift operation, we can propose a novel structure in which multipliers are replaced by adders and shift registers and embedded into single bit-serial shift registers with adders. By this structure, hardware amount can be much reduced. Lower part of Fig. 15 shows an example of the proposed structure of FIR filter in which a 21-tap band-pass filter ($H(Z) = Z^{-20} - 2Z^{-18} + 8Z^{-14} - 16Z^{-12} + 18Z^{-10} - 16Z^{-8} + 8Z^{-6} - 2Z^{-2} + 1$) is implemented. In this example, for the 16-bit width input data, 23-bit width operation is required to preserve the precision. Thus, 23-bit shift register is used for each sampling delay. 2's complement is used for negative value. Being easy to understand, upper part of Fig. 15 shows the structure without sharing shift registers among the multiplier and sampling delay shift registers. In order to remove certain shift registers of the multiplier, it is

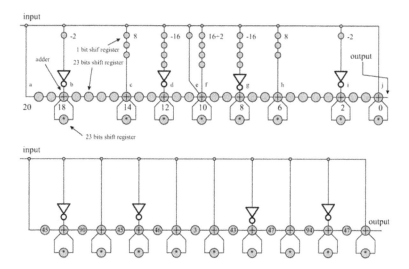

Fig. 15. Bit-serial FIR filter

enough to shift the position of corresponding adder. Another 23-bit shift registers which comes with each 1-bit adder is used for indicating the data separation.

5   Proposal of New PCA Architecture

As mentioned above, we can compose the datapath by using only shift registers and simple state machines which include 1-bit arithmetic operations. We also mentioned that all-purpose information processing architecture must consit of two parts, i.e. built-in part and plastic part, and that information porcessing itself consists of strage, transfer and processing functions.

PCA is an architecture in which strage and processing functions are mapped on plastic part, and transfer operation is mapped on built-in part. We adopted FPGA as plastic part of PCA-1 because FPGA's configuration SRAM can be regarded as strage function itself and of course configured FPGA has certain processing function. However, if processing function is composed by shift registers and state machines, plastic part of PCA just becomes what consits of only shift registers and state machines, because shift register is strage itself in bit-serial manner. We propose new PCA architecture in which plastic part consists of shift registers and state machines. In PCA-1, object is a circuit configured in plastic parts of some PCA cells. In new PCA, object is a range which includes some PCA cells instead. Fig. 16 shows new PCA's PCA cell. Outer 4 circles are state machines as built-in part, and the central circle is a plastic part. The plastic part has an SRAM which is used as a combinatorial function of state machine, and as strage of shift registers. There are no connections between plastic parts of neighboring PCA cells. Functions of routing commands such as "east","west","north","south" are same as PCA-1. Routing "pp" command does not exist. "Config" command configures not only plastic part, but also built-in part. By "open" command, object becomes what is configured by "config" command. "Close" command releases PCA cells from the object.

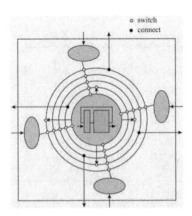

Fig. 16. New PCA architecture

6   Conclusions

In this paper, we have proposed the new design and organization of an asynchronous bit-serial multiplier, divider and FIR filter, and revealed that these circuits can be implemented only by state machines and shift registers. For the asynchronous bit-serial multiplier, we have described how the circuits are mapped on to PCA-1 which is dynamically reconfigurable architecture. In addition, based on the evaluation and analysis of the bit-serial datapath design, we have proposed new architecture of PCA.

References

1. K. Oguri, N. Imlig, H. Ito, K. Nagami, R. Konishi, and T. Shiozawa: General purpose computer architecture based on fully programmable logic. Proc. International Conf. Evolvable Systems (ICES'98) (1998) 323–334
2. K. Nagami, K. Oguri, T. Shiozawa, H. Ito, and R. Konishi: Plastic cell architecture: A scalable device architecture for general-purpose reconfigurable computing. IEICE Trans. Electron **E81-C**(9) (1998) 1431–1437
3. N. Imlig, T. Shiozawa, R. Konishi, K. Oguri, K. Nagami, H. Ito, M. Inamori, and H. Nakada, "Programmable dataflow computing on PCA," IEICE Trans. Fundamentals, vol.E83-A, no.12, pp.2409–2416, Dec. 2000.
4. M. Sahni and T. Nanya: On the CSC property of signal transition graph specifications for asynchronous circuit design. Proc. ASP-DAC (Feb 1998) 183–189
5. T. Nanya: Asynchronous microprocessor architecture and design. Proc. FED-PDI Joint Conference on 21th-Century Electron Devices (FPC'98) (June 1998)
6. J.V. Woods, P. Day, S.B. Furber, J.D. Garside, N.C. Paver, and S. Temple: AMULET1: An asynchronous ARM microprocessor. IEEE Trans. Comput. **46**(4) (April 1997) 385–398
7. R. Konishi, H. Ito, H. Nakada, A. Nagoya, K. Oguri, N. Imlig, T. Shiozawa, M. Inamori, and K. Nagami: PCA-1: A fully asynchronous, self-reconfigurable LSI. Proc. 7th Int. Symposium on Asynchronous Circuit and Systems (ASYNC 2001) (March 2001) 54–61
8. H. Ito, R. Konishi, H. Nakada, K. Oguri, A. Nagoya, N. Imlig, K. Nagami, T. Shiozawa, and M. Inamori: Dynamically reconfigurable logic LSI — PCA-1. Proc. 2001 Symposium on VLSI Circuits (June 2001) 103–106
9. M. Inamori, H. Nakada, R. Konishi, A. Nagoya, and K. Oguri: A method of mapping finite state machine into PCA plastic parts. IEICE Trans. Fundamentals **E00-A**(4) (April 2002) 804–810
10. C.L. Seitz: System Timing. in C. Mead and L. Conway: Introduction to VLSI Systems. Addison-Wesley, ISBN 0-201-04358-0 (1980) 218–262
11. S.H. Unger: Asynchronous Sequential Switching Circuits. John Wiley & Sons (1969)
12. I.E. Sutherland: Micropipelines. Commun. ACM **32**(6) (June 1989) 720–738
13. J. Cortadella, M. Kishinevsky, A. Kondratyev, L. Lavagno, and A. Yakovlev: Petrify: A tool for manipulating concurrent specifications and synthesis of asynchronous controllers. IEICE Trans. Inf. & Syst. **E80-D**(3) (March 1997)
14. I. David, R. Ginosar and M. Yoeli: An efficient implementation of boolean function as self-timed circuits. IEEE Trans. Comput. **41**(1) (1992) 2–11

15. T.H. Meng: Synchronization Design for Digital Systems. Kluwer Academic Publishers, ISBN 0-7923-9128-4 (1991)
16. C.J. Myers: Asynchronous Circuit Design. John Wiley & Sons, ISBN 0-471-41543-X (2001)
17. T. Isshiki: High-Performance Bit-Serial Datapath Implementation for Large-Scale Configurable Systems. Ph.D. Thesis, Tokyo Institute of Technology (April 1996)
18. Y. Okuyama and K. Kuroda: Simulation framework for circuits on plastic cell architecture (PCA). IPSJ SIG Notes **2001-SLDM-101**(42) (May 2001) 15–22
19. N. Weste and K. Eshraghian: Principles of CMOS VLSI Design: A System Perspective. Addison-Wesley, 2nd ed. (1993)
20. M.A. Hasan and V.K. Bhargava: Bit-serial systolic divider and multiplier for finite fields GF(2m). IEEE Trans. Comput. **41**(8) (1992) 972–980

Reconfigurable Logic:
A Saviour for Experimental
Computer Architecture Research

John Morris

Department of Electrical and Electronic Engineering, The University of Auckland,
Auckland, New Zealand
j.morris@auckland.ac.nz

Abstract. Design of state-of-the-art processors now requires budgets
beyond the means of even the most generously funded research laboratories. Academic architecture research was in danger of becoming limited
to partial simulations of full systems to 'prove' new ideas. However, increases in the complexity of readily available reconfigurable devices has
meant that it is still possible to design *and build* interesting systems in
our laboratories, *but* these systems must take into account the limitations of the technology! There are several constraints on applications
which can exploit the technology effectively and thus make realistic research projects: principally, they must have sufficient parallelism (either
simple or pipelined) and depend on relatively little fast memory. Minor
constraints are to have relatively simple control paths, use mainly integer
arithmetic and have regular functional blocks.
The large logic capacity of modern devices also allows 'proof of concept'
systems for radical new architectures (or re-incarnations of abandoned
ones!) to be built.

Keywords: Reconfigurable logic, programmable hardware, stereo correspondence, data flow, asynchronous logic.

1   Preamble

Current technology allows a designer to place up to 10^8 transistors on a single
die: consequently design *and implementation* of a state-of-the-art processor has
become a formidable task, requiring a budget far beyond that of even the best-
funded academic research laboratories. Some would argue that implementation
is no longer necessary – everything can be simulated given enough computer
cycles. However, even on a powerful processor, thorough testing and verification
through simulation of a complex system may take an impracticably long time.
This leads many to question the value of computer architecture research outside
the laboratories of the large semiconductor companies: universities don't have
the budgets or the time to embark on large projects. At best we can carry out
partial simulations (which contain many approximations to the behaviour of the
physical systems being studied) of modules of full systems.

A. Omondi and S. Sedukhin (Eds.): ACSAC 2003, LNCS 2823, pp. 69–85, 2003.

Programmable hardware has existed for decades now: it has been used extensively by digital designers for 'glue' logic connecting complex chips because it can replace several conventional logic devices. It saves development time because it is quicker for an engineer to write down the logic equations and pass them through a compiler than to draw the circuit diagram. Although the programmable devices themselves are generally more expensive than the logic devices that they replace, this is often outweighed by production cost savings in fewer types of devices, reduced inventory, *etc.*It has also saved many a red face (and many development dollars) because programmability allows design errors to be corrected without requiring a new circuit board to be laid out and fabricated.

Recently, programmable devices containing the equivalent of several million gates have appeared: this means that systems which are interesting from a research point of view can be designed *and implemented*. In this context, I define 'interesting' as 'sufficiently complex'. The reconfigurable or programmable nature of these devices allows multiple experiments to test concepts to be made without incurring high costs or long lead times for support hardware – circuit boards, connectors, test harnesses, *etc.*A critical factor remains though: how to effectively use this technology for research? The available devices will never be able to match the capabilities of a custom VLSI circuit: reconfigurability introduces overheads into programmable logic that ensure this. Thus full capability state-of-the-art processors will remain the domain of the large semiconductor manufacturers and those content with approximate simulation. In this paper, I will argue that a domain which I will label 'attached processors' is an area in which many interesting architectural studies may be made and proof of concept devices built. In this domain, a designer of custom hardware is still competing against faster, cheaper off-the-shelf general purpose processors, so it is necessary also to identify the characteristics of problems that are amenable to effective solutions in reconfigurable hardware. I will conclude with one example – the correspondence problem in stereo vision – where understanding of the limitations of reconfigurable hardware led to a simple modification of the basic algorithm used (with no performance penalty) which could be effectively implemented in a readily available commercial device.

2   Programmable Hardware

Programmable hardware has evolved in capability and performance – tracking processor capabilities for many years now. Designers have a wide spectrum of devices that they can draw upon – from ones that provide a handful of gates and flip-flops to ones with nearly 10 million gates[1]. In addition, modern devices provide

- Considerable on-chip memory, partially overcoming an inability of early devices to solve problems that required more than a few memory bits

---

[1] 2003 value: apply Moore's Law for 2004 on!

- Large numbers of I/O pins – permitting high data bandwidths between a custom processor and its environment
- Multiple I/O protocols, such as LVDS, GTL and LVPECL – enabling high speed serial channels between the device and other components of a system *and*
- General purpose processor cores.

Configurability has a cost though: a configurable circuit is more complex and has longer propagation delays than a fixed one: this translates to a slower maximum clock frequency. This tradeoff is discussed further when we consider whether an application is a good candidate for a reconfigurable processor compared to a general purpose commodity processor.

A number of terms have been used to describe programmable devices. Early devices were commonly called 'programmable array logic' chips or PALs, but a host of other similar terms have been used for marketing purposes. The most important group of devices are now almost universally termed 'Field Programmable Gate Arrays' (FPGAs). As with general purpose processors, designing a 'universal' FPGA is essentially an impossible task and a number of different architectural styles have been proposed and manufactured. The following sections outline the key elements of these devices.

2.1   FPGA Architectures

An FPGA's basic capability can usually be described in terms of three elements:

- Logic blocks: commonly consisting of a small number of simple and-or arrays, some multiplexers and a few flip-flops. Other features such a memory bits, look-up tables, special logic for handling the carry chains in adders, *etc.* may be present. Marketing exercises have produced a polyglot of names for these blocks: fortunately, most of them are readily understood. Examples are Logic Array Blocks (Altera APEX 20k family), Logic Elements (Altera FLEX 10KE), Macrocells (Altera MAX7000/MAX3000), Configurable Logic Blocks (Xilinx) and Programmable Function Units (Lucent Orca).
- Routing resources: a typical FPGA will provide lines of various lengths to interconnect the logic blocks. Short lines provide low propagation delay paths between neighbouring blocks: longer lines connect more distant blocks with low delay. A small number of buffered low delay lines which can interconnect large groups of logic blocks are usually provided for clocks.
- I/O buffers: special purpose logic blocks for interfaces to external circuitry. In modern devices, the I/O buffers provide a variety of electrical protocols eliminating the need to use special interface buffers. Eliminating these reduces chip-to-chip connections resulting in higher data transfer bandwidth between the reconfigurable processor and its environment.

In addition to these basic capabilities, high end devices now include

- separate memory blocks which may be configured in several ways,

- dedicated circuitry which makes fast arithmetic circuits possible: adders and multipliers are generally available,
- special purpose blocks, from the DSP modules (Altera's Stratix devices) to general purpose processor cores (*e.g.* the integer PowerPC cores in Xilinx' Virtex-II[1] or the ARM in Altera's Excalibur) *and*
- partial reprogrammability: a section of a device may be reprogrammed dynamically.

An Example: Xilinx 4000 Series. Xilinx' 4000 series devices[2] have been used in many projects and have features similar to many current devices.

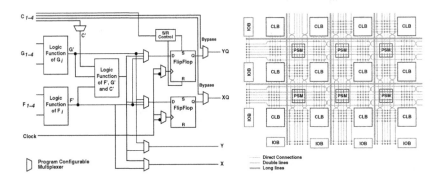

Fig. 1. Simplified diagram of the Xilinx XC4000 device showing (left) control logic block and (right) the style of the interconnection patterns. (The actual devices have additional capabilities[2])

Control Logic Blocks. Figure 1(left) shows the essential features of the 4000 series control logic blocks (CLBs). It contains three logic function blocks – each capable of implementing any boolean function of its inputs – and two flip-flops controlled by a common clock. 'Programming' the device sets the logic functions in the logic function blocks, the signal steering multiplexors and the set/reset control. There are nine basic inputs: F1-4, G1-4 and C4 (a direct data input to the flip-flops) and four outputs – two registered and two combinatorial. Paths can be chosen which bypass either or both flip-flops. Xilinx' designers have chosen to implement a moderately complex logic block. In contrast, Altera devices have simpler logic blocks with a single flip-flop[3] and Quicklogic's super cells are more complex[4]. Lucent refer to the ORCA logic block as a programmable functional unit (PFU) reflecting its complexity: 19 inputs and 4 flip-flops[5]. Additionally, CLBs can be configured to act as RAM – 16x1, 16x2 or 32x1 bit blocks. This highlights a significant drawback of early devices – inefficient implementation of memory. Using the two CLB flip-flops was an expensive way to obtain 2 bits of storage! Modern devices have dedicated RAM blocks with significant capacities.

Routing Resources. A great challenge to FPGA designers is achieving a good balance in the allocation of die area to programmable logic (the CLBs) versus routing resources. The XC4000 designers provide a combination of short lines which connect each CLB to a programmable switch matrix adjacent to it, double and quad length lines which connect every second (or fourth) switch matrix and long lines which run the entire length of a device (see Figure 1(right)). Connections through the switch matrices provide flexibility – any CLB may be connected to any other. However there is a penalty: the switch points use pass transistors which add to the propagation delay. Thus lines through the switch matrices may not be used for critical signals. The longer lines are used to reduce delays. Predicting the optimal allocation for any application is a hard task and many strategies may be seen in the commercially available devices. For example, Altera's Apex 20K devices employ a hierarchical structure, grouping basic logic elements (LEs) into logic array blocks (LABs) which are in turn grouped into MegaLABs[3]. Each block has appropriate internal routing resources.

I/O Buffers. Input/output buffers provide circuitry to interface with external devices. Apart from input buffers and output drivers, the main additional feature is the ability to latch both inputs and outputs. Limited slew rate control was also added to the output buffers – a precursor to the support for multiple electrical protocols now found in more modern designs.

Additional Features. Adders, including counters, occur on many critical paths, so the 4000 series, like most of its modern counterparts, has 'fast-carry' logic. A direct path for carry bits between CLBs reduces the critical delay in a ripple carry adder. The fast carry logic is so effective that more complex adders, such as carry look-ahead ones, are not faster and use more resources.

The special needs of global clocks are addressed by providing 'semi-dedicated' I/O pads connected to four primary global buffers designed for minimum delay and skew. The clocks of each CLB can be connected to these global buffers, a set of secondary buffers or any other internal signal. Thus multiple global and local clock domains can be established.

Problem diagnosis and boundary scan testing is facilitated through support for IEEE 1149.1 (JTAG) boundary scan logic attached to each I/O buffer.

The CLB structure lends itself to efficient implementation of functions of up to 9 inputs, but address decoders commonly require many more bits. Special decoders accepting up to 132 bits for large XC4000 devices are provided to ensure fast, resource-efficient decoding.

Virtex. The Virtex family[6] are enhanced versions of the Xilinx 4000 series. Improved process technology has allowed the gate capacity to exceed one million (8×10^6 are claimed for the largest member of the family, requiring several Mbytes of configuration data). 1.8V supply voltages allow internal clocks exceeding 400MHz to be used.

Memory. Blocks of dedicated memory can be programmed to a number of single- and dual-port configurations. Designs which were previously forced to use external memory can now run much faster.

I/O Buffers. One of the most dramatic additions to the newest devices from all manufacturers is the support of numerous electrical protocols at the I/O pins. For example, Virtex supports single-ended standards: LVTTL, LVCMOS, PCI-X, GTL, GTLP, HSTL, SSTL, AGP-2X and differential standards: LVDS, BLVDS, ULVDS, LDT and LVPECL. Support for PCI-X means that a Virtex device can implement the industry-standard PCI interface, considerably reducing the complexity of PCI cards which can now combine interface logic, control logic, some memory and external bus interfaces (*e.g.* LVDS) in a single chip.

Dynamic Reconfiguration. Virtex devices are also partially reconfigurable: individual columns may be reprogrammed.

Processor Cores. To allow us to build hybrid systems – ones which overcome some of the limitations of designs based on reconfigurable technology discussed in this paper, we now see conventional processor cores incorporated into devices. Xilinx' Virtex-II Pro devices contain hardwired PowerPC cores. Altera's NIOS processor architecture may be mapped onto their devices.

3   Reconfigurable Systems

Reconfigurable systems are easy to build: a designer has only to decide what interconnection patterns will best serve the needs of target applications – and some systems, *e.g.* UWA's Achilles, even allow that to be deferred. An enormous number of experimental and several commercial systems have been built. Guccione summarizes over 80 systems[7]. One example from our laboratory is outlined here: it's use as an interprocessor router is described in more detail elsewhere in these proceedings[8].

Achilles. In contrast to the majority of systems, which provide a fixed interconnection architecture on the 2D plane of a circuit board, the Achilles architecture provides much more flexible interconnection patterns: Tham's figure 1 in this volume[9] shows the three-dimensional arrangement in which small PCBs containing a single FPGA are arranged in a vertical 'stack'. A limited number of fixed, bussed interconnections are provided at the base of the stack – committing only about one third of the available I/O pins to fixed interconnect. A second side of the stack is used for programming and diagnostic connections: this enables the stack to be either 'gang' programmed – each FPGA is loaded with an identical program – or individually. The remaining two sides have uncommitted connections: connectors are provided for groups of 8 signals and ribbon cables are used to connect FPGAs as the target application requires. This system offers wide variations in communication patterns – at the expense of manual reconfiguration.

4   Applications

The list of applications which have already been successfully implemented in reconfigurable hardware systems is long: it includes applications from such diverse areas as:

- Image processing
- Cryptography
- Database and text searching
- Compression and
- Signal Processing.

It is generally straightforward to transfer an algorithm from a general purpose processor to reconfigurable hardware: synthesizers which convert VHDL or Verilog models into the bit streams necessary to program an FPGA-based system are available and efficient. However a successful transfer must provide a solution which is more efficient, by some criterion, than the same algorithm running on fast commodity general-purpose processors. Reconfigurable hardware generally runs slower[2], consumes more power and costs more than commodity processors. This remains true at most points in the performance spectrum. At the low performance end, small processors, e.g. Motorola's HC11 series, have very low cost and power consumption and will perform simple control and data processing tasks effectively. A modern FPGA can outperform the processors at the low end of the performance spectrum, but there are also a host of general purpose embedded processors, e.g. the PowerPC based devices, which will provide the additional processing power while still consuming less power and costing less. At the high performance end of the spectrum, the internal clock speeds of FPGAs lag behind those of commodity processors and thus their sequential processing capability does not match that of, for example, a state-of-the-art Pentium or SPARC processor. However, whilst it is clear that reconfigurable hardware will not provide efficient solutions for all problems, there are areas in which it is extremely efficient.

The general characteristics of successful applications are:

a. Sufficient parallelism: The processing algorithm must have sufficient inherent parallelism to allow multiple processing pipelines to be created. This parallelism can be either direct or pipelined.

b. Low storage requirements: Whilst modern FPGAs have blocks of dedicated memory, capacities are measured in Mbits not Mbytes! External memory can be added and wide buses employed to provide high bandwidth, but this uses valuable I/O pins and the path to external memory is likely to become a bottleneck and limit performance.

c. 'Decision-free' processing patterns: Multiplexors in the data paths will readily handle simple switches of the dataflow between down-line functional

---

[2] However Tsu et al.argue that there is no inherent reason why an FPGA should be slower[10]

blocks, but complex decision trees will generally not map efficiently to hardware. When there are large numbers of branches, inevitably many paths are little used – and thus expensive to implement in fixed hardware relative to their benefit. In particular, error handling logic will generally be complex relative to its frequency of use. Complex decision logic is efficiently handled in high performance modern processors which move common logic to cache at the expense of little used code. When branches have similar probabilities, speculative execution ensures good average rates of instruction completion. However, this criterion for successful hardware implementation is a flexible one: if high throughput for all possible processing paths is required, then the resources devoted to implementing all paths (including little used ones) may be justified. Devices are starting to appear which contain general-purpose processor cores; these address this problem and allow hybrid solutions in which complex control flow graphs may be efficiently implemented in the cores and combined with data paths which effectively use the general resources of an FPGA. Dynamically reconfigurable logic may also provide effective solutions when there are complex decision trees.

d. Ability to use local (*i.e.* between neighbouring devices) data paths in problems which are large enough to require multiple devices. Most systems provide high bandwidth paths between nearest neighbours with lower bandwidth multiple device buses and global interconnects. The 3-D Achilles design provides more device-device data path flexibility but at a cost – wiring patterns must be set up manually for each application[11].

e. Integer arithmetic: Whilst it is possible to implement arbitrary precision floating point processors in FPGAs, the number of logic blocks required and hence the delays introduced by data paths between logic blocks make them expensive in area and low in performance compared to those found in superscalar processors[3]. On the other hand, the ability to easily implement arbitrary precision integer arithmetic allows a reconfigurable system designer to pack more functional units of higher performance into a given area by choosing the minimum required word length.

Some brief notes on a selection of applications follow to illustrate these points.

4.1   Image Processing

Real time image processing presents a classic application for custom processors. A stream of pixels emanating from a camera can be passed through a wide deep pipeline – performing unrelated operations (*e.g.* threshholding and greyscale conversion) in parallel and more complex operations (*e.g.* masking) in deep pipelines. Basic operations require little storage and the relatively inefficient memory on an FPGA suffices. A masking operation, such as applying a 3×3 mask to a group of neighbouring pixels, requires the storage of two scanlines in a shift register and is feasible in large FPGAs. The reverse process, visualisation –

---

[3] Superscalar processor manufacturers invest large amounts to win benchmark competitions. Man-years of effort may be used to optimise individual circuits and layouts.

or the processing of machine generated images for display, is already the domain of special purpose processors, but market volumes have justified use of ASICs[4]. Stereo vision applications can provide yet another parallel processing path: a case study in this area appears in section 8.

4.2   Encryption/Decryption

Symmetric encryption algorithms are easily and efficiently implemented in FP-GAs: they require a number of 'rounds' of application of simple operations. Each round can be implemented as a pipeline stage. As an example, TwoFish[12] requires 16 rounds of lookup table accesses which can be implemented as a 16-stage pipeline. This allows a stream of 32-bit input data words to be encrypted at very high input frequencies with a latency of 16 cycles. In a study of four AES candidates, Elbirt *et al.* report an order of magnitude difference between FPGA-based implementations and the best software ones[13]. However they also note that that for one AES candidate, CAST-256, FPGA implementations were slower than their software counterparts. This emphasizes that the performance advantage of commodity processors can only be overcome when the problem matches the capabilities of FPGA-based custom processors. By adding further pipeline stages within each round, Gaj and Chodowiec were able to achieve throughputs greater than 10Gb/s for five of the AES candidate algorithms (12Gb/s using a 95MHz internal clock for Rijndael, the eventual winner of the AES competition)[14].

4.3   Compression

Using a systolic array style (*i.e.* a deep pipeline) for the LZ algorithm, Huang *et al.* were able to obtain throughputs 30 times greater than those achievable with commodity processors[15], even though their Xilinx XC4036s were clocked at 16MHz *vs* 450MHz for the fastest software version. Huang *et al.* believe that even better relative performance would be obtained from modern FPGAs, for example Altera's APEX 20K devices have built-in content addressable memories which would speed up matching input strings with the dictionary.

4.4   Arithmetic

When designing a reconfigurable system, the widths of arithmetic function units – and hence their propagation delays – can be constrained trivially to the number of bits actually required for the application. This saves space, logic resources and time. Designers also have considerable flexibility when complex arithmetic expressions must be evaluated; they can choose a single-stage combinatorial circuit or increase throughput by adding registers and forming a pipeline. This

---

[4] However, prototyping designs which are destined for ASICs is a major application for reconfigurable processors. They can be used to ensure that a design is correct and that the silicon will function correctly first time. Some foundries will take FPGA based designs and convert them directly to ASICs.

can often be done at essentially no cost: the logic blocks contain flip-flops already, so there is no space penalty and negligible time penalty. An application requiring floating point arithmetic may be a poor candidate for a reconfigurable system – to achieve performance comparable to that offered by a commodity processor will require significant effort. However, reconfigurable systems are excellent at processing streams of data from sensors: this data will be fixed point and readily handled by the same circuits used for integer arithmetic.

CORDIC. Trigonometric functions of fixed point data may be implemented with CORDIC arithmetic. CORDIC algorithms are iterative and use only shifts and adds. There is a large desgin space. Bit-serial designs are simple and compact, but take many cycles: this is adequate if the data rate is relatively slow. An iterative bit-parallel design will require more space but fewer cycles. Finally, unrolling the iterative loop by one or more stages produces a target through-put/space balance.

4.5   String and Text Matching

Genetic sequencing is producing enormous databases to be searched. Thus hardware to accelerate the comparison of new sequences with those in existing databases has been sought. A measure known as the edit distance is used to compare sequences. A simple dynamic algorithm can compute the edit distance in $\mathcal{O}(mn)$ time (m, n = length of source and target sequences respectively), but if the calculation is carried out on a processor array, then all operations on the diagonal may be performed in parallel. A single board Splash 2 machine achieved a factor of 20 speedup over a CM-2 – a massively parallel processor![16]

Similarly, full text searching of documents for relevance has sufficient parallelism to make FPGA-based hardware effective. When document content cannot be adequately described by keywords, a searcher supplies a list of relevant words and requires that every word of every document be checked against the list in order to build a relevance score for each document. Gunther *et al.* used 'data folding'; they built match circuitry for each word and incorporated it into a fixed matching structure. This is an example of the potential of partial reconfiguration: circuit patterns corresponding to the relevant words are loaded for each new search. Matching in hardware also does not need to be limited to direct character-by-character matching: it is possible to implement simple regular expressions allowing, for example, matching on the root of a word only[17]. Parallel text matching hardware means that we are limited only by the rate at which documents can be read from disc – independent of the number of search items.

4.6   Simulations

Cellular automata map readily to reconfigurable systems. They involve arrays of cells: each cell is a simple finite state machine whose behaviour depends only on its current state and the state of cells in its immediate environment. Milne gives an example of traffic system simulation using his generalized cellular automata concept which removes some of the constraints in simple models[18].

Petri net models are also used extensively in simulation studies: again there is abundant low level parallelism to be exploited – the firability of each transition can be evaluated simultaneously. Petri net models are based on simple units – places and transitions. It is possible to create generic models in VHDL for these units, paving the way to automatic generation of VHDL code from natural visual representation of Petri nets, which can be compiled and downloaded to suitable hardware. A single Achilles stack is able to accommodate a model containing of the order of 200 transitions[11].

5   Reconfigurable Processors *vs* Commodity Processors

Special purpose hardware has to compete with the rapid performance increase of commodity processors. Despite their relative inefficiency for many applications, if the special purpose hardware provides a speedup of, say only 2, then Moore's Law will ensure that the special purpose hardware's advantage is lost in a year[5]. When assessing whether an application will benefit from use of a reconfigurable processor, one has to remember:

- **Raw Performance.** The raw performance of FPGA based solutions will always lag behind that of commodity processors. This is superficially reflected in maximum clock speeds: an FPGA's maximum clock speed will typically be one-third or less of that of a commodity processor at the same point in time. This is inevitable and will continue: the reconfiguration circuitry loads a circuit and requires space, increasing its propagation delay and reducing the maximum clock speed.
- **Parallelism.** Thus an application must have a considerable degree of inherent parallelism which can be used effectively. The parallelism may be simple (multiple computations performed on the same data in parallel) or deeply pipelined.
- **Memory.** Although recent devices (*e.g.* Altera's APEX 20K[3]) have significant dedicated memory resources, the total number of memory bits remains relatively small and insufficient for applications which require large amounts of randomly accessible data. This means, for example, that, whilst detecting edges in an image arriving as a pixel stream from a camera is feasible, segmentation of the image is considerably more difficult. For edge detection, a simple 9-stage pipeline will apply a 3×3 mask at the pixel clock rate. Segmentation, on the other hand, needs random access to the whole image. Whilst an FPGA with auxillary memory might handle this, it is unlikely to have a significant advantage over a general purpose processor.
- **Regularity.** A processing pipeline with large numbers control flow branches may not be efficiently implemented. In such a pipeline, the large number of branches which are rarely taken all take up considerable space – lenghtening

---

[5] I have (somewhat arbitrarily) shortened the 'break-even' point from the 18 months of Moore's Law, because we need to factor in the extra cost of custom hardware *vs* using cheap commodity hardware.

data paths and challenging placement algorithms. Paths with large numbers of blocks of variable size also present a (albeit less severe) problem for an FPGA's fixed routing resources.

6 Dynamic Reconfiguration

The potential to be able to dynamically reconfigure a running circuit opens up a completely new field of architectural research. Most devices have required a complete new configuration program to be loaded every time – usually by paths with limited bandwidths requiring thousands of cycles to completely reprogram a device. However some devices provide limited dynamic reprogramming capabilities, *e.g.* Xilinx' Virtex family[6].

Two reconfiguration models have been proposed: (a) a program module is replaced by streaming a a new one from an external source and (b) the DPGA model[19]. A DPGA device would hold several configurations in the configuration memory for each logic block and allow the context to select one dynamically. The flexibility gained from this arrangement allows much more effective gate utilisation – at the expense of the additional space for the configuration memory and context selection logic.

7 Hybrid Systems

Hybrid systems couple a conventional processor and an area of uncommitted logic that may be configured to suit the demands of algorithms in which the conventional processor cannot exploit data or pipeline parallelism. Berkeley's Garp[20] contains a MIPS processor core and 32×23 array of logic blocks. A 24th column of logic blocks is responsible for communication outside the array. Logic blocks take up to 4 2-bit inputs and produce 2-bit outputs: a row of the array can thus process up to 4 46-bit words. Garp's designers hypothesize that the reconfigurable section may be used effectively for the critical kernels found in most code: hard-wiring the control logic will reduce instruction fetch over-heads and better exploit parallelism. Memory queues – which stream data to and from memory – were added because many applications process streams of data. Results from the Garp simulator on a wavelet image compression program showed an overall speedup of 2.9 compared to the MIPS processor. Individual kernels showed speedups up to 12, observed when a kernel had high exploitable instruction level parallelism and the configuration loading time could be amor-tized over many compute cycles. Garp's also showed significant speedups over a 4-issue superscalar processor, indicating that it was able to exploit more ILP, sustaining up to 10 instructions per cycle.

8 Application Example – Stereo Correspondence

The correspondence or matching problem dominates research into fully auto-mated stereo vision systems; it requires the comparison of pixels (or regions of pixels) to determine matches between corresponding segments of two images. The distance between matching regions in the left and right images (the disparity) combined with camera system geometry enables reconstruction of a 3D scene. Lacking the ability of a human brain to 'jump' to the obvious match, a machine must try all possible disparities in order to find candidate matches between pixels or to correlate regions. Disparities approach infinity for objects close to the camera lens, but in practical applications it is possible to put a lower bound on an object's closest approach to the camera. This results in a need to consider objects with disparities from 0 pixels (*i.e.* at infinity) to of the order of 10-100 pixels at the closest permissible approach.

Thus this problem has all of the required attributes for an efficient pipeline parallel implementation: parallelism of 10 to 100 or more; simple calculations (comparing pixel intensities) and regularity – the same correlation operators are applied to each pixel.

Research over several decades has led to dozens of proposals for stereo matching algorithms: here, I will consider only the implementation of the 'sum of absolute differences' (SAD) – one of the simplest algorithms, because it has been proven to be one of the most efficient[21, 22] SAD is an area-matching correlation algorithm in which the cost of a match,

$$cost(\delta, p, q) = \sum_{x, y \subset w(p, q)} |I_L(x, y) - I_R(x - \delta, y)|$$

where the summation is taken over a square window of pixels, $w(p, q)$, surrounding the pixel of interest – I_L, I_R are the intensities of pixels in the left and right images, respectively. The disparity of a pixel in the left image is determined by finding the minimum cost as the window in the right image is moved further to the left (*i.e.* as the disparity is increased).

In real images, the presence of noise requires the use of large matching windows: 9×9 is usually needed for reliable matching. A block diagram of a hardware implementation of the SAD algorithm is shown in Figure 2 and Figure 3. It shows many of the required characteristics for efficient implementation on FPGAs:

– abundant parallelism – of the order of the disparity range at a high level, with additional parallellism within the adder of the disparity calculator block,
– deep pipelining – individual pixels are shifted through a shift register which must be long enough to hold several rows of each image,
– regularity – long shift registers and identical disparity calculator blocks allow for efficient layout
– simple regular interconnection patterns
– integer arithmetic, with the ability to make the adders within the disparity calculators just wide enough to ensure no bits of precision are lost

With a 9×9 window, the shift registers need to hold up to 9×10^5 bits (9 scanlines of 8-bit pixels from a 5Mpixel colour camera): this will tax the memory capacity of a modern FPGA.

However, a study of the problem revealed that software algorithms use square matching windows simply because it is convenient to do so. Simulation has shown

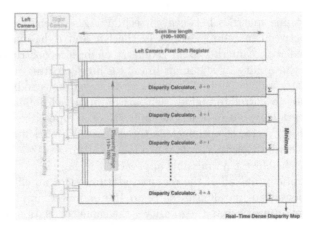

Fig. 2. Block diagram for real-time dense disparity map calculator

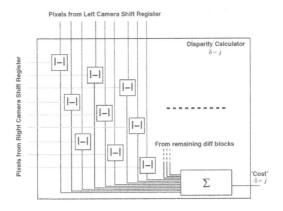

Fig. 3. Disparity calculator: this figure assumes a 3 row correlation window. Only the 3 left-most columns of absolute difference ('| − |') elements are shown.

that long narrow windows along the scanlines are equally effective[21]. In a hardware implementation, fewer scan lines need to be stored in the shift registers (3 will suffice), reducing memory needs to 30% of those initially required. The circuits shown in Figures 2 and 3 will now fit into a single commercially available device, obviating the need to shift portions of the storage into external devices.

Thus, a simple modification to the original algorithm guided by the constraints for effective FPGA implementation led to an feasible device. Dense accurate disparity maps in real-time are now possible for applications like collision avoidance.

9   New Architectures

The stereo application just described – as well as the (partial) list of suitable applications listed in Section 4 – demonstrates that reconfigurable logic provides plenty of opportunities for discovering *and proving through implementations* new computation structures. But what about research into entirely new architectural styles? For example, dataflow architectures and processors based on asynchronous circuits as well as a host of proposals for multi-threaded architectures have all been discussed in the literature. The large capacity of modern FPGAs makes it feasible to build 'proof-of-concept' machines with radically new architectures. Such machines will inevitably be limited in some way. For example, large caches have been necessary to overcome limitations in bandwidth between CPUs and memory: it is unlikely that an FPGA will ever provide us with as fast and as large a cache as a custom design can. However, the effect of cache on performance has been studied extensively and we should be able to translate performance demonstrated with an FPGA-based, but cache-less, implementation of a new architecture to that achievable with a full custom design – with sufficient confidence to justify the expense of producing the custom design.

10   Conclusions

In this paper, I have tried to set out the general characteristics of problems which architecture researchers can realistically attack – without requiring a budget that only a handful of large companies can provide. A key requirement is clearly sufficient exploitable parallelism, either as raw or pipeline parallelism.

Reconfigurable systems are always competing against the inexorable rise in power of general purpose processors. Although reconfigurable devices track processor performance as device technology improves, they lack the commercial impetus propelling commodity processors forward and stay behind their better funded cousins in raw performance. Thus, when considering a special purpose processor, one must keep in mind the point at which commodity processors will be when the design is complete. Commodity processors even have limited parallel processing capabilities with technologies such as MMX and Altivec but these are limited to very regular computations. A reconfigurable system – with its ability to implement multiple parallel data paths – will generally be better at matching the 'shape' of a multiple step algorithm, but I suggest that, generally, ~ 10 fold parallelism must be present for an effective design.

Whilst many problems fail to meet the criteria set out here and thus can be more effectively solved using commodity processors, there are many domains contain problems which are well suited to reconfigurable processors and thus bases for novel new architectural solutions. Focussing on 'attached processor' applications, I have also barely touched three areas of considerable further research potential:

- dynamically reconfigurable systems
- hybrid systems combining conventional processors with special purpose ones on a single surface *and*
- 'proving' entirely new architectures.

Thus, design *and implementation* of relevant and interesting systems should not be abandoned in our research laboratories.

References

1. Xilinx Inc.: Virtex-II Platform FPGAs. http://www.xilinx.com (2002)
2. Xilinx, Inc.: XC4000 data book. Xilinx, Inc. (1997)
3. Altera Corp.: APEX 20K Programmable Logic Device Family Data Sheet. http://www.altera.com/literature/lit-apx.html (2001)
4. QuickLogic Corp.: QuickLogic: Beyond Programmable Logic. (2001)
5. Lucent Technologies: ORCA Series 2 Field-Programmable Gate Arrays. (1999)
6. Xilinx, Inc.: Virtex-II 1.5V Platform FPGA Family. http://www.xilinx.com/partinfo/ds013-2.pdf (2001)
7. Guccione, S.: List of FPGA-based computing machines. www.io.com/~guccione/HW_list.html (1999)
8. Tham, S., Morris, J.: Performance of the achilles router. In Omondi, A., Sedukhin, S., eds.: Advances in Computer Systems Architecture (ACSAC'2003). (2003)
9. Tham, C.K.: Achilles: A high bandwidth, low latency, low overhead network interconnect for high performance parallel processing using a network of workstations. PhD thesis, The University of Western Australia (2003)
10. Tsu, W., Macy, K., Joshi, A., Huang, R., Walker, N., Tung, T., Rowhani, O., George, V., Wawrzynek, J., DeHon, A.: HSRA: High-speed, hierarchical synchronous reconfigurable array. In: Intl Symp on Field Programmable Gate Arrays (FPGA-99). ACM/SIGDA, NY, ACM Press (1999) 125–134
11. Morris, J., Bundell, G., Tham, S.: A scalable reconfigurable processor. In: Fifth Australasian Computer Architecture Conference ACAC'2000. (2000)
12. Schneier, B., Kelsey, J., Whiting, D., Wagner, D., Ferguson, N.: Comments on Twofish as an AES candidate. In NIST, ed.: The Third Advanced Encryption Standard Candidate Conference, April 13–14, 2000, New York, NY, USA, Gaithersburg, MD, USA, National Institute for Standards and Technology (2000) 355–356
13. Elbirt, A.J., Yip, W., Chetwynd, B., Paar, C.: An FPGA implementation and performance evaluation of the AES block cipher candidate algorithm finalists. In NIST, ed.: The Third Advanced Encryption Standard Candidate Conference, Gaithersburg, MD, NIST (2000) 13–27
14. Gaj, K., Chodowiec, P.: Fast implementation and fair comparison of the final candidates for advanced encryption standard using field programmable gate arrays. Lecture Notes in Computer Science **2020** (2001) 84
15. W.J. Huang, N.S., McCluskey, E.J.: A reliable lz data compressor on reconfigurable coprocessors. In: IEEE Symposium on Field-Programmable Custom Computing Machines. (2000)
16. Hoang, D.T.: Searching genetic databases on splash 2. In D.A. Buell, J.A., Kleinfelder, W., eds.: Splash 2: FPGAs in a custom computing machine, Los Alamitos, IEEE Computer Society Press (1996)

17. Gunther, B., Milne, G., Narasimhan, L.: Assessing document relevance with run-time reconfigurable machines. In Arnold, J., Pocek, K.L., eds.: IEEE Workshop on FPGAs for Custom Computing Machines, Napa, CA (1996) 10–17
18. Milne, G.J.: Reconfigurable custom computing as a supercomputer replacement. In: Proc. 4th International Conference on High-Performance Computing. (1997)
19. DeHon, A.: DPGA utilization and application. In: ACM/SIGDA International Symposium on Field Programmable Gate Arrays, Monterey, CA (1996) 115–121
20. Callahan, T.J., Hauser, J.R., Wawrzynek, J.: The Garp architecture and C compiler. Computer **33** (2000) 62–69
21. Leclercq, P., Morris, J.: Robustness to noise of stereo algorithms. In Ferretti, M., ed.: Proc ICIAP'2003. (2003)
22. Scharstein, D., Szeliski, R.: A taxonomy and evaluation of dense two-frame stereo correspondence algorithms. Intl Jnl of Computer Vision **47** (2002) 7–42

Design and Implementation of Java Processors

Amos R. Omondi

School of Informatics and Engineering, Flinders University,
Bedford Park, SA 5042, Australia,
Amos.Omondi@flinders.edu.au

Abstract. Java is now firmly established and widely used in many areas and applications, ranging from mobile phones and consumer-electronics devices to desktops. As the language has become more widely used, so has the need increased for high-performance execution of Java code. Naturally, this has led to the consideration of architectural issues to support a language that is not particularly well-suited to the design of high-performance hardware. This poses certain challenges that are discussed in this paper.

1 Introduction

All implementations for the execution of applications written in the Java language are based on an abstract machine, the *Java Virtual Machine* (JVM) [1]. A straightforward implementation of the JVM is as a software interpreter, which has the advantage of requiring relatively little memory but the major drawback of a lack of execution performance. For better performance, many implementations are based on a Just-In-Time (JIT) compiler that produces code for a conventional (or "native" host) processor. JIT-generated code when executed essentially simulate the JVM much faster than interpretation, because use is made of the high-performance hardware techniques employed in current microprocessors. However, many standard compiler-optimizations are not in JIT because they would increase the compilation time; consequently execution rates on JIT code does not match those for conventional languages. (Off-line compilation partially addresses this but can be used only in limited environments.) In addition, JIT compilation results in larger memory requirements that may not be met in small low-cost devices. Hardware implementations (full or partial) have the potential to greatly increase the performance on Java programs while at the same time minimizing memory requirements and power consumptions. With such implementations, translation is avoided and hardware can be optimized to execute Java code more efficiently than is possible with conventional processors. The JVM is, however, not ideally suited to hardware implementation, and this paper discusses some of the issues involved.

With the advent of Sun's picoJava [2], a hardware implementation of the JVM, there was a significant increase in research on hardware JVMs and much hope that this would significantly impact execution of Java code in many environments. However, it quickly became clear that real progress would be slow — that

A. Omondi and S. Sedukhin (Eds.): ACSAC 2003, LNCS 2823, pp. 86–96, 2003.

it is quite difficult to realize a full Java processor that can match conventional processors in performance, cost, etc. (Many of the difficulties encountered are familiar from the 1980s, when there was much work in the design of "high-level language" machines.) Nevertheless, there remains a need for high-performance execution of Java code on a wide variety of platforms and, in particular, for embedded systems with tight constraints on memory usage and power consumption. This latter area continues to be attractive, and there are several commercial offerings currently on the market. Examples include processors from Aurora VLSI [3], aJile Systems [4], Naozumi Communications [5], NanoAmp Solutions [6], Multiplicity [7], Zucotto Wireless [8], and Vulcan Machines [14]. These range from simple accelerators, that work on only a subset of the JVM, to more complex architectures that are intended to speed up almost all JVM operations. Various companies, such as ARM also offer soft cores that are integrated with their existing products [9]. Also, realizations are no longer restricted to just ASIC technology. FPGAs have now become sufficiently dense and fast that it is possible to envisage FPGA implementations of the JVM. An example is the LavaCORE processor (from Derivation Systems), which targets Xilinx's Virtex FPGAs [10]. FPGAs have the advantage of providing flexibility, so that an implementation may be tailored to particular applications and environments; and those like the Virtex come with a conventional core processor that may be used for the more complicated aspects of the JVM. Another area to investigate for the use of FPGAs is hardware compilation, i.e. implementing a JIT, or similar, compiler directly in hardware [25]. Other than the obvious performance improvements in going from software to hardware, this approach may result in further gains through the ability to tailor the JIT in special cases.

It seems inevitable that there will be further development of hardware to accelerate the execution of Java programs, and what needs to be considered now are the existing challenges, especially in light of the lessons that have been learned so far. These challenges generally fall into three main areas: how to handle the most complex JVM instructions (and other associated operations); how to effectively extract parallelism (at all levels) to an extent that at least matches existing conventional microprocessors; and how to reduce power consumption in the execution of Java programs. In what follows, we first review (in Section 2) the main aspects of the JVM and highlight those that require the most attention in a hardware implementation. In Section 3, we then discuss directions that may be taken with regard to the first challenge. Section 4 deals with the second challenge and discusses a new approach to the exploitation of instruction-level parallelism.

2   The Java Virtual Machine

This section is a brief summary of the JVM and covers the memory architecture, instruction set, and other secondary components needed for the proper execution of JVM programs. It should be noted that there are several variants of the JVM, target at different environments, and the following is only the "generic" one specified in [1]. Two particular areas of interest are the implications of a stack architecture and the dynamic allocation/de-allocation of memory on a heap.

2.1 Memory Architecture

The JVM has four main memory structures:

- The *stack*, which holds frames (activation records) for invoked methods. Each frame contains an operand stack, local variables, and other information (e.g. that required for dynamic linking).
- The *method area*, which holds the bytecodes that make up the instruction stream.
- The *heap*, which holds objects created at run-time, as well as additional information required to manage them.
- The *constant pool* which corresponds to the symbol table for a conventional language. It holds numerical values that have been precomputed as well as references that require resolution.

For a high-performance machine, the stack raises certain obvious problems, but these can largely be solved as discussed below. The heap, on the other hand is more problematic, for two reasons. First, it requires garbage collection. Second, it has to be managed for concurrent access by several different threads.

2.2 Instruction Set

The JVM has around 200 instructions (bytecodes) that are of a variable-length format. Each consists of a 1-byte opcode, followed by 0 to 4 operands, with the majority having only 0 to 2 operands. The instructions fall into the following categories:

- *Load/Store* instructions, which transfer data between local variables and the operand stack.
- *Arithmetic* instructions, of the usual variety, which operate on the operand stack.
- *Type conversion* instructions for explicit casting.
- *Stack manipulation* instructions, to pop, duplicate, and swap values on the stack.
- *Object manipulation* instructions to create new class instances and arrays, to load/store array components from/to the operand stack, to access fields of classes, and to examine properties of arrays and class instances.
- *Control transfer* instructions, consisting of the usual sort of conditional and unconditional branch instructions as well as two instructions that jump according to a value from a table.
- *Method invoke* and *return* instructions.
- A few additional instructions for synchronization and exceptions.

Many of the instructions are relatively straightforward and can be implemented in hardware to execute in a single cycle. But instructions for object manipulation, table-branching, and method invocation/return are obviously much more complex. It should, however, be noted that studies show that only about 45 different bytecodes occur in the majority of dynamic instruction streams [21].

2.3   Other Features

In addition to the above, the JVM environment has other aspects that are required to run Java programs. These include a *class loader*, for the dynamic loading of class files, a *bytecode verifier*, which ensures that bytecodes can be safely executed, a garbage collector, and a *thread manager* to schedule and control the execution of multiple threads inherent in Java. These are generally time-consuming activities that would greatly benefit from any hardware support that may be practical.

3   Hardware Implementation of the JVM

The first issue that needs to be considered here is whether or not a complete stand-alone Java processor is practical. In theory, one could start by examining all aspects associated with the JVM, design a suitable ISA (essentially with the JVM ISA as a subset) and then implement that in hardware. Such an ISA would also include instructions for I/O, diagnostics and exception handling, and memory access and management (which are very restricted in the JVM). Past experience with such an approach makes it doubtful that the investment would be worthwhile; moreover, a significant part of such an ISA would be quite similar to that of conventional ones. As indicated above, a better approach would be to separate the JVM into the many instructions whose execution can be speeded up by, say, the extraction of instruction-level parallelism, as discussed in detail in the following sections, and the complex instructions and other features indicated above. (The latter suggests the use of conventional software running on conventional hardware.) Here we briefly look at the general issues.

There are three main ways in which the complex Java instructions can be handled. The first is to have such an instruction cause a trap that results in the execution of code to carry out the required functions on a conventional processor. The second a complete hardware realization, implemented, through, say, microprogramming. And the third is between these two extremes. The first approach is the most common one and is useful where the Java processor is used as a simple accelerator to a conventional processor, i.e. as a "peripheral". The advantages here are the low hardware costs and the ability to use the conventional processor to run non-Java code that may be required for other purposes, e.g. operating-systems support. The third approach is exemplified by the old, unsuccessful high-level-language machines, such as the Intel iAPX432 [11], the SOAR [12], and a variety of Lisp and Prolog machines [13]. The failure of such machines to be a success may be attributed, to a large degree, to the high hardware costs relative to the performance gained. While this may still be true to some extent, the amount of chip real-estate now available now makes it more reasonable to again explore that path, taking into account the lessons that were learned in the past attempts. Nevertheless, this approach may not be suitable for embedded systems, in which cost and power consumption are critical. For the near future the most promising direction seems to be one that lies somewhere between the first and third approach. In this "middle ground" one would seek to provide hardware support that goes beyond the basic JVM instructions and a full hardware implementation for every instructions. That is, hardware support would be provided for only part of the actions required to execute a complex instruction. A partial example of this approach is the processor cores produced by Aurora VLSI. In Aurora's processors, only fourteen JVM instructions are realized in software; all of the simpler instructions are realized completely in hardware; and partial hardware support is provided for the complex instructions.

3.1   Stack Operations

A direct implementation of a stack architecture is unlikely to be competitive, in terms of cost:performance etc, with that of a conventional register architecture; this is borne out by past experience. There are two parts to a solution to these inherent problems. The first is the use of a cache or register-file to hold a part of the top portion of the stack and then move, as needed, data between this portion and the rest of the stack in main memory. And the second is *instruction folding*, in which sequences of stack instructions are gathered into something like a conventional two-register or three-register format. A fair amount of work has been done in both cases, but more remains — for example, on the best type of cache and how to optimally manage data-movement between the cache/register file and the main memory and also how to fold instructions in a way that best facilitates the exploitation of instruction-level parallelism.

3.2   Garbage Collection

This is one of the harder challenges, especially for embedded real-time systems. In addition to the obvious performance requirements, it has also been shown that tuning garbage collection has an appreciable effect memory usage and power consumption [19]. Complete hardware implementation of a garbage collector may not be practical in all cases, although there exist microcode implementations (e.g. the aJile processors), but some partial support can be provided in many cases. But it is necessary to first determine what sort of algorithms to implement and what sort of hardware. Different types of garbage collectors suit different environments: for example, for real-time systems or those with limited memory, incremental collectors are probably better than copying ones. And directly implementing existing garbage-collection algorithms may not be the best approach: [21], for example shows how known algorithms can be usefully modified for embedded Java systems. Aspects of garbage collection for which even partial hardware support can be beneficial include counters, write barriers, and other structures and mechanisms that may be used to detect pointers to the heap and their use. It may be possible to provide additional hardware support for other aspects of garbage collection algorithms, but this requires more detailed studies of the access patterns of typical Java programs, in different environments, and of the cost:performance tradeoffs in implementing the various garbage-collection algorithms.

3.3   Exploiting Parallelism

Java programs has several levels of parallelism that can be usefully exploited for performance, on a single processor or parallel processor: instruction-level, method-level, thread-level. Effective use of instruction-level parallelism, with out-of-order execution, is necessary if performance in Java processors is to approach that in conventional processors; and exploiting parallelism at higher levels makes it easy to amortize the penalties of activities (such as garbage collection, class loading, bytecode verification) that are strictly outside primary bytecode execution. The use of a stack cache/register-file combine with folding allows the exploitation of instruction-level parallelism [16, 17, 18] but not necessarily of parallelism at higher levels. Good ways to make the best use of all available parallelism are the use of parallel processors (with instruction-level parallelism within each processor) and hardware multithreading (or similar support for multiple contexts); multithreading looks particularly promising, but in both cases much more research is required. An example of the way in which multithreading may be used for secondary is described in [21]: to meet real-time constraints, the garbage collector runs in a dedicated hardware thread.

3.4   Others

Method invoke/return, thread management, memory management, object management, and table-branching are also operations that would benefit from hard support. Apart from the obvious aspects that correspond to a conventional procedure/subroutine call, method invocation is problematic because, in general, it requires dynamic location (within class or superclass) of the invoked method. Doing this rapidly, in constant time, and at low cost is difficult. Further research is needed, and a good starting point may be techniques, such as a method cache, used in old Smalltalk and similar machines. For memory management, particular points to consider would include how best to organize the memory structures so as to give the best cost:performance and power-consumption tradeoffs. This would need to take into account the different the different types of accesses made to the memory (i.e. to the heap, constant-pool, method area, and stack) as well as the patterns and frequencies of access. Where the programs to be executed are generally fixed (e.g. in many embedded systems), advantageous use can be made of traces. As an example, of this approach, to reduce, power consumption is discussed in [15]. Objects that would benefit from some hardware support are string objects (which are frequently used) and arrays. Directions for the type of hardware that would be suitable may come from old vector processors such as the CDC Cyber 205. In general, the implementation (addressing, access, etc.) of objects is an area where further work is needed; an example of a problematic area is the relocation of objects during garbage collection. For thread management, the points to consider would be support for scheduling and context-switching, the former of which may be fine-tuned to the application environment. In all these cases, there are many ideas that have been around for some time that could provide useful starting points.

4   A New Approach to Java Instruction-Level Parallelism

In order to get the best performance in a Java processor, it is necessary to extract maximal instruction-level parallelism. Instruction folding is one way towards achieving this, but it has certain limitations. First, when implemented in hardware, as is usually the case, the parallelism is constrained by the need to minimize the instruction-window over which the folding is applied; this makes it hard to fold complex patterns. Second, it is still necessary to detect and resolve dependencies between folded instructions. Bytecode-trace parallelism is one way around these difficulties [23, 24]. A *bytecode trace* is a sequence of bytecodes that has no stack-operand dependencies with any other sequence; bytecode traces can therefore be executed in parallel, on independent operand stacks. A bytecode trace begins and ends with a *clean stack-point*, which is a point in the code at which the value of the stack is zero (assuming it nominally starts at zero). Trace extraction may be done in hardware or software; however, doing it in software has the advantage that folding may be applied to complex or nested instruction patterns. A first cut at a Java Trace Processor consists of an organization in which multiple hardware operand-stacks are employed and instructions (from different traces) are issued and executed in parallel. The implementation therefore has some similarities with both tracing and multithreading as applied to conventional processors and has been named the *Simultaneous Multi-trace Instruction-Issue (SMTI)* processor.

4.1   SMTI Processor Architecture

In order to evaluate the basic ideas, detailed simulation have been carried out, based on the processor organization sketched in Figure 1. A complete discussion of the proposed processor and the results of the evaluation will be found in [23]; what follows is a brief description.

The processing is as follows. Traces are extracted during method verification, and for each trace certain information is entered in the Basic Block Trace Table (BBTT). (In the current arrangement, traces are extracted from within basic blocks only.) This information consists of a trace-id, PC values for the start and end of the trace, basic-block-id, and other information (for folding, dependence analysis, etc.). The BBTT is subsequently accessed by the Trace-Fetch logic, to obtain bytecodes to be processed, and Trace Scheduler, in order to select a trace for execution. Bytecode-fetch is from the Bytecode Cache, which holds

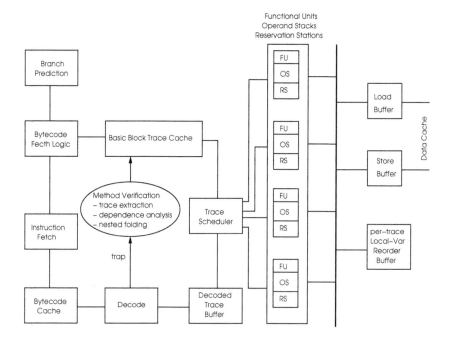

Fig. 1. Organization of an SMTI processor

folded instructions as well as unfolded (usually complex) ones. (The order of bytecode-fetching may be affected by branch prediction.) Certain instructions cause a trap when they reach the Decoder; the rest are decoded and placed in the Decoded-bytecode Trace Buffer (DTB), which consists of a buffer for each trace in progress. Instructions from the DTB are issued, in parallel, to the Reservation Stations and Functional Units for execution.

Although bytecode-traces are independent and can be executed concurrently, certain dependencies remain. Dependencies involving only local variables can be detected during bytecode verification, since they are static, and are resolved by the sequential execution of the bytecodes involved; for this, appropriate information is stored in the BBTT. Dependencies between bytecode-traces are also resolved during bytecode verification. On the other hand, dynamic dependencies, which arise from memory access of objects, can be resolved only at run-time but are processed speculatively at issue-time, on the assumption that no dependencies exist. Such dependencies are detected and resolved in the memory Load/Store Buffers No control dependencies exist between bytecode-traces, as they are extracted from basic blocks.

Trace scheduling is based on a function that depends on the availability of resources. A selected trace is assigned a dedicated operand stack and reservation station, and in each cycle one instruction is issued from each bytecode trace in the DTB. An operand stack is organized as a register file. For local variables, a set of Reorder Buffers are used to resolve write-after-read dependencies. In the case of speculatively processed bytecodes, the relevant contents in the Reorder Buffer, as well as the Load/Store Buffers and Operand Stack, are invalidated.

4.2 Evaluation

The proposed SMTI processor was evaluated by running benchmarks on a simulator based on the Kaffe JVM interpreter. The benchmarks used were taken from the SPECjvm98, Scimark, and Linpack suites. A brief summary is as follows. Evaluation on SPECjvm98 benchmarks showed that bytecode-trace extraction and folding take up around 28% of the bytecode verification time, which in turn accounts for only about 5% of the total execution time. For the number of independent traces within a basic block, ignoring memory dependencies, it was found that 75% to 95% of basic blocks have one trace, 2% to 9% have two traces, and 1% to 9% have more that three traces (with the majority of those having only three or four traces). On that basis, the simulated processor is a four-way issue one. The base for comparison was taken to be a single-issue processor with basic folding, i.e. similar to the picoJava processor. On average, over all the benchmarks, the improvement in instruction-level parallelism was around 54%, with an actual speedup of around 25Local-variable dependencies between traces within a basic block were found to be around 15speculation was less that 1

4.3 Extensions

The results obtained above may not be "spectacular", but they are sufficiently promising for further work. There are three four avenues. The most immediate is to extend the area in which bytecode traces are extracted. The studies reported on above assume that traces are wholly contained within single basic blocks, but there are certain cases in which traces span blocks, and including these will improve the performance. A second avenue is to extend the basic architecture to true hardware multithreading, which would enable secondary activities (such as bytecode verification, folding, garbage collection, and class loading) to be carried out more efficiently. The third is to determine how exactly to process complex bytecodes and associated operations, such as garbage collection. Different approaches are possible, depending, on, for example, whether the SMTI processor is used as an accelerator to a conventional processor or as a standalone processor. And the fourth avenue is a thorough study of the organization and effectiveness of memory structures: although some results are available for a variety of Java processors, it is not clear how these would apply to an SMTI processor, especially with multithreading. Lastly, of course, an actual realization (or proper simulation of one) is needed to evaluate cost, performance, and power consumption, in relation to existing conventional and Java processors.

5   Conclusions

Java will continue to be widely used, especially in embedded systems, and consequently there the need will increase for higher performance, as well as low power consumption. We may therefore expect corresponding development in the implementation of Java processors. In this paper we have summarised some of the issues that need to be addressed. These include the exploitation of parallelism (at different levels), the processing, complex Java instructions, and associated tasks, such as garbage collection and thread management. Hardware multithreading appears to be promising, and, as a starting point, we have described an architecture that essentially extracts "micro-threads" from a stream of bytecodes.

Acknowledgements

The main concepts of the SMTI processor are due to Achutharaman Rangachari (Sun Microsystems, India), who also wrote the simulator and carried out the simulations.

References

25. T. Lindholm and F. Yelin. 1999. *The Java Virtual Machine Specification*. Addison-Wesley, Massachusetts, USA.
25. J. M. O'Connor and M. Tremblay. 1997. "picoJava-I: the Java virtual machine in hardware". *IEEE Micro*, vol. 17, pp 45–53.
25. http://www.auroravlsi.com
25. http://www.ajile.com
25. http://www.naozumi.com
25. htpp://www.nanoamp.com
25. http://www.mplicity.com
25. http://www.zucotto.com
25. http://www.arm.com
25. http://www.derivation.com
25. R. Johnson. 1981. "The Intel iAPX-432: an architecture for Ada". In; *Proceedings, Symposium on High-Level Computer Architecture*.
25. D. Under. 1984. "Architecture of SOAR: Smalltalk on RISC". In: *Proceedings, 11th International Symposium on Computer Architecture*.
25. ICOT. 1984. *Fifth Generation Computer Systems*. Ohmsha, Japan.
25. http://www.vulcanmachines.com
25. S. Tomar et al. 2001. "Use of local memory for efficient Java execution". In: *Proceedings, International Conference on Computer Design (ICCD'01)*.
25. K. Scott and K. Shadron. 2000. "BLP: applying ILP techniques to bytecode extraction". In: *Proceedings, Workshop on Hardware Support for Objects and Microarchitecture for Java*.
25. R. Radhakrishnan, D. Tala, and L. K. John. 2000. "Allowing for ILP in an embedded Java processor". In: *Proceedings, International Symposium on Computer Architecture*.
25. M. Watheq El-Kharashi et al. 2002. "The JAFARDD processor: a Java architecture based on a folding algorithm, with reservation station, dynamic translation, and dual processing. *IEEE Transactions on Consumer Electronics*, vol. 48, no. 4, pp 1004–1015.

25. G. Chen at al. 2002. "Tuning garbage collection in an embedded Java environment". In: *Proceedings, 8th International Symposium on High-Performance Computer Architecture.*

25. R. Radhakrishnan et al. 2001. "Java runtime systems: characteristics and architectural implications". *IEEE Transactions on Computers*, vol. 50,, no. 2, pp 131–146.

25. S. Fuhrmann et al 2001. "A real-time garbage collection for a multithreaded Java microcontroller". In: *Proceedings, 4th International Symposium on Object-Oriented Real-Time Distributed Computing.*

25. T. Hignera et al. 2001. "Region-based memory management for Java". In: *Proceedings, 4th International Symposium on Object-Oriented Real-Time Distributed Computing.*

25. R. Acutharaman, R. Govindarajan, G. Hariprakash, and A. Omondi. 2003. Exploiting Java-ILP on a simultaneous multi-trace instruction-issue (SMTI) processor. In: *Proceedings, IPDPS -International Parallel and Distributed Symposium* (Nice, France, April 2003).

25. R. Achutharaman, G. Hariprakash, A. Omondi, R. Govindarajan. 2002. Bytecode Traces: Exploiting Java-ILP. In: *International Conference on Architecture of Computing Systems* (Karlsruhe, Germany) pp 117–124.

25. G. Hariprakash, R. Achutharaman, A. Omondi. 2002. Hardware Compilation for High Performance Java Processors. In: *International Conference on Architecture of Computing Systems* (Karlsruhe, Germany) pp 125–134.

MOOSS: CPU Architecture with Memory Protection and Support for OOP*

Radim Ballner and Pavel Tvrdík

Department of Computer Science and Engineering, Faculty of Electrical Engineering,
Czech Technical University, Karlovo nám. 13, 121 35 Prague 2, Czech Republic,
xballner@hwlab.felk.cvut.cz, tvrdik@fel.cvut.cz

Abstract. Present microprocessors are optimized for fast execution of basic arithmetic operations and fast data transfers between the CPU and the memory. HW support for semantical constructions of higher programming languages is usually very weak, especially, for object-oriented programming (OOP) even though OOP is becoming the mainstream programming technique. The main problem is to solve the trade-off between higher-level features (e.g., memory protection) and performance.
In this paper, we describe a design of a novel microprocessor architecture, called MOOSS, that provides an efficient HW support for memory protection, exception handling and method calls.

1 Introduction

The accessibility of computer systems through the Internet and widespread use of multiuser operating systems (OSs) and high-level programming languages (HLLs) make the issue of security and privacy uttermost important. The investments into computer protection against malicious hackers are huge, and still the losses, due to exploits, are significant. Why are the current OSs insecure? Common OSs, like MS Windows or Unix, are based and written in C or C++. The C language contains constructs whose semantics is very close to the semantics of machine instructions and therefore compilers can generate very efficient code, but at the same time, these constructs introduce many problems with *memory leaks* and *writing outside array bounds* (*buffer* or *stack overflows*). These overflows are usually consequences of insufficiently checked user input data or of bad use of string formatting routines of the standard C library. In a better case, the result of such an overflow can be a destruction of data and program crash. In a worse case, it can allow a hacker to get an *unauthorized access* to the OS. Many examples of these attacks against almost all common OSs (MS Windows, Linux, Solaris, Free-BSD, etc.) running on various microprocessors (x86, SPARC, Power-PC, etc.) can be found on the web site [1].

How to solve this problem? The first way could be to *abandon* common languages with *pointer arithmetic*, such as C/C++, and use languages that use

---

* This research has been supported by IGS ČVUT under grant CTU0307813/2003 and by MŠMT under research program #J04/98:212300014.

A. Omondi and S. Sedukhin (Eds.): ACSAC 2003, LNCS 2823, pp. 97–111, 2003.

references and perform *range checking*, such as Java [2] or C# without the unsafe mode. The main drawback of this solution is that all SW and even the OS should be *rewritten* in those languages. This is *practically impossible* today. For example, Java has immense requirements and compatibility problems. On the other hand, C# is more efficient, but due to performance reasons, it supports so called *unsafe mode* that allows using pointer arithmetic and bypassing the memory protection.

The second option is to implement HW primitives that would enforce range checking and help garbage collecting directly in the CPU. The new CPU architecture should also implement primitives that allow more efficient implementation of OO HLLs, which are becoming the mainstream. We have identified the 6 following requirements on a CPU architecture that supports secure and efficient OOP:

1. structured memory to distinguish between binary data and pointers,
2. range checking in a given memory block,
3. garbage collecting (e.g., reference counting),
4. method invocation and exception handling for OO HLLs,
5. separate privilege levels for kernel and user, and
6. the efficiency.

The evolution of microprocessor HW shows that a complex CPU with a wide range of features does not lead to good solutions (shift from CISC to RISC). One extreme example is Intel iAPX432 [3], a nicely designed OO CPU, but with very poor performance. Our goal is to design as simple as possible Load/Store CPU with a reasonable support for OOP and memory protection, whose performance would be comparable with modern CPUs.

2   Previous Results

Memory protection has always been an important part of CPU design. A common approach to memory protection in almost all modern CPUs is HW support for *paging*, which doesn't solve above mentioned issues.

Some CPUs support *segmentation*. It is a "coarse-grained" approach because the CPU is able to recognize only *whole* segments. Moreover, the number of segments in the system is usually limited by the CPU, thus the segments are not useful for representation of HLL data structures. Segmentation can be easily combined with paging. A good example of this approach is Intel x86 architectures [4] in the *protected* mode.

A "fine-grained" approach is represented by *tag architectures*. Data of all or some basic types (e.g., integer, floating-point, pointer) are marked by *tags*. These tags are bit strings attached to the data defining their type. Partial support for tags has been implemented for example in a SPARC microprocessor [5]. The representation of structured data is more complex. Another approach can be found in the *Mondrian Memory Protection* [6] that assigns tags to memory blocks that can have various lengths. This solution offers very good memory protection, but it does not solve the issues of OOP support.

The most complex approach is represented by *capability-based systems*. They represent complex solution for resource protection, especially from the viewpoint of an OS. They provide a single mechanism to address both primary and secondary memory and both HW and SW resources. They define a token (capability) which specifies the permission to a given resource. Capabilities are stored in the *capability lists*. Examples of capability-based systems are in [7, 8]. Capability-based systems are usually complex and the overhead is high, mostly due to the need to search in capability lists. To speed-up, simplify, and avoid extra storage the permissions can be stored directly in the *guarded pointers* that can be loaded directly into CPU registers [9].

3 Our Solution

We have designed a CPU architecture called *MOOSS* (Memory Object and Operating System Support) that implements the set of features mentioned in Section 1. In the following sections, we briefly introduce the main features of the MOOSS architecture. Due to the space limits, we can describe only the key features of the architecture and present results of the first benchmarking [10].

3.1 Memory Model

In general, the MOOSS architecture uses enhanced segmentation memory model. In contrast to common segmentation systems, such as [4], the MOOSS segments, called *Object Memory Segments*, *OMSs*, are structured. This is the key feature to distinguish between binary data and pointers. This can be achieved by implementation of tags or by dividing OMS into several sections where each part can hold only specific data. We have chosen the second variant, because the type of stored data can be recognized without reading them into the CPU, but only by checking the section bounds. Moreover, the memory requirements are smaller. Each OMS is described by a *descriptor* that contains the logical address of the OMS, access rights (AR), several limits, and other information.

Descriptors are not stored in special tables, but they are freely allocated in the memory address space. This feature overcomes the disadvantage of standard descriptor tables, whose sizes define the upper bound on the number of segments. Since there are no descriptor tables in the MOOSS architecture, a descriptor cannot be identified by an index into a table, but by its *reference*. A reference is a 32-bit string consisting of 2 parts:

- `Descriptor address` = the 29 topmost bits of the 32-bit *logical address* of the descriptor. The 3 lowest bits of the address are filled with zeroes.
- `ttt` = the 3-bit *type* of the descriptor.

The descriptor type specifies the purpose of the OMS.

- Type **Data** describes an OMS that can contain only binary data. *Examples of use*: bitmaps, strings, numeric data.

- Type `RefArray` describes an OMS that can contain only an array of references. *Examples of use*: array of references to strings, array of references to objects.
- Type `Object` describes an OMS that consists of 2 parts: binary data and an array of references. To support OOP, each descriptor of type Object also has a field that can contain a reference to the class. *An example of use*: an instance of an object in an OO HLL.
- Type `Run` describes an OMS that can contain only executable code and references to descriptors of type `Data` and `RefArray`, respectively, which are related to the code. The associated OMSs can contain static data, such as constant strings or constant arrays (see Figure 1).

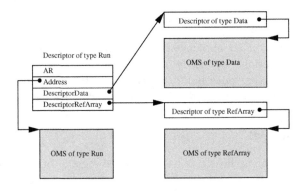

Fig. 1. Supported links between code and data

- Type `JumpTable` describes an array of entry points of subroutines (methods). *An example of use*: method table of a class.
- Type `Local` describes an OMS that consists of 3 parts: binary data, an array of references, and an array of indirect references. These OMSs are used for storing local variables or variables passed to a subroutine as parameters. These OMSs and their descriptors are only constructed on the stack and define method stack frames [11].
- Type `Stack` describes an OMS that can contain binary data (pushed and popped by user instructions), OMSs of type `Local` or `Exception`, and their descriptors.
- Type `Exception` and its OMS is constructed on the stack when an exception is raised. It is similar to the descriptor of type `Local`, e.g., it contains a return address pair.

To provide basic support for garbage collecting, 3 types of descriptors (`Data`, `RefArray`, `Object`) contain *reference counters*. The counters are incremented and decremented automatically by the CPU. When a reference counter reaches zero, an exception is prepared for raising. Since it would be very inefficient to handle the exception immediately, the MOOSS architecture uses *postponed exception handling mechanism* that delays exception handling until the number of descriptors to be freed reaches 32. Then the CPU creates a descriptor and OMS of type `Exception` on the stack and stores the references of the freed descriptors into its reference part.

3.2   ISA

Registers. In the current design, the MOOSS architecture contains 16 integer registers (`Ixx`) for integer arithmetic operations and for memory indexing and 16 floating point registers (`Fxx`). The MOOSS is a strictly Load/Store machine and all data stored in the memory can be accessed only through *reference registers*. A reference register caches a subset of descriptor data similarly to segment registers of x86 in the protected mode. Currently, the MOOSS architecture contains 16 general purpose reference registers. The relationship between reference registers, descriptors, and references is depicted on Figure 2.

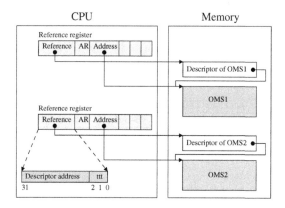

Fig. 2. The relationship between descriptors, OMSs, and reference registers

The first three reference registers have special meaning. Reference register `A00` is called `THIS` and contains a reference to the current object, which is usually represented by an OMS of type `Object`. It corresponds to variable `this` in C++ or `self` in Object Pascal.

The second reference register `A01`, called `PARAM`, contains a reference to an OMS of type `Local` that contains parameters passed to the called subroutine and is created together with its descriptor on the stack by the `local` instruction. Common CPUs store return addresses directly on the stack. In case of a stack overflow, the return address can be overwritten and this is one of the basic hacker techniques for OS exploits [1]. To avoid this risk, the MOOSS CPU does not store return addresses directly on the stack, but in a descriptor of type `Local`. When a subroutine is called, the descriptor loaded into the `PARAM` register is used for storing the return address pair: for normal return and exceptional return (see Section 3.4).

The third reference register AO2, called LOCAL, contains a reference to an OMS of type Local, containing local variables (a *stack frame*). It has similar meaning as the EBP register of Intel x86.

Besides general-purpose registers, MOOSS contains special-purpose registers for stack (STD, STI), program counter (PCD, PCI), status flags (FLAGS), and exception handling (EXD, EXI, EXTBL).

Instruction Set. The MOOSS architecture is a strict Load/Store architecture. Arithmetic instructions operate only on registers, there are no arithmetic instructions with memory operands like in Intel [4] or Motorola [12] microprocessors.

Conventional RISC architectures have instructions of the same length, usually 32 bits. This allows simplifying the prefetch unit and increasing performance. The drawbacks of this approach are that some instructions must include useless bits and the size of immediate operands is limited. MOOSS instructions can be from 1 to 7 bytes long. They are divided into 7 *groups* by their lengths. The *1st byte* of each instruction specifies its opcode and its group (see Table 1), and therefore, its length.

Table 1. The 1st byte of instruction encoding

1st byte	0xxxxxxx	10xxxxxx	110xxxxx	11100xxx	11101xxx	11110xxx	11111xxx
Group	2-byte	3-byte	4-byte	5-byte	6-byte	7-byte	1-byte
Used	80	32	23	8	4	2	8
Maximal	128	64	32	8	8	8	8

- x = opcode specification
- Used = the number of currently implemented instructions in the group.
- Maximal = the maximal number of instructions in the group.

This encoding allows the prefetch unit to fetch instructions effectively into the queue without a complex decoding. The reason for our decision to design instructions of different lengths was our observation that almost 50% of instructions need just 2 bytes and most of the remaining instructions need 3 or 4 bytes. MOOSS programs we have written or compiled had average instruction length 3. Therefore, we could consider an alternative design of the MOOSS ISA with fixed 4-byte instruction format. However at the moment, we need more empirical results from more comprehensive benchmarks to see whether this would not enlarge size of the program significantly. Of course the number of general purpose registers (integer, FP, reference), could be increased to more than 16. This problem has been left open for the future work now.

3.3 Support for Structured Memory to Distinguish between Binary Data and Addresses

The MOOSS architecture allows storing references only in the designated parts of an OMS. The example on Figure 3 shows how the semantics of the `load` instruction depends on the destination register (integer or reference).

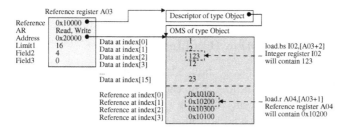

Fig. 3. An example that shows distinguishing between data and references

Instruction `load.bs I02,[A03+2]` loads a signed byte at offset 2 of the *data part* of the OMS referred to by reference register `A03` into integer register `I02`. Instruction `load.r A04,[A03+1]` loads reference register `A04` from the descriptor referred to by the 2nd reference in the *reference part* of the OMS referred to by reference register `A03`.

This mechanism is systematically incorporated into the MOOSS ISA and it makes any misinterpretation of references and binary data (non-reference data) impossible.

3.4 Support for Stack Operations and Subroutines Calls

A detailed description of the MOOSS stack and subroutine call support can be found in [11].

The stack is represented by two registers: `STD` (reference register) and `STI` (integer register with the offset of the top of the stack). The stack is structured and its organization protects stored data and it does not allow misinterpreting binary data and references.

The MOOSS architecture provides instructions for 4 types of calls implementing the *early binding* mechanism and one instruction for *late binding* mechanism.

We have designed these call mechanisms with the goal to provide efficient support for both conventional subroutine calls and method invocations in OO HLLs and OSs. The OO HLLs can use the following mechanism: the contents of the `THIS` register, which contains the current object context, can be replaced when a method is being called and restored during the return from the method [11]

When a subroutine is called, the return address pair is stored into the descriptor of type `Local` referred to by the `PARAM` reference register. The *return address pair* consists of a *normal* return address defined by the contents of (PCI, PCD) registers and *exceptional* return address defined by the contents of (EXI, EXD) registers, where PCI and EXI are integer registers containing offsets and PCD and EXD are reference registers, loaded from descriptors of type Run.

The return from a subroutine is performed by the ret instruction. Which return address will be used depends on the exception flag (see Section 3.5). The flag can be set automatically when a soft exception occurs or it can be set by a special instruction.

3.5   Support for Exception Handling

All modern OO HLLs like C++, Java, C#, or Object Pascal define semantical constructs for exception handling. But the HW support for exception handling in common CPUs is very poor. When an exception occurs, the runtime libraries have to examine the stack and unroll it to the point where the exception is caught. Stack unrolling can be a time-consuming operation and if the stack is corrupted, then it can lead to a program crash.

Due to systematic rolling and unrolling of the stack frames, the MOOSS stack is always in a consistent state. It guarantees *safe* exception handling. The MOOSS architecture defines two kinds of exceptions:

Soft Exception. It is generated by special instructions in the program. It provides support for exception handling in OO HLLs. If a soft exception occurs, the execution is transfered to the point defined by the register pair (EXI, EXD). These registers are accessible to application programs and their contents can be modified by non-privileged instruction loadexc. Soft exceptions set an exception flag in the status register. The exception flag controls behavior of the return mechanism from subroutines (see Section 3.4).

Hard Exception. It is generated when an instruction performs an illegal action or causes a CPU error. It indicates an error in the program (e.g., an attempt to write into an OMS that has no access rights for writing). A hard exception jumps to a service routine whose entry point is defined in the OMS of type JumpTable. The reference to its descriptor is specified by the EXTBL register. Privileged instructions are needed to change the EXTBL register.

Let us discuss exception handling on the following example of a code in a C-like language.

```
void A()
{
    int a=10;int b=20;
    int c=a/b;
}
```

An equivalent code in the MOOSS assembly language follows.

```
; prologue
00000243 local1    LOCAL,12,0,0   ;create space for local variables
00000248 clear     LOCAL          ;clear the space
0000024A loadexc   0000026B       ;define exception address
```

```
; body
0000024F loadc.s    IO0,10
00000252 store.ls   [LOCAL+0],IO0  ;store 10 in a local variable
00000256 loadc.s    IO0,20
00000259 store.ls   [LOCAL+4],IO0  ;store 20 in a local variable
0000025D load.ls    IO0,[LOCAL+0]
00000261 load.ls    IO1,[LOCAL+4]
00000265 div        IO0,IO1        ;divide IO0 by IO1
00000267 store.ls   [LOCAL+8],IO0
; epilogue
0000026B locdstr    LOCAL          ;remove local variables
0000027D ret                       ;return
```

This simple code raises no exception. Assume that variable b is assigned zero. Then the instruction at address 0x00000265 raises a hard exception DIVISION BY ZERO. The CPU creates a descriptor of type Exception and stores the return address pair into it. In our case, the normal return address is set to the address of the next instruction (contents of the PCD register, and the PCI = 0x00000267 register), and the exceptional address is set to the address specified by the EXD and EXI = 0x0000026B registers (the value previously set by the loadexc instruction at address 0x0000024a). Then, the CPU transfers control to the exception handler. In this trivial case, the handler can only set the exception flag in the status register and perform return from the exception by the rete instruction. The execution will continue with the function epilogue at address 0x0000026B.

3.6   Support for Privilege Levels

Modern CPUs must somehow distinguish between kernel code and user code, typically by defining at least two privilege levels. A notable exception is Intel x86 [4], which defines 4 levels. The MOOSS architecture defines 3 privilege levels. The privilege level (PL) is defined in the status register of the CPU.

- Level 0 = the most privileged level for the OS kernel. Privileged instructions (e.g., loading stack registers) can only be used at this level.
- Level 1 = the trusted level for run-time libraries and for communication between level 0 and level 2.
- Level 2 = the least privileged level used for user application software.

The privilege level can be changed by a call via a JumpTable. An OMS of type JumpTable is an array of entry points of subroutines. Each entry point consists of an address and the privilege level of the called subroutine. When the call is performed, the old privilege level is stored together with the return address pair in the corresponding descriptor of type Local loaded into the PARAM register. It is automatically restored after the return. The current privilege level can be changed only by one in both directions, e.g., a code at level 2 can call a code only at levels 2 or 1. The stack is shared between all privilege levels and the stack control mechanisms disallow destruction of data from another privilege level.

4 Performance Evaluation

In contrast to conventional microprocessors, the MOOSS architecture has HW support for structured memory and OOP, which, of course, requires some overhead. On the other hand, the arithmetic part of the MOOSS architecture is conventional and allows execution with no slowdown. Even a memory operation on binary data (non-reference data) with a loaded reference register can be executed without extra penalties. To perform a quantitative evaluation of the MOOSS architecture, we have designed a simple OO HLL, called *SOL*, written a compiler, and developed a MOOSS architecture emulator.

4.1 SOL

The *SOL* (Simple Object Language) programming language is a case-sensitive OO HLL that has syntax similar to Java or C++. It has no pointer arithmetic. It supports simple inheritance, exception handling, and polymorphism based on the early binding. The *SOL* programming language does not support all features supported by Java or C# (e.g., properties), but it provides a basic OO framework. A complete definition of the *SOL* syntax by a grammar is beyond the scope of this paper. The current *SOL* compiler generates a non-optimized code.

4.2 Design Decisions for the Emulator

A pilot emulator of the MOOSS architecture was designed with the following assumptions:

1. The CPU is able to transfer 256-bit data from the cache in one cycle.
2. All data are ready in the cache (no cache-misses).
3. All branch predictions are successful.
4. The in-order scalar instruction pipeline consists of 8 stages: `Fetch`, `Decode`, `Compute effective address`, `Check AR and limits`, `Load reference counters`, `Execute`, `Recount reference counters`, `Write back`.
5. All ALU operations take 1 cycle, except for multiplication and division.
6. Reference counters (see Section 3.1) are stored in a special Reference Counter Cache (RCC), which contains references to descriptors and the values of the counters.
7. All calls of runtime library functions (e.g., string concatenation, memory allocation, etc.), executed by the `rtcall` instruction, consume a constant number of cycles.

Memory Access. All memory accesses are performed through reference registers. The 1st part of Table 2 shows the number of cycles needed for loading/storing a reference register from/to memory and for reading/storing binary data using a loaded reference register.

The exact CPI of reference operations (`load` or `store`) depends on the descriptor type and on the need to update reference counters in RCC (one `load` or `store` can cause 2 updates).

Table 2. CPI of `Execute` phase of `Load/Store`, `local/locdstr`, and `call/ret` instructions

Instruction	CPI	Semantics
`load.r Axx,[Ayy+offset]`	1-2	Load `Axx` from the OMS specified by `Ayy+offset`
`store.r [Ayy+offset],Axx`	1-2	Store the reference from `Axx` into the OMS specified by `Ayy+offset`
`load.r Ixx,[Ayy+offset]`	1	Load `Ixx` with long from the OMS specified by `Ayy+offset`
`store.r [Ayy+offset],Ixx`	1	Store long from `Ixx` into the OMS specified by `Ayy+offset`
`local Axx,data,ref,indirect`	2+	Create a stack frame CPI depends on the values of parameters `ref` and `indirect`.
`locdstr Axx`	2	Destroy the stack frame specified by the `Axx` register
`call offset`	1	Call the subroutine at the `offset` from the program counter
`call [Axx+offset]`	1-3	Call the subroutine specified by the jumptable
`call [Axx+offset],Ayy`	1-3	Call the subroutine specified by jumptable and reload `THIS` by the `Ayy` register
`ret`	1-4	Return from the subroutine and destroy the stack frame specified by the `PARAM` register

Subroutine Calls. The 2nd and 3rd part of Table 2 show CPI for instructions used in subroutine call sequences.

4.3 Methodology for Performance Evaluation

We have measured the performance of the MOOSS architecture using several benchmarks. We have tested memory access operations, reloads of reference registers, and invocations of methods. Since the MOOSS architecture was implemented so far only as a SW emulator, the only reasonable metrics is the *total number of cycles per program* (ICP). The values measured and computed with the benchmarks are summarized in Tables 3–5: Line 1 is the ICP for the MOOSS. Line 2 is the total number of executed MOOSS instructions. Line 3 is the average CPI on MOOSS. Line 4 is the ICP for the Intel for the native implementation of the same algorithm. Line 5 is the ratio of Intel ICP to MOOSS ICP.

All measurements were performed on the Mobile Intel Celeron with the Windows XP OS. The C source code was compiled by the MS Visual Studio 6 into the release version with no optimization. Note that Intel Celeron is able to complete more instructions in 1 cycle, whereas the MOOSS emulator simulates a strictly in-order scalar pipeline.

4.4 Benchmarks

Bubble Sort. The first benchmark was the bubble sort. We have tested 2 versions: `Bubble1` for sorting integer numbers and `Bubble2` for sorting Unicode strings. The input array was sorted in the reverse order.

Figure 4 shows the source code of `Bubble1` written manually in the MOOSS assembler (`Bubble1_M`) and in *SOL* (`Bubble1_S`), which was translated with our pilot non-optimizing *SOL* compiler. The results are presented in Table 3. We have run the tests for 10, 100 and 1000 items to show that there is no influence of L1 Intel CPU cache (it faces only compulsory misses).

```
Bubble1_M(long tosort[],ulong items)
{
  asm
  {
      load.l  I07,[items]       ;number of items into I07
      load.r  A03,[tosort]      ;reference to items into A03
      loadc   I08,4             ;constant 4 into I08
  _loop:
      mov     I02,I07           ;copy I07 into I02
      xor     I03,I03           ;clear I03
  _innerloop:
      load.l  I04,[A03+I03]     ;load the first value
      load.l  I05,[A03+I03+4]   ;load the second value
      cmp     I04,I05           ;compare values
      jgeu    _noswap           ;jump if I04>I05
      store.l [A03+I03+4],I04   ;store values in opposite
      store.l [A03+I03],I05     ;order
  _noswap:
      add     I03,I08           ;add I08 to I03
      dec     I02               ;decrement I02 by one
      jgu     _innerloop        ;if I02>0 then loop continues
      dec     I07               ;decrement I07 by one
      jgu     _loop             ;if I07>0 then loop continues
  }
}
```

```
Bubble1_S(long tosort[],ulong items)
{
    ulong        i,j;

    for(j=0;j<items;j++)
    {
        for(i=0;i<items-j-1;i++)
        {
            if tosort[i]<tosort[i+1] swap tosort[i],tosort[i+1];
        }
    }
}
```

Fig. 4. The integer bubble sort in MOOSS instructions and *SOL*

Table 3. Results for the integer bubble sort

	Bubble1_M	10 items	100 items	1000 items
1	MOOSS ICP	451	44956	4499506
2	MOOSS ins.	446	44951	4499501
3	Avg. CPI	1.01	1.00	1.00
4	Intel ICP	393	26155	2511056
5	Intel/MOOSS	0.87	0.58	0.56

	Bubble1_S	10 items	100 items	1000 items
1	MOOSS ICP	2167	219607	21996007
2	MOOSS ins.	1897	189907	18999007
3	Avg. CPI	1.14	1.16	1.16
4	Intel ICP	1890	124317	12530628
5	Intel/MOOSS	0.87	0.56	0.57

Table 4. The results for the string bubble sort

	Bubble2_M	10 items	100 items	1000 items
1	MOOSS ICP	828	86726	8742251
2	MOOSS ins.	525	54101	5434751
3	Avg. CPI	1.56	1.60	1.61

	Bubble2_S	10 items	100 items	1000 items
1	MOOSS ICP	3022	304297	30342247
2	MOOSS ins.	2112	208897	20792347
3	Avg. CPI	1.42	1.46	1.46

The results for `Bubble2` are shown in Table 4. The string at index x has been initialized to value "x". The *SOL* source code `Bubble2_S` is the same like the code on Figure 4, except that the input array parameter is `unco tosort[]`. This benchmark demonstrates the impact of frequent loading of reference registers and of calling the runtime library routine for Unicode string comparison. Note the difference between the manually written code and the translation of the *SOL* code by our non-optimizing compiler.

List Traversal. The second benchmark `ListTraver` was a traversal of a list of objects to demonstrate the performance of frequent method invocations. The *SOL* source code is on Figure 6. A list of 100 objects `ListTest` is created on lines 8–12. Each of these objects contains only a reference to the next item in the list and `long` variable that is initialized to the position of the item in the list (by a constructor invoked by the `new` statement on lines 5 and 10). Method `View` of object `ListTest` has no parameters and performs only one assignment to a variable and returns. We have measured two modifications of this code. Modification 1: without line 16, i.e., only a traversal of the list is done. Modification 2: with line 16, a list traversal and method invocations.

The results are in Table 5.

```
Bubble2_M(unco tosort[],ulong items)
{
    asm
    {
        load.l  I07,[items]     ;load number of items into I07
        dec     I07             ;decrement I07 by one
        load.r  A03,[tosort]    ;load reference to items into A03
        loadc   I08,4           ;load constant 4 into I08
_loop:
        mov     I02,I07         ;copy contents of I07 into I02
        xor     I03,I03         ;clear I03
_innerloop:
        load.r  A14,[A03+I03]   ;load reference of the first value
        load.r  A15,[A03+I03+4] ;load reference of the second value
        rtcall  RT_CMP_UNCO     ;call runtime library
        jgeu    _noswap         ;jump if I04>I05
        store.r [A03+I03+4],A14 ;store values in opposite
        store.r [A03+I03],A15   ;order
_noswap:
        add     I03,I08         ;add I08 to I03
        dec     I02             ;decrement I02 by one
        jgu     _innerloop      ;if I02>0 then continue in loop
        dec     I07             ;decrement I07 by one
        jgu     _loop           ;if I07>0 then continue in loop
    }
}
```

Fig. 5. The Bubble2_M code

```
1
2 ListTraver(unco argv[])
3 {
4   long        i
5   ListTest    start=new ListTest(0)
6   ListTest    list
7   list=start
8   for(i=1;i<100;i++)
9   {
10      list.next=new ListTest(i)
11      list=list.next
12  }
13  list=start
14  while(list!=NULL)
15  {
16      list.View();
17      list=list.next;
18  }
19 }
20 View()
21 {
22   Long a=id
23 }
```

Fig. 6. The source code of the list traversal in *SOL*

Table 5. The results of the list traversal

	ListTraver	Modification 1	Modification 2
1	MOOSS ICP	1213	3314
2	MOOSS ins.	809	2209
3	Avg. CPI	1.50	1.50
4	Intel ICP	943	2135
5	Intel/MOOSS	0.78	0.64

4.5   Assessment of the Benchmark Results

The benchmark results indicate that the Intel ICP is about 60% of the MOOSS ICP. It is a consequence of the fact that our pilot MOOSS emulator simulates a strictly sequential instruction pipeline and therefore can complete at most one instruction in 1 cycle, whereas the Intel CPU can retire 3 instructions in 1 cycle. The average CPI on the MOOSS architecture is around 1.5 in the worst case, even for benchmarks where subroutine calls are frequent.

Of course, much more experiments with benchmarking must be done in order to get sound empirical evidence that the overhead of program executions on the MOOSS is very small compared to the level of advanced HW features the MOOSS architecture provides.

Note that we have assumed no cache misses in the MOOSS architecture, but this assumption does not apply to a code running on the Intel processor. Therefore, we have used small testing data to reduce the the cache misses and to get comparable results.

5   Conclusions and Future Work

In this paper, we have briefly described briefly some features of the MOOSS architecture we have recently designed. We have also described a model of the MOOSS processor implemented as a SW emulator.

The MOOSS architecture has HW support for the key mechanisms listed at the end of Section 1 needed for efficient implementations of OO HLLs and for building secure OSs. It provides tools for fine-grained memory protection and helps garbage collection in OO HLLs such as Java or C#.

The design of the MOOSS architecture processor is an on-going project. Since the core of the MOOSS processor architecture is conventional, the whole suite of known ILP techniques can be used for designing a high-performance MOOSS CPU core. But the existence of OMSs and their descriptors and reference registers brings new challenges. The performance could be significantly improved by implementing aggressive ILP for reference counting operations and the related issue is the design of RCC. The quality of a code generated by the compiler also has a great impact on the performance, especially utilization of load/store instructions for reference registers.

Note that the MOOSS architecture can be used for any programming language, but it is not advisable for languages with pointer arithmetic like C or C++, because the MOOSS architecture can natively distinguish between pointers and binary data. Languages supporting pointer arithmetic (e.g., C/C++) can emulate pointers by creating a global heap in one big OMS of type Data and accessing stored data by indexes. However, even in this case, where CPU cannot check array bounds directly, the system cannot be exploited by stack or heap overflows, since the return addresses and method tables are still protected by the CPU.

The design of a secure OO OS (implemented preferably in the *SOL* language) is also crucially important. Another, of course more long-term, research goal is to design the MOOSS processor in VLSI.

Other information about MOOSS architecture can be found on the web [10].

References

1. http://www.phrack.org.
2. M. Grand, *Java Language Reference, 2nd Edition.* O'Reilly, June 1997.
3. I. H. Witten and J. G. Cleary, "An introduction to the architecture of the Intel iAPX," *Software & Microsystems*, vol. 2, pp. 29–34, April 1981.
4. *Pentium Processor User's Manual: Volume 3 Architecture and Programming manual*, 1994.
5. *RISC Family User's Guide RISC 7C600*, June 1988.
6. E. Wittchel, J. Cates, and K. Asanovic, "Mondrian memory protection," *ASPLOS 2002*, 2002.
7. L. Lopriore, "Capability based tagged architectures," *IEEE Transactions on Computers*, vol. 33, pp. 786–803, September 1984.
8. http://www.cs.washington.edu/homes/levy/capabook/.
9. N. P. Carter, S. W. Keckler, and W. J. Dally, "Hardware support for fast capability addressing," *ASPLOS 1994*, 1994.
10. http://moon.felk.cvut.cz/~xballner/mooss/.
11. R. Ballner and P. Tvrdík, "Towards CPU architecture with efficient support for HLLs." Submited to ICCD 2003.
12. T. Harman, *The Motorola Mc68020 and Mc68030 Microprocessors: Assembly Language, Interfacing, and Design.* Prentice Hall, January 1989.

Reducing Access Count to Register-Files through Operand Reuse

Hiroshi Takamura, Koji Inoue, and Vasily G. Moshnyaga

Dept. of Electronics Engineering and Computer Science, Fukuoka University,
8-19-1 Nanakuma, Jonan-ku, Fukuoka 814-0180, Japan,
{takamura,inoue,vasily}@vlab.tl.fukuoka-u.ac.jp

Abstract. This paper proposes an approach for reducing access count to register-files based on operand data reuse. The key idea is to compare source and destination operands of the current instruction with the corresponding operands of the previous instructions and if they are the same, skip the register file activation during the operand fetch thus saving energy consumption. Simulations show that by using this technique we can decrease the total number of register-file accesses up to 62% on peak and by 39% on average in comparison to a conventional approach with only 3% processor area overhead.

1 Introduction

1.1 Motivation

Reducing energy consumption of microprocessors is necessary for extending battery lifetime of portable and wearable computing devices. In today's microprocessors, register files contribute to a substantial portion of energy dissipation [1]. In Motorola's M.CORE architecture, for example, the register file consumes 16% of the total processor power and 42% of the data path power [2]. Therefore optimizing the register files for low-energy consumption is important.

To the first order, the energy dissipation of a SRAM based register file can be expressed by:

$$E = (N_r + N_w) * E_{acc} \tag{1}$$

where, N_r and N_w are the total number of register-file reads and writes, respectively, in a program; E_{acc} is average energy consumption per register-file access. In register files, most of energy per access (E_{acc}) is burned when driving the high capacitance of the bit-lines, which are heavily loaded with multiple storage cells, and so require a large energy for charging/discharging.

This paper focuses on the reduction of number of accesses to the register file as a mean to lower the register file energy consumption.

1.2 Related Research

Previous works [2-6] have shown that many register values are used only once [3], indicating that they may be unnecessarily written back to the register file.

A. Omondi and S. Sedukhin (Eds.): ACSAC 2003, LNCS 2823, pp. 112–121, 2003.

To reduce the register file accesses, Hu and Martonosi [4] proposed buffering the results between the functional unit and the register file in a value-aged buffer, in order to read the short-lived values from the buffer not the file. Since the buffer is smaller than a typical register file, it has better energy characteristics. Zyuban and Kogge [5] advocated the register file partitioning, suggesting register-file split architecture based on the opcode steering. Tseng and Asanovic [6] showed that many operands could be provided by the bypass circuitry [7], meaning that the corresponding register-file reads are redundant. The work proposed several techniques, such as caching of the register file reads, precise read control, latch clock gating, storage cell optimization, bit-line splitting, etc. Although this paper had demonstrated the benefits of bypassing for low-power, it did not exploit the relation between the bypassing and data reuse, as well as effects of operand bypassing on the register file writes.

Recent works [9,10] have showed the importance of instruction and data reuse for low power microprocessor design. The basic observation here is that many instructions produce the same results repeatedly. By buffering the input and output values of such instruction, the output values of an instruction can be obtained via a table lookup, rather than by performing all the steps required to process the instruction. Simpler forms of reuse that do not require tracking of actual values are shown in [9]. Not performing all the steps of instruction processing can also benefit energy consumption [10]. Instruction reuse can also salvage some speculative work that is otherwise discarded on a branch mis-prediction.

1.3   Contribution

In this paper we propose a data-reusing approach for reducing access count to register-files. The approach compares source and destination operands of the current instruction with the corresponding operands of the previous instructions and if they are equal, then it dynamically omits the unnecessary register file accesses to save energy. Simulations show that based on this technique we can decrease the total number of register-file reads and writes in the conventional five-stage pipeline up to 62% in comparison to a conventional approach.

This paper is organized as follows. The next section discusses the background and presents our data reusing technique. Section 3 shows the experimental results. Section 4 summarizes our findings and outlines future work.

2   The Proposed Approach

2.1   Observation

Our approach is based on the observation that there is a large number of unnecessary register file accesses in program execution due to both the locality of references and short lifetimes of variables. Consider the following instruction sequence in conventional five-stage pipeline (IF, ID, EX, MEM, WB) [7]:

add \$t0, \$s1, \$t1 (i)
mul \$t3, \$s1, \$t1 (ii)
add \$t1, \$t1, \$s1 (iii)
sub \$t1, \$s1, \$t1 (iv)
lw \$t2, 20(\$s1) (v)
sub \$t4, \$t1, \$t1 (vi)

Suppose that the most-left operand in an instruction shows the destination register; the other operands are the source registers, respectively. During the code execution, the traditional RISC architecture performs two reads and one write for all the instructions but (v), which requires one read and one write operation. So, the total number of the register-file accesses is seventeen with $N_r=11$ and $N_w=6$. Because the conventional RISC does not pay attention to the operand reuse, the first operand ($s1$) of the instruction (i) is fetched six times in the pipeline regardless it has not been updated during the execution. Since activating the register-file consumes energy, the amount of energy dissipated by these unnecessary accesses becomes significant.

Similarly, there are redundant register-file accesses on write. For example, the result generated by the instruction (iii) is used and updated by the next instruction (iv). That is, the result of the instruction (iii) is provided to the instruction (iv) by forwarding to exclude the RAW data hazard in pipeline, and the instruction (iv) overwrites $t1$ in the register file. Thus write operation for the instruction (iii) becomes unnecessary. In order to reduce energy dissipation we must eliminate such redundant accesses.

2.2   Our Proposal

The main idea of our approach is to compare source and destination operands of the current instruction with the corresponding operands of the previous instructions and if they are equal, then dynamically reuse the operands, skipping the register file accesses. To support the operand reuse, we propose the following implementation schemes.

READ Access

For two consecutive instructions ($j - 1$ and j) the source operands of $j - 1$ can be re-used by the instruction j as follows:

1. The source operands of the instruction $j - 1$ and instruction j are compared in the IF stage of the instruction j.
2. If their source operands are equal, the register-file read access is not performed in the ID stage of instruction j. To implement this, we assume that the source operands of the instruction $j - 1$ are kept in the ID/EXE pipeline registers.
3. Otherwise the operand fetch with register-file activation of instruction j is performed as same as the conventional scheme.

We distinguish three modes of the operand reuse on read:

R-mode: Both source operands of the instruction $j - 1$ match in pairs the corresponding operands of the next instruction j, so they can be reused by j with the same order. This mode is illustrated by the first two instructions of the above example. Both source operands ($s1$ and $t1$) of the instruction (i) are reused by the instruction (ii). Although the same operands are also used by the third instruction in the code, their order is different and, hence requires register file activation during the operand fetch. Thus for the given code, the total number of the register-file accesses in this mode is fourteen (N_r=8 and N_w=6).

S-mode: This mode provides swapping the source operands during their reuse. Namely, it that the first (or second) source operand of instruction $j - 1$ can be reused as the second (or first) source operand of instruction j. Because of the swapping, the total number of the register-file accesses for the example code is reduced to ten (N_r=4, N_w=6). The swapping does not require a large hardware and can be easily controlled by a modified forwarding unit or a compiler-based register allocation scheme.

J-mode: This mode allows the instruction j to reuse the source operands of the in-struction $j - 2$. That is, we jump the instruction $j - 1$ for the source operand reuse. In the code example, the instruction (v) does not have the second source operand. In this scheme, the second source operand of the instruction (iv) can be reused as that of the instruction (vi). As result, thirteen register-file accesses (N_r=7 and N_w=6) are required for the code execution. To implement this approach, we need small control-logic modification, because the ID/EXE pipeline register has to keep the read operand data at least in two clock cycles.

RSJ: This is a combination of the R and S and J modes. In the example code, it reduces the total number of register-file accesses to seven (N_r=2 and N_w=5).

WRITE Access
To omit the register-file write access we propose:

1. To compare the destination operand of instruction j with the destination operands of two previous instructions ($j + 1$, $j + 2$) before the instruction j enters the WB pipe-stage. (The restriction to two instructions ($j + 1$) and (j+2) is caused by a limited two-stage forwarding (from MEM or EXE to ID) of the conventional five-stage pipeline. In a longer pipeline, more execution results can be considered).
2. If there is a match with at least one of the destination operands, the register-file write-access for the instruction j is not performed.
3. Otherwise, the write-back with register-file activation of instruction j occurs.

Based on this rule, we do not access the register-file for writing the result of the instruction (iv) in the example code (Section 2.1) thus saving the register file energy consumption.

3   Experimental Evaluation

We used Flexible Architecture Simulation Tool (FAST) to evaluate the number of accesses to register file. The tool provided cycle-accurate instruction simulation on a single-issue five-stage pipelined RISC-type microprocessor (similar to MIPS [2]). The simulator traces user-level instructions and records register file access information as well as instruction operands reuse frequency. We assumed that register-file performs one write and two reads per cycle regardless of the instruction type and pipeline state. We experimented with nine typical SPEC95 and MediaBench programs tested on various data sets. Table 1 illustrates our benchmark workload. Each benchmark was run to completion. The results have been determined in terms of the ratio of reused source operands to the total number of source operands; and the reuse frequency for the first and the second source operands, respectively, and the reuse frequency for the register-file writes.

Table 2 profiles the source operand reuse observed for the tested programs. In this table, R, S, J, RSJ denote the operand reuse modes, $Rs1$ and $Rs2$ define the reuse ratio (in %) of the first and the second operands, respectively, to the total amount of source operands used in the code. We see that the reuse ratio for the first source operand is much higher (up to 53.8%) than for the second source operand (up to 17.9%). This is especially evident for the (com_t) program, which involves many operand reads. Figure 1 shows the reduction ratio in terms of the register-file reads achieved by the proposed approach in comparison to the conventional one. In the figure R, S, J, and RSJ denote the reuse modes. As we see the amount of register file reads is reduced from 15% ($pegc$) to 63% (com_t). The R-mode allows the maximum operand reuse, saving the total number of register file reads by 15%-53%, while the S-mode and J-mode improve the results by a

Table 1. Benchmarks and descriptions

Benchmark {Data set}	Description	Symbol	Instruction Count
adpcm_d	Adaptive PCM voice decoding	add	8,024,540
adpcm_e	Adaptive PCM voice encoding	ade	6,602,451
compress{train}		com_n	63,719,628
compress{test}	An in-memory version of a UNIX file	com_t	4,275,434
compress{big}	compression	com_b	83,180,240,140
go{test}	A go-playing program	go	24,522,085,063
mpeg{mei16v2}		mpd_m	62,345,741
mpeg{tennis}	A Mpeg2 video decoding program	mpd_t	667,957,333
mpeg{verify}		mpd_v	10,711,481
mpeg{trace}		mpd_d	62,343,421
mpeg{clinton}	A Mpeg2 video encoding program	mpe	1,463,074,731
pegwit{my.pub}	Public key generation	pegc	16,444,080
pegwit{trace}	A public key encryption	pege	38,408,699
pegwit{pegwit}	A public key decryption	pegd	21,454,539

Table 2. Percentage of source operand reuse (read)

Benchmark	R		S		J		RSJ	
	Rs1	Rs2	Rs1	Rs2	Rs1	Rs2	Rs1	Rs2
ade	17.4	8E-05	17.4	2.4	17.4	1.5	29.4	3.94
add	15.9	8E-05	17.6	5.8	15.9	5.8	25.1	7.48
com_n	24.1	0.95	27.2	6.5	26.1	2.0	35.7	8.05
com_t	53.0	0.023	54.3	2.8	53.8	1.5	58.6	4.11
com_b	25.3	0.03	28.1	7.1	27.0	1.6	35.3	8.26
go	26.0	0.015	27.6	7.3	26.5	4.8	32.0	10.1
mpd_m	26.0	0.05	27.5	7.3	26.5	4.8	32.0	10.0
mpd_t	27.1	0.87	30.3	5.6	27.7	3.2	36.5	7.35
mpd_v	26.1	1.05	29.0	5.3	26.5	3.6	36.5	7.23
mpd_d	27.1	0.88	30.3	5.6	27.7	3.2	36.5	7.35
mpe	11.0	2.84	17.9	4.0	11.2	15.0	20.1	16.8
pegc	22.7	0.26	25.2	0.7	22.9	1.3	27.8	1.81
pege	21.5	0.42	24.0	2.5	21.6	2.8	27.3	4.74
pegd	22.4	0.2	24.3	2.7	22.5	0.8	28.5	4.54

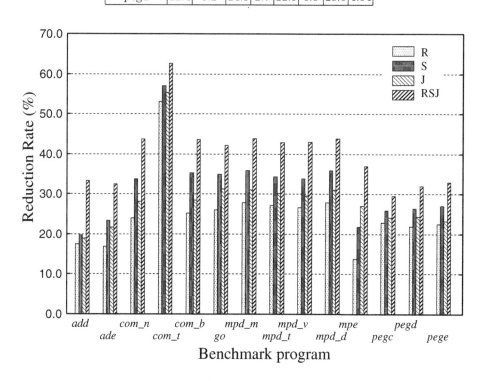

Fig. 1. Reduction of the register-file reads

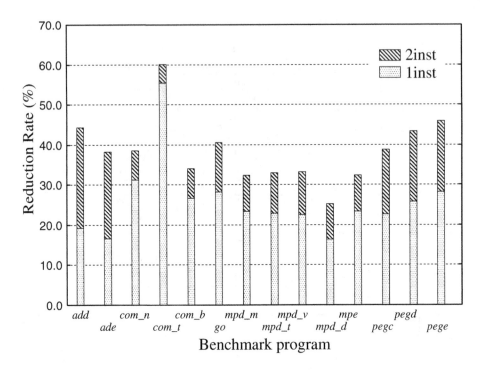

Fig. 2. Reduction of the register-file writes

few percents only. The best results (up to 63%) are achieved by the RSJ-mode that combines all the reuse options.

Figure 2 plots the reduction ratio for the register file writes observed in comparison with the conventional approach on the tested programs. The results are shown in terms of the number of previous instructions scanned for the reuse: one (1*inst*) and two (2*inst*). We see that though the results vary with the programs, the proposed method reduces the total number register-file writes by 1/3, on average. Due to keeping the short time variables out of the register file our method saves up to 62% (the *compress{big}* benchmark) of the total number of the register-file writes when two previous instructions are scanned and 55%, when only one previous instruction is considered.

Figure 3 shows the reduction rate in terms of the total number of register-file accesses (for both reads and writes). In this figure WR, WS, WJ and WRSJ denote combinations of the write reuse with the read reuse modes (R, S, J and RSJ), respectively. We observe that the proposed data reuse approach is very efficient and allows us to save up to 62% of the total number of the register file accesses for *com_t* benchmark program and by 39% on average.

We evaluated hardware overhead caused by the proposed approach. In this evaluation, we described a simple RISC microprocessor in Verilog-HDL and synthesized it by Synopsys Design Compiler. A 0.35 μm process technology was assumed. Figure 4 shows the normalized area consumption in comparison to a

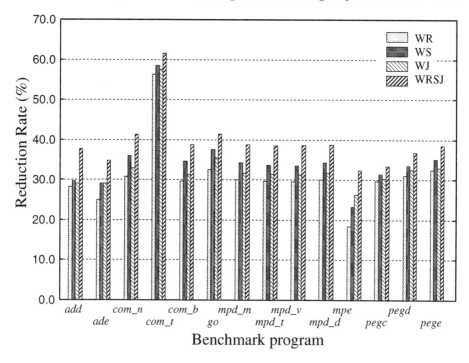

Fig. 3. Reduction of the register-file reads and writes

conventional organization, i.e. which does not support the proposed operand reusing method. In this evaluation, we did not take account of wire area because it strongly depends on the layout generation algorithm. As we can see from the figure, the hardware overhead takes about 1.7% of the total processor area when only operand reuse on read is considered. When both reading and writing accesses are reused, the hardware overhead is about 3.2%.

4   Conclusions

In this paper we proposed a technique to lower the register-file energy consumption based on operand data reuse. According to experiments, the proposed technique can decrease the total number of register-file accesses by 39% on average and 62% on peak. In this work we have not presented the energy overhead caused by the data reuse. Also the investigation has been restricted to a simple RISC architecture. We have to notice that though the operand reuse on read is acceptable for both simple RISC and super-scalar processors, the operand reuse on write access requires an extra architectural support for precise interrupts. Preventing the register-file writes might complicate maintaining the correct architectural state during exceptions (or interrupts). In this case, buffering the response to interrupt for two or three cycles might be an answer. However, it

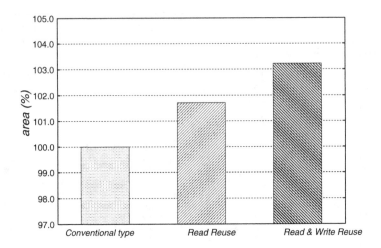

Fig. 4. Area estimation results

should be investigated in more details. This work as well as the energy estimation of the proposed approach will be conducted in the near future.

Acknowledgements

The research was supported in part by The Ministry of Education, Technology, Science, Sports and Culture of Japan, Grant-in-Aid for Scientific Research C(2) No.14580399, Grant-in-Aid for Creative Basic Research (A) No.14GS0218, and Grant-in-Aid for Encouragement of Yong Scientists (A) No.14702064. We are greatful for their support.

References

1. D. R. Gonzales. "Micro-RISC architecture for the wireless market", *IEEE Micro*, vol.19, no.4, pp.30-37, July/August 1999.
2. J. Scott. "Designing the low-power M_CORE architecture", *Proc. Power Driven Micro-architecture Workshop*, held in conjunction with ISCA98, Barcelona, Spain, June 1998.
3. M. Franklin and G. S. Sohi. "Register traffic analysis for streamlining inter-operation communication in fine-grain parallel processors", *Proc. 25th Annual Int. Symp. Microarchitecture*, Dec.1992, pp.236-245.
4. Z. Hu and M. Martonosi. "Reducing register file power consumption by exploiting value lifetime characteristics", *Proc. of Workshop on Complexity-Effective Design*, held in conjunction with 27th ISCA, Vancouver, Canada, June 2000.
5. V. Zyuban and P. Kogge, "Split register file architectures for inherently low power microprocessors", *Proc. Power Driven Micro-architecture Workshop (ISCA98)*, Barcelona, Spain, June 1998.

6. J. Tseng and K. Asanovic. "Energy-efficient register access", *Proc. of the 13th Symposium on Integrated Circuits and System Design*, Manaus, Amazonas, Brazil, Sept.2000, pp. 377-382.

7. J.L Hennessy and D.A.Patterson, *"Computer Architecture: A Quantitative Approach"*, 2nd Edition, Morgan Kaufmann, 1996.

8. P. Y. Hsu. "Designing the TFP microprocessor". *IEEE Micro*, vol.14m no.2, pp.23-33, April 1994.

9. A.Sodani and G. Sohi, "Dynamic instruction reuse", *Proc. 24th Annual Int. Symp. Computer Architecture (ISCAS-97)*, June-July 1997, pp.194-205.

10. E. Taples and D.Marculescu, "Power reduction through work reuse", *Proc. ACM/IEEE Int. Symp. Low-Power Electronic Design*, Huntington Beach, CA, 2001, pp.340-345.

SimAlpha Version 1.0:
Simple and Readable Alpha Processor Simulator

Kenji Kise[1,2], Hiroki Honda[1], and Toshitsugu Yuba[1]

[1] Graduate School of Information Systems, University of Electro-Communications,
1-5-1 Chofugaoka Chofu-shi, Tokyo 182-8585, Japan,
{kis,honda,yuba}@is.uec.ac.jp
[2] "Information Infrastructure and Applications", PRESTO,
Japan Science and Technology Corporation (JST)

Abstract. We have developed a processor simulator SimAlpha Version
1.0 for research and education activities. Its design policy is to keep the
source code readable (*enjoyable and easy to read*) and simple. SimAlpha
is written in C++ and the source code consists of only 2,800 lines. This
paper describes the software architecture of SimAlpha by referring to its
source code. To show an example of SimAlpha in practical use, we present
the ideal instruction-level parallelism of SPEC CINT95 and CINT2000
benchmarks measured with a modified version of SimAlpha.

1 Introduction

Various processor simulators[2, 7] are used as tools for processor architecture
research or processor education. The environment in which a processor simulator
can perform is improving dramatically due to the increased speed of PCs and the
growing use of PC clusters. However, the time needed for simulator construction
increases as the architectural idea to be implemented increases in complexity.
In many cases the evaluation finishes within several weeks, although several
months are needed for the construction of the simulator, even if the simulator
is developed with existing tools. SimpleScalar Tool Set[4] is a famous processor
simulator used for purposes such as processor research and education. But, since
SimpleScalar can be implemented in high-speed simulations, it is not a code that
can easily be modified.

SimAlpha Version 1.0 is an Alpha[6] processor simulator. Its code is easy
to understand and easy to modify. SimAlpha has a function equivalent to the
functional simulator of SimpleScalar/Alpha or a sim-safe program. Although it
is not the clock-level simulator of pipeline processing or out-of-order execution,
the described code should be considered an extension to these.

SimAlpha has a different policy from SimpleScalar. The SimAlpha simulator
is described from scratch. It uses C++ and the code size is small at about 2,800
lines. In order to make it readable, neither global variables nor goto statements
nor conditional compilation is used. The aim of SimAlpha is to show the implementation of a processor simulator with a different policy. A processor simulator
is an important tool, and it is advantageous to choose the most suitable tool,

A. Omondi and S. Sedukhin (Eds.): ACSAC 2003, LNCS 2823, pp. 122–136, 2003.

given many choices. As a tool for processor research and education, SimAlpha offers another choice.

2   Preparation of SimAlpha

This section explains the structure of an original execution image file, the simulation speed, and the verification policy of SimAlpha.

2.1   Execution Image File

To run SimAlpha, application or benchmark programs have to be prepared. SimAlpha reads an execution image file in its original format. It does not read Alpha binary files. By adapting the simple original format, knowledge of executable formats such as ELF and COFF is not necessary.

```
/* SimAlpha 1.0 Image File */
/*** Registers ***/
/@reg 16 0000000000000003
/@reg 17 000000011ff97008
/@pc  32 0000000120007d80
/*** Memory    ***/
@11ff97008 11ff97188
```

Fig. 1. Example of the SimAlpha execution image file.

An example of an execution image file is shown in Figure 1. This execution image file is in text format and consists of two parts. It is created from an Alpha binary file. In the first part, values are assigned to some of the registers. In the example of Figure.1, the hexadecimal value 3 is assigned to the 16th register, the value 11ff97008 is assigned to the 17th register, and the value of 120007d80 is assigned to a program counter. Registers without these specifications are initialized with the value 0. Moreover, all of the floating point registers are also initialized with the value 0. In the second part, the value of some memory is assigned in the same manner. In the example of Figure.1, the value 11ff97188 is assigned to the memory of address 11ff97008. The content of all unspecified memory is initialized with the value 0.

2.2   Benchmark Programs and Organization
of PC Used for Evaluations

A total of 20 benchmark programs, including 8 from SPEC CINT95 and 12 from CINT2000[1], are used to evaluate SimAlpha for this paper. The reduced input set of MinneSPEC[3] from the University of Minnesota is used on the 9 benchmarks of CINT2000. In the other benchmarks, an input parameter is adjusted so that the number of simulated instructions is reduced. The binary of SPEC CINT95 is generated using a DEC C compiler with the optimization option of O4. The binaries of SPEC CINT2000 are downloaded from the SimpleScalar web site.

Data such as simulation speed is measured using the Pentium III 1GHz PC with 512MB memory running Red Hat Linux 7.2. The executed instructions of each benchmark are summarized in the second column of Table.1.

Table 1. The number of executed instructions, simulation speed, ideal instruction-level parallelism measured using the modified SimAlpha.

Program	code(million)	MIPS	ILP	Program	code(million)	MIPS	ILP
099.go	138	1.12	64.2	124.m88ksim	127	1.12	10.5
126.gcc	150	1.12	41.8	129.compress	142	1.14	56.6
130.li	208	1.11	20.0	132.ijpeg	172	1.21	107.0
134.perl	153	1.10	43.3	147.vortex	184	1.07	32.0
164.gzip	596	1.19	16.9	175.vpr	17	1.00	25.1
176.gcc	551	1.10	47.1	181.mcf	188	1.12	53.1
186.crafty	4,264	1.10	108.0	197.parser	611	1.10	30.9
252.eon	94	0.93	49.7	253.perlbmk	200	1.05	8.4
254.gap	1,169	1.12	32.1	255.vortex	147	1.06	29.3
256.bzip2	1,819	1.12	43.6	300.twolf	91	1.00	21.9

2.3   Simulation Speed of SimAlpha

The compiler of egcs-1.1.2 with the optimization option of O2 is used to compile SimAlpha.

SimAlpha has a function equivalent to the functional simulator of SimpleScalar/Alpha or a sim-safe program. We ran the 20 benchmark programs on SimAlpha and sim-safe, and calculated the average simulation speed. The simulation speed for SimAlpha is 1.1 MIPS (Million Instructions Per Second), compared to 3.1 MIPS for sim-safe.

It is a drawback of SimAlpha that a simulation takes about 3 times as long as a SimpleScalar simulation. However, in many cases the development of a simulator dominates project time. If the time of simulator development can be shortened, the slow simulation speed does not become a problem.

2.4   Verification of SimAlpha

During the development of SimAlpha, compatibility with SimpleScalar was carefully confirmed.

Whenever the simulator executed one instruction, all values of the architecture state (a program counter, 32 integer registers, 32 floating point registers) of SimAlpha and the architecture state of SimpleScalar were compared. We confirmed that the two architecture states were identical during the 20 benchmark simulations.

In order to simplify the verification procedure, a way to embed the object of SimAlpha into another simulator is offered. Moreover, since SimAlpha does not use any global variables, two or more simulation images can easily be generated in one process. By using these functions, any bug of the simulator under development is discovered at an early stage. Also, by using these functions one can confirm the justification of the simulator.

3   SimAlpha Internals

In this section, in order to show the high readability of the source code, the internal structure of SimAlpha is explained showing actual C++ code (not pseudocode).

First, we start with an explanation of the main function. Then, we explain how the constructor of the object chip generates seven objects. After seeing the definition of some important classes, the definition and code of the class instruction, which play an important role, are explained.

3.1   Main Function

The main function of SimAlpha is shown.

```
int main(int argc, char **argv){
  if(argc==1) usage();
  char *p    = argv[argc-1]; /* program name */
  char **opt = argv;         /* options      */

  simple_chip *chip =  new simple_chip(p, opt);
  while(chip->step());
  delete chip;

  return 0;
}
```

After setting the program name and options, the chip of a simple_chip type object is generated. The member function step executes one instruction and returns the value of 0 when all of the instructions have been consumed (when the simulation has been completed). The simulation is advanced by repeating the while loop until the function step returns the value 0. When the loop finishes, the object chip is released, and its destructor displays the simulation result.

3.2   Class simple_chip

The definition and constructor of class simple_chip are shown.

```
class simple_chip{
  system_config     *sc;
  evaluation_result *e;
```

```
  debug              *deb;
  system_manager     *sys;
  instruction        *p;
 public:
  memory_system      *mem;
  architecture_state *as;
  simple_chip(char *, char **);
  ~simple_chip();
  int step();
};

simple_chip::simple_chip(char *prog, char **opt){
  sc  = new system_config(prog, opt);
  e   = new evaluation_result;
  as  = new architecture_state(sc, e);
  mem = new memory_system(sc, e);
  deb = new debug(as, mem, sc, e);
  sys = new system_manager(as, mem, sc, e);
  p   = new instruction(as, mem, sys, sc, e);
}
```

The constructor of a simple_chip generates seven objects. The destructor displays the simulation result, and then it releases the seven objects.

The code of the member function step of class simple_chip, which performs the stepwise execution, is shown.

```
int simple_chip::step(){
  p->Fetch(&as->pc);      /* pipeline stage 0 */
  p->Slot();              /* pipeline stage 1 */
  p->Rename();            /* pipeline stage 2 */
  p->Issue();             /* pipeline stage 3 */
  p->RegisterRead();      /* pipeline stage 4 */
  p->Execute(&as->pc);    /* pipeline stage 5 */
  p->Memory();            /* pipeline stage 6 */
  p->WriteBack();

  /* split a conditional move,see README.txt */
  execute_cmovb(p, as);

  e->retired_inst++;
  house_keeper(sys, sc, e, deb);

  return sys->running;
}
```

One instruction is executed by calling seven functions corresponding to seven pipeline stages and then calling the eighth function of WriteBack in order. Although only the capability of a function-level simulator is offered in SimAlpha Version 1.0, in consideration of the readability and extendibility of a code, the operation of an instruction was divided and described for eight stages, referring to the instruction pipeline of Alpha21264[6].

A conditional move instruction (CMOV instruction) is split into two new instructions for two input operands. Function execute_cmovb processes the second split instruction of the CMOV instruction.

3.3   Definition of Some Important Classes

Class data_t expressing data. The calculation results are stored in a register file or memory. These results are defined as the collection of class data_t objects. The definition and code of class data_t are shown.

```
class data_t{
  uint64_t value;
 public:
  int cmov;
  uint64_t ld();
  int    st(uint64_t);
  int init(uint64_t);
};

int data_t::init(uint64_t d){ value = d; cmov  = 0; return 0;}
uint64_t data_t::ld(){ return value; }
int data_t::st(uint64_t d){  value = d; return 0;}
```

Function st is used to store a data value into a data_t type object. Function ld is used to read a data value. Function init is used to generate a new object.

Architecture state. The definition and constructor of the class architecture_state, which consists of a program counter, an integer register, and floating point registers, are shown.

```
class architecture_state{
 public:
  data_t pc;    /* program counter      */
  data_t r[32]; /* general purpose regs */
  data_t f[32]; /* floating point  regs */
  architecture_state(system_config *, evaluation_result *);
};
```

Class evaluation_result. The data under evaluation is saved in an evaluation_result type object. Although the value of the evaluation_result type object is updated during the simulation, these values do not affect the behavior of the simulation. The definition of class evaluation_result is shown.

```
class evaluation_result{
 public:
```

```
    uint64_t retired_inst;
    int used_memory_block;
    time_t time_begin;      /* start time stamp */
    struct timeval tp;      /* start time stamp */
    struct timezone tzp;    /* start time stamp */
    evaluation_result();
};
```

Each variable stores the executed number of instructions, the number of pages used in the main memory, and the time when the simulation started.

Class system_config. Information on the system configuration is stored in a system_config type object. These values are defined before the start of the simulation and, in principle, do not change during the simulation.

3.4   Class Instruction

This section explains the definition and code of the class instruction. Since the function Rename has no code, its explanation is omitted. The definition of the class instruction is shown.

```
class instruction{
    evaluation_result   *e;
    architecture_state *as;
    system_manager      *sys;
    memory_system       *mem;
    INST_TYPE ir; /* 32bit instruction code  */
    int Op;       /* Opcode field            */
    int RA;       /* Ra field of the inst    */
    int RB;       /* Rb field of the inst    */
    int RC;       /* Rc field of the inst    */
    int ST;       /* store inst ?            */
    int LD;       /* load inst ?             */
    int LA;       /* load address inst ?     */
    int BR;       /* branch inst ?           */
    int Ai;       /* Rav is immediate ?      */
    int Bi;       /* Rbv is immediate ?      */
    int Af;       /* Rav from floating-reg ? */
    int Bf;       /* Rbv from floating-reg ? */
    int WF;       /* Write to the f-reg ?    */
    int WB;       /* Writeback reg index     */
    data_t  Npc; /* Update PC or PC + 4      */
    data_t  Imm; /* immediate               */
    data_t  Adr; /* load & store address    */
    data_t  Rav; /* Ra                      */
    data_t  Rbv; /* Rb                      */
    data_t  Rcv; /* Rc                      */
  public:
    int Fetch(data_t *);
```

```
int Fetch(data_t *, INST_TYPE);
int Slot();
int Rename();
int Issue();
int RegisterRead();
int Execute(data_t *);
int Memory();
int WriteBack();
INST_TYPE get_ir();
int data_ld(data_t *, data_t *);
int data_st(data_t *, data_t *);
instruction(architecture_state *, memory_system *,
            system_manager *, system_config *, evaluation_result *);
};
```

The values of the private variables are calculated as the function corresponding to the pipeline stages are called, and the processing of the instruction progresses. Fourteen variables defined as the int type hold the decoded value from
the instruction code ir. A data_t type variable holds the value loaded from the
memory or registers files, or holds the value to be stored in the memory or
register files.

Instruction fetch stage. The code of an instruction fetch is shown.

```
int instruction::Fetch(data_t *pc){
  mem->ld_inst(pc, &ir);
  Npc.init(pc->ld() + 4);
  return 0;
}

int instruction::Fetch(data_t *pc, INST_TYPE ir_t){
  ir = ir_t;
  Npc.init(pc->ld());
  return 0;
}
```

Two Fetch functions exist. The code shown above is the function Fetch for the
usual instruction (instruction other than CMOV). This function loads 4 bytes
of instruction from the address which the program counter specifies, and stores
it in the variable ir. Then, the address of the next instruction is stored in Npc.

The code shown below is used to fetch the second split instruction in a
conditional move instruction. Therefore, the function Fetch will be called with
the instruction code as one of the arguments.

Slot stage. The code of a slot stage is shown.

```
int instruction::Slot(){
  Op  = (ir>>26) &  0x3F;
```

```
RA  = (ir>>21) &  0x1F;
RB  = (ir>>16) &  0x1F;
RC  = (ir    ) &  0x1F;
WF  = ((Op&MSK2)==0x14 || (Op&MSK2)==0x20);
LA  = (Op==0x08 || Op==0x09);
LD  = (Op==0x0a || Op==0x0b || Op==0x0c ||
       (Op&MSK2)==0x20 || (Op&MSK2)==0x28);
ST  = (Op==0x0d || Op==0x0e || Op==0x0f ||
       (Op&MSK2)==0x24 || (Op&MSK2)==0x2c);
BR  = ((Op&MSK4)==0x30);
WB  = (LD || (Op&MSK2)==0x08 || Op==0x1a ||
       Op==0x30 || Op==0x34) ? RA :
       ((Op&MSK3)==0x10 || Op==0x1c) ? RC : 31;
Af  = (Op==0x15 || Op==0x16 || Op==0x17 || Op==0x1c ||
       (Op&MSK2)==0x24 || (Op&MSK3)==0x30);
Bf  = ((Op&MSK2)==0x14);
Ai  = (Op==0x08 || Op==0x09 || LD);
Bi  = (BR || (Op&MSK2)==0x10 && (ir & BIT12));
/** For the CMOV Split Code (CMOV1) **/
if(cmov_ir_create(ir)){ RB = RC; Bi = 0; }
return 0;
}
```

   The values of some variables are decoded using the instruction code fetched in
the previous stage. Instead of assignment of the decoded values to variables, the
code can be described using a macro. Although an improvement in simulation
time is expected by using a macro, the method of variable assignment was chosen
for code readability. The description of Verilog-HDL is similar to the above
description. Therefore, part of the C++ code can be reused for Verilog-HDL.

Issue stage. The code of an issue stage is shown. Here, an immediate Imm is
created according to the type of instruction.

```
int instruction::Issue(){
  DATA_TYPE Lit, D16, D21, tmp, d21e, d16e;
  d21e = ((ir & MASK21) | EXTND21) << 2;
  d16e = (ir & MASK16) | EXTND16;

  Lit = (ir>>13) & 0xFF;
  D21 = (ir & BIT20) ? d21e : (ir&MASK21)<<2;
  D16 = (ir & BIT15) ? d16e : (ir&MASK16);
  if(Op==0x09) D16 = (D16 << 16);

  tmp = (LA||LD||ST) ? D16 : (BR) ? D21 : Lit;
  Imm.init(tmp);
  return 0;
}
```

Register read stage. The code of a register read stage is shown. The values of Rav and Rbv are each selected from an immediate value, a floating point register file, and an integer register file.

```
int instruction::RegisterRead(){
  Rav = Ai ? Imm : Af ? as->f[RA] : as->r[RA];
  Rbv = Bi ? Imm : Bf ? as->f[RB] : as->r[RB];
  return 0;
}
```

Execution stage. The code of an execution stage is shown. Three data values are updated in the execution stage. The arithmetic and logic instruction calculates the value of Rcv by considering Rav and Rbv as input. A load/store instruction calculates the memory reference address Adr. A branch instruction calculates the branch target address Tpc.

```
int instruction::Execute(data_t *Tpc){
  /*** Update Rcv ***/
  if(BR || Op==OP_JSR){ Rcv=Npc; }
  else if(!LD){
    ALU(ir, &Rav, &Rbv, &Rcv);
  }
  /*** Update Adr ***/
  Adr.init(0);
  if(LD || ST){
    ALU(ir, &Imm, &Rbv, &Adr);
  }
  /*** Update Tpc ***/
  *Tpc = Npc;
  if(Op==OP_JSR){
    *Tpc = Rbv;
    Tpc->st(Tpc->ld() & ~3ull);
  }
  if(BR){ BRU(ir, &Rav, &Rbv, &Npc, Tpc); }
  return 0;
}
```

Memory access stage. The code of a memory access stage is shown. In the store instruction, the value of Rav is stored in memory. In the load instruction, the loaded value is saved at Rcv.

```
int instruction::Memory(){
  if(ST) data_st(&Adr, &Rav);
  if(LD) data_ld(&Adr, &Rcv);
  return 0;
}
```

Writeback stage. The code of a writeback stage is shown. In the instruction which generates a result, Rcv is stored in a register file, and the instruction completes execution. An execute_pal function is called when the instruction currently executed is PAL(Privileged Architecture Library) code.

```
int instruction::WriteBack(){
  if(Op==OP_PAL){
    sys->execute_pal(this);
  }

  if(!WF && WB!=31) as->r[WB] = Rcv;
  if( WF && WB!=31) as->f[WB] = Rcv;
  return 0;
}
```

3.5   Memory System

The memory system of SimAlpha Version 1.0 does not contain cache. It is implemented as a simple organization of the main memory only. The address of the Alpha AXP architecture is 64 bits in width. But, in SimAlpha Version 1.0, 32 bits of the higher ranks of an address are disregarded, and only 32 bits of the low rank are used. In the code generated by the compiler, since the value of the higher 32 bits is fixed to 0x00000001, it does not become a problem by such implementation.

4   Practical Use of SimAlpha

This section gives an example of the SimAlpha practical use. SimAlpha is modified to measure ideal instruction-level parallelism. The parallelism is acquired only after considering data dependency as a restriction. The value to be measured has the same meaning as the oracle instruction-level parallelism in [5].

4.1   Extension of Class data_t

The data treated by SimAlpha is defined as a data_t type object, not as a standard unsigned long long type value. In order to measure ideal instruction-level parallelism, class data_t is modified so that the value (this will be called the rank) equivalent to the height of the data flow graph is calculated and stored.

Physical memory is defined as an array of the object of class data_t. Since a load-and-store instruction refers to memory with a granularity of 1-8 bytes, there are some choices in the granularity that expresses the rank of the data in memory. Here, data with the 8-byte aligned unit is defined as one object.

The definition of class data_t, modified to measure ideal instruction-level parallelism, is shown. The uint32_t type variable rank was added to class data_t. The rank is stored in this variable. In the constructor, the variable rank is initialized by the value 0.

```
class data_t{
  uint64_t value;
 public:
  int cmov;
  uint32_t rank;   /* This line is inserted. */
  uint64_t ld();
  int   st(uint64_t);
  int init(uint64_t);
};
```

4.2 Calculation Method of Rank and Ideal Instruction Level Parallelism

The calculation method of a rank is shown in Figure 2. When an arithmetic and logic instruction is executed, the rank of output data Rcv is obtained by adding the operation latency to the maximum of the rank of the two input operands, Rav and Rbv. In the load instruction, rank is calculated by adding the memory reference latency and the address computation latency to the rank of Rbv. In the store instruction, the maximum of the Rav data written in memory and the rank obtained by address computation is considered to be the rank of the data.

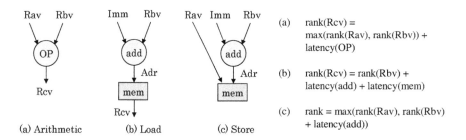

(a) rank(Rcv) = max(rank(Rav), rank(Rbv)) + latency(OP)

(b) rank(Rcv) = rank(Rbv) + latency(add) + latency(mem)

(c) rank = max(rank(Rav), rank(Rbv) + latency(add))

(a) Arithmetic   (b) Load   (c) Store

Fig. 2. The calculation method of the rank for each instruction type.

During a simulation, the maximum rank of all the data is updated apart from the rank for each of the data. The maximum of the ranks at the time when a simulation is completed expresses the height of the data flow graph, whose nodes are all the executed instructions. Therefore, ideal parallelism can be calculated from the number of executed instructions and the height of the data flow graph (the maximum of the ranks). The restriction that the data cannot be moved across a system call is added.

In the following evaluations, operation latency and memory reference latency are assumed to be one clock cycle when calculating a rank.

4.3   Extension of SimAlpha

SimAlpha was modified in order to measure ideal parallelism. Many portions of the modification consist of the calculation of a rank at the time the data is being generated. Only 26 lines of code is modified.

Except for the function st_8byte and the code which displays the result, the modified code is explained. The comment /* Added */ in the code indicates that the line has been appended.

The code of the modified execute stage is shown. After the calculation in ALU, the addition of the operation latency 1 to the maximum of the rank of the Rav and Rbv is assigned as a rank of the Rcv.

```
int instruction::Execute(data_t *Tpc){
  /*** Update Rcv ***/
  if(BR || Op==OP_JSR){ Rcv=Npc; }
  else if(!LD){
    ALU(ir, &Rav, &Rbv, &Rcv);
    Rcv.rank = (Rav.rank>Rbv.rank) ? Rav.rank : Rbv.rank; /* Added */
    Rcv.rank += 1; /* ALU latency */                     /* Added */
  }
  /*** Update Adr ***/
  Adr.init(0);
  if(LD || ST){
    ALU(ir, &Imm, &Rbv, &Adr);
    Adr.rank = (Imm.rank>Rbv.rank) ? Imm.rank : Rbv.rank; /* Added */
    Adr.rank += 1; /* ALU latency */                     /* Added */
  }
  /*** Update Tpc ***/
  *Tpc = Npc;
  if(Op==OP_JSR){
    *Tpc = Rbv;
    Tpc->st(Tpc->ld() & ~3ull);
  }
  if(BR){ BRU(ir, &Rav, &Rbv, &Npc, Tpc); }
  return 0;
```

The code of the modified memory stage is shown. In the store instruction, the rank of the data is calculated before storing Rav. In the load instruction, the code which calculates the rank of the loaded Rcv data is appended.

```
int instruction::Memory(){
  if(ST){
    Rav.rank = (Adr.rank > Rav.rank) ? Adr.rank : Rav.rank;  /* Added */
    if(Rav.rank <e->systemcall_rank)                         /* Added */
      Rav.rank = e->systemcall_rank;                         /* Added */
    data_st(&Adr, &Rav);
  }
  if(LD){
    data_ld(&Adr, &Rcv);
    Rcv.rank = (Adr.rank>Rcv.rank) ?    Adr.rank : Rcv.rank; /* Added */
```

```
    Rcv.rank += 1; /* Load latency */                        /* Added */
  }
  return 0;
}
```

The code of the modified writeback stage is shown. If data is copied to a
register file, the maximum of the ranks is calculated. Moreover, since instruction
scheduling over a system call is forbidden, the rank of the data cannot become
smaller than the maximum rank at the time of the last system call.

```
int instruction::WriteBack(){
  if(Op==OP_PAL){
    sys->execute_pal(this);
    e->systemcall_rank = e->max_rank;                        /* Added */
  }

  if(WB!=31){                                                /* Added */
    if(e->max_rank < Rcv.rank)  e->max_rank = Rcv.rank;      /* Added */
    if(Rcv.rank < e->systemcall_rank)                        /* Added */
       Rcv.rank = e->systemcall_rank;                        /* Added */
  }
  if(!WF && WB!=31) as->r[WB] = Rcv;
  if( WF && WB!=31) as->f[WB] = Rcv;
  return 0;
}
```

4.4   Evaluation Result of Ideal Instruction Level Parallelism

The measurement result of ideal instruction-level parallelism (ILP) is shown in
Table 1. We also summarize the executed code and the simulation speed (MIPS)
in Table 1.

The amount of accessed memory during the simulation increases by appending the variable rank, as shown in the modified class data_t. Moreover, in spite of
the increased processing for calculating a rank, a serious increase was not seen at
simulation time. The simulation speed after modification was about 1.1 MIPS.

The measurement results of ideal instruction-level parallelism showed low
parallelism in 124.m88ksim and 253.perlbmk. In the other benchmark, parallelism exceeding 15 was shown and we confirmed the high parallelism of 108 in
186.crafty. The data shown here is important in order to know the potential parallelism of a program. In addition, it can also be used for preliminary evaluations
of the compilers or of compiler optimizations.

In the example, class data_t is modified to store a rank. By extending SimAlpha using the same technique, the memory and branch behavior can be obtained.

5   Summary

The processor simulator SimAlpha Version 1.0 was developed for processor architecture research and processor education. In this paper, in order to show the

high readability of the code, the software architecture of SimAlpha was explained using the actual C++ code.

As an example of the practical use of SimAlpha, the evaluation method of ideal instruction-level parallelism was explained. The function for measuring ideal instruction-level parallelism was implemented with a small code modification of only 26 lines. The ideal instruction-level parallelism of SPEC CINT95 and CINT2000 was measured using the modified version of SimAlpha, and the result was reported.

Historically, the development of SimAlpha for the C version began in March, 1999. Development of SimAlpha for the C++ version began in June, 1999. Now we are implementing SimAlpha of the Verilog-HDL version, which works on an FPGA board. This version will be helpful when the simulation speed is important.

SimAlpha Version 1.0 is a function level simulator. We have the plan to construct cycle-accurate performance simulators modeling various out-of-order superscalar processors. It is another challenge to implement the complex processor models with readable and simple source code.

The source code of SimAlpha Version 1.0 and the source code of the modified version of SimAlpha to evaluate ideal instruction-level parallelism are downloadable from the following URL.

```
http://www.yuba.is.uec.ac.jp/\char 126kis/SimAlpha/
```

References

1. Standard Performance Evaluation Corporation. SPEC benchmark suites. http://www.spec.org/.
2. The MicroLib.org Project Homepage. http://www.microlib.org/.
3. AJ KleinOsowski and David J. Lilja. MinneSPEC: A New SPEC Benchmark Workload for Simulation-Based Computer Architecture Research. In *Computer Architecture Letters*, volume 1, June 2002.
4. Doug Burger and Todd M. Austin. The Simplescalar Tool Set, Version 2.0. Technical Report CS-TR-1997-1342, University of Wisconsin-Madison, June 1997.
5. Monica S. Lam and Robert P. Wilson. Limits of Control Flow on Parallelism. In *19th Annual International Symposium on Computer Architecture*, pages 46–57, May 1992.
6. R. E. Kessler. The Alpha 21264 Microprocessor. *IEEE Micro*, 19(2):25–36, March 1999.
7. Shubhendu S. Mukherjee, Sarita V. Adve, Todd Austin, Joel Emer, and Peter S. Magnusson. Performance Simulation Tools. *IEEE Computer*, 35(2):38–39, February 2002.

Towards an Asynchronous MIPS Processor

Qianyi Zhang and Georgios Theodoropoulos

School of Computer Science, University of Birmingham,
Birmingham B15 2TT, United Kingdom,
{qyz,gkt}@cs.bham.ac.uk

Abstract. Synchronous VLSI design is approaching a critical point, with clock distribution becoming an increasingly costly and complicated issue and power consumption rapidly emerging as a major concern. Hence, the last decade has witnessed a resurgence of interest in asynchronous digital design techniques as they promise to liberate VLSI systems from clock skew problems, offer the potential for low power and high performance and encourage a modular design philosophy which makes incremental technological migration a much easier task. This paper discusses an asynchronous version of the MIPS microprocessor, presenting the techniques that have been devised to address data and control hazards.

1 Introduction

Conventional synchronous architectures use design techniques based on global clocking whereby all the functional units operate in lockstep under the control of a central clock [16]. As VLSI technology advances and systems become larger, faster and more complex, timing problems become increasingly severe and account for more and more of the design and debugging expense. Increased clock speeds make on-chip clock skew significant and inter-chip skew a major problem. One solution to clock-related timing problems is to use asynchronous design techniques without any global synchronization signals to control the rate at which different elements operate. Other potential advantages of asynchronous logic, are low power consumption, high performance and support for a modular design philosophy which makes incremental technological migration a much easier task. As a result, the last decade has witnessed a resurgence of interest in asynchronous systems.

An asynchronous system may be designed as a set of functional modules (subsystems), which communicate only when it is necessary to exchange information. The operation of the system does not proceed in lockstep, but rather is *asynchronous*; each sub-system operates at its own rate synchronising with its peers only when it needs to exchange information. This synchronisation is not achieved by means of a global clock but rather, by the communication protocol employed. This protocol is typically in the form of local request and acknowledge signals which provide information regarding the validity of data signals.

Various asynchronous digital design techniques have been developed, which are typically categorised by the timing model, the signalling protocol and the

A. Omondi and S. Sedukhin (Eds.): ACSAC 2003, LNCS 2823, pp. 137–150, 2003.

data transfer technique they employ. In his influential 1988 Turing award lecture, Ivan Sutherland introduced *Micropipelines*, a new conceptual framework for designing asynchronous systems [25]. The Asynchronous Online Logic Home Page maintained by the AMULET group at the University of Manchester provides continuous, up to date information regarding asynchronous systems research [1].

A number of asynchronous architectures have been developed [28] including one at CalTech [14], NSR [4] and Fred [22] at the University of Utah, STRiP at Stanford University [6], Sun's Counterflow pipeline processor [24], FAM [5] and TITAC [17] at Tokyo University and Institute of Technology respectively, Hades at the University of Hertfordshire [7], Sharp's Data-Driven Media Processor [23] and the series of asynchronous implementations of the ARM RISC processor (AMULET1 [29], AMULET2e [10], AMULET3i [11] and SPA [21]) developed by the AMULET group at the University of Manchester.

Contributing to this effort, we have embarked on work to develop an asynchronous implementation of the MIPS architecture. This work forms part of a larger project which aims to develop an integrated framework for formal verification and distributed simulation of Asynchronous Hardware, utilising Balsa, a CSP-oriented synthesis tool developed at the University of Manchester [2]. The project is jointly undertaken by the Modelling and Analysis of Systems group at the University of Birmingham and the AMULET group at the University of Manchester and is funded by EPSRC[1]. This paper discusses the initial findings of our investigation, and presents the techniques that have been devised to address data and control hazards.

2   MIPS Architecture

For our purposes, we are using the base MIPS application architecture as described in [13, 18] and as exemplified by the R3000 processor.

MIPS R3000 is a 32 bit microprocessor consisting of two tightly-coupled processors, namely a full 32-bit RISC CPU, and a system control co-processor, referred to as CP0 as shown in Fig. 1. The processors are implemented on a single chip and can be extended with three off chip co-processors. The CPU has thirty two 32-bit general-purpose registers, two 32-bit registers for multiplication and division results, one program counter (PC), and a control logic unit. The datapath includes an ALU, a Shifter, a Multiplier/Divider, an Address Adder, and a PC incrementer.

The CP0 co-processor includes exception and control units and memory management hardware for address translation in the form of an on-chip 64 entry Translation Lookaside Buffer.

MIPS datapath is built around a five stage pipeline consisting of (Fig. 2): Instruction Fetch (IF), Decode/Register File Read (ID), Execution or Address Calculation (EX), Memory Access (MEM), Register Write-back (WB). It is a Harvard architecture utilizing two memory ports one for instruction fetches and one for data accesses.

---
[1] http://www.cs.bham.ac.uk/~gkt/Research/par-lard/

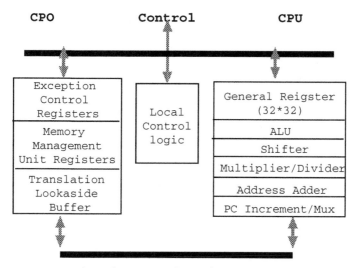

Fig. 1. MIPS R3000 Functional Blocks

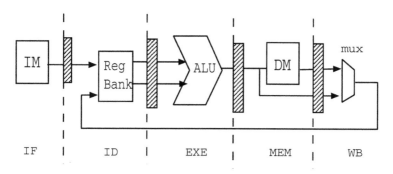

Fig. 2. MIPS Datapath

I-TYPE:	Opcode	rs	rt	immediate		
J-TYPE:	Opcode	target				
R-TYPE:	Opcode	rs	rt	rd	sa	funct

Fig. 3. MIPS Instruction Formats

MIPS supports three types of instructions: *I-TYPE* (immediate), *J-TYPE* (jump) and *R-TYPE* (register), as illustrated in Fig. 3. *rs, rt, rd* are operand register numbers, *immediate* is either an immediate operand or an offset for branch/memory address calculation, *target* is the jump target offset, *funct* is a supplement to Opcode and *sa* is a shift amount for shift operations.

For more information on the MIPS processor, the reader is referred to e.g. [13, 18].

3   Towards an Asynchronous Design

Our main objective for designing an asynchronous MIPS, is to use it as a test case for our integrated formal verification and distributed simulation environment. Within this environment, designs are specified in terms of Balsa, a CSP-based Hardware Description Language, at the Register Transfer level, as it is at this level that the communication and computation semantics of CSP can capture the concurrent, nondeterministic behaviour of asynchronous hardware [26]. Consequently, our effort to design an asynchronous MIPS targets the Register Transfer Level.

Balsa generates purely asynchronous macromodular circuits similar to those of Philip's Tangram [20]. Descriptions of RTL Balsa designs are translated into implementations in a syntax directed-fashion with language constructs being mapped into networks of parameterised instances of "handshake components" each of which has a concrete gate level implementation. It is technology independent (e.g. channel connections can be implemented using speed-independent or delay-insensitive schemes)and it targets standard cell and FPGA technologies for producing gate-level netlists. For our MIPS design, we have assumed a 2-phase bundled data signalling protocol.

Another important decision that was taken was to initially adhere to the five stage pipeline of the synchronous MIPS. A five stage pipeline design will provide a basis for comparison with previous attempts to develop an asynchronous MIPS most notably that undertaken at Caltech [15] which chose to adopt a three stage pipeline arguing that this would exploit better the potential advantages of asynchronous logic. Furthermore, the five stage pipeline introduces challenging hazard-related problems that call for innovative asynchronous solutions.

Three main problems with regard to the asynchronous MIPS design have been addressed: distributing the control, dealing with data hazards and tackling control hazards. The next sections describe these problems and the solutions that have been devised.

3.1   Distributing the Control

Asynchronous logic calls for distributed control schemes, which facilitate the concurrent, asynchronous operation of the system.

Assuming a correct implementation of the communication protocol, at the Register Transfer Level, an asynchronous system may be viewed as a network of concurrent modules communicating via synchronous, unbuffered communication. The modules are data-driven; each module will start computation as soon as data is available on its input wires, and will signal when its result has been computed. Within this framework, control signals are bundled together with the corresponding data, accompanying the latter through the pipeline. Thus, at the Register Transfer Level, a general asynchronous pipeline with processing may be viewed as depicted in Fig. 4. The sending register outputs its contents, consisting of data and control bits, onto the data bus and produces a request event (request wires are indicated in the figure by solid lines, while acknowledge

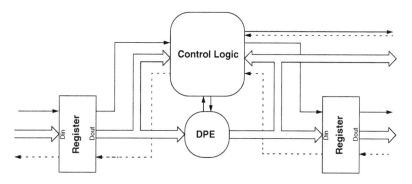

Fig. 4. Asynchronous Pipeline: A High Level View

wires are denoted by dotted lines). The control bits are used by the control logic to direct the request event to its correct destination activating, if necessary, the data processing elements (DPEs, e.g. ALUs, multipliers, shifters etc.) of the datapath. Data passes through the DPEs and propagates to the next stage.

Synchronous MIPS utilises a centralised control unit in ID stage as depicted in Fig. 5a. This unit produces the necessary control signals which propagate through the pipeline together with the data to drive circuits in the different stages of the datapath. This scheme provides a natural basis to generate and distribute the control information in the asynchronous design.

Figure 5b illustrates the asynchronous design. A main Decode unit is placed in the ID stage to perform the instruction decoding and generate the control signals required for the different stages; these signals will thereafter follow the data through the pipeline (Fig. 6) driving a set of decentralised local control circuits.

4   Dealing with Data Hazards

In pipelines systems, there are situations where the next instruction, although it has been prefetched and has entered the pipeline, it cannot or must not execute in the following cycle. One such situation arises when an instruction depends on the results of a previous instruction still in pipeline and is referred to as data hazard. Figure 7 shows a sample MIPS code[2] where a data hazard will occur because of the write back delay to register $2.

Two main approaches have been developed to deal with this problem in synchronous architectures. The first, simple albeit slow, approach stalls the pipeline by locking the Register Bank until the needed operand is written back. The second, referred to as forwarding, attempts to get the missing item earlier from the internal resources.

Efforts have been made to utilise these techniques in asynchronous designs too however asynchronous forwarding has proved a very challenging problem

---

[2] The example has been taken from [18]

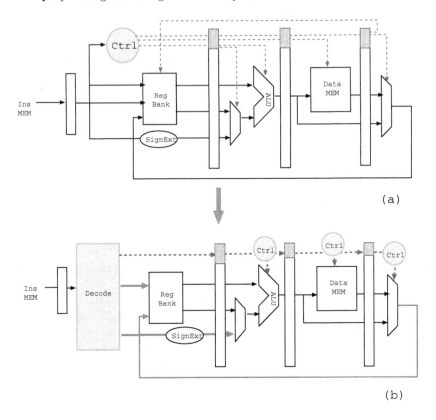

Fig. 5. Distributing the Control

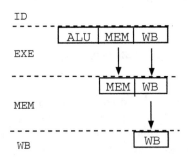

Fig. 6. Passing the Control in Different Stages

[10]. The AMULET1 microprocessor used register locking [19]. AMULET2 combined limited forwarding measures by employing a "last result register" at the output of the ALU and a "last loaded value" register at the output of memory [10]. AMULET3 uses a reorder buffer implemented as asynchronous FIFO [12]. The reorder buffer hides the load latency by receiving memory data in an arbitrary order at random, reordering them in the buffer and then forwarding

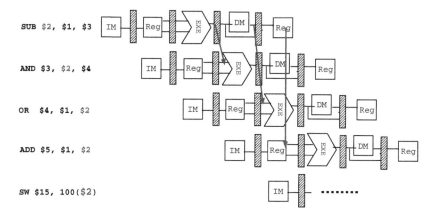

Fig. 7. Data Hazards: An Example

them back if necessary. Sun's Counterflow Processor has a radically different solution whereby the results are sent "backwards" up the pipeline to meet following instructions which propagate in the opposite direction and thus resolve register dependencies rapidly [24]. Another inovative idea has been exploited in SCALP, an asynchronous superscalar machine which attemped to avoid register storage and only forward results by using a purpose designed instruction [8].

4.1   Forwarding in MIPS

MIPS uses forwarding to handle the data hazard problem as illustrated in Fig. 8a. The operand of ALU has three sources, namely Register Bank or a forwarded result from EX and MEM stages. The decision as to which source the ALU should use at any particular moment is taken by a centralised control unit which drives the multiplexers at the ALU input.

Referring to the example in Fig. 7, the following behaviour will be exhibited:

- For instruction AND, operand ($2) is forwarded from EX stage of instruction SUB
- For instruction OR, operand ($2) is forwarded from MEM stage of instruction SUB
- For instruction ADD, we can separate the ID stage into two substages: first do decode and write back to register, then read from register files
- For instruction SW, a data hazard will never happen, since the instruction SUB has already executed.

4.2   An Asynchronous Forwarding Mechanism for MIPS

Since all the aforementioned asynchronous forwarding mechanisms exploit the particular characteristics of the respective architectures, they cannot be applied in MIPS and therefore, a new mechanism is required. In Caltech's asynchronous

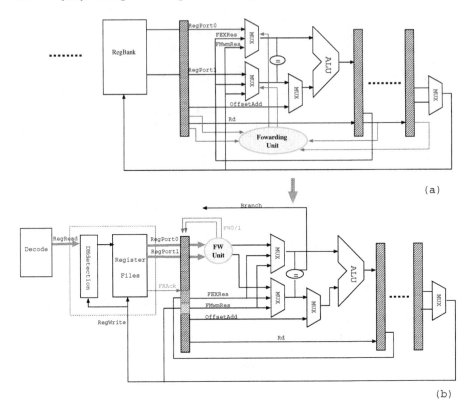

Fig. 8. Register Bank with Result Forwarding

MIPS, the use of a three instead of a five stage pipeline greatly simplifies the problem. In that system, a "bypass" unit is introduced inside the register bank to bypass the required operand when a data hazard occurs.

The objective here is to develop a mechanism that would allow the centralised Forwarding Unit (Fig. 8a) to be removed and have the control signals that drive the multiplexers at the ALU somehow sent down the pipeline bundled with the corresponding data. The control signals should specify which stage will potentially forward a result (the result may come from two places: ALU output in MEM stage and memory result in WB stage) and whether the result will be forwarded or whether it is needed. The fundamental problem is that forwarding depends on knowledge of global state, while in a distributed non-deterministic system such as an asynchronous architecture, global snapshots of the state are not easily or efficiently obtained. The solution devised does not depend on global current knowledge but rather on knowledge of the past.

Indeed, by observing the sequence of instructions as they pass through, a data hazard can be detected when performing a register read at the ID stage. The output from the register bank is a good candidate to carry this hazard control information to the multiplexers in the EXE stage. The action of the multiplexer

RegNo	Flag	
	Clean	Index
0	1	/
1	0	2
...	...	...
31	/	/

Fig. 9. Data Hazard Detection Table

will then be to choose the valid data or acknowledge the forwarded result. This does not introduce additional synchronization between the ID and EXE stages. The synchronization between EXE and MEM/WB stages can be removed by employing a buffer for the forwarded results. The pipeline structure with the forwarding is shown in Fig. 8b.

To achieve data hazard detection, another unit is introduced in the register bank as depicted in Fig. 8b. The unit utilises a table (called Data Hazard Detection Table - DHDT) which keeps a record of all the passing intructions which will do a register write back and are still in the pipeline. The structure of the table is shown in Fig. 9. It contains three bits of information for each register referred to as the register *Flag* and consisting of: one bit *Clean*, indicating whether the register is pending to be written; and two bits *Index* essentially indicating which instruction will rewrite the register (or, in other words, which stage will forward the result). At most four instructions can be at any time in the pipeline from ID to WB stage, and therefore two bits are enough for the Index field. This scheme introduces a total of $(2+1)*32=96$ additional bits in the register bank. The algorithm makes use of another two bits to point to the current instruction in the register bank, called *CurIndex*, which is incremented by one (module 4) every time a new instruction enters the register bank.

As depicted in Fig. 8b, the forwarding control information that is required at the EX stage, can now be bundled together with the data from the register bank. *RegRead* is a 18-bits channel with the first 3 bits indicating whether this instruction needs to do a register read/write while the following 15 bits give the corresponding register address. *RegWrite* contains two fields, 5 bits for register address and 32 bits for the write back data. *RegPort0* and *RegPort1* contain two fields, a 32-bit register data and a 2-bit control field with data forwarding information passed to the EX stage.

The forwarding algorithm includes three parts:

1. *Initialization:* set *CurIndex* to zero.
2. *Write Register:* two actions are performed when a *RegWrite* signal is sent;
   (a) write new value to the corresponding *register[i]*
   (b) set *Flag.clean[i]* to True
3. *Read Register:* three actions are performed when a *RegRead* signal is sent:
   - change the register's *Flag*. Check whether *register[i]* is pending to be written back. If so set *Flag.Clean[i]* to False and Flag.Index[i] to *CurIndex*
   - read register: data hazard is checked simultaneously with register reading

if *Flag.Clean[i]* is True then read from *register[i]*
else
if *Flag.Index[i]* equals to *CurIndex-1* then the result is forwarded from
EX
if *Flag.Index[i]* equals to *CurIndex-2* then the result is forwarded from
MEM
else wait for a *RegWrite* signal, then output the new value directly and
simultaneously write back into register.
– increase *CurIndex* by 1.

4.3   A Constructive Proof

The proposed mechanism has been simulated in Balsa and proved correct. As
a constructive proof, Fig. 10 presents a series of snapshots of the DHDT and
forwarding logic inside the Register Bank for the instruction sequence shown in
Fig. 7.

Instruction	*CurIndex*	*DHDT*	*Operation*
SUB $2, $1, $3	0	... (1, 1, /) (2, 0, 0) (3, 1, /)	Flag[2].clean=1,Flag[3].clean=1, Using data from RegBank as operands
AND $3, $2, $4	1	(2, 0, 0) (3, 0, 1) (4, 1, /)	$2 not clean, Index[2]=CurIndex-1, using the forwarded result from MEM stage
OR $4, $1, $2	2	(2, 0, 0) (3, 0, 1) (4, 0, 2)	$2 not clean, Index[2]=CurIndex-2, using the forwarded result from MEM stage
ADD $5, $1, $2	3	(2, 0, 0) (3, 0, 1) (4, 0, 2) (5, 0, 3)	$2 not clean, Index[2]=CurIndex-3, waiting for a result coming back
SW $5, 100($2)	0	(2, 1, /) (3, 0, 1) (4, 0, 2) (5, 0, 3)	$2 should be valid again, otherwise waiting for a result coming back

Fig. 10. Data Hazard Example

5   Dealing with Control Hazards

In conventional, von Neumann machines, instructions are executed sequentially,
from consecutive memory locations unless a control hazard, namely the execution of an instruction such as a branch or a jump, or the occurrence of an unpredictable event, such as an exception, changes the flow of control. In a pipelined

architecture, if a control hazard occurs, the prefetched instructions following a hazard must be discarded and removed from the pipeline before instructions from the new stream (e.g. the branch target address or the exception vector address) are executed. Pipeline stall, branch prediction and delayed branches are techniques that have been devised to deal with this problem.

In MIPS, there are two types of instructions that can cause transfer of control, conditional BRANCH and unconditional JUMP. MIPS uses delayed branches, inserting NOPs or instructions not dependent on the branch to avoind flushing the pipeline. In the context of this paper, we do not examine exceptions.

In synchronous pipelined systems, the depth of prefetching, namely, the number of instructions that have entered the processor and thus must be discarded in the case of a control hazard, is defined by the clock cycles and is therefore deterministic. In an asynchronous microprocessor however, where the prefetch unit is completely autonomous and decoupled from the rest of the processor, the exact number of the prefetched instructions is nondeterministic and therefore unpredictable. In this case, the depth of the prefetching depends on the precise point that the interruption of the prefetching by the branch target or the exception vector address takes place. The processor must be able to distinguish between instructions originating from the branch or the exception target, which may thus be executed, and instructions already prefetched when the hazard took place, which must therefore be thrown away.

Different approaches have been followed in different asynchronous processors to deal with this problem [27]. A very neat and efficient solution was devised for the AMULET1 processor. This technique uses a single bit to "colour" the state of the processor at any particular moment. The colour bit changes every time a transfer of control takes place in the processor. Each instruction address issued to memory, carries the current operating colour of the processor, which will be used to mark the corresponding fetched instruction. When a control hazard occurs (branch or exception), the colour of the processor changes, causing a change in the colour of instructions subsequently fetched from the new target address. The colour bit of an instruction which arrives at the datapath for execution, is compared with the current colour of the processor. If a match is found, the instruction belongs to the current valid instruction stream and is thus executed, otherwise it is discarded. Thus, all the prefeched instructions following the hazard will be discarded until an instruction from the new valid instruction stream (i.e. the branch target) is encountered.

In AMULET1, the change of the processor colour, the occurrence of a control hazard with the generation of the new transfer address and the decision as to whether an instruction should be discarded (comparison of the respective colour bits) all take place in the same pipeline stage (the ALU). In MIPS however, control hazards may potentially occur in more than one stage. In particular, we consider the case where conditional branches are taken in the EXE stage while unconditional jumps are executed in ID stage. In this case, an improved technique is required, as due to the distributed nature of the system, it is not

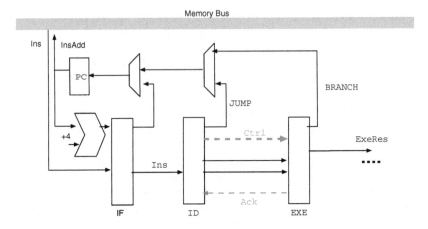

Fig. 11. Dealing with Control Hazards

clear which stage should maintain the state colour bit, or how can a stage know that the colour has been changed by a different stage.

The solution that has been initially adopted is to have the state "colour" bit exchanged between the ID and EXE stages, piggybacking it onto the request bundle (ID to EXE, to inform EXE that a Jump has taken place) and the acknowledgement signal (EXE to ID, to inform ID that a branch has been taken) as illustrated in Fig. 11. The basic operation of the algorithm is as follows:

- If a Branch is taken: the decision is made at EXE, which changes its copy of the "colour" bit, issues the new Branch target address with the new "colour" (which via an arbiter will be sent to memory and to the PC unit), and sends an Acknowledgement back to ID, piggybacking the new colour.
- In the case of a Jump: the Jump is executed at the ID stage, a new target address is sent to memory, and the new "colour" will be sent to EXE with the next data bundle.

If a jump follows immediately after a branch, the algorithm would not work. However, this will never happen: Since the MIPS compiler will either insert a NOP instruction or some other instruction after the Branch.

An alternative, more generic, distributed colouring scheme has also been devised as part of our work and is currently being evaluated [27].

6 Summary

This paper has presented a Register Transfer Level design for an asynchronous implementation of the MIPS processor. It has described the distribution of control logic and has presented the techniques that have been devised to address data and control hazards. Future work will focus on developing these techniques further, model the system in Balsa, evaluate, improve and finally synthesise it.

Ultimately, our goal is to use it as a test case to evaluate the integrated framework for formal verification and distributed simulation of asynchronous hardware, currently under development jointly at the Universities of Birmingham and Manchester.

References

1. *The AMULET Group*, URL: `http://www.cs.man.ac.uk/amulet/index.html`
2. *The Balsa Asynchronous Synthesis System*, URL: `http://www.cs.man.ac.uk/amulet/projects/balsa/`
3. G. Birtwistle, A. Davis, eds., *synchronous Digital Circuit Design*, Springer Verlang, 1995.
4. E. Brunvand, *The NSR Processor*, Proceedings of the 26th Annual Hawaii International Conference on System Sciences, Maui, Hawaii (1993), pp. 428-435.
5. K. R. Cho, K. Okura, K. Asada, *Design of a 32-bit Fully Asynchronous Microprocessor (FAM)*, Proceedings of the 35th Midwest Symposium on Circuits and Systems, Washington D.C. (1992), pp. 1500-1503.
6. M. E. Dean, *STRiP: A Self-Timed RISC Processor*, Technical Report CSL-TR-92-543, Computer Systems Laboratory, Stanford University, July 1992.
7. C. J. Elston, et al., *Hades - Towards the Design of an Asynchronous Superscalar Processor*, Proceedings of the 2nd Working Conference on Asynchronous Design Methodologies, London(1995), pp. 200-209.
8. P.B. Endecott, *SCALP: A Superscalar Asynchronous Low-Power Processor*, PhD thesis, Dept. of Computer Science, Univ. of Manchester, 1995
9. S. B. Furber, *Computing Without Clocks*, In [3], pp. 211-262.
10. S. B. Furber, et. al., *AMULET2e: An Asynchronous Embedded Controller*, Proceedings of Async '97 Conference, IEEE Computer Society Press(1997), pp. 290-299.
11. J. D. Garside, et. al., *AMULET3 Revealed*, Proceedings of Async'99 Conference, IEEE Computer Society Press(1997), pp. 51-59.
12. D.A. Gilbert, J.D. Garside, *A result forwarding mechanism for asynchronous pipelined systems*, IEEE Proc.Int. Symp. Advanced Research in Asynchronous Circuits & Syst.,1997, pp 2-11
13. G. Kane, J. Heinrich, *MIPS RISC Architecture*, Prentice-Hall, 1992
14. A. J. Martin, et al., *Design of an Asynchronous Microprocessor*, Proceedings of the Decennial Caltech Conference on VLSI, Advanced Research in VLSI 1989, pp. 351-373.
15. A.J. Martin, A. lines, R. Manohar, M. Nystroem, et. al. *The Design of an Asynchronous MIPS R3000 Processor*, IEEE, IEEE Computer Society Press, 17th Conference on Advanced Research in VLSI, 1997, pp. 164-181
16. C. A. Mead, L. A. Conway, *Introduction to VLSI Systems* (Addison Wesley, 1980).
17. T. Nanya, et al., *TITAC: Design of a Quasi-delay-Insensitive Microprocessor*, IEEE Design and Test of Computers, 11(2)(1994), pp. 50-63.
18. D.A. Patterson, J.L. Hennessy, *Computer Organization & Design*, second edition,Morgan Kaufmam, 1998
19. N. C. Paver et al., *Register Locking in an Asynchronous Microprocessor*, Proceedings of ICCD 1992, October 1992, pp. 351-355.
20. A. M. G. Peeters. *Tangram99 talk.* In ACiD WG Workshop - University of Newcastle upon Tyne, UK. Edited by: M. B. Josephs and A. V. Yakovlev. Philips Research, 18-19 January 1999.

21. L.A. Plana, P.A. Riocreux, et. al. *SPA - A Synthesisable Amulet Core for Smart-card Applications*, Proceedings of Async'2002, pp. 201-210

22. W. F. Richardson, E. Brunvand, *Fred: An Architecture for a Self-Timed Decoupled Computer*, Technical Report UUCS-95-008, University of Utah, May 1995. Available at: `ftp://ftp.cs.utah.edu/techreports/1995/UUCS-95-008.ps.Z`

23. *Sharp's   Data-Driven   Media   Processor*,   URL: `http://www.sharpsdi.com/DDMPhtmlpages/DDMPmain.html`

24. R. F. Sproull, I. E. Sutherland, C. E. Molnar, *The Counterflow Pipeline Processor Architecture*, IEEE Design and Test of Computers, 11(3)(1994), pp. 48-59.

25. I. E. Sutherland *Micropipelines*, Communications of the ACM, 32 (1)(1989), pp. 720-738.

26. G. Theodoropoulos, *Modelling and Distributed Simulation of Asynchronous Hardware*, Simulation Practice and Theory Journal, Elsevier. (7) (2000) 741-767

27. G. Theodoropoulos, Q. Zhang *A Distributed Colouring Algorithm for Control Hazards in Asynchronous Pipelines*, submitted to the 36th International Symposium on Microarchitecture (MICRO-36), December 3-5, 2003, San Diego, CA, USA.

28. T. Werner, A. Venkatesh, *Asynchronous Processor Survey*, IEEE Computer, 30(11)(1997), pp. 67-76.

29. J.V. Woods, P. Day, S.B. Furber, J.D. Garside, N.C. Paver, and S. Temple, *AMULET1: An Asynchronous ARM Microprocessor*, IEEE Transactions on Computers 46 (4)(1997) pp.385-398.

On Implementing High Level Concurrency in Java

G. Stewart Itzstein and Mark Jasiunas

School of Computer and Information Systems, University of South Australia,
Adelaide, South Australia 5095,
itzstein@cs.unisa.edu.au

Abstract. Increasingly threading has become an important architectural component of programming languages to support parallel programming. Previously we have proposed an elegant language extension to express concurrency and synchronization. This language called Join Java has all the expressiveness of Object Oriented languages whilst offering the added benefit of superior synchronization and concurrency semantics. Join Java incorporates asynchronous method calls and message passing. Synchronisation is expressed by a conjunction of method calls that execute associated code only when all parts of the condition are satisfied. A prototype of the Join Java language extension has been implemented using a fully functional Java compiler allowing us to illustrate how the extension preserves Join semantics within the Java language. This paper reviews the issues surrounding the addition of Join calculus constructs to an Object Oriented language and our implementation with Java. We describe how, whilst the Join calculus is non-deterministic, a form of determinism can and should be specified in Join Java. We explain the need for a sophisticated yet fast pattern matcher to be present to support the Join Java compiler. We also give reasons why inheritance of Join patterns is restricted in our initial implementation.

1 Introduction

Java has made concurrent programming using threads widely available to mainstream programmers. However, this situation has just re-emphasised what many experienced concurrent programmers already knew, that concurrent programming is inherently difficult. It is easy to make a mistake in a complex application that uses low-level synchronisation constructs such as monitors [15]. Object Oriented designs doesn't necessarily make concurrent programming easier. A poorly designed concurrent object oriented program can easily obscure the behaviour of threads running in parallel. Unlike processes in operating systems, which are protected by memory management software (other than those explicitly given all privileges), Java uses a type system to protect users from executing unsafe operations. However, the Java type system does not protect the user from concurrent access to shared variables. For example, programming a thread pool using only monitors can be a non-trivial task. The programmer needs to pass references

A. Omondi and S. Sedukhin (Eds.): ACSAC 2003, LNCS 2823, pp. 151–165, 2003.

to (usually objects implementing the runnable interface) a job dispatcher. This job dispatcher via some central registry of workers finds which threads are idle and signals a thread that a job is waiting. The worker thread then collects the job and runs it returning the outcome via some shared variable. Implementations of this pattern can be quite difficult with shared data being vulnerable to corruption due to double updates.

With the increasing interest in concurrent applications such as enterprise information systems, distributed programs and parallel computation there seems to be a need to provide a higher-level abstraction for concurrency and synchronisation. This would provide the ability to directly represent much higher-level abstractions in concurrent programs.

The Join Java compiler generates standard byte-code allowing compiled code to run on any Java platform. The core compiler used for Join Java compiler was based upon the extensible compiler developed by Zenger [24]. Thread synchronisation in Join Java is as straightforward as writing and calling standard Java methods. We have previously shown [16, 17] how Join Java incorporates concurrency semantics from the formal Join calculus [9] and that this may allow a more rigorous investigation of the behaviour of implementations, potentially reducing subtle errors.

It could be argued that many of the advantages claimed above can be achieved by using a pre-compiled library of high-level concurrency classes. In fact a number of approaches have been taken in this direction [13, 23], a lot of which follow the approach of Hoares [14] Communicating Sequential Processes. However extending the language rather than supplying a library allows the compiler to better utilise resources to support concurrency, as the synchronisation mechanism is an integral part of the language. For example, mandatory use of libraries are difficult to enforce, a programmer may choose to use one feature but not another (or even forget to call a method at the correct time) which leads to potential undiagnosed problems at runtime. Further information about these problems can be found in [4]. If the language is implemented as a pre-processor any syntax errors are related to the programmer in terms of the output of the pre-processor not the source file that the programmer is familiar with.

In this paper when we refer to Java we mean the language itself and not necessarily the many libraries (such as the API [12] or Triveni [5]) that have been added to support particular application domains.

The paper begins by providing a motivation and background for the language extension. Section two provides a brief overview of Join Java. In section three we look at some of the language semantic issues we encountered implementing Join semantics into the Java language. Section four examines the pattern matcher that the Join Java extension uses to resolve method calls at runtime. Section five draws some conclusions and briefly examines possible future work.

1.1   Motivation

Why introduce yet another language extension into Java? More and more programmers have to deal with problems with both concurrency and the related synchronization. Most modern production languages supply support for concurrency and synchronization using language technology that is nearly 30 years old [15]. The reasons for this are two fold. Firstly language developers try to make the language as expressive as possible by implementing low-level language constructs. If the programmer requires high-level concurrency semantics they are assumed to be able to implement these as a library. Providing a higher-level concurrency semantics allow the programmer to *choose* to use either the high-level construct or the low-level construct. In this way we support the programmer choosing an appropriate balance between performance and safety. A similar implementation to Join Java called Polyphonic C# has been recently announced [2]. We however believe that Join Java has more straightforward syntax and semantics than the Polyphonic C# proposal. Our implementations syntax restricts the expression of different behaviours to a single place in the Join pattern. We have also introduced an **ordered** modifier that provides a simple priority ordering to declarations. This gives the programmer choice in the type of determinism this way simplifying the declaration of some problems. We examine this more closely later in the paper.

1.2   Join Calculus

In this section we give an overview of the Join calculus [9] and introduce some of the terminology we have adopted. Join calculus can be regarded as a functional language with Join patterns. The Join Java extension semantics are based on the Join algebra originally proposed by Fournet. This calculus can be thought of as both a name passing calculus (i.e. processes and channels have identifiers) and a core language for concurrent and distributed programming [18]. Traditionally Join operational semantics are specified as a reflexive chemical abstract machine (CHAM) [3, 18]. Using this semantic the state of the system is represented as a "chemical soup" that consists of active definitions and running processes [18]. Potential reactions are defined by a set of reduction rules. When the soup contains all the terms on the left hand side of a reduction rule the terms react and generate all the terms on the right hand side of the reduction rule.

In Join Java we call the individual terms on the left hand side of the reduction rule, *Join fragments*. We call the entire left-hand side of the reduction rule a *Join pattern* and the entire rule a *Join method*. When all the fragments required to fulfil a Join pattern exist in the soup (in our case a pattern matcher object) the body of the Join method is executed.

Join patterns can also be viewed as guards on the message passing channel. When all the fragments of the Join pattern are called the "guarded" message (in Join Java these are the parameters of the call) is transferred between callers of the Join fragments. The standard Join calculus does not support synchronous Join fragments however, a formal translation based on CPS [1, 22] is available from [9, 18] INRIA to convert expressions conaining synchronous names to asynchronous fragments. Join calculus patterns can thus be mapped directly to Join Java patterns.

2   Join Java

In this section we will introduce the syntax of our super-set of Java. Join Java makes a number of syntactic additions to Java. The main two being the addition of Join patterns and the addition of an asynchronous return type signal.

A Join method (see Fig. 1) in Join Java gives the guarded process semantics of the Join calculus to Java. That is the body of a Join method will not be executed until all the fragments of a Join pattern are called. If Join patterns are defined with pure Java return types such as **void** or **int** they have blocking semantics. If the return type of the leading fragment is the new type **signal** the method header is asynchronous (an early return type). Trailing Join fragments are always asynchronous in the current version of the language, that is they will not block the caller. A non-Join Java aware class can call methods in a Join Java class even if the return type is **signal**. In the case of a **signal** return type the caller will return immediately. In Fig. 1 we can see a example of a Join method declaration within a Join Java class.

```
final class SimpleJoinPattern {
    //will return value of x to caller of A
    int A() & B() & C(int x) { return x; }
}
```

Fig. 1. Join Method Declaration

In Figure 1 the method would be executed when calls are made to all three methods (*A() B()* and *C(int)*). A call to method *A()* will block the caller at the method call until methods *B()* and *C(int)* are called due to the requirement that a value be returned of type *int*. When all method fragments have been called the body of the corresponding Join method is executed returning the *int* value to the caller of *A()*. The message passing channel in the example is therefore from the caller of *C(int)* to the caller of *A()* as there is an integer value passed from the argument of *C(int)* to the return type of *A()*. The call to *B()* only acts as a condition on the timing of the message passing. One thing to note is that the fragments *A*, *B* and *C* do not have method bodies of their own. The invocation of a fragment does not invoke any method body. Only when a complete set of fragments that form a Join pattern have been called does a body execute. The main advantage of the Join patterns in the language is message passing. In Fig. 1 we see that a simple unidirectional communication channel exists between the caller of *C(int x)* and *A()*. The call to *A()* will be blocked until a call to *C(int x)* and *B()* exists. When that occurs the argument *x* is passed from the caller of *C(int x)* to the caller of *A()*.

A further change to Java that relates to the introduction of Join patterns is the addition of two class modifiers **ordered** and **unordered**. These modifiers alter the behaviour of the pattern matcher for the Join patterns of the current class. Firstly, **unordered** (the default behaviour for a Join Java class) exhibits random behaviour that simulates non-determinism when confronted with multiple possible matches. For example Fig. 2 shows a Join Java class in which we have two transitions and a constructor. When an object of type UnorderedExample is created, Join fragments *A()* and *B()* are called followed by fragment *S()*. The pattern matcher has a non-deterministic choice to make. Both transitions one and two can be matched but not both. With the **unordered** modifier the pattern matcher will make a random determination which method to complete. However if the modifier was changed to **ordered** the pattern matcher will give precedence to the first pattern that is defined in the class (hence the designation **ordered**), in this case transition one.

```
final class UnorderedExample {
   //Constructor
   UnorderedExample() { B(); A(); S(); }
   signal A() & S() { System.out.println("Transition1"); }
   signal B() & S() { System.out.println("Transition2"); }
}
```

Fig. 2. Join Method Declaration

The final major change to Java is the introduction of a **signal** return type indicating that the method is asynchronous. Any method with a **signal** return type specifies that on being called a thread will be created and started. In reality the compiler optimizes this thread creation to only create threads when necessary. For instance only for a Join method with a **signal** return type for the leading fragment will a thread will be created; in all other cases no thread will be created. This is often a convenient way of creating independent threads of execution without having to create subclasses of threads with shared variables to pass arguments in. Figure 3 shows an example declaration of a thread with argument x.

```
final class SimpleJoinThread {
   /*code that uses x*/
   signal athread(int x) { }
}
```

Fig. 3. Join Method Declaration

2.1   Language Syntax

The first issue we examined was how do we express the Join calculus in Join Java. Our primary requirement was that we had to try and express the Join calculus so that it would be intuitive to the user. For this we looked at a number of syntactic variants [7, 8] of the Join calculus to find one that seemed to be sympathetic to the Java language syntax. We eventually settled on a syntax similar to that proposed by Odersky that was later implemented in the Funnel language [20, 21]. It is worth noting that the syntax concurrently developed by

Benton at Cambridge [2] for C# has a number of similarities to our language. However, there are two main differences. The Polyphonic C# language allows the synchronous method (in Polyphonic C# a Chord) to be any one of the fragments where in Join Java we restrict this to being the first fragment only. Whilst this allows flexibility in the writing of the methods we felt that by locking the synchronous/asynchronous choice to the first fragment we make it more obvious to the programmer or code reader what the synchronization behaviour of the Join Pattern is. Of course in Polyphonic C# the author can simply reorder the method to place the synchronous method first however, this freedom would lead to more unreadable code. Secondly Polyphonic C# does not support the specification of the deterministic policy for resolving ambiguous reductions of the Join Patterns. We have implemented the **ordered** and **unordered** keywords because we believe the programmer may want more control over the evaluation of Join patterns. In this way the programmer will have control of the policy for evaluating ambiguous reductions. Future work mentions possible improvements to the determinism modifier. For a more complete coverage of the Join Java language see [17] and [16].

3   Language Semantic Issues

In this section we are going to look at the three main semantic issues that have arisen during the implementation of Join Java. These issues are firstly how we handle the possibly detrimental combination of inheritance and high-level concurrency. Secondly how do we handle the non-determinism in the Join calculus in which the high-level concurrency and synchronization are based upon? Finally if we are implementing Join in our language how do we support the *return-to* construct that the calculus supplies when the Java language does not support multiple return values?

Inheritance in Join Java is supported by the standard Java language. However, we do not allow Join patterns to be inherited. The reason for this is that it has been observed that the semantics of inheriting Join patterns [11] in an earlier non-mainstream Object Oriented language led to subtle behavioural differences. The main one of which is the inheritance anomaly initially described by Matsuoka [19]. This is likely to lead to more error prone and unexpected side effects unintended by the programmer. It could be suggested that this makes the language non-object oriented. However, there are a number of examples where Object Oriented languages introduce features into the language where these features either restrict or change the Object Oriented nature of the language. For example static modifiers change the nature of the language from that of Object Oriented data structure to something akin to procedural data structures. In the future we are going to pursue the interaction of the inheritance anomaly with Join Java. We note that our synchronization mechanism is at the method level and hence should reduce the possibilities of inheritance anomalies appearing [6]. We also note that inheritance is omitted in the polyphonic C# proposal for presumably the same reasons.

Another difference between Join Java and earlier non-object oriented Join calculus implementations is the single return structure. That is having blocking semantics (**void, int** etc...) in two or more fragments of a Join pattern. There are two reasons why we made the restriction to the current version of the language. Firstly the Java language does not have a cognitive construct for multiple return paths from a single method, that is to say there is no **return-to** construct. This means that programmers of the Java language would have difficulty in connecting this idea to the language. The second issue we observed with implementing the **return-to** construct is the complexity (and hence the speed) of the pattern matcher increases significantly due to the overhead of tracking multiple localities of method call origins. We have found that by paying the small penalty of extra Join patterns you can implement bi-directional channels as two single direction channels anyway.

During the implementation of benchmark examples for the compiler we found that the non-deterministic nature of the language made solving certain problems more difficult (see [16] for a state machine and Petri-net example). This deficiency was solved by the introduction of determinism to the language via the class scoped **ordered** modifier. Simply put when a Join class has the **ordered** modifier switched on and a situation occurs when two or more Join patterns could execute preference is given to the first one defined in the class. If the **ordered** modifier is not switched on the pattern matcher will make a pseudo-random choice of which pattern to execute.

4 Pattern Matching

A major component of the Join Java extension is the pattern matcher that is used at runtime to decide which Join calls are matched together to execute Join method bodies. A prototype pattern matcher has been implemented in the form of a runtime library that integrates closely to the compiled code from the Join Java compiler. The pattern matcher implements dynamic channel formation as defined in the CHAM [10] operational semantics. The matcher forms the core of the runtime system. For every class containing a Join pattern a separate pattern matcher is generated. Each time a method is executed in one of these Join-enabled classes the signature and arguments of the call is sent to the pattern matcher for processing. The pattern matcher will determine if the Join fragment along with any previous calls completes a Join method. In the case where it does not complete a Join pattern the pattern matcher will queue the new fragment. If the fragment is of asynchronous type, control is returned to the caller. Otherwise the call is a synchronous style call and the caller is made to wait until the fragment is used in a complete pattern. This section details the pattern matcher component of the runtime support library. It describes the operation and importance of this part of the system. The pattern matcher needs to be very fast and memory efficient. We mention a number of previous designs such as state based and bitmap implementations, and finally we talk about our prototype tree matcher. Pattern matcher policies are introduced and the relative merits of each type of matching policy are elaborated. We give reasons for our choice of policy and how that affects the predictability of programs.

The pattern matcher takes as its input a stream of requests to form channels in the form of calls to Join fragments. Each fragment provides only partial information for the construction of a channel. It is the roll of the pattern matcher to monitor calls to the Join fragments. When there are enough fragments to complete a Join method the pattern is said to be completed and the arguments for all the fragments are passed to the body of the Join pattern along with the return location. The pattern matcher itself does not perform any operations on the data it simply maintains references to all waiting fragments and the origin of the calls of any synchronous fragments. The pattern matcher can be viewed as a type of scheduler when more than one pattern is potentially completed after a Join fragment call. In this case the pattern matcher requires a policy on determining what pattern to complete. Another way of viewing the pattern matcher is a mechanism for marshalling the parameters required for the body of each Join pattern. Each call to a Join fragment has a unique set of real parameters that are stored and then forwarded when ready.

When the pattern matcher is asked to process a new Join fragment there may be two or more possible patterns that can be completed by the fragment. For example given two Join patterns **A&C** and **B&C**, when the program is run an **A** and a **B** is called followed by a **C**. In the Join calculus there is non-deterministic choice as to what pattern should be chosen. The pattern matcher should be guided by a policy in this case. An example policy might be longer Join patterns are completed first. This policy could result in starvation of shorter patterns in some cases. The implementer of the pattern matcher must be careful that the algorithm does not introduce unexpected biases into the pattern matcher. Any choice other than the purely pseudo non-deterministic (random) policy should be predictable to the programmer.

The pattern matcher is implicitly a searching problem. That is when a new fragment arrives it has to be checked to see if there are any completed patterns. It will therefore always take some finite time to find a match. The Join Java pattern matcher needs to maintain state information about the callers of the blocking and non-blocking methods. This makes the search problem somewhat unusual requiring an especially constructed solution. The speed of the search is dependant on the number of patterns and fragments in each pattern as well as the algorithm chosen and the prevailing policy. Of course some optimizations are possible in the search process to reduce execution time. However, each different search algorithm has some limitation that makes it non-ideal for some set of problems. In all cases we should aim to have the pattern matcher whose performance degrades predictably as the size of the Join Java program increases. As we will explain later usually implies a limit on the number and size of patterns that can be registered.

A further design decision is whether to invoke the pattern matcher as a library call to a runtime system thereby doubling the method call overhead and argument passing. An alternative is to extend the JVM with new byte codes so that the pattern matcher is implemented as an extended virtual machine. The advantage to the latter is that the matching code is implemented on the native level. This would increase the performance at the expense of portability. A native method call for the pattern matcher is also an option however, this would of course be the slowest approach with no discernible advantage as the boundary between the native environment and the Java environment is slow to negotiate. In our prototype we have chosen to use the library call approach.

There are two ways of implementing the pattern matcher either by using a threaded and unthreaded model. When a fragment arrives at the pattern matcher, should it take over the call for processing with its own runtime or should it borrow some of the callers' runtime. By borrowing some of the callers' runtime we simplify the design of the matcher. We just have to lock the mutator and accessor methods of the pattern matcher whenever there is a change to the state of the data structure so that the integrity of the pattern matcher is maintained. In our implementation we have chosen the unthreaded model for simplicity.

4.1   Compiler Interface to the Pattern Matcher

The compiled version of the Join Java program will create an instance of the pattern matcher for each class that contains Join or asynchronous methods. This is done the moment the first call to a fragment is made. The compiler generates *join.system.joinPatterns alllocal = new join.system.joinPatterns(this);* to create an instance of the pattern matcher. The compiler adds a new Join pattern to the pattern matcher data structure with the method call *alllocal.addPattern(new int[]2, 3, true);* The second segment of code shows how the definition of a Join Pattern is passed to the pattern matcher. The first argument is an array of **int** that shows the Join fragment ids that take place in the pattern. These are in the order they are defined in the class. The second argument is a boolean that defines whether the pattern is a synchronous (true) or asynchronous (false) Join pattern. When this *addPattern* method call is made the Join pattern is added to the data structure and the individual Join fragments are linked to all the existing patterns that reference the fragment in the data structure including the one that has just been added. Join pattern addition is only done once in the runtime life of the Join class and requires a traversal of the pattern matcher data structure which modifies the data structure accordingly.

When a Join fragment is called the pattern matcher is invoked with the *addSyncCall()* for synchronous fragments and *addCall()* for asynchronous fragments. This method searches the data structure for a completed Join pattern. There are two possibilities for any identified Join pattern that is involved with the Join fragment. First if the other Join fragments in the referenced pattern have not been called yet the pattern does not complete. In this case the instance of the call is registered in the data structure and the pattern matcher method call returns and blocks the fragment caller if it is synchronous otherwise the method simply returns asynchronously. The second possibility is that one or more patterns are completed by the Join fragment that was just passed to the pattern matcher. In this case the policy settings of the pattern matcher may need to be checked to select which of the multiple patterns that the call has completed will be returned for execution. Of course there is no policy needed if only one pattern is matched. The pattern that is selected to fire is then returned to the callee along with the fragments (with their arguments) and those fragments are removed from the data structure. It is possible and sometimes likely that there will be multiple instances of each Join fragment waiting for completion. It is advisable that these fragments be removed in FIFO order due to fairness. Once the Join fragments that have been selected to cause the completion of the pattern have been identified by the policy; the reference to these are passed back to the callee. This allows the thread associated with the fragments to be unblocked by notify calls. The following code is executed when an synchronous Join fragment is called. *join.system.returnStruct retval= all.addSynchCall(new java.lang.Object[] new java.lang.Integer(par1), 0, this);* The return structure contains the arguments for the pattern (collected from the various fragments) and the completion status. If the completion status is **true** the return structure is passed to a dispatch method in the Join class that executes the appropriate Join pattern body. If the completion status is **false** the caller is blocked until the completion status becomes **true**. The *addCall* (for async return types) acts in a similar way except the caller is not blocked.

4.2   Pattern Searching

There are three major facets of the implementation of the pattern matcher. First there is the data structure used in the pattern matcher to store the status of the pattern matching pool, next there are the algorithms that traverse and search for elements in this data structure and finally there are the policies that resolve non-deterministic/deterministic situations in the pattern matching process. Most of the discussion in the remainder of this section concentrates on the techniques for pattern matching we designed. Firstly we briefly examine previous approaches to pattern matching in this application domain. We then examine how we implemented algorithms for searching for completed patterns in our runtime system. Finally we cover a potential optimization that could be used for our system in order to overcome problems with state space explosion and runtime delays.

4.3   Previous Approaches to Pattern Matching

There are a number of approaches that have been taken in constructing a pattern matcher to achieve the semantics of the Join calculus. The simple approach is to design the pattern matcher to record the state of the pool. We then record all possible Join patterns (reductions) in a list. These possible patterns are then linearly compared against the current state of the pattern matcher. If there is a match the pool is updated and the result is returned. However, this approach breaks down, as search is expensive on every call to the pattern matcher. A second more sophisticated approach to pattern matching is that used by the original Join language [7] used a state machine to represent all possible states the pool could be in. However the designers found that state space explosion was a problem and they used state space pruning and heuristics to attempt to reduce the problem. The second version of their language used a bit field to represent the status of the pattern matching. Each pattern reduction was compared with the current state of the calls via an XOR call atomically. Whilst this approach sped up pattern matching enormously the solution is not scalable beyond the predefined maximum size of the bit-field. The state space implementation consumed a lot of memory and the bit field solution was limited on the upper end by the max number of digits and hence Join fragments that the Join patterns could have.

4.4   Tree Based Pattern Matcher

In our pattern matcher we have tried to find a middle ground between the space complexity of a state-based solution and the time complexity of a linear solution. We have achieved this by using a tree structure to represent the static structure of the patterns of a Join class. The idea of our approach is to limit the search space during the runtime of the program. We therefore designed the data-structure with the idea of a localized searching in mind. In our data-structure interior nodes represent patterns and leaves represent Join fragments. The root acts as an index to both leaves and interior nodes for fast access. In Fig. 4 we see an example with three Join patterns and six fragments. The most interesting fragment is **B** as it is shared by two patterns **A&B** and **B&C&D**. This design allows us to trade the state-space explosion problem with a slightly longer matching time. However we further optimize the search time by only checking the part of the tree that is directly affected by the occurrence of the Join method fragment call. Using our example from the figure when a **C** is called only **B&C&D** is checked for completion. If **B** is called both **A&B** and **B&C&D** are checked for completions. This is achieved by connecting the leaves to multiple interior nodes so that when a fragment arrives it is quick to check if that new fragment completes any Join patterns. In the pattern matcher a list of all fragments are stored in the root of the node so that when a call arrives we can immediately access the correct location in the tree without the need to traverse the data-structure. In this way we optimize the pattern matching process to only search the part of the tree

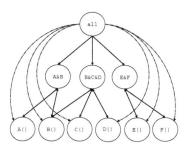

Fig. 4. Internal Representation of Tree Pattern Matcher

that contains patterns affected by the arrival of the new fragment. That is if a Join method call occurs it only checks patterns that contain that Join method fragment.

The Join calculus has a non-deterministic matching semantic on reduction of rules. However as related earlier, in the pattern matcher we have extended the semantics to support deterministic reduction. We did this via the **ordered** modifier. When the pattern matcher is in deterministic reduction mode it will match all possible patterns in the pool rather than the first randomly selected match. The pattern matcher will then choose which pattern to complete based upon the order in which they were defined in the Join class. The worst-case scenario for this pattern matcher is if a Join fragment occurs in every Join method. This will lead to every pattern being searched. We believe this is not likely to happen in the general case as most Join method fragments would have locality, that is most Join fragments only take part in a few Join patterns.

4.5   Precalculated Pattern Matcher

The second major pattern matcher we developed was designed to optimize the speed of execution for a limited number of fragments. This pattern matcher calculated every possible state that the pattern matcher could exist in and in the event of a change in the state space would immediately know the appropriate pattern to execute. The state of the pattern matcher is expressed as a series of bits used to represent an integer value. This integer value gives a position in the precalculated array that resolves to a completed pattern. The array is thus expressed as a linear array with a magnitude of 2^n where n is the number of fragments in the Join class. The state of the pattern matcher at any point in time can be expressed as a sequence of bits indicating the presence or absence of a particular fragment. For example, a Join class containing five fragments (**a** through **e**), there are 32 possible states *00000* through to *11111*. If there was an **a** and a **c** waiting the bitfield would be *10100*. The design of the precalculated pattern matcher is illustrated in Fig. 5. In the event that more than one fragment is waiting the bit field will still only be 1. Therefore 1 represents some (one or more) fragments waiting in the pattern matcher and 0 means no fragments waiting in the pattern matcher. Because the state can be converted into an index via trivial bit manipulation, retrieval of completed patterns is performed quickly. When initialization occurs (in the prototype when the first fragment is called), the pattern matcher calculates all possible states the pattern matcher could be in and calculates the resultant completed patterns from those states.

The major advantage of this approach is that the pattern matcher design has a constant delay when retrieving completed patterns. This is because after the precalculation of states is done no searching needs to be performed during runtime. The state of the pattern matcher is stored as a position in the precalculated array. Consequently the time fluctuations other matching algorithms suffer from is removed.

This pattern matcher has two disadvantages. Firstly, In the event of a large number of fragments (larger than 16 fragments) the precalculation period takes

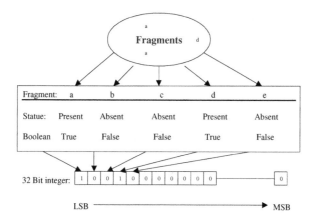

Fig. 5. Precalculated Pattern Matcher

an increasingly long time to populate the array. However, as this can be done at compile time this penalty is not as great as first appearances would suggest. The second disadvantage is the memory footprint of the pattern matcher is relatively large compared to previous implementations. The number of fragments that can be handled by the pattern matcher is limited by the memory that can be allocated to the precalculated array. The system has been tested using up to 16 Join fragments (requiring a 256k precalculated array).

Initial benchmarking of the pattern matcher has indicated that performance is adequate in the majority of cases. The greatest delay is the initial call that generates the precalculated table. However, as we stated earlier in any final implementation this would be done at compile time rather than runtime. Once the initial call has completed the speed of the method calls and the resultant pattern matching seems to be close to that of normal Java.

4.6 Symmetry

Most of the pattern matchers we have examined have had limitations in state space explosion or alternatively are expensive at runtime. Consequently it is interesting to look at what optimization we can make to the algorithms to improve the runtime speed. One such approach we have been looking at is that of symmetry. The idea of symmetry is to locate similar patterns within the pattern matcher and group them together. For example, if we had the following patterns a()&b(), a()&c(), a()&d() we would end up with 2^4 possible states. However, if we examine the patterns we see that all of them are fairly similar being of the form a()&α() where α is b, c or d. We could then store the pattern a()&α() in the pattern matcher. When a call to b,c or d occurs we store a call to α. Consequently the state space is limited (in this case) to 2^2 possible states hence reducing state space explosion. The disadvantage of this approach is we pay a penalty of interpretation when we find a complete pattern as we need to figure out which fragment **a**, **b** or **c** has been called.

5   Conclusion and Future Work

In this paper we have provided a brief overview of the Join Java language. We showed how that with two small additions to the syntax of Java we have added a powerful concurrency synchronisation mechanism to the language. We then reflected on some of our experiences with implementing the Join Java compiler and runtime. We have shown how the language itself carries out a lot of the work synchronising interactions and handling communications without making the programmer worry about low-level operations (the use of **wait** and **notify** are virtually unnecessary as they are completely handled by the runtime system of the language). This should reduce the occurrence of errors in software increasing quality for little cost.

Join Java better represents concurrency as it allows other formalisms to be directly expressed in the language with a minimum change from the core Java language. The structure of Join Java allows message passing to be easily implemented between different processes without having to concern oneself with the low level details of the message passing implementation.

In every implementation of a Join type language the critical factor to the success of the language is the pattern matcher. Whilst designing the various pattern matchers we came to the conclusion that no single pattern matcher can ever efficiently solve all possible configurations of patterns and fragments. To this end we are spending considerable effort on this component of our compiler looking for novel solutions in order to increase the speed without compromising scalability, speed or memory size. This has proved difficult but we feel that our first few pattern matchers are a good start in this direction. We would like to thank Professor Martin Odersky and Matthias Zenger from Ecole Polytechnique Federale de Lausanne for their assistance with this research.

We are refining further pattern matcher algorithms so we can explore how to increase the speed of matching. We are also designing an artificial test-rig that will simulate the behaviour of a Join program at runtime so that performance can be measured and compared against different situations in a repeatable way. We are further developing a large set of Join Java programs so that we can do full regression testing on the compiler itself.

References

1. Andrew W. Appel. *Compiling with Continuations*. Cambridge University Press, Cambridge, MA, 1992.
2. Nick Benton, Luca Cardelli, and Cédric Fournet. Modern concurrency abstractions for csharp. In *in Proceedings of FOOL9*, 2002.
3. G. Berry and G. Boudol. The chemical abstract machine. *Theoretical Computer Science*, 1(96):217–248, 1992.
4. Peter A. Buhr. Are safe concurrency libraries possible? *Communications of the ACM*, 38(2):117–120, 1995.
5. C. Colby, L. Jagadeesan, R. Jagadeesan, K. Laufer, and C. Puchol. Design and implementation of triveni: A processalgebraic api for threads + events. In *International Conference on Computer Languages. 1998.* IEEE Computer Press, 1998.

6. Lobel Crnogorac, Anands Rao, and Kotagiri Romamohanarao. Classifying inheritance mechanisms in concurrent object-orinted programming. In Eric Jul, editor, *ECOOP'98 - European Conference on Object Oriented Programming*. Springer - Lecture Notes in Computer Science 1445,, 1998.
7. F. le Fessant and L. Maranget. Compiling join patterns. In U. Nestmann and B. C. Pierce, editors, *HLCL '98 in Electronic Notes in Theoretical Computer Science*, volume 16, Nice, France, 1998. Elsevier Science Publishers.
8. Luc Maranget F. L. Fessant and Sylvain Conchon. Join language manual, 1998.
9. C. Fournet, G. Gonthier, J. Lvy, L. Maranget, and D Rmy. A calculus of mobile agents. *Lecture Notes in Computer Science*, 1119, 1996.
10. Cedric Fournet and Georges Gonthier. The reflexive cham and the join-calculus. In *Proc. 23rd Annual ACM Symposium on Principles of Programming Languages*, volume January, pages 372–385. ACM Press, 1996.
11. Cedric Fournet, Cosimo Laneve, Luc Maranget, and Didier Remy. Inheritance in the join calculus. In S. Kapoor and S. Prasad, editors, *FST TCS 2000: Foundations of Software Technology and Theoretical Computer Science*, volume 1974, pages 397–408, New Delhi India, 2000. Springer-Verlag.
12. James Gosling and H McGilton. The java language environment, 1995.
13. Gerald Hilderink, Andre Bakkers, and Jan Broenink. A distributed real-time java system based on csp. In *Third IEEE International Symposium on Object-Oriented Real-Time Distributed Computing, ISORC 2000*, pages 400–407, Newport Beach, California, 2000. IEEE.
14. C. A. R. Hoare. Communicating sequential processes. In R. M. McKeag and A. M. Macnaghten, editors, *On the construction of programs – an advanced course*, pages 229–254. Cambridge University Press, 1980.
15. C.A.R Hoare. Monitors: An operating system structuring concept. *Communications of the ACM*, 17(10):549–557, 1974.
16. G Stewart Itzstein and Kearney David. Applications of join java. In *Proceedings of the Seventh Asia Pacific Computer Systems Architecture Conference ACSAC'2002*, pages 1–20, Melbourne, Australia, 2002. Australian Computer Society.
17. G Stewart Itzstein and David Kearney. Join java: An alternative concurrency semantic for java. Technical Report ACRC-01-001, University of South Australia, 1 January 2001 2001.
18. Luc Maranget, F. L. Fessant, and Sylvain Conchon. Jocaml manual, 1998.
19. S Matsuoka and A Yonezawa. Analysis of inheritance anomaly in object-oriented concurrent programming languages. In P Agha, P Wegner, and A Yonezawa, editors, *Research Directions in Concurrent Object-Oriented Programming*, pages 107–150. MIT Press, 1993.
20. Martin Odersky. Functional nets. In *European Symposium on Programming*, volume 1782, pages 1–25, Berlin Germany, 2000. Springer Verlag.
21. Martin Odersky. Programming with functional nets. Technical 2000/331, Ecole Polytechnique Fédérale de Lausanne, March 2000 2000.
22. Guy L Steele. *Rabbit: A Compiler for Scheme*. Masters, MIT, 1978.
23. P. H. Welch. Java threads in the light of occam-csp. In P. H. Welch Bakkers and A. W. P., editors, *Architectures, Languages and Patterns for Parallel and Distributed Applications*, volume 52 April http://www.cs.ukc.ac.uk/pubs/1998/702 of *Concurrent Systems Engineering Series*, pages 259–284. WoTUG IOS Press, Amsterdam, 1998.
24. Matthias Zenger and Martin Odersky. Implementing extensible compilers. In *ECOOP 2001 Workshop on Multiparadigm Programming with Object-Oriented Languages*, Budapest, 2001.

Simultaneous MultiStreaming
for Complexity-Effective VLIW Architectures[*]

H. Pradeep Rao[1], S.K. Nandy[1], and M.N.V. Satya Kiran[1,**]

Computer Aided Design Laboratory, SERC, Indian Institute of Science,
Bangalore 560 012, India,
{pradeep,nandy,kiran}@cadl.iisc.ernet.in

Abstract. Very Long Instruction Word (VLIW) architectures exploit instruction level parallelism (ILP) with the help of the compiler to achieve higher instruction throughput with minimal hardware. However, control and data dependencies between operations limit the available ILP, which not only hinders the scalability of VLIW architectures, but also result in code size expansion. Although speculation and predicated execution mitigate ILP limitations due to control dependencies to a certain extent, they increase hardware cost and exacerbate code size expansion.
Simultaneous multistreaming (SMS) can significantly improve operation throughput by allowing interleaved execution of operations from multiple instruction streams. In this paper we study SMS for VLIW architectures and quantify the benefits associated with it using a case study of the MPEG-2 video decoder. We also propose the notion of virtual resources for VLIW architectures, which decouple architectural resources (resources exposed to the compiler) from the microarchitectural resources, to limit code size expansion. Our results for a VLIW architecture demonstrate that: (1) SMS delivers much higher throughput than that achieved by speculation and predicated execution, (2) the increase in performance due to the addition of speculation and predicated execution support over SMS averages around 12%. The minor increase in performance might not warrant the additional hardware complexity involved, and (3) the notion of virtual resources is very effective in reducing no-operations (NOPs) and consequently reduce code size with little or no impact on performance.

1 Introduction

Programmable media processors for the embedded domain demand high performance and impose additional design specifications such as low power and fast time to market. In order to meet these specifications, there is a trend to move toward complexity effective processors, whose benefits are manifold. Complexity effective designs (1) reduce design, verification and test times, enabling quick time to market, (2) allow high frequency operation, and (3) are shown to meet low power budgets.

---

[*] This work is partially supported by a research grant from STMicroelectronics.
[**] Satya Kiran is currently at the Indian Institute of Technology, New Delhi, India.

A. Omondi and S. Sedukhin (Eds.): ACSAC 2003, LNCS 2823, pp. 166–179, 2003.

In order to meet the performance specifications, designers resort to scaling clock frequencies and/or exploit more parallelism. Two key architectures that exploit parallelism at the instruction level are superscalar and VLIW. Aggressive out-of-order superscalar processors detect instruction level parallelism (ILP) at runtime using extensive hardware support. Studies have shown that this hardware is highly complex and is not scalable [14].

In contrast, VLIW architectures depend on the compiler to detect and exploit ILP. Consequently, the hardware implementation complexities for VLIW architectures are low and are increasingly popular as platforms for embedded system designs [5][15]. In this paper, we study the performance of aggressive compiler techniques such as the superblock [6] and the hyperblock [7] for VLIW architectures, using the MPEG-2 decoder as a case study. The performance of these techniques is critically dependent on hardware support for speculation and predicated execution [16]. Based on our experiments, we identify scalability and code size expansion as potential bottlenecks associated with the use of these techniques.

In this paper we also propose and evaluate schemes to address the above mentioned bottlenecks. To increase scalability, we propose simultaneous multistreaming (SMS) – an adaptation of simultaneous multithreading for VLIW architectures. Simultaneous multithreading is a technique originally proposed to increase superscalar processor utilization in the face of long latencies and limited per-thread parallelism. Simultaneous multithreading achieves higher throughputs by simultaneously issuing instructions from multiple independent tasks to fill the slack in the schedule which can be attributed to (1) dependencies between operations and (2) long operation latencies. We describe and evaluate SMS in the following sections.

We also introduce the notion of *virtual resources* to limit code size expansion with increasing VLIW issue widths. While several encoding schemes have been proposed in literature to limit code size expansion in VLIW architectures, they often result in increase in decoder complexity or require a redesign of the instruction decode logic. Virtual resources decouple architectural resources (resources exposed to the compiler) from the microarchitectural resources, without any increase in complexity and with little or no effect on performance.

The rest of the paper is organized as follows: We begin in section 2 with a description of our experimental methodology and the workload used in the evaluations. Section 3 describes the compiler techniques considered in this study and the hardware support required to make these optimizations effective. In this section, we also identify the bottlenecks associated with these optimizations and describe the use of virtual resources. In section 4, we describe SMS, along with semantics that ensure the correctness of the scheme. The simulation results for SMS using the MPEG-2 decoder as a case study, is presented in section 5. We present related work in section 6 before we conclude in section 7 with directions for future work.

2   Methodology

This section describes the simulation methodology and the workload used to obtain the performance results. A schematic of our experimental flow is shown in Fig.1.

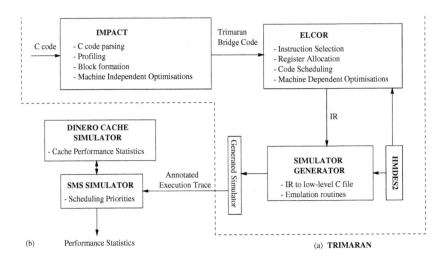

Fig. 1. Experimental Setup

2.1   Simulation

Our simulation framework is built around the Trimaran compiler infrastructure [1] schematically shown in Fig.1. Trimaran uses the IMPACT compiler [9] as it's front-end for C. The compiler front-end performs C parsing, code profiling, block formation and traditional optimizations. It also exploits support for speculation and predicated execution using superblock and hyperblock optimizations. The compiler back-end and the simulator generator are parameterized by the machine description HMDES [4]. The Trimaran back-end ELCOR [10] performs instruction selection, register allocation and machine dependent code optimizations for the HPL-PD [3] architecture. HPL-PD is a hypothetical architecture conceived at HP Laboratories for ILP research and provides support for speculation and predicated execution amongst a host of other architectural techniques intended to make the compiler effective at exploiting higher levels of ILP. The Trimaran simulator generator generates a low level C file which is compiled using the native C compiler and linked with a library of emulation routines to generate the simulator binary (compiled code simulator [1]).

We have instrumented the emulator library with trace generation routines. The benchmarks are compiled with Trimaran and linked with the modified emulator library. The traces generated on the execution of the compiled simulator for each stream input are then used as input to our SMS simulator which simulates

Table 1. Assumed operation latencies

Operation	Latency
L1 cache access	2
L2 cache access	7
ALU	1
Integer/Float Multiply	3
Integer/Float Divide	8

simultaneous multistreaming by scheduling instructions from the traces. The SMS simulator is coupled with the DineroIV cache simulator [8] to obtain cache performance. The benchmarks are run to completion to obtain the traces. The assumed operation latencies are indicated in Table 1. The assumed operation latencies are described in the machine description and is used by the compiler to schedule operations.

2.2   Workload

Streaming applications offer good data level and task level parallelism, which is often difficult to extract from a sequential program description. Under the assumption that this parallelism is explicitly extracted by the user and specified using parallel program models, simultaneous multithreading could result in significant improvements in performance by increasing functional unit utilization against lower ILP levels and long latencies (e.g. cache misses). Multiple threads could be spawned from: (1) a single program working on different input data sets with each data set being treated as a thread (uniprogrammed workload), (2) multiple programs each working on a distinct data set (multiprogrammed workload) and (3) different communicating tasks each of which belong to a single distinct program.

In the first two cases there are no dependencies between threads and hence the time involved in synchronization is also absent. However in the third case, synchronization between tasks could introduce additional waiting time, which can be mitigated by a context switch to a completely different thread. To decouple the effects of multithreading and synchronization on the performance, and to demonstrate the potential of SMT, we only consider workloads of the first two kinds in this paper. Further, we use the notion of a *stream* to clearly indicate each thread, e.g. in the first case, a set of operations on each data input would constitute a stream. In the second case the set of operations belonging to each program constitutes a stream. In order to evaluate our workload we use the following standard input sets [23] for the MPEG-2 decoder: rocket.mpg, bicycle.mpg, smoker.mpg, alien.mpg, flight.mpg, hulahoop.mpg, berger.mpg and tennis.mpg. Each MPEG encoded data input is considered as a stream and the VLIW instructions involved in the decoding of each input data set constitutes an instruction stream.

The simulations were run to completion, i.e., the simulation stops when all the streams have completed their execution. Only the first seven frames of each clip is used for simulation, as the objective is to evaluate the effect on architectural parameters.

3   Compiler Optimizations

This section describes the compiler optimizations in brief. The compiler optimizations considered in this paper can be categorized into: (i) classical/basicblock (BB), (ii) superblock (SB) and (iii) hyperblock (HB) optimizations. Classical optimizations [24] perform traditional local optimizations and include constant propagation, copy propagation, constant folding, strength reduction etc. These optimizations do not necessitate any additional microarchitectural support.

Superblock optimizations [6] form superblocks, add loop unrolling and compiler controlled speculation, in addition to the basicblock optimizations. A superblock is a structure with a single entry, multiple exits for the control flow. In other words a superblock has no side entrances. Compiler controlled speculation allows greater code motion beyond basic block boundaries, by moving instructions past conditional branches. The correctness of code thus scheduled depends on the speculation model assumed and the processor support for speculation. As processor support for speculation leads to complex hardware implementations, we assume the general speculation model [13] in our experiments. The general speculation model enforces lesser restrictions on the instructions that can be speculated without significantly increasing the hardware support required. In this model all potentially excepting instructions have a non-excepting version, and this version is used in the schedule when a potentially excepting instruction is to be speculated. The non-excepting versions for all potentially excepting instructions adds to the additional hardware support.

Hyperblock optimizations add predicated execution (conditional execution/if-conversion) to superblock optimizations. Predicated execution can eliminate all non-loop backward branches from a program. A hyperblock is a set of predicated basicblock in which control may enter from the top, but may have multiple side exits. Hyperblocks are formed using modified if-conversion and are described in detail in [7].

3.1   Virtual Resources

In this section, we motivate and describe the use of virtual resources. We begin by analyzing the bottlenecks associated with the use of aggressive compiler techniques such as the superblock and hyperblock optimizations.

Fig. 2 and Fig. 3 plot the speedup and code size respectively, for the MPEG-2 decoder, across varying issue widths for the three compiler optimizations paths described earlier. The aim of this experiment was to illustrate the upper bound on the HPL-PD performance with the use of aggressive compiler optimizations. Hence, we assume: (1) perfect caches and (2) uniform and fully pipelined functional units i.e., any operation can be executed on any functional unit and the throughput of any functional unit is utmost one per cycle.

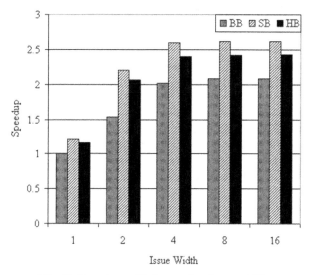

Fig. 2. Speedup with increasing issue widths.

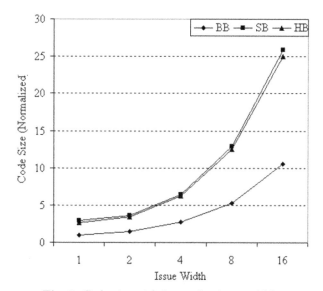

Fig. 3. Code size with increasing issue widths.

We observe from Fig. 2, that superblock optimization results in the highest performance benefit across differing issue widths, for the MPEG-2 decoder. We also note that the increase in speedup beyond 4 functional units is less than 2%, when the functional units are doubled. However, the code size (Fig. 3) almost doubles when the functional units are doubled beyond 4 functional units. Also, aggressive compiler techniques such as superblock and hyperblock optimizations have higher code size requirements than simple basicblock optimizations. The low speedups for an extremely parallel application such as the MPEG-2 decoder is attributed to the fact that this version of the application [12] was not parallelized in any manner, unlike other reported work [18].

In order to contain code size expansion, we decouple the architectural parameters (parameters that are exposed to the compiler) from the microarchitectural parameters (parameters that describe the hardware). In other words, the static code is compiled for an issue width smaller than the issue width available on the microarchitecture. We call the compiler's view of the issue width as *virtual resources*, and is specified using the machine description. To ease our explanation, we call the code thus scheduled as *virtual code*, and the code scheduled for the actual (microarchitectural) resources as *actual code*.

As there exists little performance benefit beyond 4-issue even with aggressive compiler optimizations exploiting hardware support for speculation and predicated execution, we use 4 issue slots as the virtual resource. Table 2 shows the percentage reduction in code size and the percentage decrease in performance due to the use of 4 virtual resources on an 8-issue and 16-issue VLIW. We find that virtual resources significantly limit code size expansion with negligible impact on performance across the different optimization paths. Moreover, this is achieved by recompiling the code for the pre-determined number of virtual resources and without any changes to the decoding hardware. Considering the benefits of using virtual resources, we choose 4-issue virtual resource as our design point to generate static code for later experiments. The issue width (functional units) mentioned in later experiments correspond to actual microarchitectural resources, unless mentioned otherwise.

The restriction of issue width using virtual resources leads to slack in the issue bandwidth. The additional issue slots available due to additional microarchitectural resources can be effectively utilized by simultaneously issuing instructions from other streams, logically leading to SMS, which is described and evaluated in the following sections.

Table 2. Effect of virtual resources on code size and performance

Issue Width	8		16	
	% saving in code size	% decrease in performance	% saving in code size	% decrease in performance
BB	97.17	3.69	293.73	3.7
SB	99.99	0.75	300.76	0.9
HB	98.66	1.01	297.54	1.33

4   Simultaneous MultiStreaming for VLIW Architectures

Our base VLIW architecture is derived from the HPL-PD architecture, with necessary support for SMS added. These include (1) multiple program counters to enable multiple instruction fetch per cycle and mechanisms to issue instructions based on some priority, (2) separate register files per stream and (3) separate return address stack for each stream.

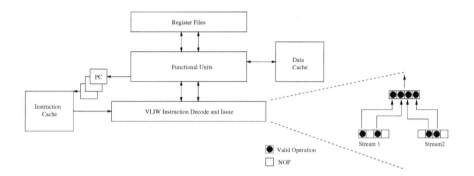

Fig. 4. Simultaneous Multithreading for VLIW architectures

Fig.4 shows our VLIW architecture modified to support SMS. The compiler generates a static schedule for a program, while conforming to the *MultiOp* format [16]. Each MultiOp instruction specifies the concurrent issue of multiple operations, i.e. each MultiOp instruction can be visualized as having slots equal in number to the issue width, within which the compiler encodes parallel operations. All operations within a MultiOp can execute simultaneously without checking for dependence or resource violations, and the compiler guarantees this.

The Trimaran compiler generates a static sequence of MultiOp instructions. The instruction decode and issue stage fetches MultiOp instructions from each stream (which corresponds to each data input) and decodes them as shown in Fig.4. In order to utilize the functional units effectively, only valid operations that are not NOP's are issued for execution. The issue of an operation from a MultiOp is determined by the availability of an issue slot. The issue of operations from multiple streams also hides long latencies, e.g., when the execution of a stream is delayed in the event of a cache miss (during which several issue slots go empty). Issuing operations from alternate streams helps increase functional unit utilization and consequently the operation throughput (measured in terms of operations issued per cycle) increases. In some instances a few operations in a particular MultiOp instruction might issue while the rest could be delayed due to lack of issue slots. Thus the dynamic MultiOp instruction as seen by the execution unit due to SMS differs from the static MultiOp instruction generated by the compiler, due to different inputs and due to the runtime behavior of the stream.

In order to ensure that issuing operations by *splitting* MultiOp does not violate correctness, we adhere to **LEQ** [16] semantics. An operation with LEQ semantics has its latency constrained between one and its assumed latency (architecturally visible latency). In contrast, operations with **EQ** semantics sample inputs and write outputs at precise virtual times. Though EQ semantics generate better schedules, as they provide more determinism for the compiler, EQ semantics require some means to capture the state of the microarchitecture when interrupted or when the code is split. The hardware complexity required to maintain the *preciseness* of state could potentially override the benefits associated with the use of EQ semantics. On the other hand, code scheduled with LEQ operations can be readily split without the need for additional hardware as the effective latencies after the split lie within LEQ schedule constraints.

Table 3. MultiOp schedule with virtual registers and the schedule optimized via EQ semantics

1	v2=op1(v1)		
2		v6=op3(v8)	
3			v7=op4(v6)
4	v3=op2(v2)		

(a)

1	r2=op1(r1)		
2		r2=op3(r8)	
3			r7=op4(r2)
4		r3=op2(r2)	

(b)

Consider for example the MultiOp instruction schedule using virtual registers (before register allocation) $v_1 .. v_7$ as shown in Table 3(a). All operations have a latency of one except for operation 1 which has a latency of 3 cycles. Operation 2 is dependent on the result of operation 1 and can only be scheduled within a MultiOp instruction that issues after the latency of operation 1 has expired. If scheduled before this latency has expired then operation 2 sees a value of v_2 not computed by operation 1 but instead the previous value of v_2. The schedule can be optimized to reduce register pressure with the use of EQ semantics as the precise read and write instants are known, i.e., virtual registers v_2 and v_6 can be allocated to a single physical register r_2 to obtain the schedule as shown in Table 3(b), as their lifetimes do not overlap. The problem with this schedule is that it would generate incorrect results, if we were to split the instruction after operation 1. The unavailability of issue slots after the split could potentially lead to operation 4 being issued after the latency of operation 1 (already issued) has expired. Thus operation 2 now sees an incorrect value of register r_2. Schedules conforming to LEQ semantics do not give rise to such inconsistencies when a MultiOp instruction is *split* and its operations issued at different instants. Thus, LEQ semantics ensure correctness.

However, another issue with our scheme that exists even when LEQ semantics are used, arise due to bidirectional dependencies between operations in a MultiOp instruction. For example, an exchange copy generates incorrect results when the individual operations are split and issued at different instances. This problem can be overcome by buffering results until all operations in the same instruction have sampled their inputs. However this additional buffering could affect latency and/or clock speeds. An efficient implementation could exclude bi-directional dependencies, wherein the compiler ensures that the only allowed dependencies between operations within a MultiOp instruction are from left to right, enabling hardware schemes such as SMS to split operation issue.

5   Simulation Results

This section presents some results from our study of SMS for VLIW architectures.

In order to demonstrate the scalability of SMS, we determined the performance speedup for SMS for upto 8 streams. The plot of speedup for three sets of streams (2, 4, and 8 streams) is shown in Fig. 5. For each set of streams the speedup using differing issue widths is also shown. The SMS (with virtual code) speedup is on an architecture that does not provide any support for either speculation or predicated execution, and is reported with respect to the aggregate execution time for all streams on an architecture without SMS support(with actual code). For purposes of comparison we also show the speedup attained by superblock and hyperblock optimizations with respect to basicblock optimization on VLIW machines with equivalent issue widths.

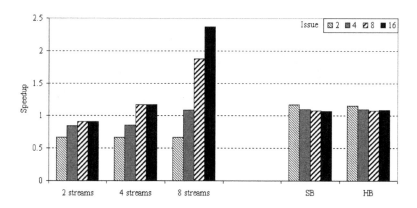

Fig. 5. Speedup with SMS and without support for speculation or predicated execution.

As the virtual code is scheduled for a 4 issue machine, we do not find any speedup on machines with 4 issues or fewer. But this compromise in performance is with a significant saving in code size as discussed earlier. However, the presence of a large number of streams boosts performance, as issue slots are filled by instructions from alternate streams.

With microarchitectural resources greater than 4, we find that the performance increases almost linearly with the number of streams. We also note that the SMS performance is more scalable and significantly higher than that obtained by either superblock or hyperblock optimizations.

We also performed experiments to determine if added hardware support for speculation and predicated execution over SMS leads to significant improvements in performance. These results are tabulated in Fig. 6 and Fig. 7 respectively.

We find that superblock optimizations, exploiting support for speculation does not increase performance significantly as indicated by Fig. 6. The performance improvement averages 12% with a maximum speedup of 22% obtained with an 8-issue VLIW and with 8 streams.

Similar to the case with speculative execution, the added support for predicated execution does not result in a significant improvement in performance (Fig. 7). These results indicate that the improvement in performance due to support for speculation and predicated execution, over SMS may not justify the increase in complexity. The complexity associated with speculation and predicated execution is discussed in detail in [16].

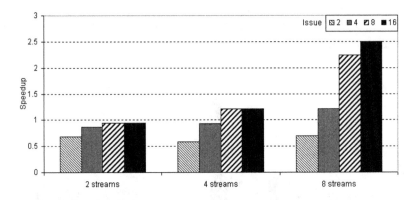

Fig. 6. SMS speedup with additional support for speculation (SB).

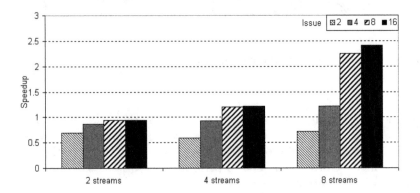

Fig. 7. SMS speedup with additional support for predication (HB).

6   Related Work

Studies by Tullsen et.al. [2] [17] explore the effects of SMT on a superscalar core for SPEC92 applications. They considered multiprogrammed workloads in their study of SMT, which helped to decouple synchronization effects from SMT. Their study analyzes and suggests schemes to ease the instruction fetch bottleneck associated with SMT. Ozer, Conte et.al, [18] studied the effect of SMT in the context of VLIW architectures. They tried to extract parallelism between tasks with a sequential program by spawning speculative threads. These speculative threads are then simultaneously multithreaded and hardware support is required to support speculative execution. Due to the granularity of the threads(tasks within a program), the achieved improvements are marginal and could possibly involve high hardware costs to support their scheme. Several other schemes for multithreading [20] [21] [22] that were studied, use variations of the above workloads and synchronization schemes.

Fritts et.al. [19], evaluated static and dynamic scheduling performance for applications from the mediabench [12] suite of applications. They found that statically scheduled VLIW architectures and in-order superscalar processors perform comparably, while dynamic out-of-order scheduling performs significantly better. They also found that though hyperblock optimizations have the best performance, its minimal improvement over out of order superscalar scheduling might not warrant the additional cost involved in conditional execution.

Our work borrows heavily from previous related research but differs and contributes in the following respects: (1) We adapt SMT to VLIW architectures while emphasizing correctness and requiring minimal architectural support, (2) we generalize our workload to accommodate data level parallelism, (3) we compare SMS with aggressive compiler techniques, such as superblock and hyperblock optimizations, that exploit far-flung parallelism, (4) we study SMS performance on media applications, using MPEG-2 as a case study, (5) we explore an optimization to limit code size expansion by decoupling architectural and microarchitectural resources, (6) we evaluate SMS performance when used with superblock and hyperblock optimization.

7   Conclusions and Future Work

In this paper, we study aggressive compiler optimizations that use the superblock and the hyperblock, whose performance is critically dependent on hardware support for speculation and predicated execution. We find that the speedup obtained with these techniques do not scale well beyond an issue width of 4, while the code size continues to increase super-linearly. We propose simultaneous multi-streaming for VLIW architectures and show that SMS performance scales with increasing issue widths. To counter the effects of increasing code size, we propose that architectural resources be decoupled from microarchitectural resources with the use of virtual resources. Our results show that virtual resources effectively limit increase in code size, with little or no impact on performance. Unlike encoding schemes that increase decoder complexity, the use of virtual resources does not require a redesign of the decoder, making this scheme complexity effective.

Moreover, virtual code can be executed on a SMS-VLIW processor. This complexity-effective arrangement addresses both non-scaling performance and code size expansion associated with the use of aggressive compiler optimizations on VLIW architectures.

Our results also indicate that the performance obtained with additional support for speculation and predicated execution over SMS might not justify the additional hardware complexity. A microarchitectural study on the complexity of these schemes would lead to complexity-effective processors delivering the desired level of performance for media applications.

Acknowledgements

We thank the anonymous reviewers for their comments on improving this work.

References

1. The Trimaran Compiler Infrastructure. http://www.trimaran.org.
2. Dean M. Tullsen, Susan J. Eggers, Joel S. Emer, Henry M. Levy, Jack L. Lo and Rebecca L. Stamm. Exploiting Choice: Instruction Fetch and Issue on an Implementable Simultaneous Multithreading Processor. In *23rd Annual International Symposium on Computer Architecture*, May 1996.
3. Vinod Kathail, Michael S. Schlansker, B. Ramakrishna Rau. HPL-PD Architecture Specification: Version 1.1. Technical report HPL-93-80, HP Laboratories, Feb 2000.
4. John C. Gyllenhaal, W.W. Hwu, B. Ramakrishna Rau. HMDES Version 2.0 Specification. *Technical Report*, IMPACT-96-3.
5. Margarida F. Jacome, Gustavo de Veciana. Design Challenges for New Application-Specific Processors. In *IEEE Design & Test of Computers*. April - June 2000.
6. W.W. Hwu, Scott A. Mahlke et.al. The Superblock: An Effective technique for VLIW and Superscalar Compilation. In *The Journal of Supercomputing*, pg 224-233, May 1993.
7. Scott A. Mahlke, David C. Lin, William Y. Chen, Richard E. Hank, Roger A. Bringmann. Effective Compiler Support for Predicated Execution Using the Hyperblock. In *27th International Symposium on Microarchitecture*, pg 217-227, Nov 1994.
8. Edler J., M. Hill. Dinero IV Trace-Driven Uniprocessor Cache Simulator. http://www.neci.nj.nec.com/homepages/edler/d4
9. W.W. Hwu et.al. The IMPACT project, http://www.crhc.uiuc.edu/IMPACT.
10. S. Aditya, V. Kathail, and B. R. Rau. Elcor's machine description system: version 3.0. Technical Report HPL-98-128 (R.1), HP Laboratories, Oct 1998.
11. Michael S. Schlansker, B. Ramakrishna Rau. EPIC: An Architecture for Instruction-Level Parallel Processors. Technical Report HP-1999-111, HP Laboratories, Feb 2000.
12. Chunho Lee, Miodrag Potkonjak et.al. MediaBench: A Tool for Evaluating and Synthesising Multimedia and Communication Systems. In *30th International Symposium on Microarchitecture*, pg 330-335, Dec 1997.

13. R.A. Bringmann, S.A. Mahlke and Wen-Mei Hwu. A Study of the Effects of Compiler-Controlled Speculation on Instruction and Data Caches. In *Proceeding of the 28th Annual International Conference on System Sciences*, Jan 1995.
14. Subbarao Palacharla, Norman P. Jouppi, James E. Smith. Complexity-Effective Superscalar Processors. In *24th International Symposium on Computer Architecture*, pg 206-218, June 1997
15. Texas Instruments TMS320C62x processor. http://www-k.ext.ti.com/sc/technical-support/tools/dsp/ftp/c62x.htm.
16. Michael S. Schlansker, B. Ramakrishna Rau, Scott Mahlke et. al. Acheiving High Levels of Instruction-Level Parallelism with Reduced Hardware Complexity. Technical Report HPL-96-120, HP Laboratories, Nov 1994.
17. D. M. Tullsen, S. J. Eggers, H. M. Levy. Simultaneous Multithreading: Maximising on-chip Parallelism. In *22nd AnnualInternational Symposium on Computer Architecture*, pg 392-403, Jun 1995.
18. E. Ozer, T. M. Conte, and S. Sharma. Weld: A Multithreading Technique Towards Latency-Tolerant VLIW Processors. In *8th International Conference on High Performance Computing*, Dec 2001.
19. Jason Fritts, Wayne Wolfe. Evaluation of Static and Dynamic Scheduling for Media Processors. In *MICRO-33 MP-DSP2 Workshop*. ACM, Dec 2000.
20. R. G. Prasadh and C. L. Wu. A Benchmark Evaluation of a Multithreaded RISC Processor Architecture. In *International Conference on Parallel Processing*, pg I:84-91, Aug 1991.
21. S. W. Keckler and W. J. Dally. Processor Coupling: Integrating Compile-time and Run-time Scheduling for Parallelism. In *19th International Symposium on Computer Architecture*, Dec 1995.
22. Richard Partridge. Cray Launches X1 for Extreme Supercomputing. Technology Trends, D. H. Brown Associates, Nov 2002.
23. The Berkeley Multimedia Research Center. http://bmrc.berkeley.edu/
24. A.V. Aho, R. Sethi, J.D. Ullman. Compilers: Principles, Techniques and Tools. Pearson Education Pte. Ltd., 2001.

A Novel Architecture for Genomic Sequence Searching and Alignment

Paul Gardner-Stephen* and Greg Knowles

Flinders University, School of Informatics & Engineering,
GPO BOX 2100, Adelaide 5001, Australia,
gardners@infoeng.flinders.edu.au, gknowles@infoeng.flinders.edu.au

Abstract. Blast[2], FASTA[4] and related algorithms are popular tools for searching genomic data. Accelerating these tools is an increasingly important goal as the growth of the databases outstrips Moore's Law[6]. Many of the existing hardware designs are little more than direct translations of existing algorithms from the software to hardware domain[3, 7]. In this paper we summarise a novel approach which we have implemented in VHDL and synthesised, with the aim of validating an efficient algorithm and virtual hardware search system which produces near perfect results compared to NCBI Blast 2.2.3. Speed and quality comparisons of the VHDL simulations with respect to NCBI Blast 2.2.3 are included.

1 Introduction

1.1 An Introduction to Searching Genomic Databases

Searching genomic databases consists of finding similarities between the database and a query sequence, both of which are formed of a small alphabet of possible symbols. In this paper the searching of DNA databases is considered. These consist of the alphabet G,A,C and T, representing the nucleotides which constitute a DNA strand. The length of genomic databases is typically in the billions of nucleotides. The query sequences are typically much smaller, usually several thousand nucleotides or less.

Such databases may also include additional symbols which represent uncertainty regarding the true nature of a base. The most common of these is N, signifying that the nucleotide is completely unknown. Treatment of such symbols is not attempted in this paper.

Exact Sub-string Matching. Exact sub-string matching consists of locating contiguous corresponding symbols between a query and subject sequence. That is to find all congruent regions between the sequences. For example:

query sequence: CGA CTG ATC TAG
subject sequence: CGT GTA GCT AGC AGT GTA GTC TAG CGT ACG TGC

---

* Author for correspondence.

A. Omondi and S. Sedukhin (Eds.): ACSAC 2003, LNCS 2823, pp. 180–192, 2003.

sequence matches:
CG (query offset 0) matches subject offsets 0,24 and 31:
CGt gta gct agc agt gta gtc tag CGt aCG tgc

..
TCTAG (query offset 7) matches subject offset 19:
cgt gta gct agc agt gta gTC TAG cgt acg tgc
etc...

Non-exact Sub-string (Non-gapped) Matching. Non-gapped matching aims to locate non-exact non-gapped sub-string matches. These matches may include transpositions or transformations, but not insertions or deletions. Thus one or more bases may be replaced with exactly the same number of substituted bases, but the total number must remain constant. That is, to find all congruent and also similar, though non-congruent regions between the sequences. For example:

query sequence: CGA CTG ATC TAG
subject sequence: CGT GTA GCT AGC AGT GTA GTC TAG CGT ACG TGC
sequence matches:
CGACT (query offset 0) matches subject offset 0 :
CGt gTa gct agc agt gta gtc tag cgt acg tgc

..
TCTAG (query offset 7) matches subject offsets 2,14 and 19:
cgT gTA Gct agc agT gTA GTC TAG cgt acg tgc
etc...

Various rules are applied to determine at what level of similarity a match is considered significant. These typically involve a *reward* score for corresponding symbols in the sequences, and a *penalty* score for differing symbols.

For instance, comparing CGACT with CGTGT using reward and penalty scores of 1 and -3 respectively would result in a score of -3 (Table 1).

This is the level of searching performed by Blast version 1.

Table 1. Non-gapped comparison of CGACT and CGTGT

C	G	A	C	T
C	G	T	G	T
+1	+1	-3	-3	+1

Gapped Matching. Gapped matching introduces the concept of gaps caused by insertions or deletions. In addition to the reward and penalty scores typically associated with non-gapped matching, *gap creation* and *gap extension* penalties are often used.

For example, CGACT and CGAAGCT can be aligned, if gaps are added into the query sequence (Table 2).

Table 2. Gapped comparison of CGACT and CGAAGCT

C	G	A	-	-	C	T
C	G	A	A	G	C	T
+1	+1	+1	-5	-2	+1	+1

Assuming a gap creation score of -5, and a gap extension score of -2 the example above would have a final score of -2.

This is the type of search performed by Blast version 2 and Smith-Waterman.

Dynamic Programming. Gapped extension greatly increases the complexity of the search. In order to find the optimal solution to a given gapped search, dynamic programming techniques are typically employed.

This approach consists of generating a dynamic programming space which has the query and subject sequences as axes. Each discrete cell in the space is then evaluated, relying on the values of cells nearer the origin than itself. For example in Table 3, the value of the fifth cell in the second row is arrived at by finding the maximum score which is possible by considering the cells immediately left, above and above-left, i.e:

$$score = max \begin{pmatrix} -5 + gap\,extend = -7 \\ -10 + gap\,create = -15 \\ -8 + reward = -7 \end{pmatrix}$$
$$= -7 \ .$$

Once the maximum score in the search space has been found, the path taken to obtain that score can be determined by tracing backwards to reveal the optimal alignment of the two sequences. Such alignments can be either global or local. For a local alignment the path is not required to traverse from the origin (top left in Table 3) to the end point of the space.

In the example evaluated dynamic programming space of Table 3, a locally optimal path would be CGA=CGA. The globally optimal path would be CGA–CT=CGACT. Note that there may be multiple optimally scoring paths.

Table 3. Example evaluated dynamic programming space

	C	G	A	A	G	C	T
C	1	-4	-6	-8	-10	-12	-14
G	-4	2	-3	-5	-7	-9	-11
A	-6	-3	3	-2	-4	-6	-8
C	-8	-5	-2	0	-5	-3	-5
T	-10	-7	-4	-5	-3	-8	-2

2   Architectural Overview

This section provides a high level overview of the architecture designed to perform efficient genomic sequence searching and alignment. Figure 1 illustrates the context and location of each unit described.

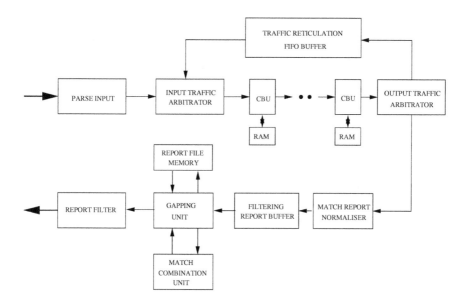

Fig. 1. High level overview of architecture

2.1   Parse Input

The Parse Input Stage accepts ASCII input, including embedded control characters and the polynucleotide sequence to be searched for (query sequence), followed by a control character and the sequence database to be searched through (subject sequence or database).

2.2   Systolic Array of Processing Elements (CBUs)

The Processing Elements perform the actual sequence comparison. Each PE consists of three stages which in parallel:

1. Compare one stored query sequence symbol with one subject sequence symbol.
2. Determine whether to create a match, extend a match, terminate a match or do nothing.
3. Emit a match report if a match has been terminated.

Each stage takes one cycle, excepting when a match report is emitted in which case an additional cycle is required. This results in a stall which is propagated back along the pipe-line. Back-tracking or flushing of the pipe-line is never required due to the serial nature of the work. The pipe-line has been simulated with up to 1000 processing elements in VHDL with Synopsys Scirocco.

The probability of any given processing element stalling in any given cycle can be determined precisely from the minimum congruent region length. The probability of the entire pipe-line stalling is directly proportional to its length. Thus it is possible to determine the maximum useful length of the pipe-line beyond which extension yields diminishing returns. However, given current FPGA capacities, Moore's Law and the estimated size of the processing elements, this limit is not likely to be reached for several years - rather FPGA capacity will be the limiting factor.

2.3   Virtual Hardware and Traffic Reticulation

For situations where the query sequence is longer than the number of PEs, a Virtual Hardware regime is employed.

Each PE refers to a memory (SYMFILE in Fig. 2) which stores the array of state information for each pass. All state information is written back to this file each cycle. The most recently used, the next monotonically addressed and zero addressed values are cached so that the read cycles do not delay the pipe-line.

The use of such memories makes efficient usage of these resources typically found on modern FPGAs, allowing a virtualisation factor of 128 or more on a typical large FPGA (e.g. Altera Stratix family) with a only a moderate (less than two-fold) increase in the required area per processing element.

The Input Traffic Arbitrator, Output Traffic Arbitrator and Traffic Reticulation FIFO manage the repeated passage of each subject sequence word through the pipe-line, and the associated pass number tagging. Acceptance of new data into the pipe-line is permitted immediately the current traffic has been completely processed and begins to exit. This ensures preservation of order and prevents the pipe-line from emptying during this process.

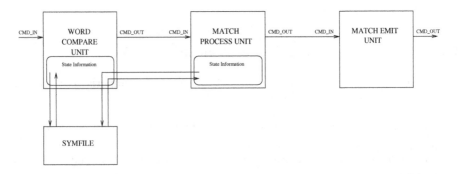

Fig. 2. Overview of Processing Element, including state flow for virtual hardware

Siphoning of Match Reports between Virtual Hardware Passes. The Output Traffic Arbitrator also siphons off any match reports which arise rather than subjecting them to multiple passes through the pipe-line. This serves two purposes; firstly to remove the idle bubbles which they cause in the pipe-line thus avoiding a build up over subsequent passes, and secondly to obtain an optimal ordering for the Gapping Unit, which will be discussed later.

The Match Report Normalisation Unit converts the match reports from their compact pipe-line form which is used for space efficiency into a more verbose format which includes where it starts and ends in the query and subject sequences.

At this point the architecture effectively performs the equivalent of Blast 1.

Optimising Match Report Production Order. The order in which the matches are generated and processed is significant in that it affects the number of recent matches which are required for consideration to produce combined (gapped) reports.

The systolic array configuration of the architecture ensures that match reports are delivered to the Gapping Unit ordered by their end point in the subject sequence. This is advantageous as only match reports produced previously will have an earlier end point in the subject sequence. Thus the most recent match at any point only requires consideration against previous reports for the formation of compound matches.

This sort issue becomes more complex for the virtual hardware configuration where only part of the pipe-line is running at any point in time. In this case, the order of match delivery becomes partially sorted by the query sequence due to the subsequent passes of the data through the pipe-line. This change in the sort order is beneficial, the consequence being that match reports with similar end points in the subject sequence are sorted by end point in the query sequence. The window for combining reports is related to the distance between the start point of one match report and the end of recent match reports in the subject and query sequences. The modified sorting means that the match reports are dispatched effectively ordered by the sum of the difference in the subject and query sequences.

Thus, the earlier the match report was dispatched, the less likely it is to be suitable for combination with the match report in question. The end result being that the Gapping Unit requires only a surprisingly small number of the most recent match reports to form most possible combined match reports.

2.4   Gapping and Filtering

The described architecture takes advantage of the fact that Blast normally only reports matches which include an 11 base pair congruency. The Filtering Report Buffer contains the most recent n match reports. When an 11 base pair or longer match report is received by the Filtering Report Buffer, the m match reports it contains immediately prior to and following that report are released to the Gapping Unit, where $0 \leq m \leq n$. Larger values of m provide greater sensitivity in certain circumstances. Conversely smaller values of m result in shorter execution times. All other match reports are discarded.

Only releasing match reports in the vicinity of an 11 base pair or longer match report reduces the work load of the Gapping Unit by an order of magnitude or more. This is significant as the Gapping Unit requires 16 or more cycles per Match Report it receives. This delay is the result of the sequential consideration of the match report with the most recent 16 match reports received, via the Match Combination Unit. This is necessary to determine if any match reports can be joined to form combined reports consisting of those congruent regions and the incongruent region in between. This process is recursive in that any compound match reports produced are fed back into the Gapping Unit, thus resulting in an additional 16 cycle delay.

Regardless of whether a match report results in combined match reports or not, when the Gapping Unit has finished processing it passes the match report to the Output Filtering Unit. This unit verifies that the report is not a duplicate or sub-set of the last report, and that it meets minimum length requirements imposed by the operator.

3 Method

3.1 VHDL Implementation and Synthesis

The architecture was prototyped in VHDL. Simulated was performed using Synopsys Scirocco, and Synthesis with MentorGraphics Leonardo Spectrum. The synthesis target was the Altera Stratix EP1S80F1508C-6 device (79,040 LC) with a pipe-line of 10 processing elements and the supporting units to gauge area and timing requirements both with and without the virtual-hardware scheme.

3.2 VHDL Simulations

Fifty-six test cases were randomly generated using excerpts from the Human Genome[1] of between 54,123 and 9,622,958 bases for the subject sequence. The query sequence was a randomly selected sub-set of 50 to 94 bases from the above excerpt. These test cases were run through NCBI Blast 2.2.3[2] and behavioural simulations of the described architecture were performed using Synopsys Scirocco.

4 Results

4.1 Synthesis Results

Synthesis was performed for the architecture with and without the virtual hardware system. Refer to Tables 4 and 5 for relative areas and critical paths of the ordinary and virtual-hardware versions of the architecture respectively. The virtual hardware version requires less than double the area (620 versus 351 LCs) per

Table 4. Summary of synthesis results of selected architecture components. Generated using MentorGraphics Leonardo Spectrum, targeting a Altera Stratix EP1S80F1508C-6 device (79,040 LC). 10 PE's and no virtual-hardware

Component	Critical Path	LC count & percent
CBU (each)	6.4ns	351 (0.44%)
Other Units	na	7,167 (9.07%)
Total with 10 CBU	9.00ns	10,677 (13.51%)

Table 5. Summary of synthesis results of selected architecture components. Generated using MentorGraphics Leonardo Spectrum, targeting a Altera Stratix EP1S80F1508C-6 device (79,040 LC). 10 PE's with virtual-hardware

Component	Critical Path	LC count & percent
CBU (each)	8.22ns	620 (0.78%)
Other Units	na	3,420 (4.32%)
Total with 1 CBU	8.86ns	4,040 (5.11%)
Total with 10 CBU	9.14ns	9,615 (12.16%)

processing element (CBU). The timing characteristics for the architecture are also reasonably preserved at 9.14ns, up from 9.00ns. An indication of the size of the supporting logic is given in the difference in area required by the other units. These supporting structures were refined during the process of implementing the virtual-hardware scheme as reflected in the reduced area requirement for these units (3,420 versus 7,167 LCs) despite the additional logic added to support the virtual-hardware operation.

4.2   Speed and Coverage Comparison

The speed comparison consisted of comparing the execution time of Blast with the simulated execution time of the architecture with 100 processing elements, assuming the conservative clock speed of 100MHz. The simulations were performed using a behavioural model in Synopsys Scirocco. The speed comparison was done for all fifty-six tests.

The match coverage comparison consisted of comparing the percentage of bases in the subject sequence which each application found, compared to those found by the other, a score of 100 being perfect. This is referred to as the coverage comparison. The architecture simulations required approximately five CPU weeks on a Sun Blade 1000 with UltraSparc-III 750MHz processor.

A summary of the results can be found in Figs. 3, 4 and Table 6. Note that the Blast tests were run on both Sun UltraSparc-III 750MHz (8MB L2 cache) and AMD Athlon 1.4GHz (256KB L2 cache) processors. The performance of each system was within 2%, with the UltraSparc being faster. The results shown are those from the UltraSparc-III processor.

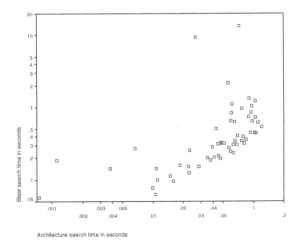

Fig. 3. Scatter plot of log of Blast and Architecture execution times

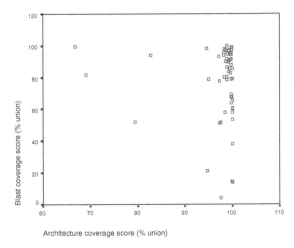

Fig. 4. Scatter plot of Blast and Architecture coverage scores

Table 6. Summary statistics of Blast and the architecture's relative performance

	Architecture	Blast
Total run time	3.28	23.67
Mean run time	0.055	0.401
Min run time	0.008	0.014
Max run time	0.12	6.75
Mean coverage score	97.35	77.45
Min coverage score	66.72	4.01
Max coverage score	100	99.84

Table 7. Linear regression of contributors to architecture execution time

Linear regression coefficients for proposed architecture

	Unstandardised			
	B	Std. Err	t	sig
(Constant)	-1.380E-02	.003	-5.029	.000
Subject length	2.170E-08	.000	87.150	.000
Query length	2.140E-04	.000	6.281	.000
Hits found	2.158E-06	.000	6.267	.000

Table 8. Linear regression of contributors to Blast execution time

Linear regression coefficients for Blast

	Unstandardised			
	B	Std. Err	t	sig
(Constant)	.224	.237	.944	.349
Subject length	8.456E-09	.000	.406	.686
Query length	-5.09E-03	.003	-1.742	.087
Hits found	1.783E-03	.000	33.692	.000

4.3   Analysis of Execution Times

Here we used a linear regression model to profile the performance of the described architecture and Blast (Tables 7 and 8).

Given that the database length was typically ~10^7 bases, Blast and the architecture were similarly influenced at 8.456×10^{-9} and 2.17×10^{-8} seconds per base respectively (B coefficient column). A similar relationship is evident for the query sequence length. The major difference is in the effect of the number of hits found where Blast suffered almost three orders of magnitude greater effect than the architecture: 1.783×10^{-3} versus 2.158×10^{-6} seconds per hit found.

This model produces significant results at the 95% confidence level for Blast only against the number of hits found, with the ratio of the standard error to the estimated coefficient generally small as indicated by the t column. Conversely the model for the architecture is significant for all dependent variables tested (sig column), with consistently larger B coefficients than their associated standard errors.

4.4   Performance of Gapping Unit and Input Report Filtering

As previously noted, it is possible to determine the probability of any one of the processing elements stalling during any given cycle. Thus it is possible to determine the average number of cycles required for the pipe-line to proceed, and hence process one base of the subject sequence. By comparing this theoretical speed against the actual speed it is possible to gain an appreciation of the order of time the Gapping Unit is requiring, remembering that it requires at least 16 cycles per match report delivered to it.

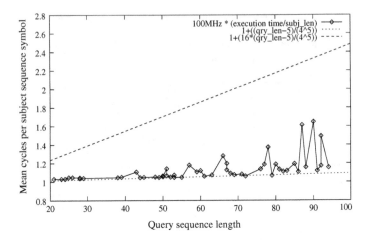

Fig. 5. Actual cycle costs compared to theoretical minimum and expected costs without Input Report Filtering

Figure 5 depicts the query sequence length versus the theoretical cycle cost per base (lower dashed line), and the computed cycle cost per base from the tests (solid line).

It can be seen that the lower bound for the execution time quite closely follows the predicted value. In comparison, the expected cost of the Gapping Unit is described by:

$$avg\,cycles = 1 + 16 \times \frac{query\,len - n}{4^n}$$

This accounts for the base one cycle cost plus 16 cycles for each match report generated. n represents the minimum match length, hence for an alphabet size of four (A,C, G & T) the probability of a match occurring in any given cycle will be the number of opportunities ($query\,length - n$) divided by the probability of a report occurring at each ($\frac{1}{4^n}$).

Thus for the tests performed with $n = 5$, and a query sequence length of between 20 and 100 bases:

$$avg\,cycles_{20} = 1 + 16 \times \frac{20 - 5}{4^5} = 1 + 0.23 = 1.23$$

$$avg\,cycles_{100} = 1 + 16 \times \frac{100 - 5}{4^5} = 1 + 1.48 = 2.48$$

However, the actual cost was much nearer the theoretical minimum than the expected cost (upper line of graph). This shows the effectiveness of the input match report filtering and buffering process in avoiding excessive stalling of the pipe-line due to Gapping Unit induced delays.

5 Conclusions

5.1 Performance as Evidence for Validity of Approach

The architecture presented here found, on average matches which covered 97.35% of the output from Blast. This suggests that the approach taken is valid.

The speed comparison is also favourable, indicating that even when clocked at only $\frac{2}{25^{th}}$ the rate of Blast it still performs on average around six times faster, and hence around 75 times faster on a parity clock basis. Further, there were individual cases where the architecture performed around 50 to 100 times faster than Blast likely due to the more variable execution time of that heuristic algorithm - providing a performance increase of 600 to 1200 times on a parity clock basis.

The filtering of input to the Gapping Unit, and the advantageous sorting effect which the Virtual Hardware feature provides, are contributors to the good speed performance.

5.2 Different Execution Time Characteristics

Empirical evidence suggests that the large speed differences occur when the search returns a large number of hits. Such cases occur only occasionally, however overall they contribute 80-95% of the total execution time to a given batch of searches. We have also shown that the described architecture exhibits execution time which is almost completely predictable by the size of the search, while execution time of Blast is predominantly predicted by the number of hits (Table 7).

This combined with the better execution times suggest that such an architecture may be of use to genomic database search service providers for whom superior aggregate execution time and predictability are advantageous characteristics.

5.3 Virtual-Hardware Scheme

The virtual-hardware scheme has only moderate effect on the processing element density possible on a given device when employed on a typical FPGA device. Further, the static overheads were completely mitigated by refining the other functional units.

5.4 Future Work

From our experience in this preliminary project, we expect that by refining our architecture and using the latest generation of FPGAs we will be able to obtain more than order of magnitude speedup on the results presented here. Increasing the buffering into the Gapping Unit could potentially reduce the peaks in Fig. 5 by preventing the pipe-line from stalling when the Gapping Unit is operating. Further speed improvements could be obtained by utilising a number of FPGAs or ASICs performing portions of the search in parallel. Indeed genomic sequence searching lends itself easily to such parallelism.

Interestingly, the presented architecture often found matches covering much more of the subject sequence than Blast, as evidenced by the low minimum and average coverage scores of Blast. This suggests that the architecture is presently more sensitive than Blast, whilst still being faster.

In conclusion, this work shows that an alternative to the traditional dynamic programming approaches to genomic database searching exists.

Acknowledgements

The author would like to acknowledge the support of the CSSIP (Australian Co-operative Research Centre for Signal, Sensor and Information Processing) Firmware project.

References

1. Human Genome, Working Draft as at 19 June 2002, ftp://ftp.ncbi.nih.gov/ repository/UniGene/Hs.seq.all.gz
2. Blast 2.2.3 (May 13 2002): Altschol, Stephen F., Thomas L. Madden, Alejandro A. Schaffer, Jinghui Zhang, Zheng Zhang, Webb Miller, and David J. Lipman (1997), "Gapped BLAST and PSI-BLAST: a new generation of protein database search programs", Nucleic Acids Res. 25:3389-3402.
3. Speeding Up Genome Computation With a Systolic Accelerator (1998), Dominique Lavenier The, http://citeseer.nj.nec.com/lavenier98speeding.html
4. Rapid and sensitive sequence comparison with FASTP and FASTA: Pearson, W. R., Methods in Enzymology 183:63–98, 1990.
5. The Fasta and Blast programs: Galisson, 2000.
6. Time Logic Corporation technology overview, http://www.timelogic.com/-technology.html
7. Time Logic Corp. DeCypher algorithms, http://www.timelogic.com/-decypher_algorithms.html

A Reconfigurable Multi-threaded Architecture Model

Sebastian Wallner

Department of Distributed Systems, Technical University Hamburg-Harburg,
Schwarzenbergstrasse 95, D-21073 Hamburg, Germany,
`wallner@tu-harburg.de`

Abstract. Reconfigurable computing devices promise to deliver the performance of application-specific hardware along with the flexibility of general-purpose microprocessors. It is still a technology with confined dedications due to restricted hardware resources, high cost of developing and upgrading applications. Hardware virtualization with appropriate configuration techniques can be applied to significantly reduce these problems.
This paper presents a novel architecture model for reconfigurable execution which virtualizes hardware resources to remove the fixed-size constraints present in conventional reconfigurable devices. The architecture maps computation threads via a pipelined configuration technique onto available physical hardware. Some application examples demonstrate that the proposed architecture concept provides performance and application flexibility.

Key words: Reconfigurable Architectures, Computation Threads , Hardware Virtualization, Pipelining, Datapath Processor

1 Introduction

Fine-grained reconfigurable devices offer great flexibility. They enable the architecture to be modified to closely match the computational problem and offer high performance. However, fine-grained reconfigurability exacts a high price in performance and silicon area. It is estimated that only a few percent of the area of a typical FPGA is available for usable logic [1]; the rest is needed for interconnections and configuration memory. Furthermore, the cost of generating and maintaining software for reconfigurable hardware is significantly higher than for general purpose computers. There are some attempts to reduce these overheads by using coarse-grained reconfigurable processing cells or even simple programmable processors [2, 3].

In this paper, a reconfigurable architecture is presented for computationally intensive applications in wireless communication- and multimedia video and audio streaming environments that significantly reduce the addressed problems. The architecture is based on a synchronous multifunctional pipeline flow model using coarse-grained reconfigurable processing cells and configurable data paths.

A. Omondi and S. Sedukhin (Eds.): ACSAC 2003, LNCS 2823, pp. 193–207, 2003.

For run-time- and partial reconfiguration, a pipelined configuration technique via descriptors is deployed [4]. Descriptors represent small configuration templates abutted to instruction operation-codes in conventional Instruction Set Architectures (ISA).

The architecture is adaptable to larger problems in a spatial- or temporal manner. It allows to execute parts of an application by configuring the hardware between each execution stage. For this purpose, several descriptors can be sliced into fixed-size computation threads that, in analogy to virtual memory pages, are swapped onto available physical hardware within a few clock cycles. The architecture supports data level parallelism as used in vector and MMX architectures [6], as well as thread-level parallelism and thread interleaving realized in chip multiprocessors and multi-threaded processors. The approach results in a flexible reconfigurable hardware architecture with performance and function flexibility which manages the hardware virtualization process with minimal supporting hardware.

Other reconfigurable architectures have been introduced, which partition and time-multiplex large applications as compute pages [7, 8]. Their page communication is buffered through a small, fixed set of device registers. Hence when the application is larger than the physical hardware, the execution time may be dominant by the reconfiguration time. Their virtualization concepts gets inefficient due to the limited page communication resources. The proposed architecture approach avoids this inefficiency by utilize a fast pipelined configuration technique with coarse-grained processing cells. It directly feeds back partial results to the physical pipeline.

Similar to the solution in this paper is PipeRench from CMU [9, 10]. PipeRench defines a reconfigurable fabric paged into horizontal stripes which communicate vertically as a pipeline. The execution model fully virtualizes stripes and enables hardware scaling to any number of physical stripes. Although the stripes communicate through input-output registers, PipeRench's pipelined configuration scheme hides excessive reconfiguration overhead. The sequential reconfiguration scheme with a configuration word is well suited for simple feed-forward pipelines. However, this scheme is not practical for mapping heterogeneous computation graphs with feedback loops. It may waste available parallelism when wide computation graphs are squeezed into linear sequences of stripes. The proposed architecture does not have this restrictions. A heterogeneous computation graph can be divided into computation threads which are then processed temporally to the reconfigurable processing array.

Pipelined configuration for commercial FPGAs has also been described [15]. To date, there is no mechanism present for control of the reconfiguration- and data stream with respect to the hardware virtualization.

The outline of the paper is as follows: In the next section the microarchitecture of the hardware model is introduced. Section 3 describes the descriptor structure and explains the hardware virtualization concept with the configuration technique in more detail. Section 4 introduces the architecture components and the datapath structure. In section 5 some application examples and performance results are given. Section 6 discusses future directions for programming the reconfigurable architecture and implementing the reconfigurable processing cell array in a processor architecture. Some concluding remarks are given in section 7.

2 Architecture Model

The architecture allows the virtualization of reconfigurable computing resources by dividing an application up into several computation threads and time-multiplexing the threads onto available physical hardware.

2.1 Hardware Overview

The microarchitecture consists of a configuration manager and an array of configurable coarse-grained processing cells linked to each other via broadcast- and pipelined data buses. It is fragmented into four parallel stripes which can be configured in parallel via descriptor buses. Figure 1 shows a cluster with overall 16 processing cells.

Every stripe has available an independent $256 * 48$ bit dual port scratch-pad memory and a $64 * 24$ bit descriptor memory. In order to adjust configuration cycles, three pipeline registers for every stripe are implemented.

The configuration manager operates as a static microcoded scheduler. It controls the hardware virtualization process, initiating descriptors and handles the data from the I/O buses. Additionally, it manages four independent data se-

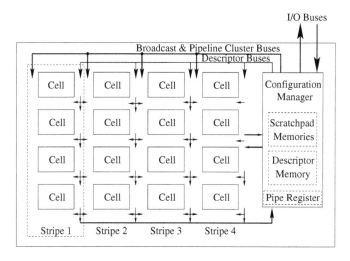

Fig. 1. The overall structure of a cluster with the configuration manager and 16 processing cells. The configuration manager includes the dual port scratch-pad memories, the descriptor memory and the pipeline register files.

quencer units for the local scratch-pad memories. If hardware virtualization is needed, the configuration manager controls the data feedback of partial results.

In the following, the descriptor structure is introduced before the configuration concept and the architectural details will be explained.

3   Descriptor Structure

Descriptors are templates for configuration which are decoded in a processing cell similar to an instruction operation-code in a conventional processor architecture. They contain the specification for the configuration process and the processing cell function. The descriptor operation code comprises a descriptor identification bit, a 10 bit function and data source entry and 13 bits of cell configuration data. Figure 2a) shows the overall descriptor organization.

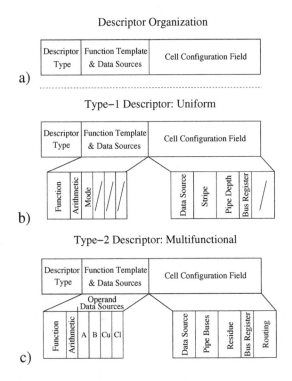

Fig. 2. An illustration of the descriptor organization is shown in 2a). The 24 bit descriptor body includes the descriptor identification bit, a function and data source entry and a cell configuration field for the configuration process. Figure 2b) shows the type-1 uniform descriptor. The crossed entries are not used. Figure 2c) shows the type-2 multifunctional descriptor. There is an operand data source selection field for the broadcast data buses A, B and the pipeline cluster buses Cu, Cl. Cu and Cl means the upper and lower half of the 48 bit pipeline bus C.

There is a uniform and a multifunctional descriptor. The uniform descriptor can be used to construct simple feed-forward pipelines. It saves configuration memory since several processing cells can be configured with only a single descriptor. The multifunctional descriptor allows the construction of heterogeneous computation graphs and more complex functions from several processing cells. The descriptor structures are shown in Figs. 2b) and c).

The function and data source entry of the uniform descriptor is constructed as follows:

- micro-code address for the processing cell configuration (Function),
- signed/unsigned arithmetic (Arithmetic),
- operating width declaration ; 48- or two 24 bit processing in parallel (Mode).

The remaining entries are not used. The cell configuration field holds the specification for the configuration process. It includes the:

- broadcast data bus selection (Data Source),
- stripe number specification (Stripe),
- number of cells to be configured (Pipe Depth),
- assignment of a local processing cell register (Bus Register).

The following entry is not used. The function and data source entry of the multifunctional descriptor is constructed as follows:

- micro-code address for the processing cell configuration (Function),
- signed/unsigned arithmetic (Arithmetic),
- specification of the operand data sources (A,B,Cu,Cl).

The cell configuration field entry includes the:

- broadcast data bus selection (Data Source),
- pipelined data bus specification (Pipe Buses),
- address for the cell to be configured (Residue),
- assignment of a local processing cell register (Bus Register),
- data path routing code (Routing).

3.1   Configuration Execution and Virtualization

The configuration technique via descriptors is accomplished through a pipelined self-configuration process which is based on a local run-time reconfiguration (RTR) concept [12]. A descriptor circulates through the stripe and configures the processing cells. Figure 3 shows the configuration of one stripe in four clock cycles. The configuration process is discriminate with respect to the proposed descriptor types:

- A type-1 uniform descriptor is able to configure several processing cells with a single function. It circulates like a token through the stripe and allows concurrent configuration and calculation.

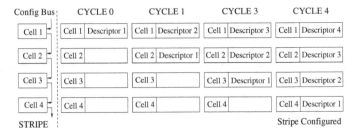

Fig. 3. Principle of the pipelined configuration process. The figure shows the configuration of a stripe with four processing cells. In this example the stripe is fully configured at the fourth clock cycle.

- A type-2 multifunctional descriptor is able to configure only one dedicated processing cell. To configure a stripe, several configuration cycles are needed.

The architecture allows pipeline-oriented execution controlled through a data-stationary pipeline control mechanism [13]. The concept allows to create high speed pipelines due to the lack of a central control unit and small decoder overhead [5]. The architecture is able to map an application of any size to the given physical resources. The fixed resource limitations are overcome by virtualizing the computational, communication and memory resources of the reconfigurable hardware. A large application can be divided into computation threads and mapped onto a small physical pipeline. Computation threads consists of short sequences of one or more descriptors that configure the processing cells by Time Division Multiple Access (TDMA). The architecture is not limited to implementing homogeneous computations. A multifunctional pipeline composed of several descriptors can be constructed which approve different computations at different pipeline stages on the parallel realized stripes.

The configuration manager allows partial configuration while other processing cells are calculating. It assists configuration interleaving and miscellaneous configuration with both descriptor types. Intermediate results remain stored in the appropriate pipeline stages. There is no need for supplemental storage.

4   Architecture Components

The reconfigurable architecture consists of several components for processing and controlling the datapath and the configuration process.

4.1   Processing Cell Structure

A processing cell, shown in Fig. 4, comprises an Arithmetic Logic Unit (ALU), a descriptor controller which manages the self-configuration process and a 24 bit local register.

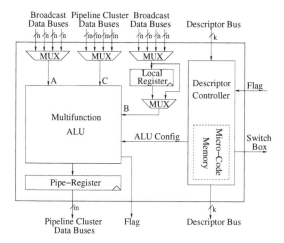

Fig. 4. The overall processing cell structure with a multifunctional ALU, a descriptor controller unit and a local processing cell register. The register can be used to store coefficients during the configuration process.

One Operand	Two Operand	Three Operand	Four Operand
– Barrelshift (48 Bit)	– 48/24|24 Bit Add/Sub/Mul– (signed/unsigned) – Boolean – Average – Absolute – Min/Max	– 24 Bit add/sub – MAC – MAC (symmetrical) – Absolute– Difference	– 24 Bit add/sub – Real Butterfly (24 Bit)

Fig. 5. Overview of the most important ALU functions with different operands. The expression 24|24 marks two 24 bit parallel computations in one processing cell.

4.2   Multifunction ALU

The processing cell is comprised of a multifunctional 48 bit fixed-point ALU with three source buses and one destination bus. The ALU consists of a 24 bit signed/unsigned multiplier which is separable into two independent 12 bit multiplier units. There are two 24 bit adders with saturation logic implemented. The adders are cascadable via a carry line to a 48 bit adder unit. A 24 bit word is chosen since many algorithms in the target application fields need 12 to 24 bit processing [14].

The ALU provides a variety of complex functions with a different number of operands which will be typically used in the application domains. It supports multiply and accumulate (MAC), absolute and average value, absolute differences, boolean functions and the real-valued butterfly calculation. In addition, there is a 48 bit barrel shift- and a min/max select-unit. Figure 5 gives an overview of the ALU functions. The ALU has a flag output which indicates saturation. The flag assigns the following processing cells in the pipeline either to work on, or to pass on partial data.

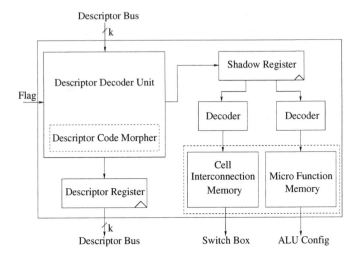

Fig. 6. The descriptor controller unit includes the descriptor decoder with the code-morpher, a shadow register which holds the descriptor opcode and the interconnection and function micro-code memories. The descriptor code-morpher unit modifies the cell configuration field when passing a processing cell.

4.3   Descriptor Controller and Configuration

Every processing cell consists of a descriptor controller unit. It includes a descriptor decoder with a code-morpher, a shadow register which contains the descriptor opcode and a micro-code memory for the function- and interconnection codes. Figure 6 shows the internal structure. The descriptor controller performs the following configuration tasks:

1. checking the descriptor type and the cell configuration field,
2. storing the descriptor in the shadow register according to the descriptor type,
3. decoding the descriptor function- and interconnection entry,
4. updating the pipe depth/residue entry in the cell configuration field via the descriptor code-morpher to indicate that the processing cell has been passed.

Figure 7 shows the configuration process of both descriptor types via a flow chart.

4.4   Datapath Composition and Routing

The processing cells in a cluster are connected via 48 bit pipelined data buses. In order to broadcast data simultaneously to the processing cells, four independent 24 bit broadcast data buses for every stripe are implemented. Figure 8 shows the cluster data path structure. For high routing flexibility, the architecture has a switch matrix based on switch-boxes, which allows flexible horizontal and vertical point to point connections among processing cells. The switch-box allows to split the pipelined data buses via multiplexer in two equivalent halves due to the 24 bit parallel computation in a processing cell.

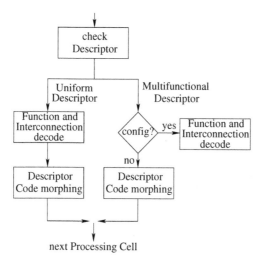

Fig. 7. Illustration of the descriptor controller tasks of both descriptor types during the configuration process.

5   Applications and Performance

In order to analyze the hardware virtualization concept and the flexibility of the reconfigurable processing array, it is necessary to map some "hand-compiled" applications.

At first, a filter application example and then more complex structures will be mapped for demonstration.

5.1   Stream-Based Application Example

A Finite Impulse Response (FIR) filter is mapped where the architecture takes advantage of the regular nature of the computation [11]. The convolution sum for an N-tap FIR filter is defined as:

$$y(i) = \sum_{k=0}^{N-1} h(k)x(i - k) \tag{1}$$

where $h(x)$ denotes the filter coefficients and $x(i - k)$ the input samples. Figure 9 shows a systolic realization form which is practically for mapping to the architecture. To illustrate the flexibility of the datapath network, a sixteen tap 24 bit systolic FIR-filter on a cluster is mapped. The filter coefficients are situated in the scratch-pad memories while the samples are on the I/O Bus. To map the FIR-filter, the configuration manager needs to address four uniform MAC descriptors in parallel. Additionally, it has to control the data sequencer units to make the FIR-filter coefficients available. The application uses two broadcast data buses of every stripe to get the samples and filter coefficients.

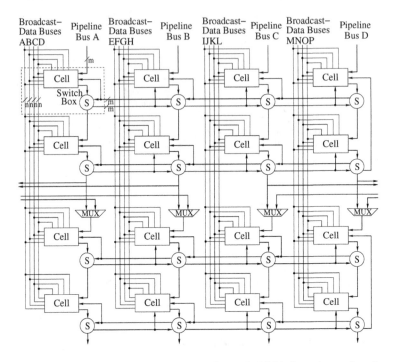

Fig. 8. An illustration of the cluster data paths with 24 bit broadcast data buses, 48 bit pipelined data buses and the switch-box units S. Multiplexers in the middle of every stripe may split the cluster in two equivalent halves to better exploit the processing cell array. The descriptor buses for configuration have been omitted for clarity.

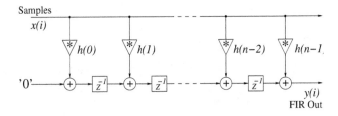

Fig. 9. Systolic dataflow graph for a N-tap systolic FIR-filter realization. $h(x)$ represents the filter coefficients while z^{-1} denotes the delay elements.

In the application, the filter calculation and the configuration process with the uniform MAC descriptor start simultaneously. This results in a configuration time of zero. During the configuration process, the filter coefficient data is stored in the local processing cell register. The filter coefficients reside in the local processing cells for the whole filter process.

When the processing cells are not able to map the whole filter length, the configuration manager works in place by feeding back the partial filter results. In this case, additional uniform MAC descriptors are needed for calculation.

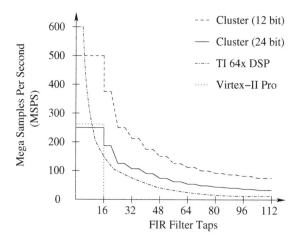

Fig. 10. Performance comparison of a systolic FIR-filter realization with 12- and 24 bit filter coefficients on a cluster with 16 processing cells compared to a TI64x DSP and a Xilinx Virtex-Pro FPGA with 16 embedded multipliers.

To be able to compare the architecture with other architectures, a VHDL description of a cluster with sixteen processing cells is synthesized. The underlying process was a 0.18 micron CMOS-process based on the UMC library. A first speed grade estimation gave about 250 MHz clock frequency. Figure 10 shows the performance of the architecture with different filter lengths. As shown, an FIR-filter with less than 16 taps runs at the full clock rate of 250 MHz. Larger filters demonstrate a graceful degradation of performance due to the need of TDMA processing. The specific performance reduction in Fig. 10 results from the data path structure shown in Fig. 8. The architecture can process two separate FIR-filter channels with 12 bit filter coefficients in a single processing cell. This results doubles the performance.

A cluster outperforms the Texas Instruments TMS320C64x, a commercial DSP that runs at 600 MHz and contains four parallel 16 ∗ 16 bit integer multipliers, on filter larger than a few taps [16]. For filters with small numbers of taps, the high clock frequency of this device yields extremely high performance. This performance decays rapidly with an increasing number of taps due to the presence of only four parallel multipliers. The proposed architecture exhibits similar the same degradations of performance as the DSP when hardware virtualization is needed. Compared to a Xilinx Virtex-II Pro FIR pipeline realization using 16 parallel embedded 16 bit multipliers and 268 MHz clock frequency, nearly the same performance is expected when the filter length will not exceed 16 taps [17]. Filter with more than 16 taps are only feasible with additional hardware.

5.2 Virtualization Example

A 24 bit implementation of a typical sub-system found in wide band programmable modulator ASICs is illustrated [18]. It is composed of a complex systolic

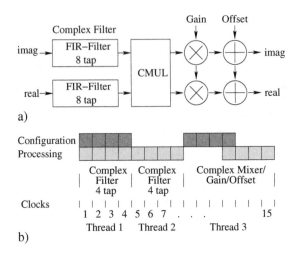

a)

b)

Fig. 11. Illustration of a virtualization process with three computation threads. The example maps an 8 tap complex filter, a complex mixer and a gain and offset calculation onto two parallel stripes. The figure illustrates the partially overlapped configuration and calculation cycles. During the configuration of the complex mixer and the gain and offset calculation structure, the 8 tap FIR-filter results must be stored in the pipeline register files.

FIR-filter realization, a complex multiplier/mixer structure and a final gain and offset calculation unit. Figure 11 a) shows the structure. The application is mapped onto two parallel stripes. For this purpose, the sub-system is divided into three computation threads which are mapped temporally to the processing cells. The execution comprices three tasks:

- calculating the complex FIR-filter with the first four FIR-filter coefficients,
- calculating the filter with the second four filter coefficients and
- performing the complex multiplication and the gain and offset calculation.

Figure 11 b) illustrates the allocation of the configuration and calculation cycles. In order to map the complex FIR-filter, two uniform MAC descriptor are required. To assemble the complex multiplication in parallel, two MULTIPLIER and two MULTIPLIER/ADD multifunctional descriptors for every stripe are needed. The gain and offset calculation needs two multifunctional MULTIPLIER and ADDER descriptors, respectively. To map the whole sub-system, 10 descriptors are needed. The configuration manager feeds back the partial results after one thread is calculated. It controls the data sequencer of the scratch-pad memories to provide the coefficients.

The latency time ($T_{Latency}$) to process the sub-system is composed of the number of process threads, the configuration cycles and the pipeline latency. The time required to process a computation is:

$$T_{Latency} = [K(N + (C - 1))]T \qquad (2)$$

where K is the number of threads, N is the number of pipeline stages, C is the configuration cycles and T is the time for one pipeline clock cycle.

The complex FIR-filter is realized by two uniform MAC descriptors which have an overlapped configuration and calculation time. The number of clock cycles is $2(4 + 0) = 8$. The number of clock cycles needed to configure and compute the complex multiplication and the gain and offset calculation is $1(4 + 3) = 7$. The whole sub-system can be calculate in effective 15 clock cycles. The application only needs three configuration cycles which results in 20 % configuration overhead for this application example. Due to the low configuration time overhead, the reconfigurable architecture can achieve high performance when hardware virtualization is needed.

6   Future Directions

The most important open question is how to incorporate the reconfigurable architecture into a larger processing system with a conventional ISA processor architecture. One approach is to treat the proposed reconfigurable architecture as a co-processor. Another more refined way is an implementation in a dedicated heterogenous processor architecture which can better exploit the high parallelism of the reconfigurable processing array.

In such a system, several different resource units and a general purpose processor operate as dedicated functional units controlled by a specialized Micro-Task Controller unit (MTC). The general purpose processor may work synchronously in dedicated time slots or asynchronously to the rest of the processing system. Such an implementation would significantly increase the application domain. The architecture could be used for both general processing as well as computationally intensive applications, such as digital signal processing in high speed digital communication engineering and multimedia video- and audio applications.

The status of the project is as follows: The reconfigurable architecture model with two clusters in VHDL has been implemented and the functionality has been verified. Currently, a prototype is being developed and mapped onto a UMC standard-cell 0.18 micron 6 layer CMOS process.

The next step would be to develop and implement the reconfigurable architecture in the heterogenous processor architecture with appropriate processing resources, the design of the micro-task controller unit and the interconnection structure.

The next challenge is the programming of the reconfigurable architecture. A visual programming language like simulink [19] may help to construct applications in graphical form. The advantages of such a description are as follow:

- it is natural for digital signal processing,
- a maximum of parallelism is possible,
- it is modular and hierarchical,
- the same description can be used for simulation and implementation.

For this purpose, a library is currently designed which includes dedicated function blocks for the target application fields. Additional, an add-on tool for simulink is established which converts the applications automatically into several computation threads which are then translated into a set of descriptors.

7   Conclusions

In this paper, a novel reconfigurable architecture model for computationally intensive applications in wireless communication environments and multimedia video- and audio streaming applications was presented. The architecture features performance and application flexibility and allows run-time- and partial reconfiguration. It is capable to virtualize computing resources by partitioning an application into computation threads which are then sequentially mapped and executed onto available physical hardware. According to application requirements, computation threads can be mapped and processed in a spatial and temporal manner.

The configuration technique is based on a pipelined self-configuration process with configuration templates, called descriptors. The configuration comprises of two descriptor types: an uniform descriptor with overlapped configuration and calculation time for simple feed-forward pipelines and a multifunctional descriptor to map more complex structures.

The proposed reconfigurable architecture is a new class of device with a higher computational density then FPGAs and some novel forms of flexibility. It approves a library-based design approach which may reduce the developing-time and cost without the need of a synthesis tool.

References

1. A. DeHon: Reconfigurable Architectures for General-Purpose Computing. MIT Artificial Intelligence Laboratory Report No.1586, Oct. 1996
2. F. Mayer-Lindenberg: A Universal Architecture for Parallel Embedded Systems. Proc. of the International Conference on Parallel and Distributed Processing Techniques and Applications PDPTA'98, vol. iii pp. 1497-1503, Las Vegas, Jul. 1998
3. F. Mayer-Lindenberg: Crossbar Design for a Super FPGA Architecture. International Conference on Parallel Architectures and Compilation Techniques PACT'98, pp. 29-33, Paris, Oct. 1998
4. J. D. Hadley and B. L. Hutchings: Design Methodologies for Partially Reconfigured Systems. IEEE Symposium on FPGAs for Custom Computing Machines, pp. 78-84, Los Alamitos, California, Apr. 1995. IEEE Computer Society
5. R. Ernst: Long Pipelines in Single-Chip Digital Signal Processors-Concepts and Case Study, IEEE Transactions on Circuits an System, vol. 38, NO.1, Jan. 1991
6. A. Pelg, S. J. Wilkie U. Weiser: Intel MMX for multimedia PC's. Communications of the ACM, 40(1):24-38, 1997
7. X.P. Ling and H. Amano: WASMII: a Data Driven Computer on a Virtual Hardware. Proceedings IEEE Workshop on FPGA's for Custom Computing Machines FCCM, Apr. 1993

8. G. Brebner: The Shapable Logic Unit: A Paradigm for virtual Hardware. Proceedings of the 5th IEEE Symposium on FPGA for Custom Computing Machines FCCM'97, pages 77-86, Apr. 1997
9. S. Goldstein, H. Schmit, M. Moe, M. Budiu, S. Cadambi: PipeRench: a Coprocessor for streaming Multimedia Acceleration. Proceedings of the 26th International Symposium on Computer Architecture ISCA'99, pages 28-39, May 1999
10. Y. Chou, P. Pillai, H. Schmit, J. Paul Shen: PipeRench: Implementation of the Instruction Path Coprocessor. IEEE/ACM International Symposium on Microarchitecture (Micro-33), pp. 147-158, Dec. 2000
11. H. T. Kung: Why systolic architectures?. IEEE Computer, pages 37-45, Jan. 1982
12. S. Trimmberger D. Carberry, A. Johnosn, and J. Wong: Time Multiplexed FPGA. Proceedings of the IEEE Symposium on FPGAs for Custom Computing Machines, Apr. 1997
13. P. Kogge: The Architecture of Pipelined Computers, Hemisphere Publishing, 1981
14. R. Enzler and T. Sailer: Application Exploration Regarding a DPC Like Architecture. Technical Report, Electronics Lab, Swiss Federal Institute of Technology (ETH) Zürich, May 2000.
15. W. Luk, N. Shirazi, S. Guo, P. YK Cheung: Pipeline morphing and virtual pipelines. Field-Programmable Logic and Applications, London, England, Sep. 1997
16. Texas Instruments: TMS320C64x Technical Overview. Texas Instruments Inc, 2001
17. Xilinx Inc: "MAC-Based FIR Filter", Product Specification DS245, Nov. 2002
18. Intersil Semiconductor: HSP 50415 : Wideband Programmable Modulator (WPM). Product Description, Mar. 2000
19. Simulink: Dynamic System Simulation software , The MathWorks Inc., 1995

Reconfigurable Instruction-Level Parallel Processor Architecture

Toshiyuki Ito[1], Kentaro Ono[1], Mayumi Ichikawa[1],
Yuuichi Okuyama[2], and Kenichi Kuroda[1]

[1] The University of Aizu, Graduate School of Computer Science and Engineering
[2] NTT Network Innovation Laboratories

Abstract. This paper proposes an instruction-level parallel (ILP) processor with architecture reconfigurability. The processor can employ the optimal architecture to applications without loosing generality. Instruction-level parallelism is achieved by expanding the number of PUs depending on its load. Required features of reconfigurable hardware devices for such processors are discussed and the plastic cell architecture (PCA) is chosen as a target device for implementation of the ILP processor. Performance with reconfiguration overhead is measured and evaluated.

Keyword: dynamical reconfigurability, PCA, self-reconfigurability, VLIW, ILP Processor

1 Introduction

Today, most of multimedia applications are processed on general-purpose processors, that is, the von Neumann type processors. Although vast amount of computation and real time response are required for such multimedia applications, architecture of the general-purpose processors cannot be optimal to every application because of their generality requirements.

Pipeline hazards and memory-cpu bandwidth limitation have been problems on further performance improvement of general-purpose processors. In order to solve pipeline hazards, branch prediction and speculative execution were exploited. On the other hand, these technologies may cause complicated controls of pipelines and increase the number of pipeline stages, which can also cause performance deterioration. As to the bandwidth problem, miss hitting in cache memory access can be reduced by increasing cache memory capacity. As cache memories have regular structure and they can be easily allocated on chip area, large percentages of chip area of advanced processors are occupied by cache memories. Large cache memory size can reduce misses in cache memory accesses and accesses to low-speed main memories [1]. However, this increases critical path length and causes saturation of peak operation frequency. These kinds of technologies for high performance are based on a scheme of a single instruction stream but there arises limitation as mentioned above.

Another approach is multi-stream processing that executes multiple instructions simultaneously. This parallel stream architecture utilizes hardware re-

A. Omondi and S. Sedukhin (Eds.): ACSAC 2003, LNCS 2823, pp. 208–220, 2003.

sources efficiently and improves performance. In addition, it can reduce penalties due to miss hits in cache memory accesses and branch prediction errors. However, on this architecture, when only a single stream instruction is executed, unused hardware resources remain and they occupy chip area. Is there any way to achieve much higher performance of general-purpose processors with highly efficient hardware resource utilization?

In traditional single stream processing, deteriorating factors on performance depend on applications and the most optimal architecture is different in each application. If the architecture of the processor is flexible and adaptable to applications, general-purpose processors with very high performance can be realized [3]. Thus, reconfigurability is one of the answers for further high performance processors. However, it is required that reconfiguration overhead including time and hardware resources should not be serious obstacles for single stream processing. This kind of architecture is difficult for the traditional hardware devices. Here needs some reconfigurable devices.

In this paper, we will propose a single stream processor that can flexibly change its construction depending on applications. In the following chapters, requirements for the architecture and hardware devices will be discussed and implementation of the processor on the devices and its evaluation will be described.

2   Proposed Architecture

2.1   Basic Concept

In order to achieve high-speed single stream processing, an optimal architecture of PUs (PUs) and the most suitable number of registers should be determined beforehand. There are various functions in multi-media data processing and the most appropriate PU is different for each application. As the amount of transferred data among memories and registers varies depending on applications, the number of registers should be changed [1][2]. In addition, the number of PUs including an instruction decoder, a general-purpose arithmetic functional unit, and registers should be increased when executable instructions in parallel are given. By introducing these reconfigurable features, processing speed can be accelerated.

Reconfiguration functions need two phases, an initial configuration phase and a succeeding reconfiguration phase, for optimization. In the initial configuration phase, the minimal required arithmetic functional unit (AFU) and the number of registers are analyzed in order to estimate available hardware resources when compiling. The analysis specifies the AFU configuration with arithmetic functional modules (AFMs). In the reconfiguration phase, some hardware resources that are not loaded in the initial phase are added or modified. In this phase, PUs are increased as much as possible when instructions with high parallelism are given for simultaneous parallel execution. AFMs specific to applications can be also loaded.

2.2   Instruction Format

An instruction set similar to the very long instruction word (VLIW) is introduced to satisfy the above-mentioned features. The VLIW instruction set can simplify decoder circuits and control circuits because compilers generate executable instructions in parallel. In addition, a single word in VLIW consists of multiple instructions though the number of them is fixed. Parallelism is realized by distributing instructions in parallel. However, the instruction set employed in the proposed general-purpose single stream processor can have variable word length, which can change the degrees of parallelism depending on hardware resource utilization condition. The instruction word has a parallel-executable flag and a synchronization flag, and parallel-executable instructions are executed independently on the number of PUs. This scheme can realize our flexible parallel processing corresponding to parallelism in the instruction word. In addition, two or more instruction words can be combined for parallel stream processing in our proposal architecture.

2.3   Flow of Command Processing

The proposed processor is named instruction-level parallel (ILP) processor. Fig. 1 shows the required functions and architecture of the ILP processor. The processor consists of a program counter, an instruction memory, an instruction issue unit for instruction synchronization, instruction decoders, data registers, buffers, arithmetic function units, an I/O control unit, and a data memory. The following describes processing flow for VLIW-like instruction execution.

1. An instruction word is fetched from the instruction memory by a program counter.
2. The instruction issue unit specifies a parallel or a sequential instruction according to the header of the instruction and synchronizes instructions. It issues an instruction to an unused PU.
3. The PU decodes the instruction issued from the instruction issue unit.
4. Data in a data register is transferred to a specified AFM in the AFU.
5. Operation is executed in the AFM.
6. The processed data is stored in the data register from the AFM.

The configuration of AFMs and the number of registers are changeable depending on application. The number of the PUs consisting of AFU and registers can also be changed. Processing flows for addition or deletion of AFM and registers are listed as follows.

The Case for Registers and AFMs

1. In the initial phase, the optimal number of registers and the most appropriate AFMs are determined. Moreover, a necessary minimal AFMs and registers are beforehand arranged as a basic processing unit.

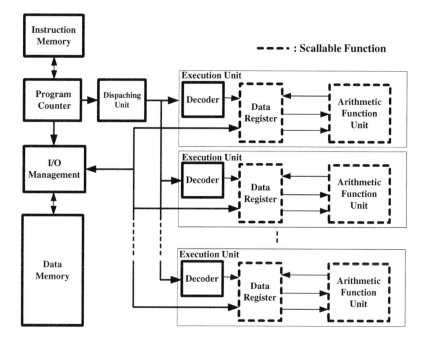

Fig. 1. Structure of Proposed ILP Processor

2. Operation starts in the basic unit with necessary minimum functions. The following processing is performed when the current AFU does not have required AFMs and/or registers (i.e., when the necessity for architecture extension is detected).
   (a) In the case of the expansion of the AFU, the empty region is checked. If there are enough regions for additional AFMs, the required AFMs will be added. Moreover, if there are not enough regions, the replacement with other AFMs will be performed. Even in such case, the minimal general-purpose AFMs, which keeps flexibility, is not changed.
   (b) In the case of registers, the increase in a register region is notified to a managing unit which manages the register region.

The Case of a Processing Unit

1. The necessary minimal architecture in the initial phase is allocated. That is, the number of PUs is 1.
2. Statistics of parallelism in instructions are taken while executing instructions.
   (a) When the current number of PUs is smaller than the degree of parallelism obtained by statistics, copy of the PU to the empty region is prepared. It is not copied, if there are not enough regions.
   (b) When the current number of PUs is larger than the degree of parallelism obtained by statistics, the PU is deleted and the region is released.

The mechanism of managing the region for architecture extension is assumed to exist already.

3   Requirements for Reconfigurable Architecture

The requirements of the device for our proposal architecture are following three.

(1) The device can expand the quantity of hardware resources.

(2) The device can allocate and free hardware resources dynamically, and has the management system of hardware resources.

(3) The device can communicate locally between functional units [5].

The item (1) means that the architecture does not need to change the data processing after expanding hardware resources. If hardware resources were not scalable, the architecture needed for each application would be inextensible. The item (2) corresponds to efficient utilization of hardware resources. Dynamic reconfiguration can construct PUs without stopping the whole system. Self-reconfiguration is preferable. This concept is that a system can reconfigure its function autonomously. The overhead of sel f-reconfiguration may become smaller than the overhead of the external reconfiguration equipped with the external system. The item (3) means that the load of communication control can be distributed. If the functional units communicated with the large-scale communication control system, the system would have a large communication load. On the other hand, when functional units communicate locally and mutually, the load of communication is small. Thus, a local communication control system is better than a l arge-scale communication control system.

4   Implementation

4.1   Requirements for Reconfigurable Devices

As a target device for implementation, Plastic Cell Architecture (PCA) is chosen. PCA is one of dynamically reconfigurable devices and its features meet some demands described in Chap. 3. PCA has a two-dimensional regular structure of unit cells called PCA cells. Each PCA cell consists of two parts, a Plastic Part (PP) and a Built-in Part (BP). The PP is a variable logic part, which is used as a set of functional circuits (hereafter they are called objects) or memory circuits (hereafter memory objects). The BP is a basic information processing part, which is used as functions of forwarding and writing data and so on. The PP and the BP of neighboring PCA cells are connected respectively. An object constructed on PPs can communicate with other objects [7][8].

PCA has two features, which are different from other existing reconfigurable architectures. One of them is dynamic reconfiguration. This feature means that objects and memory objects on PPs can reconfigure without stopping all the system. Another is self-reconfiguration. This feature means that objects and memory objects on PPs can reconfigure independently in parallel without external system's control. The BP has commands to realize self-reconfiguration.

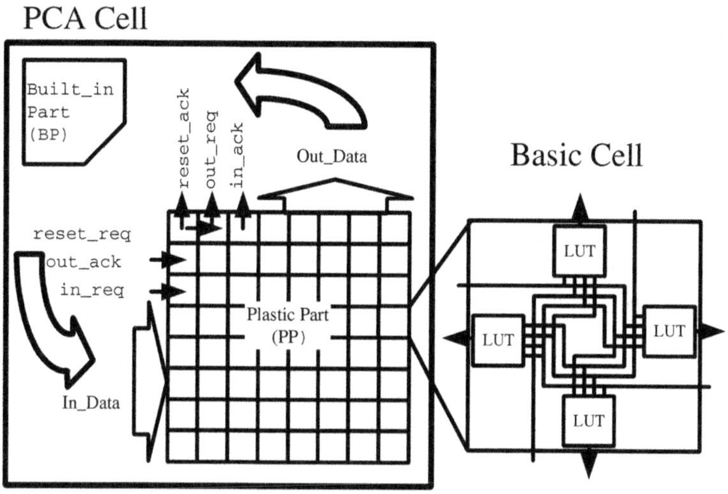

PCA Cell

Fig. 2. Structure of PCA cell on PCA-1 chip

These commands can reconfigure objects and rewrite data of memory objects independently. The self-reconfiguration can decrease overhead for intervening external processors, and can reconfigure objects and memory objects in parallel. Now, the concept of PCA has been already implemented as a real hardware chip, and the PCA prototype chip is called PCA-1 [6].

PCA can establish and delete communicating routes dynamically using BP internal commands (shown in Table 1). The dynamic routing can decrease the wiring area and achieve minimum route wiring by time-sharing routing [9].

Table 1. BP Command table on PCA-1 chip

Instruction	Code	Function
clear	0xxxx	route clear
open	1000x	connect to PP to BP
close	1001x	disconnect from PP
co	10100	read configration of PCA cell
coci	10101	copy functional circuit
ci/m	10110	copy data of memory on PCA cell
ci/f	10111	writedata of function circuit on PCA cell
west	11000	set route to west
north	11001	set route to north
east	11010	set route to east
south	11011	set route to south
pp-out	111xx	set route to PP

4.2   Functions and Structure for ILP Processor on PCA

Possible Functions and Limitations

An instruction sequencer and PUs consisting of scalable registers and functional units are implemented. Data is treated as a stream with 4-bit width because input and output data from memory modules on PCA-1 is 4-bit-width streams. Stream instructions are fetched in sequence. However, they are regarded to be fetched nearly in parallel like in VLIW because the execution time for each instruction is much larger as compared with instruction fetch time.

There are two kinds of instructions: instructions executed in sequence and those in parallel. We need to guarantee synchronization among these instructions, so the instructions should have an indicator that shows the instruction can be executed in parallel or in sequence (P/S). Sequential type instructions have to wait until the previous instruction completion. Parallel type instructions are distributed to unused PUs.

In this paper, we do not implement an access manager for scalable registers, a reconfiguration detector of functional units and a statistic analyzer of instruction parallelism.

Scalability on PCA

The number of functional units and registers should be scalable on the proposed architecture. Using the dynamical routing function of PCA, we can dynamically create and delete paths to communicate between circuits and need not to prepare permanent fixed paths [9]. The fine-grained uniform structure of PCA makes it easy to increase and decrease functional units and memory objects in a scalably fashion.

The Instruction Set

An instruction set for the proposed ILP processor consists of three fields: I/O instructions, arithmetic instructions and the next instruction address as shown in Fig. 3 [10].

- I/O Instructions indicate input and output data transfer between PCA and an outside system to communicate configuration information and data in registers.
- Arithmetic Instructions indicate arithmetic operations in PUs.
- Next Instruction Address indicates next instruction address to be processed.

Figure 4 shows an instruction including complex arithmetic operations like VLIW format, and it contains P/S indicator, operation type and register address. The operation type and register address are indicated as dynamic routing information to an objective operator or a register. We adopt indirect addressing for reducing routing information. The indirect addressing is realized by preparing some common routing information registers. The obtained routing is combination of the route in the register and the routing information in the instruction set.

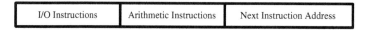

Fig. 3. Instruction set

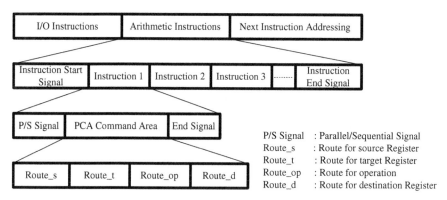

Fig. 4. Hierarchy of an instruction set for arithmetic operation

Implementation of ILP Processor on PCA

The proposed processor was designed on PCA. The whole structure of the processor is shown in Fig. 5. [10]

(1) Instruction sequencer:

An instruction sequencer takes out an instruction from instruction memories. Address information is extracted from the instruction, and the sequencer outputs the remaining commands to an I/O decoding unit. The instruction sequencer accesses a memory using the extracted address information.

(2) I/O instruction decode unit (I/O IDU):

First, the instruction sequencer extracts the I/O instructions from the input instruction. The extracted I/O instruction consists of some instructions of read/store and reconfiguration data, of circuits for optimization. After processing finishes, The I/O instruction decode unit outputs an arithmetic instruction to an instruction issue unit.

(3) The instruction Issue unit (IIU):

The unit has two jobs. One is a management of a parallel / sequential signal, another is management of instruction issue timing.

The unit extracts a P/S indicator from inputted arithmetic instructions, and judges whether the instructions should be executed in parallel, or in sequence. In addition, the IIU manages utilization of a PU, and judges instruction dispatching or waiting. After processing, it outputs instruction without the P/S indicator to a PU.

The unit manages instruction issue timing. The management function consists of a function to manage number of PUs and issued instructions. The two number maximum values are equaled. When IIU issues instruction to PU, the number of issued instruction is increased. And when IIU receives processing

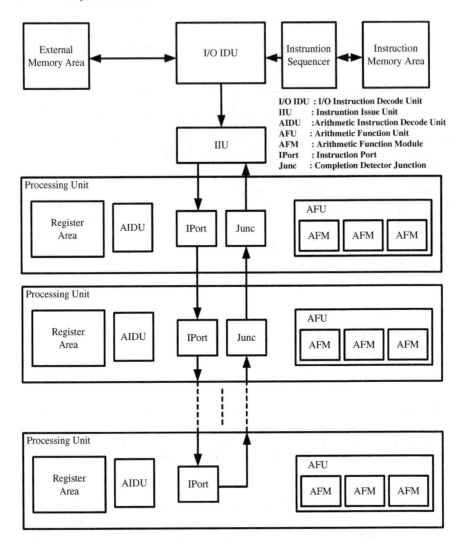

Fig. 5. Structure of ILP Processor on PCA

completion signal from PU, the number of issued instruction is reduced. If the number of PUs equals the number of issued instructions, the IIU prohibits issuing instructions to PUs.

(4) Processing unit:

After an instruction is inputted into an Instruction Port (Iport), the Iport passes the following instruction to the next PU until processing completion. The inputted instruction is decoded in Arithmetic Instruction Decode Unit (AIDU). According to decoded instruction, operand data is read out from an indicated register (or registers in two operands case) and stored in the buffer for a AFU. Subsequently, one of AFMs is chosen, and the content of a buffer is calculated.

The result is stored in a specified destination register. When PU's processing completes, a completion detector junction (Junc) issues a processing completion signal to IIU. After the Junc issued a processing completion, the Iport permits next instruction acceptance.

4.3   Simulation and Result

We selected an IIU and a PU from the various kinds of units described in the previous sections, implemented them on PCA, and simulated their behavior. As a simplified AFM, we used a through circuit, which outputs input data as it is without any modification, and simulated the forwarding operation between two registers. Tables 2, 3 and 4 show circuit sizes on PCA-1 chips, configuration time and the processing time for a single instruction word, respectively. Processing time uses the measurement time using PCA SIM II, a device simulator for PCA-1, on a computer of PentiumW 2GHz and WindowsXP.

Table 2 shows that the AIDU and the Iport unit occupy rather a larger number of cells compared to others. We need to improve them to optimize allocation of all circuits. Figure 6 shows that the configuration time takes 2.7 times longer than that of processing, because this short processing time is due to the simple through circuit as the AFM. The configuration time must be relatively smaller than processing time when the calculation is realistically complicated. As a realistic example, we will take a 4-bit-serial 16-bit-multiplier, which executes 128 vector operations with an instruction in 4.283 (msec). If we adopt the multiplier

Table 2. Circuit size on PCA-1 chip

Name of Functional Unit		Size (the number of PCA cells)	Rate
PU	AIDU	37	0.46
	Iport	22	0.27
	AFU	1	0.01
	Junc	2	0.03
	Refister Area	19	0.23
	Sum	81	100
IIU	Sum	8	100

Table 3. Configuration time

Name of Functional Unit	Time(msec)
Processing unit	1.162
IIU	0.145

Table 4. Processing time for one operation

	Time(msec)
Operation execution time in Processing unit	0.423

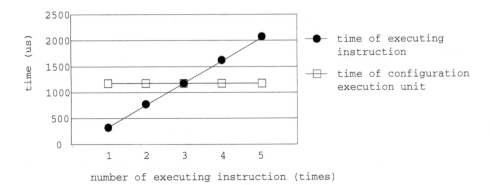

Fig. 6. Comparison of processing unit composition time and command processing speed

as a part of AFM in the ILP processor, an instruction execution time is about 4.5 (msec), and the PU configuration time is about 1.5 (msec). Thus, PU configuration time is very small compared with the whole system execution time. Moreover the configuration time can be reduced by parallel configuration.

A relation between processing time for 100 instructions and the number of PUs are shown in Fig. 7. The theoretical values are also listed. The measurement environment used PCA-1 board (The four PUs can operate on one board), and used the computer of PentiumIII and Windows2000 for input-and-output control of PCA-1 board. The theoretical values define the processing time of one PU divided by the number of PUs. The measurements values are very close to the

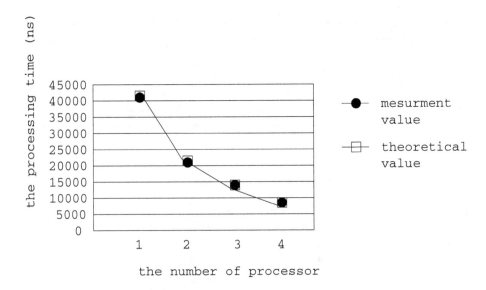

Fig. 7. Comparison of the degree of parallelism and Instruction processing speed

theoretical ones. Thus, this shows that communication overheads don't influence whole system operation, and that a degree increase of PU parallelism improves the processing speed.

5   Conclusion

An instruction-level parallel (ILP) processor with architecture reconfigurability was proposed. The processor can employ the optimal architecture for applications without loosing generality. Instruction-level parallelism was achieved by expanding the number of PUs depending on its load. Required features of reconfigurable hardware devices for such processors were discussed and the plastic cell architecture (PCA) was chosen as a target device for implementation of the processor. In implementation, an IIU and a PU were designed. In the PU, a simple through circuit was used as an AFM. Reconfiguration overhead were measured and evaluated. Assuming the architecture adopts realistic processing time, configuration time can be ignored. The implemented processor shows basic behavior of the ILP processor with reconfigurability.

Acknowledgement

The authors would like to thank Mr. Tsunemichi Shiozawa in NTT Network Innovation Lab. for his useful discussions about circuit implementation and performance evaluation of PCA-1 chip. They also appreciate Mr. Akira Nagoya, other stuff in NTT labs., Prof. Kiyoshi Oguri in Nagasaki University for their fruitful discussion and Prof. Junji Kitamichi for his helpful advices.

References

1. Y. Wu, R. Racvic, L.-L. Chen, C.-C. Miao, G. Chrysos and J. Fang, "Compiler Managed Micro-cache Bypassing for High Performance EPIC Processors", Int. Sym. on Micro architecture (Micro-35), pp. 134-145,(2002).
2. S.-K. Hsu, S.-L. Lu, S.-C. Lai, R. Krishnamurthy and K. Lai, "Dynamic Addressing Memory Arrays with Physical Locaity", Int. Sym. on Micro architecture (Micro-35), pp.161-170,(2002).
3. J.Borns and J.-L. Gaudiot, "SMT Layout Overhead and Scalability", IEEE Trans. on Prallel, and Distributed Systems, Vol. 13, No. 2, pp.142-155, (2002).
4. Y. Nakane, K. Nagami, T. Shiozawa, N. Imligy, A. Nagoya and K. Oguri, "Runtime Resource Management for the Dynamically Self-Reconfigurable Architecture PCA", Proc. on ERSA2001, pp67-72,(2001).
5. J.- E. Smith, "Instruction-Level Distributed Processing", IEEE Computer, pp.59-65, April, (2001).
6. H. Ito, K. Oguri, R. Konishi, and H. Nakada, "PCA Chip: Asynchronous Design of Dynamically Reconfigurable Logic LSI." Technical Report of IEICE,CPSY99-92, pp.65-72,(1999). (in Japanese)
7. H. Ito, R. Konishi, H. Nakada, and K. Oguri, "Dynamically Reconfigurable Logic LSI - PCA-1." Technical Report of IEICE, pp.9-16,ED2000-111, (2000). (in Japanese)

8. T. Shiozawa, K. Nagami, N. Imlig, and R. Konishi, "Applications and Design Environment for PCA", NTT Group's Research and Development Activities Vol. 49, No. 9, pp.527-536, 2000. (in Japanese)
9. N. Imlig, T. Shiozawa, K. Nagami, and K. Oguri, "Communicating Logic: Digital Circuit Compilation for the PCA Architecture", DA Symposium'99, pp101-pp.106, (1999).
10. M. Ichikawa, K. Ono, Y. Okuyama, and K. Kuroda, "A Reconfigurable and Stream-Oriented Vector Processor for Plastic Cell Architecture " Proc. 19th PERTHENON Workshop, pp. 3-12 (2001). (in Japanese)

Mapping Applications
to a Coarse Grain Reconfigurable System

Yuanqing Guo, Gerard J.M. Smit, Hajo Broersma,
Michèl A.J. Rosien, and Paul M. Heysters

University of Twente,
Faculty of Electrical Engineering, Mathematics and Computer Science,
P.O. Box 217, 7500AE Enschede, The Netherlands,
{yguo,smit,broersma,rosien,heysters}@cs.utwente.nl,
Phone: +31 53 4894178, Fax: +31 53 4894590

Abstract. This paper introduces a method which can be used to map applications written in a high level source language program, like C, to a coarse grain reconfigurable architecture, MONTIUM. The source code is first translated into a control dataflow graph. Then after applying graph clustering, scheduling and allocation on this control dataflow graph, it can be mapped onto the target architecture. The clustering and allocation algorithm are presented in detail. High performance and low power consumption are achieved by exploiting maximum parallelism and locality of reference respectively. Using our mapping method, the flexibility of the MONTIUM architecture can be exploited.

1 Introduction

In the CHAMELEON/GECKO[1] project we are designing a heterogeneous reconfigurable System-On-Chip (SoC) [12] (see Fig. 1). This SoC contains a general-purpose processor (ARM core), a bit-level reconfigurable part (FPGA) and several word-level reconfigurable parts (MONTIUM tiles; see Section 2). We believe that in future 3G/4G terminals heterogeneous reconfigurable architectures are needed. The main reason is that the efficiency (in terms of performance or energy) of the system can be improved significantly by mapping application tasks (or kernels) onto the most suitable processing entity.

The objective of this paper is to show that a design method can be used to map processes, written in a high level language, to a reconfigurable platform. The methods can be used to optimize the system with respect to certain criteria e.g. energy efficiency or execution speed.

[1] This research is supported by PROGram for Research on Embedded Systems & Software (PROGRESS) of the Netherlands Organization for Scientific Research NWO, the Dutch Ministry of Economic Affairs and the technology foundation STW.

A. Omondi and S. Sedukhin (Eds.): ACSAC 2003, LNCS 2823, pp. 221–235, 2003.

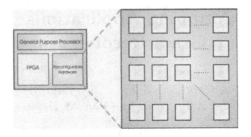

Fig. 1. CHAMELEON heterogeneous SoC architecture

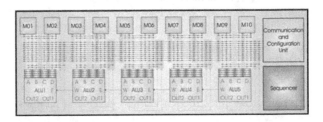

Fig. 2. MONTIUM processor tile

2   The Target Architecture: MONTIUM

In this section we give a brief overview of the MONTIUM architecture, because this architecture led to the research questions and the algorithms presented in this paper. Fig. 2 depicts a single MONTIUM processor tile. The hardware organization within a tile is very regular and resembles a very long instruction word (VLIW) architecture. The five identical arithmetic and logic units (ALU1···ALU5) in a tile can exploit spatial concurrency to enhance performance. This parallelism demands a very high memory bandwidth, which is obtained by having 10 local memories (M01···M10) in parallel. The small local memories are also motivated by the locality of reference principle. The ALU input registers provide an even more local level of storage. Locality of reference is one of the guiding principles applied to obtain energy-efficiency in the MONTIUM. A vertical segment that contains one ALU together with its associated input register files, a part of the interconnect and two local memories is called a processing part (PP). The five processing parts together are called the processing part array (PPA). A relatively simple sequencer controls the entire PPA. The communication and configuration unit (CCU) implements the interface with the world outside the tile. The MONTIUM has a datapath width of 16-bits and supports both integer and fixed-point arithmetic. Each local SRAM is 16-bit wide and has a depth of 512 positions, which adds up to a storage capacity of 8 Kbit per local memory. A memory has only a single address port that is used for both reading and writing. A reconfigurable address generation unit (AGU) accompanies each memory. The AGU contains an address register that can be modified using base and modify registers.

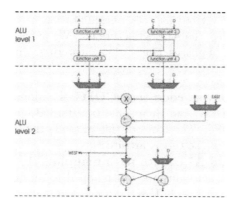

Fig. 3. MONTIUM ALU

The configuration of the interconnect can change every clock cycle. There are ten busses that are used for inter-PPA communication. Note that the span of these busses is only the PPA within a single tile. The CCU is also connected to the global busses. The CCU uses the global busses to access the local memories and to handle data in streaming algorithms. Communication within a PP uses the more energy-efficient local busses. A single ALU has four 16-bit inputs. Each input has a private input register file that can store up to four operands. The input register file cannot be bypassed, i.e., an operand is always read from an input register. Input registers can be written by various sources via a flexible interconnect. An ALU has two 16-bit outputs, which are connected to the interconnect. The ALU is entirely combinatorial and consequentially there are no pipeline registers within the ALU. The diagram of the MONTIUM ALU in Fig. 3 identifies two different levels in the ALU. Level 1 contains four function units. A function unit implements the general arithmetic and logic operations that are available in languages like C (except multiplication and division). Level 2 contains the MAC unit and is optimised for algorithms such as FFT and FIR. Levels can be bypassed (in software) when they are not needed.

Neighboring ALUs can also communicate directly on level 2. The West-output of an ALU connects to the East-input of the ALU neighboring on the left (the West-output of the leftmost ALU is not connected and the East-input of the rightmost ALU is always zero). The 32-bit wide East-West connection makes it possible to accumulate the MAC result of the right neighbor to the multiplier result (note that this is also a MAC operation). This is particularly useful when performing a complex multiplication, or when adding up a large amount of numbers (up to 20 in one clock cycle). The East-West connection does not introduce a delay or pipeline, as it is not registered.

3 Approach

The overall aim of our research is to execute DSP programs written in high level language, such as C, by one MONTIUM tile in as few clock cycles as possible. There are many related aspects: the limitation of resources; the size of total configuration space; the ALU structure etc. We propose to decompose this problem into a number of phases: translation, clustering, scheduling and resource allocation:

1 **Translating the source code to a CDFG**: The input C program is first translated into a CDFG; and then some transformations and simplifications are done on the CDFG. The focus of this phase is the input program and is largely independent of the target architecture.
2 **Task clustering and ALU data-path mapping**, clustering for short: The CDFG is partitioned into clusters and mapped to an unbounded number of fully connected ALUs. The ALU structure is the main concern of this phase and we do not take the inter-ALU communication into consideration;
3 **Scheduling**: The graph obtained from the clustering phase is scheduled taking the maximum number of ALUs (it is 5 in our case) into account. The algorithm tries to find the minimize number of the distinct configurations of ALUs of a tile;
4 **Resource allocation**, allocation for short: The scheduled graph is mapped to the resources where locality of reference is exploited, which is important for performance and energy reasons. The main challenge in this phase is the limitation of the size of register banks and memories, the number of buses of the crossbar and the number of reading and writing ports of memories and register banks.

Note that when one phase does not give a solution, we have to fall back to a previous phase and select another solution.

3.1   Some Definitions Regarding a CDFG

For the purpose of formulating our problem in a mathematical context, it is convenient to introduce a new type of graphs called **hydragraphs**[2] to model our directed acyclic CDFGs (CDFGs for short in this paper). This concept should capture and represent the operations, the inputs and outputs, as well as which inputs are used and which outputs are produced by the operations (and which outputs of a certain operation serve as inputs for one or more further operations).

A hydragraph $G = (N_G, P_G, A_G)$ consists of two finite non-empty sets of **nodes** N_G and **ports** P_G and a set A_G of so-called **hydra-arcs**; a hydra-arc $a = (t_a, H_a)$ has one **tail** $t_a \in N_G \cup P_G$ and a non-empty set of **heads** $H_a \subset N_G \cup P_G$. In our applications, N_G represents the operations of a CDFG, P_G represents the inputs and outputs of the CDFG, while the hydra-arc (t_a, H_a) either reflects that an input is used by an operation (if $t_a \in P_G$), or that an output of the operation represented by $t_a \in N_G$ is input of the operations represented by H_a, or that this output is just an output of the CDFG (if H_a contains a port of P_G).

---

[2] These graphs are named after Hydra, a water-snake from Greek mythology with many heads that grew again if cut off.

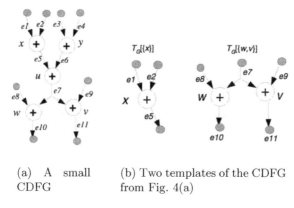

(a)   A   small
CDFG

(b) Two templates of the CDFG
from Fig. 4(a)

Fig. 4. An example.

See the example in Fig. 4(a): The operation of each node is a basic computation such as addition (in this case), multiplication, or subtraction. Hydra-arcs
are directed from their tail to their heads. Because an operand might be input for
more than one operation, a hydra-arc is allowed to have multiple heads although
it always has only one tail. The hydra-arc $e7$ in Fig. 4(a), for instance, has two
heads, w and v. The CDFG communicates with external systems through its
ports represented by small grey circles in Fig. 4(a).

A node subset $S \in N_G$ generates a hydragraph in the following natural way:
For every $v \in S$ consider the following two types of hydra-arcs of G related to v:

- (t_v, H_v), so hydra-arcs with tail v: if $H_v \not\subset S$, we introduce a new port p_v and
  replace (t_v, H_v) by $(t_v, (H_v \cap S) \cup \{p_v\})$; otherwise, we keep (t_v, H_v) as it is.
- (t_u, H_u) with $v \in H_u$, so hydra-arcs for which v is one of the heads: if $t_u \notin S$,
  we introduce a new port t'_u and replace (t_u, H_u) by $(t'_u, H_u \cap S)$; otherwise we
  keep (t_u, H_u) as it is.

Doing so for all hydra-arcs, e.g. starting from the sources in S, we obtain a
unique hydragraph which we will refer to as the **template** generated by S in
G. We denote it by $T_G[S]$ and say that S is a **match** of the template $T_G[S]$. In
the sequel we will only consider connected templates without always stating this
explicitly. For convenience let us call a template an i-**template** if the number
of its nodes is i. Similarly i-**match** and i-**node subset** are defined.

For example, in Fig. 4(b) we see two templates of the CDFG from Fig. 4(a):
the left one is generated by the set $\{x\}$, the right one by $\{v, w\}$. Compared with
the original CDFG from Fig. 4(a), in the left one, the newly added port is a
head for hydra-arc $e5$, while in the right one the newly added port is a tail for
hydra-arc $e7$.

Two hydragraphs G and F are said to be **isomorphic** if there is a bijection
$\phi : N_G \cup P_G \to N_F \cup P_F$ such that:

$$\phi(N_G)=N_F, \phi(P_G)=P_F, \text{ and } (t_v, H_v) \in A_G \text{ if and only if } (\phi(t_v), \phi(H_v)) \in A_F.$$

We use $G \cong F$ to denote that G and F are isomorphic.

We say that $S' \subset N_G$ is a **match for the template** $T_G[S]$ if $T_G[S'] \cong T_G[S]$. A hydragraph H is a **template of the hydragraph** G if, for some $S \subset N_G$, $T_G[S] \cong H$. Of course, the same template could have different matches in G.

Note that, in general, a template is not a subhydragraph of a hydragraph, because some nodes may have been replaced by ports. The important property of templates of a CDFG is that they are themselves CDFGs that model part of the algorithm modelled by the whole CDFG: the template $T_G[S]$ models the part of the algorithm characterized by the operations represented by the nodes of S, together with the inputs and outputs of that part. Because of this property, templates are the natural objects to consider if one wants to break up a large algorithm represented by a CDFG into smaller parts that have to be executed on ALUs. In this paper, we only consider connected templates.

4   Phase1: Translating C to a CDFG

In general, CDFGs are not acyclic. In the first phase we decompose the general CDFG into acyclic blocks and cyclic control information. In this paper we only consider acyclic graphs. To illustrate our approach, we use an FFT algorithm. The Fourier transform algorithm transforms a signal from the time domain to the frequency domain. For digital signal processing, we are particularly interested in the discrete Fourier transform. The fast Fourier transform (FFT) can be used to calculate a DFT efficiently. Fig. 5 shows the CDFG generated automatically from a piece of 4-point FFT code after C code translation, simplification and complete loop expansion. This example will be used throughout this paper.

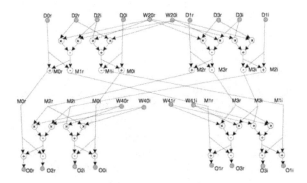

Fig. 5. The generated CDFG of a 4-point FFT after complete loop unrolling and full simplification.

5   Phase2: Clustering

The input for clustering and data-path mapping is a CDFG. In the clustering phase the CDFG is partitioned and mapped to an unbounded number of fully connected ALUs, i.e., the inter-ALU communication is not considered. A cluster corresponds to a possible configuration of an ALU data-path, which is called **one-ALU configuration**. Each one-ALU configuration has fixed input and output ports, fixed function blocks and fixed control signals. A partition with one or more clusters that can not be mapped to our MONTIUM ALU data-path is a failed partition. For this reason the procedure of clustering should be combined with ALU data-path mapping. Goals of clustering are 1) minimization of the number of ALUs required; 2) minimization of the number of distinct ALU configurations; and 3) minimization of the length of the critical path of the dataflow graph.

The clustering phase is implemented by a graph-covering algorithm [6]. The distinct configurations corresponds to distinct templates and the clusters corresponds to matches in [6]. The procedure of clustering is the procedure of finding a cover for a CDFG.

We say that a collection $(T_1, \ldots, T_k)$ of hydragraphs is a k-**tiling** of the hydragraph G if there exists a partition of N_G into mutually disjoint sets $S_1, \ldots, S_k$ such that $T_G[S_i] \cong T_i$ for all $i \in \{1, \ldots, k\}$. In that case we call $S_1, \ldots, S_k$ a k-**cover** of G. A (k, ℓ)-**tiling** is a k-tiling in which at most ℓ nonisomorphic hydragraphs appear. Similarly, we define a (k, ℓ)-**cover**.

Problem 1: Hydragraph Covering Problem

Given a CDFG G, find an optimal (k, ℓ)-cover $S_1, S_2, \ldots, S_k$ of G. It is clear that we cannot expect to solve this complex optimization problem easily. We would be quite happy with a solution concept that gives approximate solutions of a reasonable quality, and that is flexible enough to allow for several solutions to choose from. We propose to start the search for a good solution by first generating all different matches (up to a certain number of nodes because of the restrictions set by the ALU-architecture) of nonisomorphic templates for the CDFG. The second step tries to find an efficient cover for an application graph with a minimal number of distinct templates and minimal number of matches.

Problem A: Template Generation Problem

Given a CDFG, generate the complete set of nonisomorphic templates (that satisfy certain properties, e.g., which can be executed on the ALU-architecture in one clock cycle), and find all their corresponding matches.

Problem B: Template Selection Problem

Given a CDFG G and a set of (matches of) templates, find a 'optimal' (k, ℓ)-cover of G.

5.1   Template Generation

A clear approach for the generating procedure is:

1. Generate a set of connected i-node subsets by adding a neighbor node to the $(i-1)$-node subsets.
2. For all i-node subsets, consider their generated i-templates. Choose the set of nonisomorphic i-templates and list all matches of each of them.
3. Starting with the 1-node subsets, repeat the above steps until all templates and matches op to *maxsize* nodes have been generated.

In step 1, an i-node subsets can be obtained by different $(i-1)$-node subsets, which will result in unnecessarily many computations. To avoid this, we use a clever labelling of the nodes during the generation process depicted in detail in [6]:

- Each hydragraph node is given a unique serial number.
- A leading node is defined within each node subset S, which is the one with the smallest serial number.
- Within a subset S, each graph node $n \in S$ is given a **circle number**, denoted by $\mathrm{Cir}(n|S)$, which is the distance between the leading node and n within S, i.e., $\mathrm{Cir}(n|S)=\mathrm{Dis}(S.\mathrm{LeadingNode}, n|S)$.

If a $(i-1)$-node subset S and one of its neighbor node *Nei* satisfy the following conditions, $S' = S \cap \{Nei\}$ will be considered as a i-node subset, otherwise S' is thrown away.

1. $S.\mathrm{LeadingNode.Serial} < Nei.\mathrm{Serial}$;
2. $\mathrm{Dis}(S.\mathrm{LeadingNode}, Nei|S \cup \{Nei\})$ is not smaller than $\mathrm{Cir}(n|S)$ for any $n \in S$;
3. For each n which satisfies $n \in S$ and
   $\mathrm{Cir}(n|S) = \mathrm{Dis}(S.\mathrm{LeadingNode}, Nei|S \cup \{Nei\})$, $n.\mathrm{Serial} < Nei.\mathrm{Serial}$.

For each i-template S', these conditions chose a unique pair (S, Nei) such that $S' = S \cap \{Nei\}$. Thus multiple copies of S' are discarded. The proof can be found in [6].

5.2   The Template Selection Algorithm

Given G, $\Omega = \{T_1, T_2, \cdots, T_p\}$ and the matches $M(\Omega)$, the objective is to find a subset C of the set $M(\Omega)$ that forms a 'good' cover of G. Here by 'good' cover we mean a (k, ℓ)-cover with minimum k and ℓ.

Since the generated set $M(\Omega)$ can be quite large, the template and match selection problem is computationally intensive. We adopt a heuristic based on maximum independent set, and apply it to a conflict graph related to our problem, similarly as it was done in [8][10].

A **conflict graph** is an undirected graph $\tilde{G} = (V, E)$. Each match $S \in M(\Omega)$ for a template of the CDFG G is represented by a vertex v_S in the conflict graph $\tilde{G}$. If two matches S_1 and S_2 have one or more nodes in common, there will be an

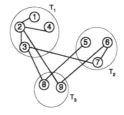

Fig. 6. A conflict graph. The weight of each node is 4.

edge between the two corresponding vertices v_{S_1} and v_{S_2} in the conflict graph $\tilde{G}$. The **weight** $w(v_S)$ of a conflict graph vertex v_S is the number of CDFG nodes $|S|$ within the corresponding match S. The vertex set of the conflict graph are partitioned into subsets, each of which corresponds to a certain template (see Fig. 6). Therefore, on the conflict graph, vertices of the same subset have the same weight. The **maximum independent set (MIS) for a subset** $T \subset V(\tilde{G})$ is defined as the largest subset of vertices within T that are mutually nonadjacent. There might exist more than one MIS for T. Corresponding to each MIS for T on $\tilde{G}$, there exists a set of node-disjoint matches in G for the template corresponding to T; we call this set of matches a **maximum non-overlapping match set**(MNOMS). To determine a cover of G with a small number of distinct templates, the templates should cover a rather large number of CDFG nodes, on average.

An MNOMS corresponds to a MIS on the conflict graph. Finding a MIS in a general graph, however, is an NP-hard problem [5]. Fortunately, there are several heuristics for this problem that give reasonably good solutions in practical situations. One of these heuristics is a simple minimum-degree based algorithm used in [7], where it has been shown to give good results. Therefore, we adopted this algorithm as a first approach to finding 'good' coverings for the CDFGs within our research project.

For each template T, an **objective function** is defined by:

$$g(T) = g(w, s),$$

where w is the weight of each vertex and s is the size of an approximate solution for a MIS within the subset corresponding to T on the conflict graph. The outcome of our heuristic will highly depend on the choice of this objective function, as we will see later.

The pseudo-code of the selection algorithm is shown in Fig. 7. This is an iterative procedure, similar to the methods in [1][3][10]. At each round, after computing an approximate solution for the MISs within each subset, out of all templates in Ω, the heuristic approach selects a template T with a maximum value of the objective function, depending on the weights and approximate solutions for the MISs. After that, on the conflict graph, the neighbor vertices of the selected approximate MIS and of the approximate MIS itself are deleted. This

1 Cover $C = \phi$;
2 Build the conflict graph;
3 Find a MIS for each group on the conflict graph;
4 Compute the value of objective function for each template; The T with the largest value of objective function is the selected template. Its MIS is the selected MIS. The MNOMS corresponding to the MIS are put into C. On the conflict graph, delete the neighbor vertices of the selected MIS, and then delete the selected MIS;
5 Can C cover CDFG totally? If no, go back to 3; if yes, end the program.

Fig. 7. Pseudo-code of the proposed template selection algorithm

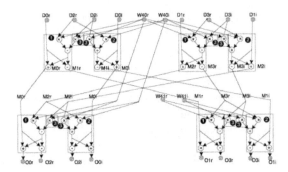

Fig. 8. The selected cover for the CDFG in 5

procedure is repeated until the set of matches C corresponding to the union of the chosen approximate MISs, covers the whole CDFG G.

We currently use the following objective function:

$$g(T) = w^{1.2} \cdot s = ws \cdot w^{0.2}. \qquad (1)$$

In this function, for a template T, ws equals the total number of CDFG nodes covered by a MNOMS, which expresses a preference for the template whose MNOMS covers the largest number of nodes. Furthermore, due to the extra $w^{0.2}$ factor, the larger templates, i.e., the templates with more template nodes, are more likely to be chosen than the smaller templates.

Each selected match is a cluster that can be mapped onto one MONTIUM ALU and can be executed in one clock-cycle. As an example Fig. 8 presents the produced cover for the 4-point FFT. The letters inside the dark circles indicate the templates. For this CDFG, among all the templates, three have the highest objective function value. The hydragraph is completely covered by them. This result is the same as our manual solution. It appears that the same templates are chosen for a n-point FFT ($n = 2^d$). After clustering, we get a clustered graph shown in Fig. 9.

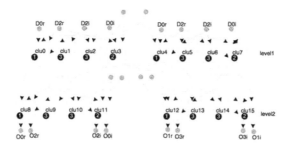

Fig. 9. The clustering result for the CDFG from Fig. 5.

6 Phase3: Scheduling

To facilitate the scheduling of clusters, all clusters get a **level** number. The level numbers are assigned to clusters with the following restrictions:

- For a cluster A that is dependent on a cluster B with level number i, cluster A must get a level number $> i$ if the two clusters cannot be connected by the west-east connection (see Fig. 3).
- Clusters that can be executed in parallel can have equal level numbers.
- Clusters that depend only on in-ports have level number one.

The objective of the clustering phase is to minimize the number of different configurations for separate ALUs, i.e. to minimize the number of different one-ALU configurations. The configurations for all five ALUs of one clock cycle form a **5-ALU configuration**. Since our MONTIUM tile is a very long instruction word (VLIW) processor, the number of distinct 5-ALU configurations should be minimized as well. At the same time, the maximum amount of parallelism is preferable within the restrictions of the target architecture. In our architecture, at most 5 clusters can be on the same level.

If there are more than 5 clusters at some level, one or more clusters should be moved one level down. Sometimes one or more extra clock cycles have to be inserted. Take Fig. 9 as an example, where, in level one, the clusters of type 1 and type 2 are dependent on clusters of type 3. Therefore, type 3 clusters should be executed before the corresponding type 1 or type 2 cluster, or they are executed by two adjacent ALUs in the same clock cycle, in which case type 3 clusters must stay east to the connected type 1 or type 2 cluster. Because there are too many clusters in level 1 and level 2 of Fig. 9, we have to split them. Fig. 10(a) shows a possible scheduling scheme where not all five ALUs are used.

This scheme consists of only one 5-ALU configuration: $C1=\{❶❸❷❸\ \ \}$. As a result, with the scheme of 10(a), the configuration of ALUs stays the same during the execution. The scheduling scheme of Fig. 10(b) consists of 4 levels as well, but it is not preferable because it needs two distinct 5-ALU configurations: $C2=\{❶❸❷❸❸\}$ and $C3=\{❶❷❸\ \ \}$. Switching configurations adds to the energy and control overhead.

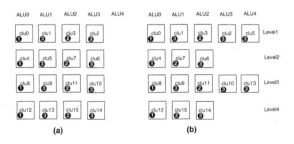

Fig. 10. Schedule the ALUs of Fig. 9

7   Phase4: Allocation

The main architectural issues of the MONTIUM that are relevant for the resource allocation phase are summarized as follows:

- The size of a memory is 512 words.
- Each register bank includes 4 registers.
- Only one word can be read from or written to a memory within one clock cycle.
- The crossbar has a limited number of buses (10).
- The execution time of the data-path is fixed (one clock cycle).
- An ALU can only use the data from its local registers or from the east connection as inputs (see Fig. 3).

After scheduling, each cluster is assigned an ALU and the relative executing order of clusters has been determined. In the allocation phase, the other resources (busses, registers, memories, etc) are assigned, where locality of reference is exploited, which is important for performance and energy reasons. The main challenge in this phase is the limitation of the size of register banks and memories, the number of buses of the crossbar and the number of reading and writing ports of memories and register banks. The decisions that should be made during allocation phase are:

- Choose proper storage places (memories or registers) for each intermediate value;
- Arrange the resources (crossbar, address generators, etc) such that the outputs of the ALUs are stored in the right registers and memories;
- Arrange the resources such that the inputs of ALUs are in the proper register for the next cluster that will execute on that ALU.

Storing an ALU result must be done in the clock cycle within which the output is computed. Preparing an input should be done one clock cycle before it is used. However, when it is prepared too early, the input will occupy the register space for a too long time. A proper solution in practise is starting to prepare an input 4 clock cycles before the clock cycle it is actually used by the ALU. When the outputs are not moved to registers or memories immediately after generated by ALUs, they will be lost. For this reason, in each clock cycle, storing outputs of the current clock cycle takes priority over using the resources. If the inputs are not well prepared before the execution of an ALU, one or more extra clock cycles can be inserted to do so. However, this will decrease the speed.

When a value is moved from a memory to a register, a check should be done whether it is necessary to keep the old copy in the memory or not. In most cases, a memory location can be released after the datum is fed into an ALU. An exception is that there is another cluster which shares the copy of the datum and that cluster has not been executed.

```
//Input: Scheduled Clustered Graph G
//Output: The job of an FPFA tile for each clock cycle
0   function ResourseAllocation(G) {
1       for each level in G do  Allocate(level);
2   }
3   function Allocate(currentLevel) {
4       Allocate ALUs of the current clock cycle
5       for each output  do store it to a memory;
6       for each input of current level
7       do  try to move it to proper register at the clock cycle which is four steps
8           before; If failed,  do it three steps before; then two steps before;  one
9           step before.
10      if some inputs are not moved successfully
11      then insert one or more clock cycles before the current one to load inputs
12  }
```

Fig. 11. Pseudocode of the heuristic allocation algorithm

We adopt a heuristic resource allocation method, whose pseudocode is listed in Fig. 11. The clusters in the scheduled graph are allocated level by level (lines 0-2). Firstly, for each level, the ALUs are allocated (line 4). Secondly, the outputs are stored through the crossbar (line 5). Storing outputs is given priority because the outputs will be lost when they are not moved to registers or memories immediately after generated by the ALUs. The locality of reference principle is employed again to choose a proper storage position (register or memory) for each output. The unused resources (busses, registers, memories) of previous steps are used to load the missing inputs (lines 6-9) for the current step. Finally, extra clock cycles might be inserted if some inputs are not put in place by the preceding steps (lines 10-11).

The resource allocation result for the 4-point FFT CDFG is listed in Table 1. Before the execution of Clu0, Clu1, Clu2 and Clu3, an extra step (step 1) is needed to load there inputs to proper local registers. In all other steps, besides saving the result of current step, the resources are sufficient to loading the inputs for the next step, so no extra steps are needed. The 4-point FFT can be executed within 5 steps by one MONTIUM tile. Note that when a previous algorithm already left the input data in the right registers, step 1 is not needed and consequently the algorithm can be executed in 4 clock cycles.

Table 1. The resource allocation result for the 4-point FFT CDFG

Step	Actions
1	Load inputs for clusters of level 1 in Fig. 10
2	Clu0, Clu1, Clu2 and Clu3 are executed; Save outputs of step 2; Load inputs for clusters of level 2.
3	Clu4, Clu5, Clu6 and Clu7 are executed; Save outputs of step 3; Load inputs for clusters of level 3.
4	Clu8, Clu9, Clu10 and Clu11 are executed; Save outputs of step 4; Load inputs for clusters of level 4.
5	Clu12, Clu13, Clu14 and Clu15 are executed; Save outputs of step 5.

8   Conclusion

In this paper we presented a method to map a process written in a high level language, such as C, to one MONTIUM tile. The mapping procedure is divided into four steps: translating the source code to a CDFG, clustering, scheduling and resource allocation. High performance and low power consumption are achieved by exploiting maximum parallelism and locality of reference respectively. In conclusion, using this mapping scheme the flexibility and efficiency of the MONTIUM architecture are exploited. We introduced a new type of graph (hydragraph) to represent a CDFG.

To date, the work does not deal with CDFGs with loops and branches, which will be done in the future work. Furthermore, the scheduling and resource allocation steps will be investigated in more detail.

9   Related Work

There have been published many related research efforts in the areas of FPGA logic synthesis. Many systems use the SUIF compiler of Stanford [13].

For multiprocessor systems, Sarkar [11] presents a clustering algorithm based on a scheduling algorithm on unbounded number of processors. Our MONTIUM is a VLIW processor instead of multiprocessor. To simplify the problem, we still employ a four phase decomposition algorithm based on the two-phased decomposition of multiprocessor scheduling introduced by Sarkar [11].

Clustering is the key parts in our decomposition. In [2][4], a template library is assumed to be available and the template matching is the focus of their work. However, this assumption is not always valid, and hence an automatic compiler must determine the possible templates by itself before coming up with suitable matchings.

[9][10] give some methods to generate templates. These approaches choose one node as an initial template and subsequently add more operators to the template. The drawback is that the generated templates are highly dependent on the choice of the initial template. The heuristic algorithm in [8] generates and maps templates simultaneously, but cannot avoid ill-fated decisions.

The algorithms in [1][3] provide all templates of a CDFG. The central problem for template generation algorithms is how to generate and enumerate all the (connected) subgraphs of a CDFG. The methods employed in [3] and [1] can only enumerate the subgraphs of specific shapes (tree shape, single output or single sink) and as a result, templates with multiple outputs or multiple sinks cannot be generated. In the MONTIUM architecture, each ALU has three outputs, so the existing algorithms cannot be used.

References

1. Srihari Cadambi, and Seth Copen Goldstein, "CPR: A Configuration Profiling Tool", *IEEE Symposium on FPGAs for Custom Computing Machines,* 1999.
2. Timothy J.Callahan, Philip Chong, Andre DeHon, and John Wawrzynek, "Fast Module Mapping and Placement for Datapaths in FPGAs", *Proc. of International Sysp. of Field Programmable Gate Arrays,* 1998.
3. Amit Chowdhary, Sudhakar Kale, Phani Saripella, Naresh Sehgal, Rajesh Gupta, "A General Approach for Regularity Extraction in Datapath Circuits", *Proc. of Internaltional Conference on Computer-Aided Design (ICCAD)* San Jose, CA, 1998, pp.332-339.
4. Miguel R. Corazao, Marwan A. Khalaf, Lisa M.Guerra, Miodrag Potkonjak and Jan M. Rabaey, "Performance Optimization Using Templete mapping for Datapath-Intensive High-Level Synthesis", *IEEE Transactions on Computer-Aided Design of Intergrated Circuits and Systems*, vol.15, No.8, August 1996, pp.877-888.
5. M. R. Garey and D. S. Johnson, *Computers and Intractability: A Guide to the Theory of NP-Completeness*, W. H. Freeman and Company, New York, 1979.
6. Yuanqing Guo, Gerard Smit, Paul Heysters, Hajo Broersma, "A Graph Covering Algorithm for a Coarse Grain Reconfigurable System", *2003 ACM Sigplan Conference on Languages, Compilers, and Tools for Embedded Systems(LCTES'03)*, California, USA, June 2003, pp.199-208.
7. Magnús M. Halldórsson, Jaikumar Radhakrishnan, "Greed is good: Approximating independent sets in sparse and bounded-degree graphs", *ACM Symposium on the Theory of Computing*, 1994.
8. Ryan Kastner, Seda Ogrenci-Memik, Elaheh Bozorgzadeh and Majid Sarrafzadeh, "Instruction Generation for Hybrid Reconfigurable Systems", *Proc. of International Conference on Computer-Aided Design (ICCAD)*, San Jose, CA, November, 2001.
9. Thomas Kutzschebauch, "Efficient Logic Optimization Using Regularity Extraction", *Proc. of the 1999 Internaltional Workshop on Logic Synthesis*, 1999.
10. D. Sreenivasa Rao, and Fadi J. Kurdahi, "On Clustering For Maximal Regularity Extraction", *IEEE Transactions on Computer-Aided Design*, vol.12, No.8,August,1993, pp.1198-1208.
11. Vivek Sarkar. *Clustering and Scheduling Parallel Programs for Multiprocessors.* Research Monographs in Parallel and Distributed Computing. MIT Press, Cambridge, Massachusetts, 1989.
12. Gerard J.M. Smit, Paul J.M. Havinga, Lodewijk T. Smit, Paul M. Heysters, Michel A.J. Rosien, "Dynamic Reconfiguration in Mobile Systems", *Proc. of FPL2002*, Montpellier France, pp 171-181, September 2002.
13. SUIF Compiler system, `http://suif.stanford.edu`.

Packing with Boundary Constraints for a Reconfigurable Operating System

Abhinandan Sharma, Martyn A. George, and David Kearney

Reconfigurable Computing Laboratory (RCL)
Advanced Computing Research Centre
University of South Australia
Mawson Lakes SA 5095
abhish@cse.iitb.ac.in
{Martyn.George, David.Kearney}@unisa.edu.au

Abstract. An operating system for reconfigurable computing is responsible for dynamically placing relocatable pre-routed cores onto an FPGA at run-time. We describe an exact algorithm proposed for use in this type of OS that pre-packs cores into rectangles for subsequent placement. The algorithm not only generates feasible packings but selects those that have a minimum distance metric to optimise inter-core communication distance within the pre-packed rectangle. The algorithm works in conjunction with other software components of the OS that are responsible for partitioning large applications into manageable "space slices" and allocating area to the pre-packed rectangles from the remaining free area of the FPGA. All of these algorithms are capable of operating in a dynamic environment where applications are queued to execute on the FPGA, and then removed when completed with full area reclaim. Thus, they inherently support partial reconfiguration, dynamic reconfiguration, and multi-user operations on a reconfigurable platform.

1 Introduction

The goal of the ReconfigMe operating system (OS) project is to support a software like development process for reconfigurable computing. The OS must therefore free the programmer/designer of reconfigurable applications from the need to commit to a location, and complete resource allocation at compile time. Thus unlike other run time systems, ReconfigMe has services to allocate FPGA resources, and in particular area, during run time. Dynamic and partial reconfiguration are natively supported in ReconfigMe. Applications are developed using any language system compatible with the manufacturer's place and route tools. Applications are compiled to a data flow graph consisting of pre-routed and placed cores which are stored in a relocatable format together with their data flow precedence constraints. When an application is invoked the operating system will load the it into space slices which are the area equivalent of time slices for a traditional OS. The cores in the data flow graph are packed into a rectangular space slice and then the space slice is loaded onto a location of free area on the FPGA. When the application completes the space slice is returned to a free list. If an application will not fit into a space slice, its data flow graph is partitioned into two or more slices. These functions of the operating systems are shown in Figure 1

A. Omondi and S. Sedukhin (Eds.): ACSAC 2003, LNCS 2823, pp. 236–245, 2003.
© Springer-Verlag Berlin Heidelberg 2003

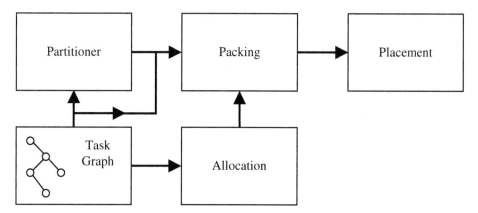

Fig. 1. A flow graph showing the basic operations of the ReconfigMe OS

The practicality of the OS implementation thus critically depends for its perform-ance on algorithms for assigning area and partitioning data flow graphs (task graphs). The current OS has split the NP hard packing task of assigning cores to available area into two phases. This has been done to reduce the complexity of the task, following research from other fields where packing has already been attempted. The two phases are called packing and allocation. In the packing phase, which is the topic of this pa-per, the rectangular cores that make up the task graph are pre-packed into rectangular boxes. The allocation phase takes the pre-packed boxes and assigns them to the re-maining (possibly concave) space on the FPGA, left after previous applications have been allocated, and perhaps in "holes" where applications that have completed have been removed to free up space. At present we do not envisage the relocation of run-ning applications on the FPGA as this is likely to be difficult to achieve (cores may not be preemptable), and time consuming (reconfiguration overheads are often high on many commercial FPGAs).

However, it is not sufficient to just place the cores into boxes and allocate the boxes anywhere that's free on the FPGA. In order for tasks placed on the FPGA to communicate with one another, the intra-task I/O cores should be close to task boundaries. Thus, the packing algorithm must not only find feasible solutions, but must select from amongst those solutions to find an arrangement that permits inter-task communications. These requirements are called boundary constraints in this pa-per. We say that a feasible packing meets boundary constraints if all of its I/O cores are adjacent to the task boundaries.

In the next section of this paper we describe previous work that has been done on exact algorithms for packing in reconfigurable computing applications. Then in sec-tion three we describe our proposal for incorporating boundary constraints into the search process for a feasible packing so that better feasible packings are favoured. In section 4 we give an example an application of the algorithm.

2 Packing and Its Application to Reconfigurable Computing

Some research into the use of packing algorithms to support reconfigurable computing applications has already been completed. For example, Grant Wigley et al [1] describe two algorithms which they use to solve the allocation problem. In their work,
these algorithms are called 'algorithm 1' and 'algorithm 2', but herein they will be
called the 'brute force' algorithm, and the 'bottom-left corner' algorithm, respectively. For both of these algorithms, the essential problem is to pack a number of
source rectangles into a larger *destination rectangle* in such a way that no two source
rectangles overlap.

The brute force algorithm maintains a list of free area contained within the destination rectangle which is similar in design to the list of free blocks often used for file
storage management. However, instead of blocks, the list will contain *units*, where a
unit is the smallest possible free region. When a request is made to pack a particular
source rectangle, the algorithm searches the free list looking for a contiguous area
large enough to satisfy the request. The source rectangle is then placed at the first free
position inside the destination rectangle. If the source rectangle overlaps another
which has been placed previously, it is progressively and deterministically moved until either the entire destination area has been scanned, or until an unoccupied region
large enough to contain it is found. In the latter case, the region found is reserved for
the selected source rectangle. The algorithm then repeats this process until the queue
of requests is depleted, or until there is insufficient free area to satisfy further requests. Given that f represents the number of free units in the destination rectangle,
and s is the unit area of a given source rectangle, the brute force algorithm has $O(fs)$
time complexity.

Consisting of a partitioning manager and a heuristic for dividing the free area of
the destination rectangle, the bottom-left corner algorithm [2] differs from the brute
force algorithm in the way that it manages the free area. In this algorithm, the free
area is stored as a list of rectangles. When a request is made to pack a particular
source rectangle, the list is searched to determine if a region large enough to contain
the source rectangle exists within the destination rectangle (note that this search is
$O(n)$, where n is the number of rectangles in the list). If found, the source rectangle is
inserted into the bottom-left corner of the corresponding rectangular region within the
destination rectangle. The space left after the insertion is subdivided into two further
rectangles according to the specified heuristic. Although efficient, this algorithm will
produce more fragmentation than the brute force algorithm. As with the previous algorithm, the bottom-left corner algorithm will continue to meet further requests until
insufficient resources remain.

A different packing algorithm that forms the basis of this paper, and which will
thus be described in more detail, is Scheper's algorithm [3]. This algorithm is more
general than the previous two in the sense that it has been designed to work with objects having any number of spatial dimensions. However, for our operating system,
we are interested in packing rectangular cores onto a planar FPGA surface and will
thus consider the two dimensional case only. Geometric information pertaining to the
set of cores in a task is obtained by taking projections from the cores of which the task
is composed, and storing the intervals thus obtained in two interval graphs; one for intervals lying along the x-axis, and one for intervals lying along the y-axis (see Figure
2). Each vertex in the interval graphs corresponds to a particular interval and contains

a weight describing its length, and, for our particular implementation, a tag indicating that the vertex is an I/O vertex, as appropriate. An edge between any pair of vertices signifies that the respective intervals overlap. It should be noted that although each of the graphs provides some spatial information for intervals lying along a particular axis, no information is stored regarding their order. As a consequence, it is necessary to provide an orientation to the pair of interval graphs to obtain a packing, where a packing is any configuration that can be represented physically (i.e. no two rectangles overlap in more than one dimension). Since there are a number of orientations for a given pair of interval graphs, it follows that they represent a *set* of packings rather than just a single packing. If all of the packings in this set are feasible, where a feasible packing is one which is entirely contained within the bounds defined by a given destination rectangle, the set is called a *packing class*. The corollary to this, is that if we can prove that a set of packings is a packing class, we can deduce that all of the packings it contains are feasible.

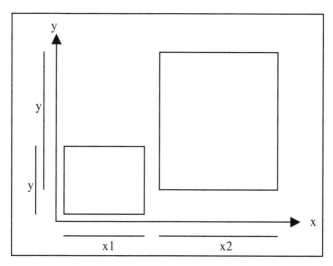

Fig. 2. Interval projections

In light of the definition of a packing class, we can conclude that in order to find a feasible packing, it is sufficient to find a packing class and then provide any orientation to its intervals. Since locating a feasible packing from a given packing class can be achieved in linear time, and since processing a packing class enables an entire set of packings to be processed simultaneously, checking the feasibility of a given packing can be performed efficiently.

In order to determine if a given pair of graphs represents a packing class, the following three properties must be satisfied:

P1. The graphs encoding the information for each of the two dimensions (x, and y) must be interval graphs.

P2. If there is an edge between a pair of vertices in one of the interval graphs, there must not be an edge incident upon either of the corresponding vertices in the other interval graph.

P3.   The weight of the maximum weighted clique in the complement of an interval graph must be less than the length of a side (in the corresponding dimension) of the destination rectangle.

With respect to the first property (P1, above), a particular graph is an interval graph if it satisfies two criteria. Firstly, it must not be possible to induce a sub-graph which is a four-cycle. This is so since a four-cycle would represent the physically impossible situation where two intervals at the outer extremities of a set of four overlap each other without overlapping both of the intermediate intervals. An orientation of intervals in a packing class is performed by taking a complement graph and converting its edges to directed edges. The resulting orientation must be transitive acyclic. This is satisfied by the second criterion which requires that if the interval graph's complement contains an odd cycle, then that cycle must contain at least one two-chord. The second of the three conditions (P2) guarantees that the source rectangles only overlap in one dimension at the most. This is necessary because the rectangles are considered to be rigid and an overlap in both dimensions would represent a physical impossibility. Finally, the complement of an interval graph contains an edge between every pair of vertices that do not overlap. This graph, in turn, is composed of a set of complete sub-graphs, or cliques, each of which depict a non-overlapping set of intervals. The maximally weighted clique corresponds to the longest set of non-overlapping intervals lying along the respective axis. The third property (P3) checks that this length does not exceed that permitted by the bounds of the destination rectangle process by which Scheper's algorithm derives packing classes, is to build a search tree in which each node contains four interval graphs. Note there are a pair of graphs, E_i+, and E_i-, for each dimension, where those for the x-dimension are denoted E_0+ and E_0-, and those for the y-dimension are denoted E_1+ and E_1-. The four graphs in the first node of the search tree will contain no edges, which signifies a packing where none of the represented cores overlap and thus lie along a diagonal. Starting at this node, the algorithm will traverse the search tree, testing for the properties previously described (P1, P2, and P3), to determine whether the set of interval graphs represents a packing class. If a particular node does represent a packing class, success has been achieved and the algorithm terminates. If, on the other hand, the current node does not contain a packing class (signified by the absence of at least one property), the algorithm adds a new node to the search tree to represent a different orientation of the same packing (and thus a different packing). The algorithm produces different packings by adding and removing edges in the interval graphs until a packing class is produced, or until it determines that a packing class cannot be derived from the initial packing.

Between pairs of vertices in a given packing, edges that are 'necessary' are added to E_i+ whilst those that are 'excluded' are added to E_i- [3]. After an edge is added to one of the four interval graphs (E_0+, E_0-, E_1+, or E_1-), an update procedure adds edges to other graphs as necessary to ensure the following:

- Cores must not be permitted to overlap in both dimensions simultaneously. Thus, when an edge is added between a pair of vertices in Ei+ for one dimension, a corresponding edge must be added between the same vertices in Ei- for the other dimension.
- Four-cycles are avoided in E_i+.
- Clique structures are avoided in E_i-.

The update procedure does this recursively until the graphs cannot be updated further.

As the search progresses, nodes will be produced that don't represent feasible packings. Whenever this occurs, the algorithm will back-track, and an attempt will be made to find a feasible packing along a different branch of the tree. The search will abort, indicating that a packing class could not be found, when the union of the $Ei+$ and $Ei-$ graphs for dimension i is a complete graph.

3 Boundary Constraints

In this section we show why we need to consider boundary constraints when implementing the packing algorithm. We then describe how the boundary constraints may be incorporated into the Scheper's algorithm and the modifications that need to be made.

Sometimes it is desirable for independent tasks to communicate with one another. If the tasks are not in close proximity with each other, this can be accomplished by arranging the tasks so that they derive input data from, and send output data to, static RAM connected to the FPGA chip. This shared RAM can then by used by the communicating tasks to exchange data. Another option is for communication channels to be routed between the separated tasks. Neither of these options is particular efficient since they require complex routes to be established which reduces the amount of FPGA area available for the placement of other tasks. Moreover, long communication routes can introduce timing errors such as clock skew.

A much more efficient approach to inter-task communication is for the allocation algorithm to arrange participating tasks adjacent to one another such that the I/O cores in pairs of communicating tasks abut. In order for this to occur, the packing algorithm must arrange the I/O cores in a task at its boundaries. These boundary constraints may be incorporated in Scheper's algorithm by modifying it so that when various orientations are applied to a packing class to yield feasible packings, those for which the I/O vertices aren't on the task boundary are discarded as infeasible.

We extend Scheper's algorithm by taking the packing class it produces, and then finding the maximal cliques in the pair of interval graphs (x and y) of which it is composed. A property of an interval graph, is that it is also a triangulated graph (a graph having no cycle greater than three which is chordless). Since a triangulated graph has a perfect elimination order which can be calculated in linear time [4], we can find all of the maximal cliques in the interval graphs using an $O(|V| + |E|)$ algorithm, where $|V|$ is the number of vertices, and $|E|$ is the number of edges in the graph. Furthermore, the cliques in each interval graph can be ordered such that for all i, the cliques containing vertex v_i are consecutive. This implies that columns of an associated clique adjacency matrix can be permuted so that its rows satisfy the consecutive ones property. Figure 3 shows an example of a such a packing with its associated x-axis adjacency matrix.

Observation of Figure 3 reveals that maximal cliques in an interval graph represent maximal sets of overlapping cores in the relevant dimension. For a given interval graph, it may be possible to obtain several clique orders which satisfy the consecutive ones property. Each of the orders obtained corresponds to a particular orientation of the interval graph. Taken together, orientations that satisfy the consecutive ones property in a pair of x and y graphs represent a feasible packing.

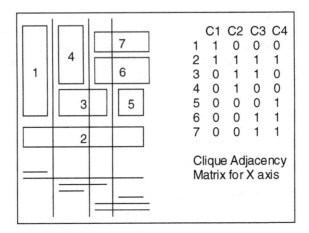

Fig. 3. Packing, and x-axis adjacency matrix

In order for a packing to meet the boundary constraints, the I/O cores should occur in the first or last cliques of the clique orders that define it. Our aim therefore, is to find four cliques, two in each graph, which together cover all of the I/O vertices. One approach to this problem is to consider all possible permutations of maximal cliques in a pair of interval graphs, and remove all of those that don't satisfy the consecutive ones property. From the remaining subset of cliques, we would then remove all of those where the outermost cliques did not cover all I/O vertices. A significant problem with this method is that exponential storage space would be initially required to store the permutations. This problem can be overcome by using an efficient data structure for storing permutations. 'PQ Trees', a data structure proposed by Booth and Leuker [5] is an example of such an efficient data structure which is especially suitable for determining clique orders in interval graphs satisfying the consecutive ones property.

The space complexity of a PQ tree is $O(|V|)$, where $|V|$ denotes the number of vertices in an interval graph. As suggested by the name, a PQ tree has two types of node, 'P', and 'Q'. The difference between the node types is that P nodes must have at least two children, and these can be permuted arbitrarily, whilst Q nodes must have at least three children, the order of which can only be reversed (e.g. 1-2-3, 3-2-1). A left to right ordering of leaf nodes is called a 'frontier'. All trees obtained by permuting the children of P nodes arbitrarily, and reversing the order of children of Q nodes are said to be *equivalent*. Given a set of equivalent trees, each would will have a unique frontier which represents a permissible permutation of the maximal cliques [4]. A *universal* tree is a PQ tree having a P node as its root, and all maximal cliques as its children. Booth et al [5] present a linear time algorithm that takes a universal tree and progressively removes all infeasible permutations. An example of x and y PQ trees for the packing shown in Figure 3, is presented in Figure 4.

Our aim is to obtain from the tree only those permutations in which the outermost cliques cover all I/O vertices. We do this after building PQ trees for both x and y dimensions, by applying a procedure to *fix* selected nodes. A node is fixed by changing its position (if required) so that it becomes an outer node on its level in the tree, and ensuring that it doesn't participate in the enumeration of subsequent permutations.

The algorithm used to fix nodes must abide by some rules. Firstly, all nodes can have no more than a single child fixed, excepting for the root node which can have up to two of its children fixed. Secondly, a maximum of two nodes can be fixed in any level of the tree. Thirdly, if a node is to be fixed, it must be possible to fix all of its ancestors. If any of these rules would be broken by fixing a node, the operation is aborted for that particular node.

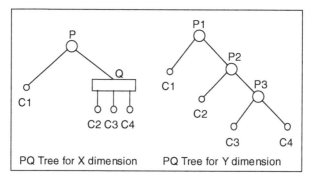

Fig. 4. PQ trees for X and Y dimensions

Our algorithm begins by selecting nodes (which we will call start nodes) to which the fix procedure will initially be applied in the pair of PQ trees. For a given I/O vertex, the algorithm finds the common ancestor of all cliques containing that vertex (participating cliques). This common ancestor is selected as a start node unless there is only one such clique, in which case the leaf node itself is chosen as the start node. If the start node is a P node, its descendents will consist only of the participating cliques, but if it is a Q node, the descendents might also be comprised of non-participating cliques. In the latter case however, the participating cliques will be adjacent to one another. Furthermore, when the start node is a Q node, if one of the participating cliques is an outer child it will also be designated as a starting node, but if none of the participating cliques is an outer child, the algorithm will be aborted with respect to the current I/O vertex only. Once all of the start nodes have been determined, the fix procedure is applied to each start node, and all of its ancestors.

At this stage, the procedure for fixing nodes pertaining to a single I/O vertex has been described. This needs to be repeated for all other I/O vertices. For this purpose we utilise a search procedure which traverses the two PQ trees applying the fix procedure to visited nodes, as appropriate, in an attempt to propagate all I/O vertices to the outer nodes. After the search concludes, all I/O vertices have migrated to the outer nodes, and we have a boundary constrained feasible packing.

4   An Example Incorporating Boundary Constraints

In this section we choose a realistic example of how a boundary constrained feasible packing can be obtained from a given packing. The packing illustrated in Figure 3 depicts our initial task with its associated arrangement of cores, while Figure 4 represents the corresponding x and y PQ trees.

Let us assume that {1, 3, 6} is the set of I/O vertices in the packing. The packing in Figure 3 does not have vertex 3 on the boundary. We execute our algorithm as follows:

1. As the adjacency matrix shows vertex 1 participates in C1, so C1 is fixed in the x PQ tree.
2. Vertex 3 participates in C2, and C3, so the common ancestor, which is a Q node, is fixed, along with C2.
3. Vertex 6 participates in C3, and C4, so we try to fix C4 since the common ancestor is a Q node.
4. We are unable to fix C4 since this would violate the rule prohibiting two children of the same node from being fixed.
5. Since our attempt to fix with respect to vertex 6 failed in the x PQ tree, we attempt the same in the y PQ tree. Vertex 6 participates in C2 for the y PQ tree, so we fix C2 and its ancestors.

The two PQ trees now represent boundary constrained feasible packings (see Figure 5) with the output clique orders: X = {1, 4, 3, 2}, and Y = {1, 3, 4, 2}, or {1, 4, 3, 2}.

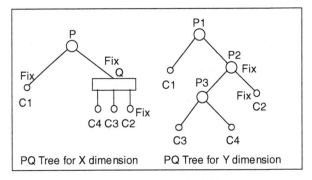

Fig. 5. Boundary constrained PQ trees

5 Conclusion

Operating systems such as ReconfigMe for FPGA based reconfigurable computing architectures must supply a service which will organise groups of tasks, or cores, into suitable arrangements so that they can then be packed into predefined rectangular areas for subsequent allocation onto the FPGA. We have described Scheper's algorithm which generally well-suited for this type of task. However, since it is desirable to place I/O cores close to the borders of the rectangular region, we have identified the need to utilise a packing algorithm which performs the same packing task, but is further constrained by the positioning requirements of the I/O cores (boundary constraints). We have shown that this can be achieved by extending Scheper's algorithm and using PQ trees to efficiently identify the subset of all feasible packings which meet this criterion.

We have also identified the need to further constrain packing arrangements which we call distance constraints. This is similar to the boundary constraints problem, but instead of arranging packings so that I/O cores are near the edges, we are interested in arranging all of the cores in a task to facilitate intra-task communication. This requires that those cores that need to communicate with one another inside a task are positioned in close proximity. Although we have not discussed distance constraints in this paper, our intention is to incorporate this related problem into our future research.

Acknowledgements

The authors acknowledge the support of the Sir Ross and Sir Keith Smith Fund.

References

1. G. Wigley & D. Kearney, 'The Management of Applications for Reconfigurable Computing using an Operating System', Seventh Asia-Pacific Computer Systems Architecture Conference, Melbourne, Australia, 2002.
2. K. Bazargan, R. Kastner, & M. Sarrafzadeh, 'Fast Template Placement for Reconfigurable Computing Systems', IEEE Design & Test of Computers, vol. 17, 2000, pp. 68-83.
3. S. P. Fekete & J. Schepers, On More-Dimensional Packing III: Exact Algorithms, Angewandte Mathematik und Informatik Universität zu Köln, 97.290, 2000.
4. M. C. Golumbic, Algorithmic Graph Theory and Perfect Graphs, Academic Press, Inc., New York, 1980.
5. K. S. Booth & G. S. Leuker, 'Testing for the Consecutive Ones Property, Interval Graphs, and Graph Planarity using PQ-tree Algorithms', Journal of Computer and Systems Science, vol. 13, 1976, pp. 335-379.

Arithmetic Circuits Combining Residue
and Signed-Digit Representations

Anders Lindström[1], Michael Nordseth[1], Lars Bengtsson[1], and Amos Omondi[2]

[1] Department of Computer Engineering, Chalmers University of Technology, Sweden
{e8call, e8mn}@etek.chalmers.se, labe@ce.chalmers.se
[2] School of Informatics and Engineering, Flinders University, Australia
amos@infoeng.flinders.edu.au

Abstract. This paper discusses the use of signed-digit representations in the implementation of fast and efficient residue-arithmetic units. Improvements to existing signed-digit modulo adders and multipliers are suggested and new converters for the residue signed-digit number system are described for the moduli $\{2^{\cdot}-1, 2^{n}, 2^{n}+1\}$. By extending an existing efficient signed-digit adder design to handle modulo operations, we are able to implement high performance modulo addition. The hardware complexity of signed-digit modulo multipliers is reduced by using a more efficient algorithm for calculating partial products. Finally, the novel converters presented makes it possible to integrate this residue signed-digit number system with conventional binary circuits.

1 Introduction

The residue number system (RNS) is often used when high speed computation is needed and where the use of the conventional binary system would limit the speed of the arithmetic circuits due to carry propagation. RNS divides an integer into a number of smaller integers (i.e. with a shorter binary representation) that can be processed in parallel independently of each other and thus reducing carry propagation. However, the remaining carry propagation can still be a limiting factor in real-time applications.

The use of the signed-digit (SD) system has recently been suggested as a way of eliminating the remaining carry propagation in RNS arithmetic [1][2]. The SD representation is a redundant number system and therefore facilitates carry-free addition [3], SD numbers can be added in constant time independent of operand-widths. Combining the carry-free properties of SD with RNS arithmetic helps simplify the implementation of crucial RNS arithmetic operations. Our work makes two main contributions: the improvements of circuits that have previously been proposed for residue signed-digit (RNS+SD) arithmetic; and the design of novel converters for the RNS+SD representation.

The improvements on existing work consist of designs for faster and smaller SD modulo adders than are currently known and in improvements, by reduction of the number of partial products, in the modulo multiplication algorithm (and

A. Omondi and S. Sedukhin (Eds.): ACSAC 2003, LNCS 2823, pp. 246–257, 2003.

corresponding implementations). In addition, we present completely new designs for RNS+SD converters based on the moduli-set $\{2^n - 1, 2^n, 2^n + 1\}$.

The rest of the paper consists of four sections, as follows. Section 2 gives a brief overview of the mathematics and algorithms used in the RNS and SD representations. Section 3 presents the improved arithmetic units and the new converters, and Section 4 discuss the results obtained from implementing these circuits in VLSI. The last section is a concluding summa.

2   Background

2.2   The Residue Number System

A residue number system is defined by a set of relative prime numbers, $\{m_1, m_2, ... m_r\}$, called the moduli. In such a system, an integer X is represented by an ordered set of r residues, $\{x_1, x_2, ..., x_r\}$, where $x_i = X$ mod m_i. If only positive numbers are permitted, then any integer in the range [0, M), where $M = m_1 \cdot m_2 \cdot .... m_r$, can be uniquely represented. If negative numbers are also allowed, then it is usual to let the dynamic range be [$-M/2$, $M/2$).

The choice of moduli is crucial to the representational efficiency and to the complexity and delay of the arithmetic unit. The moduli set $\{2^n - 1, 2^n, 2^n + 1\}$ is used throughout this paper. This is a popular moduli-set, as the restriction to powers of two (± 1) in the set makes it relatively easy to implement efficient arithmetic units and to produce generalized designs that are parameterized by operand word length.

2.2   The Signed Digit Number System

The radix-2 signed-digit number system has the digit-set $\{\bar{1}, 0, 1\}$, where $\bar{1}$ denotes -1. An n-digit SD integer $Y = [y_{n-1}...y_0]_{SD}$, $y_i \in \{\bar{1}, 0, 1\}$, has the value

$$\sum_{i=0}^{n-1} y_i \times 2^i$$

which is the same as for an unsigned binary integer except that y_i also can be -1. This makes it possible to represent an integer in more than one way. For example, the integer "6" can be represented as $[0110]_{SD}$, $[1\bar{1}10]_{SD}$, or $[10\bar{1}0]_{SD}$. Zero is, however, uniquely represented.

The binary representation of an SD digit, y_i, requires two binary bits, y_i^- and y_i^+. The binary coding used in this paper consists of [00], [01] and [10] to represent 0, 1, and $\bar{1}$ respectively. That is, $y_i = [y_i^- \ y_i^+]$, where $Y^+ = [y_{n-1}^+...y_0^+]$ and $Y^- = [y_{n-1}^-...y_0^-]$ are binary n-bit vectors. With this coding, the value of an n-digit SD integer, Y, can be written as

$$\sum_{i=0}^{n-1} y_i^+ \times 2^i - \sum_{i=0}^{n-1} y_i^- \times 2^i = Y^+ - Y^-$$

$$(1)$$

The rules for adding two SD integers, X and Y, are shown in Table 1, in which c_i denotes the carry and u_i the interim sum.

Table 1. Rules for adding SD numbers

x_iy_i	00	01	01	0$\bar{1}$	0$\bar{1}$	11	$\bar{1}\bar{1}$	1$\bar{1}$
$x_{i-1}y_{i-1}$	–	neither is $\bar{1}$	at least one is $\bar{1}$	neither is $\bar{1}$	at least one is $\bar{1}$	–	–	–
c_{i+1}	0	1	0	0	$\bar{1}$	1	$\bar{1}$	0
u_i	0	$\bar{1}$	1	$\bar{1}$	1	0	0	0

The facts that $[01]_{SD} = [1\,\bar{1}]_{SD}$ and $[0\,\bar{1}]_{SD} = [\bar{1}1]_{SD}$ are used in the rules above to avoid any carry propagation when the final sum is calculated, $s_i = c_i + u_i$, $s_i \in \{\bar{1}, 0, 1\}$ Below is an example of adding two SD integers with the rules in Table 1.

$$
\begin{array}{rll}
 & 100\bar{1}0 & (14) \\
+ & \bar{1}1\bar{1}11 & (-9) \\
\hline
 & 00\bar{1}01 & c_i \\
+ & 0110\bar{1} & u_i \\
\hline
s_i & 00011\bar{1} & (5)
\end{array}
$$

Note that since the SD system can represent a negative integer without any special sign digit, it is possible to represent any integer and its negation with an equal number of digits (unlike the ordinary binary system).

The negation of an integer is a very simple operation in the SD system, $y_i = y_i^- y_i^+$ becomes $(-y)_i = y_i^+ y_i^-$ when negated as can be seen by negating Eq. (1).

3   Arithmetic Units

In the first and second parts of this section, we suggest improvements to existing SD modulo adders and multipliers. We show that speed and area gains can be made by taking a known highly efficient SD addition cell and adapting it for residue operation. We also show that the area gains can be further improved in the modulo multipliers by using a better multiplication algorithm.

In the third and fourth part of this section, we present novel converters for the RNS+SD $\{2^n - 1, 2^n, 2^n + 1\}$ representation. Although there has been prior work on arithmetic units that combine RNS and SD notations, none of that work has dealt with the important issue of conversion between RNS+SD and conventional binary. One of the main contributions of this paper is the design of appropriate converters.

3.1 SD Modulo Addition

An implementation of the SD adder cell circuit description in [4] is used as a foundation for the presented SD modulo adder. We also considered the adder cells suggested in [5] and [6], but, when implemented and synthesized, neither had better delay, area nor power performance than the one chosen. Eq. set 2 describes the logic for this SD adder cell.

$$p_i = \overline{x_{i-1}^- + y_{i-1}^-}$$

$$xid_i = x_i^- + x_i^+$$

$$yid_i = y_i^- + y_i^+$$

$$z_{i+1} = \overline{xid_i \cdot \overline{yid_i} \cdot p_i + \overline{xid_i} \cdot yid_i \cdot p_i + x_i^+ \cdot yid_i + y_i^+ \cdot xid_i}$$

$$t_i = \overline{xid_i \cdot \overline{yid_i} \cdot p_i + \overline{xid_i} \cdot yid_i \cdot p_i + xid_i \cdot yid_i \cdot \overline{p}_i + \overline{xid_i} \cdot \overline{yid_i} \cdot \overline{p}_i}$$

$$s_i^- = t_i \cdot z_i$$

$$s_i^+ = \overline{t}_i \cdot \overline{z}_i$$

Eq. set 2. SD addition

Our SD modulo adders are based on the end-around-carry logic for SD adders described in [1] and [2], but we will now apply this basic concept to the more efficient SD adder described above.

Modulo 2^n+1 addition (where n is the word length) can be performed by including an end-around-carry in the computations described by Eq. Set 2. This inclusion is described in Eq. set 3.

$$p_0 = \overline{x_{n-1}^+ + y_{n-1}^+}$$

$$z_0 = \overline{xid_{n-1} \cdot \overline{yid_{n-1}} \cdot p_{n-1} + \overline{xid_{n-1}} \cdot yid_{n-1} \cdot p_{n-1} + x_{n-1}^- \cdot yid_{n-1} + y_{n-1}^- \cdot xid_{n-1}}$$

Eq. set 3. 2^n+1 end around carry

For modulo 2^n-1 addition, the end-around operation is much simpler:

$$p_0 = \overline{x_{n-1} + y_{n-1}}$$

$$z_0 = z_n.$$

This results in modulo adders that are just a few gates larger than the normal SD adder but which are equally fast.

The use of a more efficient SD adder cell makes the SD modulo adders presented here faster and smaller than the proposed circuit implementation described in [2] as the SD adder cell in our modulo adders only uses one bit for the carry (z_i) compared to the two bit solution in [2].

In contrast with binary residue adders, the carry-free nature of SD addition means that there is no carry propagation involved in the addition of the end-around-carry. In the specific case of a modulo $2^n + 1$ adder, the SD counterpart of the binary residue adder also has the advantage that it only needs n-digits to represent the result. If the result happens to be greater than $2^n - 1$ then the result will instead be taken from the negative range, for example

$$\langle [110] + [010] = [1000] \rangle_9 = [00\overline{1}]_{SD} = -1 = 8 - 9$$

where $\langle X \rangle_m$ is the operation $X \bmod m$. In fact, the negative range will be used whenever it is suitable.

The hardware logic needed for an SD adder can be dramatically simplified if the input to the adder is in binary representation. The rules in Table 1 can in this case be simplified to those shown in Table 2.

Table 2. Simplified rules for binary input

$x_i y_i$	00	01	10	11
c_{i+1}	0	1	1	1
u_i	0	$\overline{1}$	$\overline{1}$	0

It is also possible to reduce the complexity of the SD adder even if just one of the inputs to the SD adder is in binary representation. Table 1 may be simplified to Table 3 in this case.

Table 3. Rules for mixed input

$x_i y_i$	00	01	10	11	$\overline{1}0$	$\overline{1}1$
c_{i+1}	0	1	1	1	0	0
u_i	0	$\overline{1}$	$\overline{1}$	0	$\overline{1}$	0

The translation of Table 2 and Table 3 into logic is straightforward and can be used directly for modulo $2^n - 1$ addition by using a simple end-around-carry, $c_0 = c_n$. However, this is not feasible in the case of modulo $2^n + 1$ addition where instead Eq. set 2 and Eq. set 3 can be simplified for binary or mixed input. SD modulo subtraction with one or both inputs in binary representation can be simplified in a similar way.

3.2 SD Modulo Multiplication

We have improved on existing implementations of RNS+SD multiplication by presenting a simple way to reduce the number of partial products to be added, and, therefore, the logical complexity of the multiplier. Such a reduction has negligible effect on the operational time of the multiplier.

Modulo m multiplication is defined as

$$\langle x \cdot y \rangle_m = \langle \sum_{i=0}^{n-1} y_i \langle 2^i \cdot x \rangle_m \rangle_m$$

where n is the word length. The partial products (i.e. $y_i \langle 2^i \cdot x \rangle m$) can be summed in a tree of SD modulo adders as described in [1] and [2].

Conventional schemes for reducing the number of partial products cannot be used here as both x and y are in SD format. However, we will now show that SD arithmetic allows the number of partial products to be reduced, without the complex multiplier-recoding that is normally required in conventional schemes.

The number of partial products can be reduced to $n/2$ by considering two digits of y simultaneously as follows

$$\langle x \cdot y \rangle_m = \langle \sum_{i=0}^{\frac{n}{2}-1} \langle 2^{2i}(y_{2i} \cdot x + y_{2i+1} \cdot 2x) \rangle_m \rangle_m = \langle \sum_{i=0}^{\frac{n}{2}-1} \langle 2^{2i} \cdot rp_i \rangle_m \rangle_m = \langle \sum_{i=0}^{\frac{n}{2}-1} \langle pp_i \rangle_m \rangle_m$$

where the value of rp_i are as shown in Table 4. These values can be generated using only one SD modulo adder (to generate $3x = 2x + x$) as shift, rotation (see Eq. set 4) and negation does not require any additional gates.

Table 4. Possible values of rp_i

y_{2i+1} y_{2i}	0	1	$\bar{1}$
0	0	$2x$	$-2x$
1	x	$3x$	$-x$
$\bar{1}$	$-x$	x	$-3x$

The partial products, $pp_i = \langle 2^{2i} \cdot rp_i \rangle m$, can be generated by rotation if the moduli is $2^n - 1, 2^n$ or $2^n + 1$ by using the rules in Eq. Set 4. These rotations can be accomplished by wiring connections appropriately.

$$\langle 2^a \cdot y \rangle_{2^p - 1} = [y_{p-1-a} \cdots y_0 \, y_{p-1} \cdots y_{p-a}]$$

$$\langle 2^a \cdot y \rangle_{2^p} = [y_{p-1-a} \cdots y_0 \, 0_{p-1} \cdots 0_{p-a}]$$

$$\langle 2^a \cdot y \rangle_{2^p + 1} = [y_{p-1-a} \cdots y_0 \, (-y_{p-1}) \cdots (-y_{p-a})]$$

$$p \geq a, y = [y_{p-1} \cdots y_0]$$

Eq. set 4. Rotation

The partial products, pp_i, can then be summed in a tree of SD modulo adders. Compared to an addition tree that sums all n partial products without recoding, the top level consisting of $n/2$ adders is replaced by one adder and some logic. The suggested reduction of partial products results in lesser hardware complexity with a negligible slow down of the circuit.

3.3 RNS+SD Forward Converter

We have developed a new forward converter (i.e. for conversion from conventional binary to RNS+SD) for the $\{2^n - 1, 2^n, 2^n + 1\}$ moduli set. Essentially, the new converter structure is based on the binary-to-RNS converter described in [7] but we have adapted it for RNS+SD arithmetic. The use of SD arithmetic is very convenient because, in contrast with a conventional binary implementation, the use of simplified SD residue adders reduces the complexity of the converter.

For a $3n$-bit binary integer, Y, in the range $[0,M)$, where $M = (2^n - 1)2^n (2^n + 1)$, the vectors

$$k_0 = y_{n-1} \cdots y_0$$

$$k_1 = y_{2n-1} \cdots y_n$$

$$k_2 = y_{3n-1} \cdots y_{2n}$$

are created. With these vectors the following operations

$$p_1 = \langle k_2 + k_0 \rangle_{2^n - 1}$$

$$r_1 = \langle p_1 + k_1 \rangle_{2^n - 1}$$

$$r_2 = k_0$$

$$p_2 = \langle k_2 + k_0 \rangle_{2^n + 1}$$

$$r_3 = \langle p_2 - k_1 \rangle_{2^n + 1}$$

Eq. set 5. Modulo operations

are then performed to obtain the residues $\{r_1, r_2, r_3\}$ which is the RNS representation of Y.

The modulo operations in Eq. set 5 become trivial with the SD system and are no more complex than normal SD additions. Also, since the input, Y, is a binary integer the modulo SD adders calculating p_1 and p_2 can be greatly simplified as they will only require a few gates per bit. This results in a very small and fast (constant time) converter. Fig. 1 shows a schematic overview of the converter.

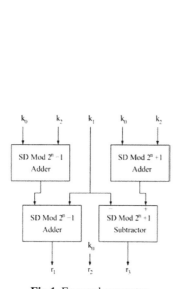

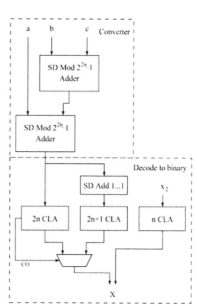

Fig 1. Forward converter   **Fig 2.** Backward converter

3.4 RNS+SD Backward Converter

A backward converter for the moduli set $\{2^n - 1, 2^n, 2^n + 1\}$ has also been developed.

The backward converter is based on a modified version of the New Chinese Remainder Theorems (CRT-1 as stated in [8]). We will present our modifications of CRT-1 and also our new SD implementation of the modified theorem in the following paragraphs. CRT-1 states

$$X = x_2 + 2^n \langle x_2 - x_3 + 2^{n-1}(2^n + 1)(x_1 - 2x_2 + x_3) \rangle_{2^{2n} - 1}$$
(6)

where $\{x_1, x_2, x_3,\}$ is the RNS representation of X. Eq. (6) can be written as

$$X = x_2 + 2^n \langle x_2 - 2^{2n}x_2 - x_3 - 2^n x_2 + 2^{n-1}(2^n + 1)(x_1 + x_3) \rangle_{2^{2n} - 1}$$
(7)

and by using the first rotation rule in Eq. set 4 with $y = [0...0x_2]$ and $a = p = 2n$ Eq. (7) simplifies to

$$X = x_2 + 2^n \langle -x_3 - 2^n x_2 + 2^{n-1}(2^n + 1)(x_1 + x_3) \rangle_{2^{2n}-1}$$

Now, by using the fact that x_3 is n-digits in the SD system the above expression can be written as

$$X = x_2 + 2^n \langle a + b + c \rangle_{2^{2n}-1}$$

where a, b and c have the digit length $2n$ and are formed by concatenation and rotation as follows

$$a = [(-x_2)\ (-x_3)]$$

$$b = [x_{1_0} x_{1_{n-1}} \ldots x_{1_0} x_{1_{n-1}} x_{1_1}]$$

$$c = [x_{3_0} x_{3_{n-1}} \ldots x_{3_0} x_{3_{n-1}} x_{3_1}].$$

Forming a, b and c can be done without using any gates but adding a, b and c will however require two $2n$-digit SD modulo adders. The last step, i.e. the computation of $x_2 + 2^n \langle \ldots \rangle_{2^{2n}-1}$, may also be done with concatenation and will thus not require any additional gates.

Converting the SD representation of X to binary can be done by using a $3n$-bit carry-look-ahead adder (CLA) (see Eq. (1)), but the fact that the lower part of X consists of the residue x_2 can be used to convert each part independently. The upper part of X, $\langle a + b + c \rangle_{2^{2n}-1}$, can be converted by a $2n$-bit CLA and the lower part, x_2, can be converted by a n-bit CLA. Any carry-outs from the CLAs can safely be ignored as the two parts are bound by their moduli.

X will be in the range $(-M, M)$ $M = (2^n - 1)2^n(2^n + 1)$ due to the fact that SD residue adders also use the negative range. If it is necessary that the output from the converter to be in the range $[0, M)$, then the positive value of $\langle X \rangle_M$ is the correct output which can be calculated by adding $(2^n - 1)2^n(2^n + 1) = [\ 1_{2n-1} \ldots 1_0 0_{n-1} \ldots 0_0]$ to X if X is negative. This is done by adding 1's to the upper $2n$-bits of X. The addition is very simple in the SD system as the rules in Table 1 can in that case be simplified to Table 5.

Table 5. Adding ones to an SD integer

$x_i y_i$	01	11	$\bar{1}1$
c_{i+1}	1	1	0
u_i	$\bar{1}$	0	0

When converting to binary, it is simplest to just first add 1's to the upper $2n$-bits of X, before converting, and then convert the result and the original $2n$-bits to binary using two $2n$-bit CLAs operating in parallel. The correct binary value can then be selected by examining the sign bit of the converted original $2n$-bits. The complete arrangement is shown in Fig. 2.

4 Implementation Results

The presented circuits have been implemented in parameterized (word length generic) VHDL (see [9]) and performance estimation with various word lengths has been carried out. The units have been synthesised and optimized for the UMC13 0.13μm standard cell library under typical operating conditions using Synopsys Design Compiler. The circuits are synthesized without timing constraints and can thus be made faster at the cost of area. Some of the results are presented in Table 6.

Table 6. Performance evaluation

n	16		32		64	
	delay (ns)	area (μm²)	delay (ns)	area (μm²)	delay (ns)	area (μm²)
SD Adder	0.49	1142.1	0.49	2277.3	0.49	4544.2
SD Mod 2^n-1 Adder	0.49	1143.8	0.49	2277.3	0.49	4544.1
SD Mod 2^n+1 Adder	0.49	1142.1	0.49	2275.5	0.49	4542.4
BIN-SD Mod 2^n-1 Adder	0.19	414.6	0.19	829.1	0.19	1658.2
BIN-SD Mod[a] 2^n+1 Adder	0.33	459.5	0.33	872.3	0.24	1694.6
Fast Binary CLA Adder[b]	0.51	1475.6	0.8	3236.4	1.4[c]	6758[c]
N	**6**		**12**		**21**	
SD Mod 2^n+1 Multiplier	2.13	2861.4	3.14	10827.1	3.73	32783.5
BIN to RNS+SD converter[d]	0.68	945.0	0.68	1852.0	0.67	3215.1
RNS+SD to BIN converter[e]	3.04	3146.9	4.63	6207.3	6.93	10798.7

[a] SD modulo adder with binary inputs
[b] Conventional binary carry-look-ahead adder for reference
[c] Linear estimation
[d] The input has the bit length 3n and the three outputs each have the digit length n.
[e] The three inputs each have the bit length n and the output has the bit length 3n.

The results confirm that the complexity of the SD modulo adders are almost exactly the same as for normal SD adders.

For the simplified SD modulo adders (those with binary inputs) used in the BIN to RNS+SD converter, the complexity is greatly reduced. This results in a very efficient forward converter, especially compared to conventional binary converters that at least have the area complexity of three CLA adders and a delay of at least two CLA adders.

The backward converter is however less efficient, since the conversion of the intermediate SD integer into binary adds some delay.

5 Conclusions

Improved RNS+SD arithmetic circuits have been presented and new RNS+SD converters for the $\{2^n - 1, 2^n, 2^n + 1\}$ moduli have been described.

By using a more efficient SD adder cell, we have been able to implement faster and smaller SD modulo adder circuits. These circuits can be simplified if one or both of the inputs are in conventional binary format.

The number of partial products have been reduced to half in our modulo multiplier which results in lesser hardware complexity and combined with the faster modulo adders also in improved speed performance.

The developed RNS+SD converters make it possible to integrate RNS+SD circuits with conventional binary systems. Converting to RNS+SD from conventional binary can be done very efficiently but the reverse operation, converting from RNS+SD to conventional binary, is a more costly operation. The reverse operation is however very suitable for pipelining in two or more steps, to reduce an otherwise perhaps limiting delay.

References

1. Shugang Wei and Kensuke Shimizu, "Fast residue arithmetic multipliers based on signed-digit number system", in IEEE 8th Conf. Electronics, *Circuits and Systems*, vol. 1, pp. 263-266, 2001.
2. Shugang Wei and Kensuke Shimizu, "A novel residue arithmetic hardware algorithm using a signed-digit number representation", *IEICE Trans. inf. & syst.*, vol. E83-D, no. 12, pp. 2056-2064, Dec. 2000.
3. Israel Koren, *Computer Arithmetic Algorithms*, 2nd edition. Natick, MA: A K Peters Ltd, 2002. ISBN: 1-56881-160-8.
4. Naofumi Takagi, "High-Speed VLSI Multiplication Algorithm with a Redundant Binary Addition Tree", *IEEE Transactions on Computers*, vol. c-34, no. 9, pp. 789-796, Sep. 1985.
5. S. Kuninobu, T. Nishiyama, H. Edamatu, T. Taniguchi and N. Takagi, "Design Of High Speed MOS Multiplier And Divider Using Redundant Binary Representation", in *IEEE Proc. 8th Symp. Computer Arithmetic*, pp. 80-86, 1987.
6. A. Vandemeulebroecke, E. Vanzieleghem, T. Denayer and P. G. A. Jespers, "A New Carry-Free Division Algorithm and its Application to a Singler-Chip 1024-b RSA Processor", *IEEE Journal of solid-state circuits*, vol. 25, no. 3, pp. 748-756, Jun. 1990.

7. B. Vinnakota and V.V.Bapeswara Rao, "Fast Conversion Techniques for Binary-Residue Number systems", *IEEE Trans. Circuits and Systems*, vol. 41, no. 12, Dec. 1994.

8. Y. Wang, "Residue-to-binary converters based on new chinese remainder theorems", *IEEE Trans. Circuits Syst. II*, pp. 197-206, Mar. 2000

9. A. Lindström and M. Nordseth. (2003, Mars). *VHDL Library of Nonstandard Arithmetic Units*. [Online]. Available: http://www.ce.chalmers.se/arithdb/

A New On-the-fly Summation Algorithm

Hooman Nikmehr and Cheng-Chew Lim

School of Electrical and Electronic Engineering, Faculty of Engineering, Computer and Mathematical Sciences, The University of Adelaide, Adelaide SA 5005, Australia,
{nhooman,cclim}@eleceng.adelaide.edu.au

Abstract. Digit recurrence operations mainly use redundant representation, mostly in signed-digit format. These operations generate results one digit per iteration from left to right. Since the final result has to be converted into 2's complement format, to eliminate the end of operation conversion delay, on-the-fly algorithms are employed. These algorithms, with no use of carry propagating adders, convert the result into the conventional format as the signed-digits are generated. Some applications like rounding non-normalized results, positive or negative offsetting, coding and cryptography require not only the original result in 2's complement format, but also to generate the original result summed with $(n)ulp^1$, where n is an integer, in the ordinary representation. This paper proposes a new algorithm applying to digit recurrence operations to generate that value on-the-fly.

1 Introduction

In a digit recurrence operation like division and square root, the result appears in digit-by-digit form at the output, most significant digit first (MSDF) [1, 2]. Almost in all cases, the digits could be selected either from a conventional digit set or a signed-digit set [3]. While the conventional digit set for the radix-r is $\{0, 1, 2, \cdots, r - 2, r - 1\}$, the allowed range for the signed-digits is $\{\overline{r-1}, \cdots, \overline{1}, 0, 1, \cdots, r - 1\}$ ($\overline{m}$ means $-m$). Selecting the result-digits from a signed-digit set not only makes the result-digit selection module simple, but also lets carry-free adders being used in the operation [4, 5]. However, since the result is used by the other parts of the system like memory or running applications, the signed-digit output needs to be converted into conventional 2's complement format at the final stage.

In some applications, the result generated by a digit recurrence operation MSDF not only needs to be reformatted into conventional 2's complement representation, but also requires to be summed with a positive or negative integer. Rounding the result when the round bit is not the last bit (e.g. when the result is not normalized) [6] and adding a positive integer to or subtracting a negative integer from the result for the purpose of coding (e.g. excess 3) are examples of such applications.

---

[1] ulp stands for unit of last position

A. Omondi and S. Sedukhin (Eds.): ACSAC 2003, LNCS 2823, pp. 258–267, 2003.

In the traditional method, the summation is implemented using a binary carry propagating adder of W bits where W represents the length of the converted number. Therefore, the worst case summation delay due to propagating a carry from the least to the most significant bit is $W\tau$ where τ denotes the binary full adder delay [7]. However, since the delay is too big comparing to one iteration of a fast digit recurrence operation [8], the ordinary summation technique heavily lengthens the total operation time.

This paper proposes an algorithm generating values on-the-fly in ordinary format, namely $Q + (n)ulp$, where n is any desired integer in the set $\{\cdots, -2, -1, 0, +1, +2, \cdots\}$, and Q denotes the result of digit recurrence operations. The new algorithm is named on-the-fly summation. The algorithm utilizes no carry propagating adder and consequently, it incurs a small delay, which is non-proportional to W, to the operation.

The paper is organized as follows. Section 2 briefly explains the mathematical outline of the summation $Q + (n)ulp$ and discusses the problem of using the traditional method. Section 3 introduces the recurrence used in on-the-fly summation algorithm and provides a proof. Section 4 compares the recurrences employed in on-the-fly conversion algorithm [9] and on-the-fly rounding algorithm [10] to the proposed algorithm. The paper continues with an example in Sect. 5, followed by addressing some implementation issues in Sect. 6. The paper ends with a short summary in Sect. 7.

2 Summation Using Carry Propagating Adders

Consider a digit recurrence operation in radix-r. Let p_i denote a result digit produced MSDF by a digit recurrence operation in i-th iteration and $p_i \in \{\bar{a}, \cdots, \bar{1}, 0, 1, \cdots, a\}$, where $\lceil \frac{r-1}{2} \rceil \le a \le r - 1$. The first k digits of the result build the digit-vector $P[k]$ in the form of

$$P[k] = \sum_{i=1}^{k} p_i r^{-i}. \tag{1}$$

Generally, at the end of every iteration, P is converted into its 2's complement equivalent digit-vector

$$Q[k] = \sum_{i=1}^{k} q_i r^{-i} \quad \text{where} \quad q_i \in \{0, 1, \cdots, r - 1\}. \tag{2}$$

The traditional approach to obtain (2) performs

$$Q[k] = Q[k-1] + p_k r^{-k} \quad \text{where} \quad Q[0] = 0 \tag{3}$$

using a carry propagating adder. Moreover, in some applications such as rounding non-normalized results, in addition to converting the result to Q, it is required to calculate $Q + (n)ulp$ where n is an integer with any desired value. The new digit-vector containing the summed value, Q_n, is formed by

$$Q_n[k] = Q_0[k] + (n)r^{-k} \text{ where } \begin{cases} Q_0[k] = Q[k] \text{ and} \\ n \in \{\cdots, -2, -1, 0, +1, +2, \cdots\}. \end{cases} \tag{4}$$

Again, the traditional approach substitutes (3) into (4) to perform

$$Q_n[k] = Q_0[k-1] + (p_k + n)r^{-k} \tag{5}$$

by means of a ripple carry adder. Considering (3) as a special case of (5) when $n = 0$, it could be found that if $0 \le (p_k + n) \le r - 1$, then appending $(p_k + n)$ to the right of old Q_0 forms new Q_n; if $r \le (p_k + n)$, then a carry propagates from right to left during the summation; if $(p_k + n) < 0$, then a borrow bounces from left to right during the summation. Although the concatenation adds no additional delay, the propagation slows down (5). Consequently, the whole recurrence operation is effectively delayed. The delay added by the propagation in the traditional method ranges from τ to $W\tau$ where τ is the delay of a binary full adder and W is the length of the digit-vectors. Obtaining Q_n without using ripple carry adders is the solution proposed in the next section.

3   On-the-fly Summation

In this section, the algorithm for generating $Q_n = Q_0 + (n)ulp$ on-the-fly, where n is negative or non-negative integer with any desired value, is introduced.

3.1   Algorithm

Let the integer $n \in \{\cdots, -2, -1, 0, +1, +2, \cdots\}$ and $-(r-1) \le p_k \le (r-1)$. The recurrence for computing Q_n on-the-fly is

$$Q_n[k] = \begin{cases} n & \text{if } k = 0 \text{ (initialize)} \\ (Q_m[k-1], s) & \text{if } k \ge 1 \text{ (update)} \end{cases} \text{ where } \begin{cases} s = ||n + p_k| - |rm||, \\ m = \left\lfloor \dfrac{n + p_k}{r} \right\rfloor \end{cases} \tag{6}$$

and (a, b) is a concatenation notation. In addition, the minimum length of the vectors, namely W, is calculated using

$$W = l + d\log_2(r) \text{ where } \begin{cases} d = \text{number of result-digits and} \\ l = \text{number of bits representing } n \\ \quad \text{in 2's complement form.} \end{cases} \tag{7}$$

3.2   Observation

It can be seen from (6) that when calculating Q_n, no carry/borrow propagating summation is required and the only processes are

- calculating m and s based on p_k, r and n, and
- concatenating s to $Q_m[k-1]$ from the right to obtain $Q_n[k]$.

Therefore, using the proposed algorithm, Q_n is generated on-the-fly (as the result digits are produced) and consequently, no additional delay incurs in the operation.

3.3   Proof

To start proving (6), (5) is rewritten in the form of

$$Q_n[k] = Q_0[k-1] + (m)r^{-(k-1)} + (-m)r^{-(k-1)} + (n+p_k)r^{-k}.$$

Therefore, since $(-m)r^{-(k-1)} = -(mr)r^{-k}$ and also from (4),

$$Q_n[k] = Q_m[k-1] + (-(mr) + (n+p_k))r^{-k}. \tag{8}$$

Now, (8) is studied in the two subranges as follow:

- **Non-negative subrange:** $mr \le (n+p_k) < (m+1)r$ **where** $0 \le m$.
  Since $-(mr) = -|mr|$ and $(n+p_k) = |n+p_k|$, and also from (8), it gives

$$Q_n[k] = Q_m[k-1] + (-|mr| + |n+p_k|)r^{-k}. \tag{9}$$

- **Negative subrange:** $mr \le (n+p_k) < (m+1)r$ **where** $m < 0$.
  Since $-(mr) = |mr|$ and $(n+p_k) = -|n+p_k|$, and also from (8), therefore

$$Q_n[k] = Q_m[k-1] + (|mr| - |n+p_k|)r^{-k}. \tag{10}$$

Combining (9) and (10) confirms the statements shown in (6) for s and Q_n. Moreover, since for the subranges

$$m \le \left(\frac{n+p_k}{r}\right) < (m+1), \tag{11}$$

comparing (11) to the definition of floor function, which is

$$\lfloor x \rfloor \text{ is the largest integer } \le x,$$

reveals that the expression for m in the recurrence is correct.

4   Special Cases of On-the-fly Summation

4.1   On-the-fly Summation with -1

Ercegovac and Lang in [9] introduce an algorithm called on-the-fly conversion. The algorithm uses the following recurrence with the assumption that P is a normalized fraction and so, $p_1 > 0$.

$$A[1] = \begin{cases} +p_1 r^{-1}(0.p_1) & \text{if } P > 0 \\ -|p_1| r^{-1}(1.(r - |p_1|)) & \text{if } P < 0 \end{cases} \quad \text{(initialize)}$$

$$A[k] = \begin{cases} (A[k-1], p_k) & \text{if } p_k \geq 0 \\ (B[k-1], (r - |p_k|)) & \text{if } p_k < 0 \end{cases} \quad k > 1 \quad \text{(update)}$$

$$B[1] = \begin{cases} +(p_1 - 1) r^{-1}(0.(p_1 - 1)) & \text{if } P > 0 \\ -(|p_1| + 1) r^{-1}(1.(r - 1 - |p_1|)) & \text{if } P < 0 \end{cases} \quad \text{(initialize)}$$

$$B[k] = \begin{cases} (A[k-1], (p_k - 1)) & \text{if } p_k > 0 \\ (B[k-1], (r - 1 - |p_k|)) & \text{if } p_k \leq 0 \end{cases} \quad k > 1 \quad \text{(update)}$$

$$(12)$$

Recurrence (12) not only reformats the result into the conventional form, but also generates the result summed with $(-1)ulp$ on-the-fly. The two values are kept in vectors A and B, consequently. Although the recurrence looks different from (6), replacing A with Q_0 and B with Q_{-1} shows that (6) is indeed identical to (6) when $n = -1$. So, on-the-fly conversion algorithm could be interpreted as a special case of on-the-fly summation algorithm.

4.2   On-the-fly Summation with $+1$

Ercegovac and Lang in [10] extend on-the-fly conversion algorithm to on-the-fly rounding algorithm. The algorithm uses notations Q and QM instead of A and B, and introduces an additional digit-vector, QP. At the end of every iteration, in addition to the result and the result summed with $(-1)ulp$, the result summed with $(+1)ulp$ is obtained in 2's complement format. This value is kept in digit-vector QP.

The algorithm initializes QP, Q and QM with $+1$, 0 and -1, respectively. To updates the digit-vectors at the end of every iteration using (12) and

$$QP[k] = \begin{cases} (Q[k-1], (p_k + 1)) & \text{if } -1 \leq p_k \leq r - 2 \\ (QM[k-1], (r - |p_k| + 1)) & \text{if } p_k < -1 \\ (QP[k-1], 0) & \text{if } p_k = r - 1. \end{cases} \quad (13)$$

Again, changing symbols Q, QM and QP to Q_0, Q_{-1} and Q_{+1} reveals that both on-the-fly rounding algorithm and on-the-fly summation algorithm when $n = +1$, produce the same results in the same manner. Therefore, on-the-fly rounding algorithm could be considered as another special case of on-the-fly summation.

5   An Example of On-the-fly Summation

Using (6), Table 1 is formed to show the updating statements required for building digit-vectors Q_0, Q_{+1}, Q_{+2}, Q_{+3}, Q_{+4}, Q_{+5}, Q_{+6}, Q_{-1}, Q_{-2} and Q_{-3} in

Table 1. Updating Q_6 down to Q_{-3} in radix-4

Vectors	New values						
	$p_k = \bar{3}$	$p_k = \bar{2}$	$p_k = \bar{1}$	$p_k = 0$	$p_k = 1$	$p_k = 2$	$p_k = 3$
$Q_{+6}[k]$	$(Q'_0,3)$	$(Q'_{+1},0)$	$(Q'_{+1},1)$	$(Q'_{+1},2)$	$(Q'_{+1},3)$	$(Q'_{+2},0)$	$(Q'_{+2},1)$
$Q_{+5}[k]$	$(Q'_0,2)$	$(Q'_0,3)$	$(Q'_{+1},0)$	$(Q'_{+1},1)$	$(Q'_{+1},2)$	$(Q'_{+1},3)$	$(Q'_{+2},0)$
$Q_{+4}[k]$	$(Q'_0,1)$	$(Q'_0,2)$	$(Q'_0,3)$	$(Q'_{+1},0)$	$(Q'_{+1},1)$	$(Q'_{+1},2)$	$(Q'_{+1},3)$
$Q_{+3}[k]$	$(Q'_0,0)$	$(Q'_0,1)$	$(Q'_0,2)$	$(Q'_0,3)$	$(Q'_{+1},0)$	$(Q'_{+1},1)$	$(Q'_{+1},2)$
$Q_{+2}[k]$	$(Q'_{-1},3)$	$(Q'_0,0)$	$(Q'_0,1)$	$(Q'_0,2)$	$(Q'_0,3)$	$(Q'_{+1},0)$	$(Q'_{+1},1)$
$Q_{+1}[k]$	$(Q'_{-1},2)$	$(Q'_{-1},3)$	$(Q'_0,0)$	$(Q'_0,1)$	$(Q'_0,2)$	$(Q'_0,3)$	$(Q'_{+1},0)$
$Q_0[k]$	$(Q'_{-1},1)$	$(Q'_{-1},2)$	$(Q'_{-1},3)$	$(Q'_0,0)$	$(Q'_0,1)$	$(Q'_0,2)$	$(Q'_0,3)$
$Q_{-1}[k]$	$(Q'_{-1},0)$	$(Q'_{-1},1)$	$(Q'_{-1},2)$	$(Q'_{-1},3)$	$(Q'_0,0)$	$(Q'_0,1)$	$(Q'_0,2)$
$Q_{-2}[k]$	$(Q'_{-2},3)$	$(Q'_{-1},0)$	$(Q'_{-1},1)$	$(Q'_{-1},2)$	$(Q'_{-1},3)$	$(Q'_0,0)$	$(Q'_0,1)$
$Q_{-3}[k]$	$(Q'_{-2},2)$	$(Q'_{-2},3)$	$(Q'_{-1},0)$	$(Q'_{-1},1)$	$(Q'_{-1},2)$	$(Q'_{-1},3)$	$(Q'_0,0)$

Note: $Q'_j = Q_j[k-1]$ where $j = -3, -2, -1, 0, +1, +2, +3, +4, +5, +6$

radix-4. Observing the table develops an ordered pattern among the cells. Between the width of the pattern and the radix, a very straightforward relation could be found. Moreover, the direction and the slope of the pattern are clearly associated with the set of the vectors involved in the algorithm. Therefore, as a secondary result, instead of using (6) to calculate the appropriate vectors and the concatenating values, the pattern could be utilized.

An example of on-the-fly summation is now studied using the updating statements shown in Table 1. Let $P = p_1 p_2 p_3 p_4 = \bar{2}01\bar{3}$ be the output of a digit recurrence operation, represented in radix-4 signed-digit form.[2] The digits are generated from left to right, one digit per iteration. Table 2 shows the content of the vectors in 2's complement binary format. Each column shows the values stored in the vectors after they are updated based on the produced result-digit. The last column on the right indicates that at the end, while $P = -127 = 111110000001$, the values are appropriately formed in the vectors.

6 Implementation

In this section, the hardware implementation of on-the-fly summation algorithm is explained through an example performing $Q_0 + (5)ulp$ and $Q_0 + (-2)ulp$. The hardware shown in Fig. 1 consists of two individual units, updating unit and control unit.

---

[2] For simplicity, instead of a fraction, P is supposed an integer

Table 2. The vectors contents in 2's complement where $P = p_1 p_2 p_3 p_4 = \overline{2}01\overline{3}$

Vectors	*	$p_1 = \overline{2}$	$p_2 = 0$	$p_3 = 1$	$p_4 = \overline{3}$
Q_{+6}	0110	0001,00	1111,11,10	1111,10,01,11	1111,10,00,01,11 $= -121 = -127 + 6$
Q_{+5}	0101	0000,11	1111,11,01	1111,10,01,10	1111,10,00,01,10 $= -122 = -127 + 5$
Q_{+4}	0100	0000,10	1111,11,00	1111,10,01,01	1111,10,00,01,01 $= -123 = -127 + 4$
Q_{+3}	0011	0000,01	1111,10,11	1111,10,01,00	1111,10,00,01,00 $= -124 = -127 + 3$
Q_{+2}	0010	0000,00	1111,10,10	1111,10,00,11	1111,10,00,00,11 $= -125 = -127 + 2$
Q_{+1}	0001	1111,11	1111,10,01	1111,10,00,10	1111,10,00,00,10 $= -126 = -127 + 1$
Q_0	0000	1111,10	1111,10,00	1111,10,00,01	1111,10,00,00,01 $= -127 = -127 + 0$
Q_{-1}	1111	1111,01	1111,01,11	1111,10,00,00	1111,10,00,00,00 $= -128 = -127 - 1$
Q_{-2}	1110	1111,00	1111,01,10	1111,01,11,11	1111,01,11,11,11 $= -129 = -127 - 2$
Q_{-3}	1101	1110,11	1111,01,01	1111,01,11,10	1111,01,11,11,10 $= -130 = -127 - 3$

Note 1: The column indicated by "*" contains the vectors initial values.

6.1   Updating Unit

The updating unit indicated on the bottom of Fig. 1 performs all the left-shifting and the concatenating operations required for calculating the digit-vectors used in the algorithm. The registers and the multiplexors are the only elements involved in the construction of the unit. The digit-vectors are realized by the edge-triggered registers with parallel-load, preset and clear features. The appropriate updating values are selected by the multiplexors and applied to the registers inputs. Then a rising-edge of the system clock stores the values in the registers, if the registers are enable. The desired results $Q_0 + (5)ulp$ and $Q_0 + (-2)ulp$ are produced by the updating unit and stored in registers Q_{+5} and Q_{-2}, respectively. The assumptions for this particular example are $r = 4$ and $d = 2$. So, according to (7), the registers have to be 8-bit wide. In addition, since the concatenating values are represented in 2 bits, the multiplexors inputs should be 6-bit wide. Table 1 can be used for finding the other information needed for implementing the updating unit including the number of required registers, types of the multiplexors, e.g. 2:1 or 3:1, the concatenating values and the manner of connectivity.

6.2   Control Unit

The control unit is shown on the top of Fig. 1. It is driven by three inputs: START, STOP and p_k. The unit starts the summation by initializing the registers through $\overline{\text{CLR}}$ (clear) and $\overline{\text{PRE}}$ (preset) signals. Then, during the updating process, it keeps $\overline{\text{EN}}$ (enable) signal active, puts appropriate values on SEL (select) signals and produces appropriately CON (concatenating) values. Finally,

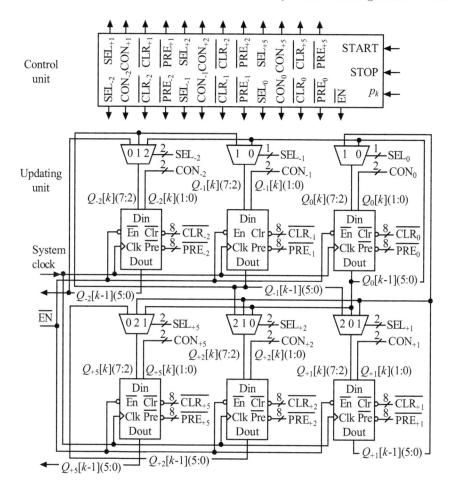

Fig. 1. A hardware implementation for the example of Sect.5; $Q_j[m](u:v)$ indicates all the bits between the position u and the position v of $Q_j[m]$

the control unit sets $\overline{\text{EN}} = 1$ to disable the registers and to end the summation process.

Designing the control unit requires a complete list of all the signals and the values generated by the unit. Table 3 shows such a list for the above example. To find how the table is used for building the control unit, one case as an example is discussed. The other cases of the table could be explained in the same way.

If $p_k = \overline{2}$ and the status is "Update", to update Q_{-2} the control unit sets $\text{SEL}_{-2} = 01$ to let $Q_{-1}[k-1](5:0)$ pass through the multiplexer. Meanwhile, the unit sets $\text{CON}_{-2} = 00$ to have $Q_{-2}[k](1:0)$ concatenated to $Q_{-2}[k](7:2)$ from the right. Then since $\overline{\text{EN}} = 0$, the next rising-edge of the system clock lets the new value load into Q_{-2}. In this stage, the updating process $Q_{-2}[k] = (Q_{-1}[k-1], 0)$ (conforming to Table 1) is completed.

Table 3. Signals and values generated by the control unit shown in Fig. 1

Signals	Initialize	$p_k = \overline{3}$	$p_k = \overline{2}$	$p_k = \overline{1}$	$p_k = 0$	$p_k = 1$	$p_k = 2$	$p_k = 3$	End
				Update					
START	1	0	0	0	0	0	0	0	0
STOP	0	0	0	0	0	0	0	0	1
$\overline{\text{EN}}$	1	0	0	0	0	0	0	0	1
SEL_{+5}	×	01	01	10	10	10	10	00	×
CON_{+5}	×	10	11	00	01	10	11	00	×
$\overline{\text{CLR}}_{+5}$	05	FF	FF	FF	FF	FF	FF	FF	×
$\overline{\text{PRE}}_{+5}$	FA	FF	FF	FF	FF	FF	FF	FF	×
SEL_{+2}	×	10	00	00	00	00	01	01	×
CON_{+2}	×	11	00	01	10	11	00	01	×
$\overline{\text{CLR}}_{+2}$	02	FF	FF	FF	FF	FF	FF	FF	×
$\overline{\text{PRE}}_{+2}$	FD	FF	FF	FF	FF	FF	FF	FF	×
SEL_{+1}	×	10	10	00	00	00	00	01	×
CON_{+1}	×	10	11	00	01	10	11	00	×
$\overline{\text{CLR}}_{+1}$	01	FF	FF	FF	FF	FF	FF	FF	×
$\overline{\text{PRE}}_{+1}$	FE	FF	FF	FF	FF	FF	FF	FF	×
SEL_0	×	1	1	1	0	0	0	0	×
CON_0	×	01	10	11	00	01	10	11	×
$\overline{\text{CLR}}_0$	00	FF	FF	FF	FF	FF	FF	FF	×
$\overline{\text{PRE}}_0$	FF	FF	FF	FF	FF	FF	FF	FF	×
SEL_{-1}	×	1	1	1	1	0	0	0	×
CON_{-1}	×	00	01	10	11	00	01	10	×
$\overline{\text{CLR}}_{-1}$	0F	FF	FF	FF	FF	FF	FF	FF	×
$\overline{\text{PRE}}_{-1}$	F0	FF	FF	FF	FF	FF	FF	FF	×
SEL_{-2}	×	00	01	01	01	01	10	10	×
CON_{-2}	×	11	00	01	10	11	00	01	×
$\overline{\text{CLR}}_{-2}$	0E	FF	FF	FF	FF	FF	FF	FF	×
$\overline{\text{PRE}}_{-2}$	F1	FF	FF	FF	FF	FF	FF	FF	×

Note 1: Values in rows $\overline{\text{CLR}}$ and $\overline{\text{PRE}}$ are in hexadecimal and the rest in binary.
Note 2: Symbol × means don't care.

7   Summary

The proposed algorithm sums $(n)ulp$, where n is an integer, to the result of any digit recurrence operation like division and square root without using carry propagating adders. The summation has a very small delay, non-proportional to the operands length. It is less than the delay of one iteration of a fast digit recurrence operation. On-the-fly algorithm for summation could be used in rounding non-normalized results, positive or negative offsetting, coding and cryptography applications.

The recurrence performing on-the-fly summation has been derived mathematically as well as through pattern identification. In addition, the two special cases of the new algorithm are compared to the two well known algorithms, on-the-fly conversion and on-the-fly rounding algorithms, and their similarity discussed. Moreover, the new algorithm is supported by a comprehensive example accompanied by an implementation scheme.

References

1. Parhami, B.: Computer Arithmetic: Algorithms and Hardware Designs. Oxford University Press Inc., New York, USA (2000)
2. Ercegovac, M.D., Lang, T.: Division and Square Root: Digit-Recurrence Algorithms and Implementations. Kluwer Academic Publisher, Norwell, MA, USA (1994)
3. Oberman, S.F.: Design Issues in High Performance Floating Point Arithmetic Units. PhD thesis, Stanford University, Electrical and Electronic Department (1997)
4. Trivedi, K., Ercegovac, M.D.: On-line algorithms for division and multiplication. IEEE Transactions on Computers **26** (1977) 681–687
5. Avizienis, A.: Signed-digit number representations for fast parallel arithmetic. IRE Transactions on Electronic Computers **EC-10** (1961) 389–400
6. Nikmehr, H., Lim, C.C.: Architectures for floating-point division. Technical Report CHIPTEC-2002/02, School of Electrical and Electronic Engineering, The University of Adelaide, Adelaide, Australia (2002)
7. Hwang, K.: Computer Arithmetic: Principles, Architecture, and Design. John Wiley & Sons, Inc., New York, USA (1979)
8. Antelo, E., Lang, T., Montuschi, P., Nannarelli, A.: Fast radix-4 retimed division with selection by comparisons. In: Proceedings of IEEE 13th International Conference on Application-specific Systems, Architectures and Processors (ASAP 2002), San Jose, California, USA (2002) 185–196
9. Ercegovac, M.D., Lang, T.: On-the-fly conversion of redundant into conventional representations. IEEE Transactions on Computers **36** (1987) 895–897
10. Ercegovac, M.D., Lang, T.: On-the-fly rounding. IEEE Transactions on Computers **41** (1992) 1497–1503

State Reordering
for Low Power Combinational Logic

Kun-Lin Tsai[1], Feipei Lai[12], Shanq-Jang Ruan[3], and Szu-Wei Chaung[2]

[1] Dept. of Electrical Engineering,
National Taiwan University, Taipei, Taiwan,
kunlin@orchid.ee.ntu.edu.tw
[2] Dept. of Computer Science and Information Engineering,
National Taiwan University, Taipei, Taiwan
[3] Synopsys Taiwan Inc.

Abstract. Circuit partition, precomputation and retiming techniques are effective in reducing power consumption of the combinational circuits. In this paper, we propose a methodology to optimize power consumption at combinational logic, named state reordering. The state reordering synthesis flow consists of three phases: first, evenly partition the output patterns based on the Shannon expansion, secondly encode the output vectors of each partition to build an equivalent functional logic. Finally, apply combine algorithm to rearrange the logic function to reduce power consumption and decrease area cost. The validity of our concept is proven by applying it to some MCNC benchmarks with simulation environment.

1 Introduction

As the portable, battery-operated, electronics market moves to computational-intensive products like cellular telephones and notebook computers, the need to focus on low-power design becomes critical to extend battery life. As a result, many low power techniques have been proposed to help designers to meet low power requirement (see [1] for a survey). In this paper, we address logic level optimization of combinational circuit for low power.

Alidina, *et al.* first proposed precomputation-based architectures, which selectively disables the inputs of a sequential circuit to obtain low power [2]. Several papers have been published since then, extending the precomputation technique to the other variant schemes. In [3], STG is partitioned into two sub-machines with unequal sizes such that smaller one is active most of the time and clock for larger one is disabled. However, the selection logic (GCB) may result in large area, and offset the power reduction. Chow *et al.* decomposed an FSM into a number of coupled submachines [4], and assigned code not only to the states in the submachines but also to the machines as well. Therefore, the selection logic could be simplified as a decoding logic. Choi and Hwang exploited Shannon expansion to partition circuit by analyzing the logic function [5]. However, the relationship between the number of partitions and power dissipation is still unclear. Ruan, *et al.* presented an effective partition algorithm in higher design

A. Omondi and S. Sedukhin (Eds.): ACSAC 2003, LNCS 2823, pp. 268–276, 2003.

level by observing the input/output behavior of the circuits [6]. The results show the relationship among number of partitions, power saving and area. Ruan, *et al.* further developed a global-encoding algorithm for low power and small area circuit design [7], which evenly partitioned the output vector by the corresponding input variables and re-assigning the output vectors of each partition to minimize the number of input vectors and Hamming distance of each partition. However, the duplicated partitions overhead offset the saving of power and area of some circuits.

Another technique for saving power is retiming, which is the process of repositioning flip-flops, originally proposed for minimizing the clock periods of digital circuits [11]. The retiming has also been proposed for reducing the power dissipation of digital circuits [12][13]. In [12], the authors proposed a heuristic algorithm to select the positions of registers for reducing the power dissipation. Lalgudi, *et al.* proposed a scheme of using two-phase level-clocking, which may reduce the power dissipation without sacrificing the clock period [13].

This paper proposes a refunction algorithm for low power combinational logic synthesis based on partition-codec architecture and retiming methodology. In the beginning, we partition a circuit based on the Shannon expansion, then encode the output patterns of each partition. Finally, we merge the partitions and reposition the registers between the REL (Refunction and Encoding Logic) and decoder for reducing the area and power. Experimental results show that our algorithm reduces more power and area than the previous studies.

The rest of the paper is organized as follows. Section 2 describes the basic partition-codec architecture and algorithm as background materials. Section 3 is the core of this paper. It presents the refunction algorithm for partition-codec architecture and gives an example to illustrate this approach. In section 4, experimental results are presented that confirm the effectiveness of our new algorithm. A conclusion is given in section 5.

2 Partition and Encoding

The concepts of entropy [16], partition-codec architecture [7] and global-encoding algorithm are described in this section. The global-encoding algorithm will be extended with the "combine" algorithm to synthesize the architecture into low power and small area.

2.1 Entropy of the Circuit

As have been shown in [16], power consumption in FSM combinational part depends on the entropy of inputs and outputs of an FSM combinational circuit. For a circuit, the average power consumption is related with the circuit area and the average entropy value over all nodes. From [16], the entropy value depends on input and output entropies and on the number of input and output nodes. It is evidently that decrease of input and output entropies of a circuit leads to decrease of the average power consumption. Based on this concept, we reduce the number of internal signals to reduce the power consumption of whole circuit.

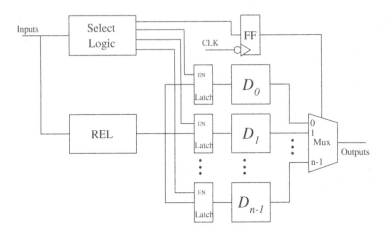

Fig. 1. Partition-codec architecture.

2.2   The Simple Partition-Codec Architecture

The partition-codec architecture is illustrated as in Fig. 1. By using a part of the original input pins, a combinational circuit can be transformed into a Shannon expansion typed circuit. For low power consideration, the signal gating idea [17] is used by selection logic to select a single decoding circuit (D_i) to be activated during operation. The inserted latches between REL and decoding blocks are used to control the input of decoding blocks, and REL (Refunction and Encoding Logic) is used to encode the input vectors. The active decoding circuit D_i decodes the value received from the REL circuit back to the original output patterns. Finally the selection logic also drives the select lines of the multiplexer to choose a correct output among the partition blocks.

2.3   The Global-Encoding Method

There are two reasons to use global-encoding method for our architecture. First, from [8], the area complexity strongly depends on the number of input, in which the average area complexity of an n-input Boolean function varies exponentially with n. Thus minimizing the number of input pins of each partition can efficiently reduce the area cost of partitions and latches. Second, in Fig. 1, most power dissipation of whole circuit is from the REL and multiplexer, it is because that these blocks are activate every clock cycle. By encoding the REL output vectors, the REL can be optimized to reduce the output entropy and area complexity.

Since both partition and encoding should be considered at the same time for finding a solution, the relationship between partition and encoding motivates the following two-phase global-encoding solution.

1. *Partition phase*: to select input variables which minimize the different output number of each partition based on Shannon expansion.

2. *Encoding phase*: the goals of this phase are to minimize the switching activity of the output/input pins of the REL/decoding (D_i) logic blocks and minimize the area of REL. Here we define N_Sti as the number of different output of partition D_i.

Example 1. Fig. 2 shows the partition process with different input variables. Fig. 2(a) shows the original truth table, if x_2 is selected, marked in gray, as the partition variable (shown in Fig. 2(d)), the output pattern will be $\{00,10\}$ when $x_2 = 0$, and $\{10,11\}$ when $x_2 = 1$. Hence the maximum number of different output patterns in both partitions is two. However, if we select x_0 or x_1 to partition the same circuit, the maximum number of different output patterns is three.

Example 2. Consider the partition result of Fig. 2. We encode the output pattern with symbol $St_{i,q}$, as shown in Fig. 3, while i represents the ith decoding block D_i and q stands for the different output pattern number in D_i. These symbols would be used to do state reordering and area optimization later. N_St_0 and

x_0 x_1 x_2	f_0 f_1	x_0 x_1 x_2	f_0 f_1	x_0 x_1 x_2	f_0 f_1	x_0 x_1 x_2	f_0 f_1
0 0 0	0 0	0 0 0	0 0	0 0 0	0 0	0 0 0	0 0
0 0 1	1 0	0 0 1	1 0	0 0 1	1 0	0 1 0	0 0
0 1 0	0 0	0 1 0	0 0	1 0 0	0 0	1 0 0	0 0
0 1 1	1 1	0 1 1	1 1	1 0 1	1 1	1 1 0	1 0
1 0 0	0 0	1 0 0	0 0	0 1 0	0 0	0 0 1	1 0
1 0 1	1 1	1 0 1	1 1	0 1 1	1 1	0 1 1	1 1
1 1 0	1 0	1 1 0	1 0	1 1 0	1 0	1 0 1	1 1
1 1 1	1 1	1 1 1	1 1	1 1 1	1 1	1 1 1	1 1
(a)		(b)		(c)		(d)	

Fig. 2. Partition with different input variables.

	x_0 x_1 x_2	f_0 f_1	encoding	N_St_i
	0 0 0	0 0	$St_{0,0}$	
D_0	0 1 0	0 0	$St_{0,0}$	2
	1 0 0	0 0	$St_{0,0}$	
	1 1 0	1 0	$St_{0,1}$	
	0 0 1	1 0	$St_{1,0}$	
D_1	0 1 1	1 1	$St_{1,1}$	2
	1 0 1	1 1	$St_{1,1}$	
	1 1 1	1 1	$St_{1,1}$	

Fig. 3.

N_St_1 are both 2 in this case. Obviously, we can use only one bit rather than three bits to represent the states in each decoding block, and it can achieve the goal of minimizing the switching activity.

As the encoding phase, we consider the possibility to merge the partition by reorganizing the REL and partition tables. We will address the problem in the next section.

3 The Combination Algorithm

In this section, we describe the combination algorithm to effectively merge the partitions and give an example to show the merging sequence.

3.1 Algorithm Overview

The combination algorithm effectively merges partitions to reduce power consumption of the selection logic and output multiplexer. It can also minimize the decoding circuit area. In this algorithm, there are four rules to help to merge the partitions:

1. if $St_{i,q} = St_{j,q}$, for all q and $i \neq j$, then merge D_i and D_j to D_{ij} (D_{ij} is a new partition block, and define $St_{ij,q}$ as the new output function).
2. if the set of $St_{i,q}$ is equal to the set of $St_{j,p}$, for $i \neq j$, only the sequence is different (ex. in Fig. 4(b) D_2 is $\{010, 000, 111\}$, and D_3 is $\{000, 010, 111\}$), then we use $St_{i,q}$ to represent the output pattern of the merged function, and re-encoding the output of $St_{j,p}$.
3. if only some partial set of $St_{i,q}$ equals some partial set of $St_{j,p}$, for all p, q, and $i \neq j$ (ex. in Fig. 4(b) $St_{4,0} = St_{5,0}$, $St_{4,2} = St_{5,2}$) and the input pins condition is satisfied, then the equal parts are selected first (ex. 011 and 110 are selected first), and plus the unequal parts of $St_{i,q}(D_4, 110)$ and $St_{j,p}(D_5, 101)$ to be the new output of the merged blocks
4. if $St_{i,q}\{000, 110, 010\} \neq St_{j,p}\{111\}$, for all q and $p(i \neq j)$, and the input pins condition is satisfied, then merge D_i and D_j to be D_{ij} and combine $St_{i,q}$ and $St_{j,p}$ as the new output of the merged block.

The input pins condition of case 3 and case 4 is $N\_St_{ij} \leq 2^{\text{REL output pin number}}$, where N_St_{ij} is the number of different output pattern of D_{ij}. This is because if $N\_St_{ij} > 2^{\text{REL output pin number}}$, it will result in additional output pins of the REL. In other words, it would increase power dissipation and area of the REL.

Example 3. Consider the partition of Fig. 2. N_St_0 and N_St_1 are both 2, and only one output pin of the REL is enough to control the output pattern of D_0 and D_1. If we merge D_0 and D_1 to D_{01}, then N_St_{01} is 3. That means that we need two output pins of REL to control the output pattern of D_{01}.

The refunction algorithm is shown below. The input of our algorithm is the subcircuits which are generated by the *global-encoding* algorithm. It outputs the

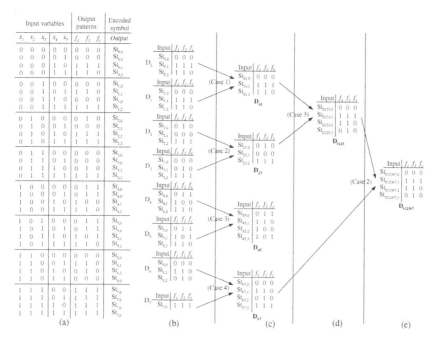

Fig. 4. An example of refunction.

REL and the partitions. The merging priority is $case1 > case2 > case3 > case4$.
The reason for setting priority for each case is that the higher priority case can
save more power and area than the case of low priority. It is possible to merge
again and again to obtain the smallest partition.

Refunction( )
{
10   **INPUT**: subcircuits after global-encoding (as shown in Fig. 4(b))
20   **OUTPUT**: REL and partitions
30   **Do-Until** no more partitions can be merged
40   **FOR** all i, j and $i \neq j$
50   { Select subcircuits D_i and D_j from the set of subcircuits
             (SS)=$\{D_0, D_1, K, D_{n-1}\}$;
60   **IF** D_i and D_j can be merged together according to one of
             four conditions
70   **THEN** {
80   merge D_i and D_j to D_{ij};
90   delete D_i from SS;
100   delete D_j from SS;
110   add D_{ij} into SS;
            }
      }
}

3.2 An Example of Refunction

There are four kinds of merging approaches used in *refunction* algorithm. As shown in Fig. 4(a), x_1 to x_5 are the input variables of the circuit and f_1 to f_3 are the outputs of the circuit. In this example, we take x_1, x_2 and x_3 to partition circuit by Shannon Expansion. We assign the symbol to the output of each partition by the order of its occurrence during bench-marking (ie. $\#St_{i,0} \geq \#St_{i,1} \geq \#St_{i,2}$ for partition D_i). In Fig. 4(b), D_0 to D_7 are the partitions done by global-encoding. In Fig. 4(c), D_{01}, D_{23}, D_{45} and D_{67} are the partitions after the first merge step. For D_{01}, the input pattern is $\{St_{01,0}, St_{01,1}, St_{01,2}\}$ and output pattern is $\{000, 111, 110\}$. After the second merge step, D_{0123} is generated from D_{01} and D_{23}, as shown in Fig. 4(d). Finally, after refunction, two partition blocks D_{012367} and D_{45} remains. For each partition now, we can use two pins to encode the symbols.

3.3 Power Saving of Partition Architecture

The major power saving comes from several parts. First, partitioning the circuit and using the gated-clock [14] avoid the unnecessary power consumption of the idle blocks. Second, we use the retiming technique to reposition registers between the REL and partition blocks, and it is useful to reduce the number of active registers at one clock period. Finally, the entropy [15][16] of the circuit is also an important key point of power reduction. During the process of partition, we change the entropy of circuit. The sum of the entropy of the REL and partition blocks is much smaller than the original one.

4 Experimental Results

The state-reordering algorithm has been implemented in C++ on a SUN SPARC station. We used SIS [10] to synthesize our partition results and estimate the power and area by mapping our design to MCNC.genlib and MCNC_latch.genlib cell libraries. Combinational logic examples from the MCNC logic synthesis benchmarks were used in the experiments. In the experiment, 5v supply voltage and a clock frequency of 20MHz was assumed. The rugged script of SIS was used to optimize most of the benchmarks.

Fig. 5 illustrates the synthesis flow of the partition-codec architecture. First, we partition the circuit into 2^k sub-circuits, where k is the input variables which we choose to do partition. Second, we re-assign the output of each sub-circuit by the *global-encoding* algorithm. Then we merge the sub-circuits by applying our *Combination* algorithm. Note that this combination algorithm returns an encoding table which maps distinct outputs to a symbol. Then, we encode the symbols by NOVA [9], which is used to do the state assignment for the symbols of the REL. Finally, SIS is used to estimate the power and area of the circuit.

Table. 1 presents the results compared to those of the circuits optimized by state ordering. Column *Original* gives the results of conventional approach,

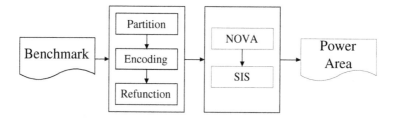

Fig. 5. The synthesis flow.

Table 1. Experimental Results

Bench mark	Original		State-reorder	
	Power	Area	PR%	AR%
t	222.2	61	50.0	49.2
apex2	2320.0	748	60.8	49.6
too_large	2283.8	738	59.4	47.8
cm85a	605.6	179	11.6	−49.8
rd73	546.0	168	38.8	32.7
cm163a	752.8	223	50.4	48.9
cmb	747.0	210	58.7	58.1
rd84	795.6	259	47.2	42.1
vg2	1363.3	387	44.3	43.4
pcle	969.5	296	8.3	−28.1
Average			43.0	29.4

which didn't use any low power technique. Column *State reorder* gives the results with reordering algorithms. The *PR%* and *AR%* in these two columns represent the power and area reduction percentage, respectively.

It is clear from Table. 1 that there is significant decrease in power obtained by state reordering algorithm. The results also show that state reordering algorithm can achieve area reduction in most cases. Because the number of partitions is decreased by state reordering algorithm, the selection logic and multiplexers become much simpler and less than that by global-encoding algorithm. On average, the power dissipation of the circuits generated by the state reordering algorithm is reduced by 43%, and the area is reduced by 29.4%. The area increase in benchmark *cm85a* and *pcle* is because the additional circuit, REL, is much bigger than the original circuit area.

5   Conclusion

An improved algorithm for synthesizing low power partition-codec architecture has been presented. Given a circuit, we first partition the circuit based on Shannon expansion, then re-assign and reorganize the partition to reduce the number of partitions for simplifying the selection logic, input latches and output multiplexers. The state reorder methodology is more suitable for circuits with equal probability of output patterns. Experimental results on a large class of benchmark circuits in MCNC benchmark suite have shown that not only power dissipation but also area can be dramatically reduced.

References

1. K. Roy and S. C. Prasad, *Low Power CMOS VLSI Circuit Design*. New York: John Wiley, 2000
2. Alidina, Jose Monteiro, Srinivas Devadas, Abhijit Ghosh and Marios Papaefthymiou, "Precomputation-Based Sequential Logic Optimization for Low Power," *IEEE Tran. on VLSI*, vol. 2, No. 4, pp.426-436, Dec. 1994.
3. S,-J.Chen, R.-J. Shang, X.-J. Huang, S.-J. Ruan and Feipei Lai, "Bipartition and Synthesis in Low Power Pipelined Circuits," *IEICE Tran. Fundamentals Electron., Commun., Comput. Sci.,* vol. E81-A, pp.664-671, Apr. 1998.
4. H. Chow, Y.-C. Ho, T. Hwang, "Low Power Realization of Finite State Machines-A Decomposition Approach," *ACM Trans. Design Automation & Electronic Systems,* vol. 1, no. 3, , pp. 315-340 Jul. 1996.
5. I.-S. Choi and S.-Y. Hwang, "Low Power Logic Synthesis Algorithm Using Multiple Partitioning Under Delay Constraints," *IEE Electronics Letters*, vol. 35, no. 7, pp. 558-560, Apr. 1999.
6. S.-J. Ruan, J.-C. Lin, P.-H. Chen, F. Lai, K.-L. Tsai, and C.-W. Y, "An Effective Output-Oriented Algorithm for Low Power Multipartition Architecture," in *Proc. IEEE Int. Conf. Electronics, Circuits and Systems*, Dec. 2000, pp. 609-612.
7. S.-J. Ruan, J.-C. Lin, P.-H. Chen, K.-L. Tsai, and F. Lai, "Synthesis of Partition-Codec Architecture for Low Power and Small Area Circuit Design," in *Proc. IEEE Int. Symp. Circuits and Systems*, May 2001.
8. K.-T. Cheng and V. D. Agrawal, "An Entropy Measure for the Complexity of Multi-output Boolean Function," in *Proc. 27th ACM/IEEE Design Automation Conf.* 1990, pp.302-305.
9. T. Villa and A. Sangiovanni-Vincentelli, "NOVA: State Assignment of Finite State Machines for Optimal Two-Level Logic Implementation," *IEEE Trans. Computer-Aided Design*, vol. 9, pp. 905-924, Sep. 1990.
10. SIS: A System for Sequential Circuit synthesis is implementd by Electronics Research Laboratory in Department of EE and CS, University of California, Berkley, 4 May 1992.
11. C.E. Leiserson and J.B. Saxe. "Retiming Synchronous Circuitry" *Algorithm*, pp. 5-35, Jun. 1991.
12. J. Monteiro, S. Devadas and A. Ghosh. "Retiming Sequential Circuits for Low Power" in *Proc. ICCAD*, pp. 398-402, 1993.
13. K.N. Lalgudi and M.C. Papaefthymiou. "Fixed-Phase Retiming for Low Power Design" in *Proc. ISLPED*, pp. 259-264, 1996.
14. L. Benini and G. D. Micheli, 'Automatic synthesis of low-power gated clock finite-state machines,' *IEEE Tran. on Computer-Aided Design of Integrated Circuits and Systems*, vol. 15, No. 6, pp.630-643, Sep. 1996.
15. M. Nemani and F. N. Najm, "High-level area and power estimation for VLSI circuits," *IEEE Trans. Computer-Aided Design*, vol. 18, pp. 697-713, Jun 1999.
16. M. Nemani and F. N. Najm, "Towards a High-Level Power Estimation Capability," *IEEE Trans. Computer-Aided Design*, vol. 15, pp. 588-598, Jun 1996.
17. G. Yeap., *Practical Low Power Digital VLSI Design*, Kluwer,1998.

User-Level Management of Kernel Memory

Andreas Haeberlen[1] and Kevin Elphinstone[2]

[1] University of Karlsruhe, System Architecture Group, 76128 Karlsruhe, Germany,
haeberlen@ira.uka.de
[2] University of New South Wales, Sydney, 2052, Australia,
kevine@cse.unsw.edu.au

Abstract. Kernel memory is a resource that must be managed carefully in order to ensure the efficiency and safety of the system. The use of an inappropriate management policy can weaken the isolation between subsystems, lead to suboptimal performance, and even make the kernel vulnerable to denial-of-service attacks. Yet, many existing kernels use only a single built-in policy, which is always a compromise between performance and generality.

In this paper, we address this problem by exporting control over kernel memory to user-level pagers. Thus, subsystems can implement their own application-specific management policies while independent subsystems can still be isolated from each other.

The pagers have full control over the memory resources they manage; they can even preempt and later restore individual pages of kernel memory. Still, protection is not compromised because the kernel converts its metadata into a safe representation before exporting it. Therefore, pagers need only be trusted by their respective clients.

We describe the model we use to page kernel memory and various techniques for obtaining a safe external representation for kernel metadata. We also report experiences with an experimental kernel that implements our scheme and outline our plans to further develop the approach.

1 Introduction

Operating systems obviously need resource management. Any multitasking or multiuser system needs to ensure resources are efficiently managed to fulfil some desired system-level policy, such as maximising overall throughput or guaranteeing availability to high priority tasks. Poor or simplistic resource management can result in underutilisation, low performance, or even denial of service.

Kernel memory is an often overlooked resource. It is required to implement higher-level resources or services for applications; examples include page tables for implementing virtual memory, buffer caches for file providing, and thread control blocks (TCB) to implement threads. Physical memory is the ultimate resource consumed by kernel memory, and thus simplistic kernel memory management is ultimately simplistic and problematic physical memory management. As demonstrated by Scout [27], a management approach encompassing all kernel memory is required to avoid denial-of-service attacks.

A. Omondi and S. Sedukhin (Eds.): ACSAC 2003, LNCS 2823, pp. 277–289, 2003.

Several operating systems manage their kernel memory carefully. Scout provides limits on kernel memory per protection domain and per *path* [27]; a path is a logical execution flow through one or more domains. Eros[26] and the Cache kernel[4] both view kernel physical memory as a cache of kernel metadata and as such can evict cache entries when cache capacity is exceeded. However, these systems share one thing in common: they all carefully manage kernel memory in such a way as to fulfil a single overall system policy. This is understandable as each system has a particular focus and is designed to meet its specific needs.

We believe these kernels are overly restrictive in their management of kernel memory and thus limit their application in areas outside their original focus. Related work has shown that applications are often ill-served by the default operating system policy[1, 28] and can benefit significantly from managing their own memory resources[7, 9, 11, 13, 15, 20]. Ideally, a kernel should be adaptable to different application areas, and even support concurrent applications with differing requirements on kernel memory management whilst preventing interference between the applications.

An example might be a real-time system running together with an insecure best-effort system. The two have very different requirements for kernel memory management: the real-time system may require preallocated and pinned memory to ensure deadlines are met, whereas the best-effort system only needs cache-like memory behaviour to meet its current needs.

Paged virtual memory has become ubiquitous in modern systems as it provides a well understood, flexible, and efficient mechanism to manage the physical memory of applications. Virtual memory has proved sufficient to manage physical memory usage between competing clients, provide recoverable and transactional memory [5, 24], provide more predictable or improved cache behaviour via page colouring [14], enable predictable access timing via pinning, and even enable secure application-controlled virtual memory by safely exporting control of basic virtual memory mechanisms [7, 17, 22]. Given the power, maturity, and understanding of applying virtual memory techniques to user-level applications, we believe virtual memory techniques can also be applied to manage kernel memory.

By paging kernel memory and safely exporting that control to user-level, we believe we can harness the power and flexibility of virtual memory to support classes of applications requiring careful management of kernel memory without targeting and thus restricting our approach to a particular application area; also, we can concurrently support different applications while ensuring isolation from each other.

Moreover, the generality of our approach allows us to unify and replace various existing mechanisms. One example is user-level persistence, which can be easily implemented when kernel metadata is fully accessible. Another example is cache colouring[14], which requires control over the in-kernel placement policy.

2   The Approach

We chose the L4 microkernel as the platform to evaluate our ideas. L4 is a small microkernel which reduces the complexity of the problem. It also has a powerful model for constructing user-level address spaces [16] which we believe can be applied to kernel memory. Our approach to kernel memory management aims to place all kernel memory logically within a kernel virtual address space, which is realised by user-level *kpagers* using the same model that is used to construct user-level virtual address spaces. We believe our approach is unique in that it allows untrusted user-level pagers to safely supply and preempt kernel memory. Before we proceed to describe our approach in more detail, a brief description of the L4 virtual address space model is warranted.

L4 implements a recursive virtual address space model which permits virtual memory management to be performed entirely at user level. Initially, all physical memory is mapped within the root address space σ_0; new address spaces can then be constructed by mapping regions of accessible virtual memory from one address space to the next.

Memory regions can either be **map**-ped or **grant**-ed. Mapping and granting is performed by sending typed objects in IPC messages. In the case of **map**, the sender retains control of the newly derived mapping and can later use another primitive (**unmap**) to revoke the mapping, including any further mappings derived from the new mapping. In the case of **grant**, the region is transferred to the receiver and disappears from the granter's address space (see Figure 1).

Page faults are handled by the kernel transforming them into messages delivered via IPC. Every thread has a pager thread associated with it. The pager is responsible for managing a thread's address space. Whenever a thread takes a page fault, the kernel catches the fault, blocks the thread and synthesizes a page-fault IPC message to the pager on the thread's behalf. The pager can then respond with a mapping and thus unblock the thread.

This model has been successfully used to construct several very different systems as user-level applications, including real-time systems and single-address-space systems [8, 10, 12, 21]. We believe it can also be used to manage kernel memory.

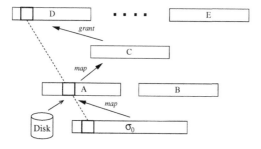

Fig. 1. Virtual memory primitives

2.1   The Basic Model

We propose the following extension to the L4 memory model to facilitate kernel memory management. While these extensions are L4 specific, they should also be applicable to other systems. We associate each thread with a *kpager* which receives kernel page faults when the kernel requires more memory for a thread. The kpager can choose to map any page it possesses to resolve the fault. Like a normal pager, the kpager can revoke the memory at any point by invoking unmap on the supplied page.

This basic model is more complicated in reality due to important differences between paging an application and paging the kernel. By paging the kernel to a user-level pager, we are storing critical information in an object backed by an untrusted, insecure pager. To succeed, we need to ensure that no kpager can obtain sensitive kernel information, nor compromise the kernel. However, it is acceptable for a kpager to obtain information associated with its clients, or to compromise its clients.

We consider kernel memory currently in use (the equivalent to memory paged in), and kernel state not in the kernel (the equivalent to memory paged out) separately. In-use memory is protected from kpager interference and examination by revoking user-level read-write access rights to the page. The kpager still logically possesses the page and can unmap it from the kernel to gain normal access once again.

Paged-out kernel memory can be freely examined and modified by the kpager. To prevent the disclosure of sensitive information, the kernel transforms the contents of a page into a safe external representation prior to exporting it back to the kpager. To avoid interference by potential kpager modifications to the exported state, the kernel validates the contents when paging it back into the kernel, and converts the contents back into its in-kernel representation. The exact transformation to and from the external representation is dependent on the particular kernel memory being exported and imported. The following section describes the classes of data we deal with.

2.2   Kernel Data Structures

In terms of ease of exporting kernel data to kpagers, we have identified three broad classes of kernel data: *safe*, *redundant*, and *sensitive*. The classes are not necessarily mutually exclusive.

Data is *safe* to export as-is if it is readily available (readable and writable) to the client. If any restrictions are placed on data availability to the client, the data is still *safe* if the restrictions can remain in place after the data is exported to and imported from the kpager.

Some kernel data can be readily reconstructed from data held by user-level applications. This *redundant* data can be exported by simply discarding the contents of the page, and returning a vacant page to the pager. One example is a page table which is discarded when exported, and rebuilt when imported via page faults to user-level pagers.

Data is *sensitive* to export if it refers to kernel internals, to clients other than those being paged by the kpager, or to client attributes not freely accessible to the client itself. Unrestricted access to *sensitive* data could compromise the kernel, detrimentally affect the clients of other kpagers, or raise the privileges of clients beyond what is directly achievable by the client or the kpager. *Sensitive* data can be exported, for example, by sealing it cryptographically before exporting it to user-level, and validating it when it is returned to the kernel.

3   Implementation

This section describes the more interesting details of our implementation. We focus on L4 on Intel's IA-32 architecture, but we believe the techniques described are readily applicable to other architectures. The IA-32 L4 kernel has the following in-kernel data structures: page tables, thread control blocks (TCBs), mappings nodes, and node tables.

3.1   Page Tables

Pages tables are *redundant* data as they are constructed by a user-level application's invocation of the map, grant, and unmap primitives. The user-level pager typically has a superset of the kernel's page table which it uses to manage its clients' virtual address spaces. Page tables are also *sensitive* data as they contain physical addresses. To avoid the potential security issues in exporting *sensitive* data, we actually export the page tables vacant.

3.2   Mapping Nodes

Mapping nodes are used to track the derivation tree of mappings that represent the current state of all address spaces in the system. This mapping database is required to implement the unmap primitive. unmap removes any mapping derived from a specified mapping and, optionally, the specified mapping itself. Like page tables, the mapping database is *redundant* data constructed by invoking map, grant, and unmap. In principle, the data structure could be exported vacant.

However, the data structure is a hierarchical tree. Thus, to export part of it vacant, any branches derived from the newly vacated part must also be invalidated to ensure unmap is correct when applied closer to the root of the tree. Hence, a simplistic approach to vacating pages from the mapping database could result in significant, cascading invalidation. We avoid this by localising mapping nodes prior to exporting them.

Localisation is a general technique we use to transform particular *sensitive* data into *safe* data. Data is exported by translating all data in the page from in-kernel references to references valid in the local user-level context of the client. When returned to the kernel, the page is validated by translating the client-local references back into kernel data. By translating the kernel data into local references, we safely export the data by restricting the contents of the page to references to objects the client can directly manipulate. Any permutation of the page returned to the kernel could have been constructed directly by the client by invoking operations on local objects.

A mapping node contains a reference to the virtual page and address space it is associated with, a reference to the page and address space from which it is derived, and reference to any further derived mappings. The mapper of the page determines the page from which the mapping is derived, and the receiver of the mapping determines the location where the received mapping is placed.

We split the mapping node into a sender-derived part and a receiver-derived part. The sender's and receiver's kpager pages the respective parts. Each part is localised with respect to the sender and receiver, thus making it examinable by the respective parties. Kpager modifications of the data can only result in situations that could have been created through cooperative application of the mapping primitives by both parties.

3.3   Node Tables

Node tables exist to provide a mapping between virtual memory regions and the corresponding nodes in the mapping database. They are closely related to page tables and have a similar structure; for each page table entry, there is a corresponding node table entry which points to the associated mapping node. Unlike page table entries, however, these pointers are not *redundant*; they are required by the kernel e.g. to locate preempted mapping nodes. Therefore we export them by localising them to the context of the client.

3.4   Thread Control Blocks

Thread control blocks (TCBs) implement kernel threads. A thread's TCB contains a thread's register set and activation stack (if in kernel mode), the thread's state (e.g. waiting or running), its scheduling parameters (time slice, priority, run queue link), and other queue links related to IPC. In order to support lazy thread switching[19], the TCBs are divided into two parts, one of which (the UTCB) is user accessible, and the other (the KTCB) resides in protected kernel memory. The content of the UTCB is modifiable at user level by the thread it implements, and thus is not protected in any way. It is *safe* and we simply export the complete contents to the kpager. Similarly, the thread's user-level register set is also *safe*.

The kernel activation stack and state is *sensitive*. In order to safely export it we use a *continuation*, a special kernel object which contains a digest of the state that is encoded in the stack. Only particular safe points within the kernel need to be represented by the continuations, and those can be safely revalidated when faulted back into the kernel. Examination of the continuation only gives a kpager coarse knowledge of the particular thread's kernel state, and modification of the exported data results in a mutation to some other valid kernel state which can only affect the client thread involved. The integrity of other threads and the kernel itself is preserved.

Scheduling parameters and implementation are *sensitive*. We are currently exploring how to safely export them. If we adopted a hierarchical proportional-share scheduling scheme with kpagers determining scheduling parameters, we could localise the scheduling parameters in terms of shares of the kpager's allocation. However, we are wary of unifying both scheduling and memory management into a single hierarchy. Currently, a copy of the scheduling parameters is kept in the kernel.

3.5   Deadlocks

In a system with pageable kernel metadata, the kernel must be prepared to handle situations where it lacks the metadata necessary to complete an operation. These situations can occur when additional metadata needs to be allocated, or when existing metadata has been paged out. In either case, care must be taken to ensure progress, i.e. to prevent the system from being caught in a deadlock.

To this end, two different problems need to be solved. First, the kernel must not deadlock *internally*, e.g. because the page fault handler itself causes a page fault. Second, the page fault messages must not cause deadlocks in the *user-level system*.

The first problem is common to all pageable kernels; it is essentially a matter of system design. In our system, we solved it by eliminating all circular dependencies between kernel data structures, and by imposing a strict hierarchy. The second problem, however, cannot be solved entirely at kernel level because the user can always create a deadlock, e.g. by establishing a circular dependency between a pager and one of its clients. The kernel can therefore only guarantee that it is *possible* to construct a deadlock-free system with reasonable effort, and that unrelated subsystems are not affected when a deadlock does occur.

In an L4 system, the only critical operation is sending a `map` message via IPC. When a kernel page fault occurs while a kpager is using this operation to resolve another page fault in one of its clients, the kpager is blocked indefinitely because it can never handle the second fault. In this case, however, the kernel can easily detect the deadlock and resolve it by aborting the operation. Both threads are notified and can use this information to avoid further deadlocks, e.g. by handling the page faults in a different order.

We use *fault ordering* to reduce the overhead induced by deadlock resolution. When the kernel detects that it needs multiple resources $r_1, \ldots, r_n$ to complete an operation, it chooses an order $(i_1, \ldots, i_n)$ such that r_{i_j} does not depend on any r_{i_k} with $k > j$. Such an order always exists because the metadata is structured hierarchically. The kernel can then effectively avoid deadlocks by requesting the resources in that order.

3.6   Other Details

We enable accounting and control of kernel memory usage by associating the memory mapped to the kernel with a resource principal. Tasks (i.e. address spaces containing one or more threads) were chosen as resource principals since most kernel data (page tables, etc.) is used to implement tasks and is shared between all threads in the task. The kernel only uses kernel memory associated with the requestor of a service. Once exhausted, the kernel can fault in more pages on behalf of a task from the task's kpager. Therefore, kpagers can accurately account and control the amount of kernel memory used by individual tasks.

Typically, a pager has a contract to implement virtual memory regions for its clients. For this purpose, it uses the mapping primitives and its physical memory resources; it also keeps a mapping between virtual page addresses and their contents, which reside either in memory or on external storage. However, while the client of a normal pager does not know the current assignment between physical pages and virtual memory regions and therefore must treat the region as an opaque object, the client of a kpager (the kernel) has full knowledge and can therefore operate on the memory as it sees fit, even access the physical frames directly. Thus, virtual page addresses become content identifiers and need not bear any resemblance to the actual virtual addresses used by the kernel. Kernel page faults can be signalled when content is not present or when more memory is required, not necessarily as a result of hardware-based page faults. This gives the kernel implementor full freedom, but still preserves the simple pager model for all user-level code.

Different kernel pages have different costs associated with revoking them from the kernel; for example, a root page directory is more costly to revoke than a leaf directory. To allow fine tuning of kpager policy, we are exploring the possibility of giving specialised kpagers information about the internal data types of a particular kernel. This can be done cleanly by assigning kernel data types to specific virtual page ranges. A specialised kpager can make use of this information, e.g. to adjust its replacement policy or to discard vacated pages instead of writing them to backing store. At the same time, a generic kpager can function correctly, albeit sub-optimally.

4   Evaluation

We have constructed an experimental L4 kernel to serve as a platform to develop and experiment with our ideas. It implements a modified L4 API and allows kpagers to page most dynamically allocated kernel memory. All memory-management related data is paged, and most TCB data is paged (all but approximately 100 bytes of an original 1 Kbyte TCB).

The kernel is stable and complete enough to run L^{4}Linux [10], a derivative of Linux 2.4.20 that was modified to run on top of the L4 microkernel. We used this system to get a first impression of performance.

4.1   Kernel Memory Usage

In order to determine the amount of kernel memory used by typical applications, we booted a standard Debian distribution on top of L^{4}Linux. After opening an

Space	Application	Threads	Resident	#P	#N	#M	#U	Metadata
30.1	σ_0	1	131.080k	3	1	8	1	52k
32.1	L^4Linux	19	129.804k	5	5	8	3	84k
214.2	pingpong	2	20k	4	4	1	1	40k
216.2	init	2	76k	5	5	1	1	48k
218.2	bash	2	52k	5	5	2	1	52k
21a.2	bash	2	392k	5	5	2	1	52k
21c.2	getty	2	80k	5	5	1	1	48k
21e.2	syslogd	2	152k	5	5	1	1	48k
220.2	portmap	2	96k	5	5	1	1	48k
222.2	klogd	2	108k	5	5	1	1	48k
224.2	rpc.statd	2	108k	5	5	1	1	48k
226.2	gpm	2	96k	5	5	1	1	48k
228.2	inetd	2	100k	5	5	1	1	48k
22a.2	lpd	2	112k	5	5	1	1	48k
22c.2	smbd	2	260k	5	5	1	1	48k
22e.2	rpc.nfsd	2	272k	5	5	1	1	48k
230.2	rpc.mountd	2	284k	5	5	1	1	48k
232.2	cron	2	140k	5	5	1	1	48k
234.2	getty	2	80k	5	5	1	1	48k
236.2	getty	2	80k	5	5	1	1	48k
238.2	getty	2	80k	5	5	1	1	48k
23a.2	cc	2	164k	5	5	1	1	48k
23e.2	emacs	2	2.700k	5	5	4	1	60k

Fig. 2. Memory usage under L^4Linux. Table shows resident set size, number of pages used for page tables (P), node tables (N), mapping database (M), user TCBs (U), and total kernel memory usage.

emacs session and starting a compile job, we obtained a snapshot of the system and analysed the usage of kernel memory (Figure 2).

We found that a typical[1] application consumes approximately 100-300kB of user memory and 40-60kB of kernel memory. We conclude that a nonnegligible portion of main memory is used as kernel memory; hence, some extra effort for managing it seems justified.

We also found that the numbers are surprisingly high and do not vary much between small and large applications. This is due to high internal fragmentation, which is largely caused by sparsely populated page tables and cannot be avoided by the kernel alone since the page table format is dictated by the IA-32 hardware. However, by replacing the standard Linux address space layout with a more compact one, the overhead could be reduced significantly, in some cases by up to 50%.

A comparison to other L4 kernels for the IA-32 shows that the effective overhead of our scheme amounts to only 1.5 frames or 6kB, which we consider sufficiently low.

---

[1] The root pager σ_0 and the L^4Linux server have atypical resident set sizes because they have all physical memory (128MB in our experiment) mapped to their address spaces. Most of that memory is mapped on to other applications.

4.2 Policy Overhead

In order to determine the temporal overhead for a simple user-level allocation policy, we measured the time required to handle a kernel page fault. To this end, we modified our kernel to support an optional in-kernel memory pool. When this pool is in use, no kernel page faults are generated.

We then ran a simple test application that causes a page fault in a previously untouched memory region. This memory region was carefully chosen so that multiple instances of kernel metadata (a page table and a node table) would be required to handle the fault. Without the in-kernel memory pool, the kernel would thus have to send two additional page faults.

| In-kernel allocator | 1 fault | 18,091 cycles ($\pm$ 100) |
| User-level allocator | 3 faults | 21,454 cycles ($\pm$ 100) |

Fig. 3. Cycles required to handle a complex page fault, for which the kernel must allocate two additional pages of kernel memory.

The experiment was performed on a dual Pentium II/400 system with 192 MB of main memory; we used the performance counters of the CPU to measure the cycles required in both cases (Figure 3). The difference of approximately 3,400 cycles is explained by the additional overhead for generating two fault IPCs, executing the user-level fault handler twice, and crossing the user-kernel boundary four times. This indicates an effective overhead of 1,700 cycles per kernel page fault on this machine.

In the previous section, we demonstrated that a typical L^{4}Linux task uses less than 60kB of kernel metadata. This is equivalent to 15 frames. We estimate that requesting these frames from a simple user-level manager, e.g. one that implements a Quota policy, causes an additional one-time overhead of $15 \cdot 1,700 = 25,500$ cycles or $64\mu s$, which we consider acceptable, especially given that our microkernel is still completely unoptimized.

5   Related Work

There has been previous work on managing kernel memory from user level. The path abstraction in Scout[27], Resource Containers[2] and Virtual Services[23] can be used to account for and limit consumption of kernel memory; all of them can be controlled from user level. The same is possible in extensible systems like SPIN[3] and VINO[6], where code can be uploaded into the kernel at runtime. However, all of these approaches use a global policy for the entire system, and neither of them supports preemption or revocation of kernel memory, except by killing the principal.

EROS[25] and the Cache Kernel[4] use a different approach in which the kernel acts as a cache for metadata and can evict objects from this cache when its capacity is exceeded. However, neither the capacity nor the allocation of these caches can be controlled by applications, and it is difficult to isolate subsystems from each other.

Liedtke has described another approach where applications can resolve a shortage of kernel memory by donating some of their own memory to the kernel[18]. However, the model is incomplete as no mechanism is provided to revoke or reclaim memory from the kernel.

The Fluke kernel can export kernel state to user level, which has been used to implement user-level checkpointing[29]. However, kernel memory itself cannot be managed.

6   Conclusions and Future Work

In this paper, we have presented a mechanism that can be used to safely export control over kernel memory to user level. Unlike previous solutions, it supports graceful preemption and revocation of kernel memory, which makes it possible to implement not only basic policies like FCFS or quotas, but also more advanced strategies such as Working Set. Also, every subsystem can implement its own custom policy, allowing it to benefit from specific knowledge about its current and future needs.

To demonstrate the feasibility of our approach, we have implemented it in an experimental kernel that supports the L4 API. The experimental kernel allows all memory-related metadata and most TCB metadata to be paged from user level. A small portion of the TCB (approximately 10%) is not paged because this would require changes to the L4 API. We plan to continue refining our design to eliminate the remaining unexported data; also, we will conduct further experiments to apply different management policies and to evaluate their performance.

We believe that our mechanism is powerful enough to be used beyond the simple control of physical memory consumption. We envisage kpagers enabling subsystem checkpointing by capturing both the kernel and user-level state of a subsystem. Kpagers should also enable paging of kernel data to backing store, thus allowing kernel memory to exceed physical memory limitations. Page coloring[14] might also be advantageous when applied to kernel memory.

In summary, we believe we can safely export management of kernel memory to user-level pagers. Our system should be flexible enough to do any or all schemes concurrently on isolated subsystems, without requiring kernel modification.

References

1. Andrew W. Appel and Kai Li. Virtual memory primitives for user programs. In *Proc. 4th ASPLOS*, pages 96–107. ACM Press, Apr 1991.
2. Gaurav Banga, Peter Druschel, and Jeffrey C. Mogul. Resource containers: a new facility for resource management in server systems. In *Proc. 3rd OSDI*, pages 45–58, Feb 1999.

3. Brian N. Bershad *et al.* SPIN: an extensible microkernel for application-specific operating system services. In *Proc. 6th ACM SIGOPS European Workshop*, pages 68–71, 1994.

4. David R. Cheriton and Kenneth J. Duda. A caching model of operating system kernel functionality. In *Proc. 1st OSDI*, pages 179–193, Nov 1994.

5. David R. Cheriton and Kenneth J. Duda. Logged virtual memory. In *Proc. 15th ACM SOSP*, pages 26–38, Dec 1995.

6. Yasuhiro Endo, James Gwertzman, Margo Seltzer, Christopher Small, Keith A. Smith, and Diane Tang. VINO: The 1994 fall harvest. Technical Report TR-34-94, Harvard Computer Center for Research in Computing Technology, 1994.

7. Dawson R. Engler, Sandeep K. Gupta, and M. Frans Kaashoek. AVM: Application-level virtual memory. In *Proc. 5th HotOS*, pages 72–77, May 1995.

8. A. Gefflaut *et al.* The SawMill multiserver approach. In *9th SIGOPS European Workshop*, Kolding, Denmark, September 2000.

9. Steven M. Hand. Self-paging in the Nemesis operating system. In *Proc. 3rd OSDI*, pages 73–86. USENIX Association, Feb 1999.

10. Hermann Härtig, Michael Hohmuth, Jochen Liedtke, Sebastian Schönberg, and Jean Wolter. The performance of μ-kernel-based systems. In *Proc. 16th ACM SOSP*. ACM, 1997.

11. Kieran Harty and David R. Cheriton. Application-controlled physical memory using external page-cache management. In *Proc. 5th ASPLOS*, pages 187–197, Oct 1992.

12. Gernot Heiser, Kevin Elphinstone, Jerry Vochteloo, Stephen Russell, and Jochen Liedtke. The Mungi single-address-space operating system. *Software Practice and Experience*, 28(9), Jul 1998.

13. John P. Kearns and Samuel DeFazio. Diversity in database reference behaviour. *Performance Evaluation Review*, 17(1):11–19, May 1989.

14. R. E. Kessler and Mark D. Hill. Page placement algorithms for large real-indexed caches. *ACM TOCS*, 10(4):338–359, Nov 1992.

15. Keith Krueger, David Loftesness, Amin Vahdat, and Thomas Anderson. Tools for the development of application-specific virtual memory management. In *Proceedings of the eighth annual conference on Object-oriented programming systems, languages, and applications*, pages 48–64. ACM Press, 1993.

16. Jochen Liedtke. On μ-kernel construction. In *Proc. 15th ACM SOSP*, pages 237–250. ACM Press, Dec 1995.

17. Jochen Liedtke. Toward real microkernels. *Communications of the ACM*, 39(9), Sep 1996.

18. Jochen Liedtke, Nayeem Islam, and Trent Jaeger. Preventing denial-of-service attacks on a μ-kernel for WebOSes. In *Proc. 6th HotOS*, May 1997.

19. Jochen Liedtke and Horst Wenske. Lazy process switching. In *Proc. 8th HotOS*, pages 15–18, May 2001.

20. Dylan McNamee and Katherine Armstrong. Extending the Mach external pager interface to accommodate user-level page replacement policies. Technical Report TR-90-09-05, Department of Computer Science and Engineering, University of Washington, 1990.

21. Frank Mehnert, Michael Hohmuth, and Hermann Härtig. Cost and benefit of separate address spaces in real-time operating systems. In *Proc. 23rd Real-Time Systems Symposium*, Dec 2002.

22. Richard Rashid *et al.* Machine-independent virtual memory management for paged uniprocessor and multiprocessor architectures. *IEEE Transactions on Computers*, 37(8), Aug 1988.

23. John Reumann, Ashish Mehra, Kang G. Shin, and Dilip Kandlur. Virtual services: A new abstraction for server consolidation. In *Proc. of the 2000 USENIX ATC*, Jun 2000.

24. M. Satyanarayanan, Harry H. Mashburn, Puneet Kumar, David C. Steere, and James J. Kistler. Lightweight recoverable virtual memory. *ACM TOCS*, 12(1), Feb 1994.

25. Jonathan S. Shapiro, David J. Farber, and Jonathan M. Smith. State caching in the EROS kernel. In *Proc. 7th Intl. Workshop on Persistent Object Systems*, pages 88–100, 1996.

26. Jonathan S. Shapiro, Jonathan M. Smith, and David J. Farber. EROS: a fast capability system. In *Proc. 17th ACM SOSP*, pages 170–185, Dec 1999.

27. Oliver Spatscheck and Larry L. Peterson. Defending against denial of service attacks in Scout. In *Proc. 3rd OSDI*, pages 59–72, Feb 1999.

28. Michael Stonebraker. Operating system support for database management. *Communications of the ACM*, 24(7):412–418, Jul 1981.

29. Patrick Tullmann, Jay Lepreau, Bryan Ford, and Mike Hibler. User-level checkpointing through exportable kernel state. In *Proc. 5th Intl. Workshop on Object Orientation in Operating Systems*, Seattle, WA, Oct 1996.

Variable Radix Page Table:
A Page Table for Modern Architectures

Cristan Szmajda[1] and Gernot Heiser[1,2]

[1] School of Computer Science and Engineering, University of New South Wales,
Sydney 2052, Australia
[2] National ICT Australia,
Sydney, Australia,
{cls,gernot}@cse.unsw.edu.au

Abstract. This paper presents a new page table structure, the *variable radix page table*, which overcomes many of the disadvantages of other page table structures. Unlike a hashed page table, the variable radix page table naturally accommodates shared segments and mixed page sizes. But unlike a multi-level page table, the radix page table is space-efficient and requires few memory references to look up, even in large and sparse address spaces. Our measurements show that the variable radix page table outperforms other page table structures, and is even competitive with a memory-based TLB cache.

Recent research has shown that thrashing of the TLB is an increasing bottleneck in modern processors: measurements of the TLB's contribution to execution time often exceed 40%. Such results sometimes even understate the full impact of TLB thrashing due to the presence of indirect overheads such as cache pollution and the effect of exceptions on the processor pipeline. By reducing the cost of TLB misses, the variable radix page table can achieve a significant overall speedup. The variable radix page table's mixed page size support also facilitates the reduction of TLB miss frequency, addressing the architectural imbalance that causes TLB thrashing. Our conclusions are also significant in the debate on the different hardware organizations in use for virtual memory.

1 Motivation

1.1 Performance

Virtual memory (VM) is almost universally supported in modern architectures and operating systems. VM has many benefits and one main cost: the overhead in time and space for maintaining and looking up page tables. In most processors, page table look-ups are cached in a hardware translation lookaside buffer (TLB). Historically, TLBs have been very effective. Clark and Emer [1] measure the contribution of TLB misses to execution time of a variety of workloads on the VAX-11/780 in the range 5–8%.

However, more recent measurements show that the TLB overhead in modern processors is surprisingly high. Huck and Hays[2], Romer et al.[3], Subramanian et al.[4], and Navarro et al.[5] all report TLB overheads which often exceed

A. Omondi and S. Sedukhin (Eds.): ACSAC 2003, LNCS 2823, pp. 290–304, 2003.

40%. Using simulations, Kandiraju and Sivasubramaniam[6] report data TLB miss *rates* in excess of 20% for some benchmarks, which translates to an extremely high overhead given that the typical cost of a TLB miss is 30 cycles or more.

What is the cause of such poor TLB performance results? The TLB is another casualty of the widening gap between processor and memory speed. Processor speed and memory sizes have been increasing steadily, but the coverage of the TLB much more slowly. Navarro et al. observe that the coverage of the TLB ten years ago was in the order of 1% of the main memory size: today it is in the order of 0.01%. There are architectural reasons why the TLB has been growing slower than the rest of the memory hierarchy. The TLB is a virtual cache, so it usually requires wider content-addressable memory (CAM) tags. The TLB must be frequently invalidated, so larger sizes bring diminishing returns. To avoid context switch invalidations, each tag is often widened further by an address space identifier. Because of their relatively small size and potential for pathological misses, the TLB often has high associativity already: as a result, TLBs are difficult to build simultaneously large, fast, and cool. Shared pages also effectively increase the amount of physical memory without reducing the number of TLB entries required to cover it. The cost of each individual TLB miss is also increasing due to deeper pipelining, the overhead of handling precise exceptions, and page tables for 64-bit address spaces.

Inertia must also be blamed. Once specified in the architecture, TLB parameters (such as the page size) are often difficult to change without introducing incompatibilities with existing system software. There is also some neglect. Much attention is paid to enhancing caches with prefetching, multiple levels of hierarchy, and better integration with the processor pipeline. The TLB does not receive nearly as much attention as the rest of the memory hierarchy.

1.2 Superpages

An easy way to improve TLB coverage is to increase the page size. However, an architecture's page size often cannot be changed in an upwards-compatible manner. Larger pages also increase fragmentation and I/O latency. Therefore, many architectures instead provide multiple page sizes: a base page and one or more *superpages*, which are power-of-two multiples of the base page size. A *superpage TLB* allows pages of different sizes to be used simultaneously, even in the same address space (provided, of course, that they do not overlap). Most current processors provide superpage TLBs to extend TLB coverage rather than attempting to build larger conventional TLBs.

The first applications of superpages in operating systems were special-purpose: kernel virtual memory, memory-mapped I/O devices, and mappings which bypass address translation. Superpages are ideal for these applications as their mappings are usually large, contiguous, and long-lived.

The more general use of superpages is inhibited by assumptions pervading the operating system. The whole VM subsystem, in its page fault handling, page replacement algorithms, and free frame management generally assumes throughout that all pages are the same size. Several approaches for the general use of superpages for ordinary applications have recently been presented, with varying extents of modification to existing operating system software. Romer et al. count TLB misses to small pages, promoting them when the miss count exceeds a threshold. Ganapathy and Schimmel[7] use a background daemon which promotes pages based on memory pressure and hints specified by the user in the executable. However, because both these schemes still allocate small pages to noncontiguous frames, the pages must first be copied into a contiguous region before promotion. Copying is such a performance penalty that Swanson, Stoller, and Carter[8] have proposed adding another TLB at the DRAM interface to optimize it. Subramanian et al. avoid copying altogether: they reserve contiguous memory for superpages by using a free frame manager based on the buddy system. Navarro et al. also use the page reservation technique, and have solved many practical issues using this scheme.

However, while several approaches exist for making use of superpages in higher layers of the VM subsystem, very little advantage of superpages is taken in the page table. Most page tables support only one or two page sizes directly. Other page sizes must typically be expanded into multiple page table entries (PTEs), each with the coverage of the base page size. For example, if the base page size is 8 kBytes, a 4 MByte superpage would require 512 PTEs. Not only does this duplication waste space, but it can make superpage promotion and demotion operations expensive. It is also a poor match for page size assignment policies which use a single page size for each process or for each segment. With most page tables, these simple policies would suffer much from PTE duplication.

1.3 Sharing

Many systems allow physical frames to be shared between address spaces. This is used for shared code segments, shared libraries, memory-mapped I/O, and interprocess communication. However, most page tables also have poor support for shared segments. The PTEs for the shared segment are usually duplicated in every page table. A page table which could represent shared segments without duplication would save space, be easier and faster to update, and friendlier to caches.

A shared page shares the same physical memory and physically-indexed cache lines, but not TLB entries. With typical address space identifier (ASID) tags, a separate TLB entry is still required for each address space which shares a page. Sharing therefore increases the coverage of memory and physically-indexed caches, but not the TLB. This makes TLB performance worse relative to the rest of the memory hierarchy. Some TLBs have more sophisticated tags which allow TLB entries to be shared between address spaces[9, 10]. The tag identifies not an individual address space but a whole *protection domain*, of which more than one address space may be a member. Whether or not the TLB supports domains directly, the motivation for improving the performance of shared segments in the page table is clear.

Another effect of shared segments is that the page tables occupy more space relative to the size of physical memory. According to Khalidi and Talluri[11], unshared page tables for shared pages can increase page table size by an order of magnitude. Since many operating systems cannot page out page tables, page table space can be a significant problem.

2   Previous Page Tables

The most common page table structures in current use fall into two broad categories: those based on radix trees and those using hashing.

2.1   Radix-Based Page Tables

Probably the most common page table structure is the *multi-level page table* (MLPT), which is essentially a shallow radix tree. To look up an MLPT, the page number is split into m fields which are used to index m arrays in turn (see Fig. 1). The choice of m and the size of the arrays is a time–space tradeoff. Choosing fields of about 10 bits wide yields a page table of manageable size. With 32-bit addresses, only two or three levels are required.

But with full 64-bit addresses, a manageable MLPT would require at least five levels. Looking up a 5LPT would require five sequential memory references: an unacceptably large overhead. Moreover, a 5LPT is not particularly space efficient either. Segments of memory scattered sparsely throughout the address space would require many arrays to be allocated, which are mostly empty space. These problems make MLPT impractical to use with 64-bit addresses. Nevertheless, the new AMD x86-64 architecture defines a 4LPT, but restricts virtual addresses to 48 bits.

MLPT enables some simple optimizations. Since an aligned superpage of appropriate size would fill a whole leaf page table level, a common technique is to factorise it into a single leaf entry in the upper level page table. Fig. 2 shows

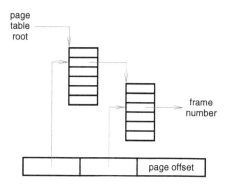

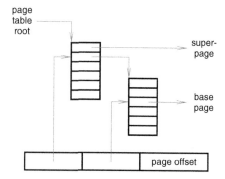

Fig. 1. A two-level page table   **Fig. 2.** Superpage representation in a two-level page table

the effect of this representation: indexing is truncated when enough bits of the page number have been translated to uniquely identify the superpage. However, the number of different page sizes that can be supported with this technique is limited. Typically the minimum supported superpage size is several MBytes, and all other page sizes must be represented by duplicating PTEs. Nevertheless, superpage factorization is common in systems using MLPT.

Another optimization to MLPT is to share whole segments by cross-linking page tables. However, similar limitations apply to this technique: each shared segment must be isolated in its own aligned region of several MBytes. If many small segments must be shared, the amount of virtual address space wasted by putting each into its own aligned region is considerable. Few systems using MLPT cross-link page tables.

The virtual linear array (VLA) page table is a variation of MLPT which mirrors the multi-level structure, but allocates the page tables in virtual memory. The page table thus appears to be a single large array indexed by virtual page number. Storing page tables in virtual memory effectively allows interior nodes to be cached in the TLB, short-circuiting page table look-up in the common case to a single (virtual) memory reference. Only if all levels miss in the TLB does the full m-level look-up take place. However, unless the necessary control is included in hardware, each miss requires an expensive nested exception to handle. TLB entries for the virtual linear array also compete with TLB entries for applications. Finally, the virtual linear array consumes a large swath of virtual address space: a finite resource. Nevertheless, VLA page tables are popular, and some architectures provide support for them either directly or by assistance with nested exceptions or multiple exception vectors.

2.2   Hashing-Based Page Tables

An alternative to ordinary page tables is the *inverted page table* (IPT), which is indexed by physical, not virtual, address. An IPT is particularly attractive with 64-bit addresses because its size is proportional to the size of physical memory, not the size of the virtual address space. Moreover, only one IPT is required for all address spaces in the system, and the reverse function (physical to virtual) is provided automatically. But unless hardware is available to search it in parallel, the IPT requires an additional *hash anchor table* to look up the IPT by virtual address. Another disadvantage of IPT is that sharing a frame between multiple address spaces is hard.

Huck and Hays[2] show that a hash table on its own performs slightly better than IPT, and removes some of its disadvantages. Their *hashed page table* (HPT) is essentially a hash table with collision chaining (Fig. 3). A HPT is somewhat larger than other page tables because the virtual address must be present in each PTE to check for hits and collisions.

The *clustered page table* (CPT) proposed by Talluri, Hill, and Khalidi[12] is a variation of HPT which stores multiple adjacent PTEs per hash bucket. This combines both hashing and radix-based approaches, applying hashing on the sparse high-order bits and array indexing on the dense low-order bits. A CPT may also use less space than a pure HPT, as only one virtual address needs to be stored per hash bucket, instead of one per PTE.

Hashing-based page tables are attractive for 64-bit address spaces as a hash function is just as efficient for large virtual addresses as small ones. Sparse address space distributions are also no problem. However, hashing has some undesirable properties. Collisions cannot be eliminated, even with a perfect hash function. Hash tables are also difficult to traverse: consider the problem of deleting an address space whose PTEs are scattered throughout an HPT. Finally, hashing does not support superpages well: common workarounds are to try multiple hash functions or to expand superpages into many base page size PTEs.

Nevertheless, the advantages of HPT are such that many recent architectures, wishing to include page table support in hardware for performance but not wishing to set an inflexible page table in stone, have included hardware support for HPT, either as a complete page table or as a cache to accelerate another page table implemented in software.

2.3   Path Compression

Path compression is an established technique for reducing the depth of radix trees[13]. Path compression works on chains of non-branching nodes, whose entries are all invalid except for one. Every such chain is abbreviated into a single entry containing just the tail of the chain and an indication that several bits of the key were skipped on the path. The skipped bits may also be stored in the entry and checked during the look-up; alternatively keys may be stored in the leaves and checking deferred till the end.

The *guarded page table* (GPT) is a multi-level page table which applies path compression (Fig. 4). In the terminology of Liedtke[14], each node is 'guarded' by skipped bits, which must compare equal with the page number key before descending further in the page table.

The GPT works well in sparse address spaces[15]. Since very few applications use more than a tiny fraction of a 64-bit address space, path compression is

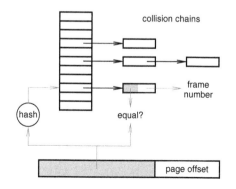

Fig. 3. A hashed page table

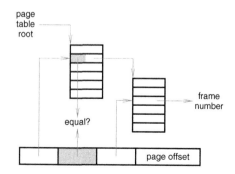

Fig. 4. A guarded page table

effective at reducing radix tree depth, especially in higher levels of the radix tree.

However, implementations of GPT have not performed well in large and dense address space regions. While Liedtke originally contemplated a GPT with variable radices, all implementations have to date used a fixed radix. Moreover, to take advantage of sparsity, and to reduce the cost of GPT updates, this radix is typically small. Elphinstone[15] determined that the optimal GPT radix over a range of look-up, creation, and deletion benchmarks is 16. As a result, GPT depth can sometimes blow out, especially for large contiguous segments.

3   Radix Page Table

3.1   Level Compression

Level compression[16] is another technique for reducing the depth of radix trees. It works by reducing complete subtrees, whose nodes are all valid, reducing them to a single, flat super-node.

The *variable radix page table* (VRPT) is a radix tree which applies both path compression and level compression (Fig. 5). Each node may skip any number of bits which are insignificant, and point to an array of any power of two in size. Each level may be a different size, and the depth of the tree may be different at different regions of the address space.

VRPT also dispenses with the need for actual guards. Instead, checking the validity of a look-up is deferred until a leaf is reached. This optimistic strategy is reminiscent of hashing, where key comparison only occurs after the hash algorithm selects a bucket. Omitting guards also greatly simplifies VRPT updates, allowing the easy restructuring of VRPT levels to arbitrary powers of two.

The combination of path compression and level compression is more effective at reducing page table depth than either technique alone. Flexible radices allow VRPT to take advantage of any regularity or structure present in the address space layout to reduce the number of required levels. There is no need to choose a compromise radix that suits both sparse and dense address spaces. If an address space contains a mixture of sparse and dense regions, the level size and depth may even be different in the different regions.

Sparse address space distributions contain many compressible paths, especially near the root of the page table. Path compression is therefore most effective near the page table root. Level compression is effective at the leaves, though is sometimes also effectively applied near the root for certain address space layouts. Large dense segments benefit the most from level compression. Regularly laid out address spaces typically require only two or three levels, even in 64-bit address spaces.

Indexing an VRPT may seem to be a complex operation, but in fact the data structure and look-up algorithm can be made simple and reasonably efficient using bit arithmetic (Fig. 6). Each page table index is extracted with two instructions: a variable left shift followed by a variable right shift. An internal node consists only of a pointer and two shift amounts. The left shift amount,

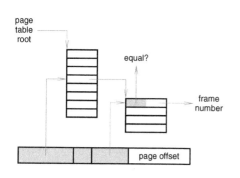

p = root of page table
v = virtual address

repeat {
    $p = p \rightarrow ptr + (v \ll p \rightarrow skip \gg p \rightarrow size)$
} **until** p points to a leaf

if $p \rightarrow virt \neq v$ {
    page fault
}

Fig. 5. A variable radix page table   **Fig. 6.** VRPT indexing algorithm

which is related to the number of bits skipped before indexing, is called *skip*. The right shift amount, which is related to the size of the following level, is called *size*. A bias is applied to *size* so that the index is 'pre-scaled' to the size of page table entries. Bits skipped in the page number are simply ignored during indexing, and are checked at the end. With a typical RISC instruction set, the inner loop can be implemented in only 7 or 8 instructions.

3.2 Radix Policy

The difficult part of implementing a flexible radix tree is choosing the radices. Nilsson and Tikkanen[17] promote or demote a level to the next power of two if it fills up or empties below certain thresholds. Elphinstone[15, p. 36] proposes using knowledge supplied from higher layers about the structure of the application. However, in the absence of such information it is difficult to guess such structure in advance from the lowest layers of the VM subsystem. Moreover, address space structure may evolve during the life of a process. The choice of radix is also a time–space tradeoff, and depends on the resources available to the system. A system with low memory pressure may be able to apply level compression more aggressively, whereas a system which is suffering from paging I/O may decide that aggressive level compression is not worth it.

    Instead, our implementation of VRPT uses a radix policy which balances memory pressure against the desire for shallow page tables. The page tables use a smart allocator, based on the buddy system, which 'greedily' allocates the largest levels possible with the available contiguous physical memory. However, it reserves the right to take back some or all of the memory if it is unused and more memory is needed. This policy requires co-operation from the code which updates page tables, but the amount of extra complexity is small. The benefit is that room is provided for growth wherever possible, avoiding expensive tree restructuring operations as an address space is populated.

    This policy also solves a subtle garbage collection problem. If higher layers unmap pages for a short time, the memory allocator may incur significant expense if the page tables are eagerly freed and quickly reallocated again. The

VRPT allocator frees such page tables lazily, only when required. The VRPT allocator also integrates easily with resource management mechanisms designed to limit the amount of kernel memory which can be consumed by each user.

4   Benefits

In addition to look-up performance, the VRPT structure has some other beneficial properties. Mixed page sizes, shared segments, and many common virtual memory update operations are simple and easy to implement relative to other page table structures.

4.1   Superpages

Section 2 described how MLPT can incorporate limited page size mixtures in an efficient way. VRPT also naturally accommodates page size mixtures, but is much more flexible, allowing the operating system to achieve the maximum benefit of superpages.

Many architectures provide a large number of page sizes, in multiples of 4 or 8. VRPT supports arbitrary page size mixtures by *superpage factorization*: superpages may be treated as variable-length keys in the radix tree, and compressed into small leaves which truncate look-up at any point in the tree. Factorization saves space and allows superpage PTEs to be quickly updated.

Factorization in VRPT is always optional. Our implementation avoids factorizing superpages if the factorized version requires as much space as the expanded version (or more). This heuristic is not motivated by a compulsion to save memory but by the observation that a smaller page table is usually also simpler and shallower. In practice this superpage expansion generally only occurs if a superpage is promoted in-place from a population consisting mostly of smaller pages. In this case, full factorization only occurs when enough pages have been promoted to justify it. This policy also avoids the pathological situations which can occur with certain page size mixtures.

The one drawback of superpage factorization is that it can increase page table depth slightly. However, for this effect to become significant, a very large number of page sizes must be present, in which case the performance benefit of the large pages far outweighs the slight increase in page table depth.

4.2   Cross-Linking

VRPT supports cross-linked page tables in a similar manner to the MLPT. But with VRPT, cross-linking is more flexible. Shared segments may be aligned on any power-of-two boundary, not just at a fixed boundary such as 4 MBytes.

Cross-linked page tables can eliminate *minor page faults*, which occur when there is a page fault on a page which is already resident in memory. A common reason for minor page faults is when shared pages are brought into the page cache by another application but not entered into every application's page table. If the shared segment is mapped by a cross-linked page table, this problem goes away.

Compared with the TLB miss handler, the page fault handler is usually a 'slow path' through the system, and is not as aggressively optimized. For this reason, minor page faults have a significant performance cost in many systems, even though they involve no actual I/O. Linux has recently addressed this problem by optimizing its page cache with a radix tree[18]. FreeBSD has instead added code to preload page tables from its page cache on address space creation[19]. Cross-linked page tables achieve the same effect as page table preloading without the added start-up cost.

4.3 Page Table Updates

When higher layers update page tables, they often do so in particular ways. The VRPT structure allows some simple optimizations for these common update patterns.

One common operation is to map, unmap, or change the protection attributes of an entire segment of memory at once. The VRPT structure allows the internal nodes to contain protection bits which qualify all underneath PTEs. These qualifying protection attributes may be accumulated during look-up by adding one extra AND instruction to the VRPT indexing loop: an instruction which may be free on a multiple-issue processor. Protection operations on whole memory segments may be implemented by modifying the internal node rather than every leaf PTE. When combined with sharing, address spaces may share segments with different protection attributes.

Another common operation is to update or invalidate all the PTEs which refer to a particular physical frame. For example, the page daemon may write-protect or pageout a frame from all address spaces. In some systems the number of PTEs referring to one frame may be large due to features such as shared libraries and the indiscriminate use of copy-on-write. Cross-linked page tables can help, but can not always be used, for example if segments are shared at different addresses or are inappropriately aligned. Searching for all the PTEs may be expensive. In some systems it is not even known at pageout time which address spaces contain a particular frame, and a brute force search is required.

A simple enhancement allows such operations to be optimized. A single pointer is added to each PTE which links together all the PTEs referring to the same physical frame. An operation on all virtual pages for a single physical frame may simply follow the linked list to find all affected PTEs. While this technique is not specific to VRPT, the inclusion of the virtual address in the VRPT leaf allows common operations such as pageout to proceed by following this list without reference to any external data structure. Other systems have a similar data external structure, such as the pv_entry structures in FreeBSD, which are actually used as machine-independent templates for generating the hardware page tables[19]. Merging this data structure into the page table itself saves considerable complexity at the cost of only one word in each PTE.

5   Performance

VRPT was benchmarked on two 64-bit architectures: MIPS64 and IA-64.

MIPS64 is a typical RISC architecture: all TLB misses are handled by trapping to software. Its TLB has been extensively studied, for example by Chen, Borg, and Jouppi[20]. Seven page sizes from 4 kBytes to 16 MBytes are supported. The hardware and experimental methodology is comparable with that of Elphinstone[15]: a 100 MHz MIPS R4700 processor running benchmarks selected from the SPEC CPU95 suite.

IA-64 is an architecture for high-performance servers, and includes many architectural features supporting fast virtual memory. The TLB is tagged by a domain (called a *protection key*). Eleven page sizes from 4 kByte to 4 GByte are supported. TLB refill hardware (called the virtual hash page table, VHPT) can be configured in one of three ways: as a hardware-walked VLA page table (short-format), as a hardware walked TLB cache (long-format), or disabled, with all TLB misses handled by software exception handlers. Our test platform used a 733 MHz Intel Itanium processor, using a custom kernel created for the purpose.

5.1   Methodology

A common methodology used in the literature is to count TLB misses and instrument the TLB miss handler, either in hardware or software. Instrumentation usually does not include effects such as the disruption of the processor pipeline and the cache misses due to displacement of cache lines by the TLB miss handler. More complex instrumentation could conceivably measure these indirect overheads, but it would be difficult to verify both the correctness of the measurements and the absence of other introduced overheads.

A better methodology which includes all the direct and indirect costs of TLB misses is to perform a second run of each benchmark in physical mode, with the TLB disabled. (Where the machine does not allow physical addressing in user mode, the effect can be simulated with very large superpages.) The relative difference between the two times is the TLB overhead.

Indirect costs are the probable explanation of the anomalous observation of Subramanian et al.[4] that the speedup due to superpages exceeded the total apparent TLB overhead.

5.2   Comparison between Page Tables

VRPT was implemented as a kernel module in the L4/MIPS microkernel[21]. For comparison, several other page table modules are also available in L4/MIPS. Fig. 7 shows the results. HPT, CPT, and GPT are implementations of the page tables described in Section 2. The implementation of GPT is also described in detail by Liedtke and Elphinstone[22]. An MLPT implementation was also available, but performed so poorly that it was excluded to avoid distorting the graph. CACHE is the same as GPT, but page table look-ups are accelerated by a 128 kByte software-maintained TLB cache in main memory[23].

On the MIPS, VRPT outperforms other page tables in terms of TLB miss overhead by a factor of two. VRPT is competitive with CACHE, even though the TLB cache in this benchmark achieves close to 100% hit rate. The number of memory references made by each page table is the main determiner of performance. Because these benchmarks are compact in their use of the address space, both CACHE and VRPT touch only one cache line per TLB reload. HPT and CPT must touch at least two to compute the hash and resolve collisions. GPT typically requires three or more levels.

Our results are generally consistent with the conclusion of Huck and Hays[2] that page table look-up is dominated by cache misses. In their simulations, 20–35% of the cycles spent in handling TLB misses are cache miss penalty cycles. They also compute cache miss rates of 2–3% for a 2LPT root, 12–15% for a 2LPT leaf, and 20–50% for an HPT. The advantages of hashing must be balanced against its reduced locality.

Not surprisingly, TLB performance is also highly sensitive to the locality of the application. *Swim*'s data segment is large, but its working set is relatively small. *Gcc* is smaller, but touches a large number of pages, perhaps due to the preponderance of algorithms operating on linked data structures.

An application's locality behaviour may benefit different levels of the memory hierarchy differently. We find little correlation between TLB miss rate and L1 cache miss rate, L2 cache miss rate, or page fault rate. This makes it difficult to compare TLB coverage with cache sizes, or to recommend a TLB size.

On the Itanium, (Fig. 8), two other page tables were also measured for comparison: 3LPT is Linux 2.5.43, which uses a three-level page table (but does not supports the full 64-bit address space). Linux was patched to use the HPT (as a TLB cache) rather than the VLA, as the latter does not support the use of superpages. (The overall performance difference between the two hardware-supported page table formats has been found to be negligible[9].) HPT is FreeBSD 5.0, which uses software TLB reload from a hashed page table.

Every effort was made to minimize the inaccuracy due to the different operating system kernels. All executables were statically linked with the same ver-

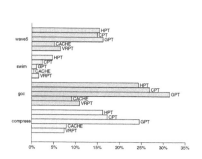

Fig. 7. Page table performance (MIPS64)

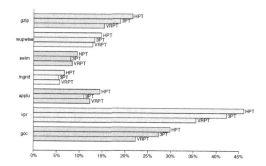

Fig. 8. Page table performance (IA-64)

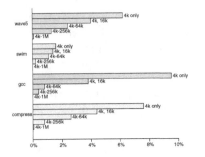
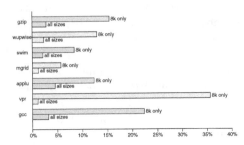

Fig. 9. The effect of superpages (MIPS64)

Fig. 10. The effect of superpages (IA-64)

sion of the standard libraries. These libraries emulate most system functionality such as file I/O. The executables were preloaded into the system's page cache by performing a dummy run before benchmarking. The benchmarks themselves are designed to have very little interaction with the system. Nevertheless, some lingering system impact may be present in these results.

Because Itanium features a hardware-loaded TLB, the results in Fig. 8 are somewhat less pronounced. The majority of hardware TLB misses hit in the memory-based VHPT, and do not require page table lookup. Moreover, the cost of taking an exception is a large component of the TLB miss overhead on this processor.

5.3   The Effect of Superpages

One of the benefits of VRPT is its ease in accommodating superpages. In order to establish the benefit of using superpages, VRPT was benchmarked against itself in one of several different configurations. The *4k only* or *8k only* configuration uses only one (base) page size. The other configurations automatically promote smaller pages to superpages where possible.

The use of 64 k and larger superpages all but eliminates the TLB overhead in these benchmarks. This shows that TLB thrashing on the MIPS processor is dominated by TLB capacity misses: conflict misses are all but eliminated by the fully-associative TLB, despite the pseudo-random replacement algorithm.

Results for the Itanium processor are similar. However, a problem with using superpages on the Itanium is that the VHPT cannot cache superpages effectively: only the base page size is cached. Therefore, all TLB misses for superpages become VHPT misses. Despite the high cost of VHPT misses on this processor, superpages reduce the hardware TLB miss rate so dramatically that they are still a win.

A limitation in these benchmark is that it assumes that memory pressure is low, and that there is no paging I/O activity. We may expect different results if the system decides to run the application partly resident in memory.

6 Conclusions

Architectural imbalances have resulted in VM overheads forming a significant bottleneck for many workloads. The contribution of TLB misses to execution time often exceeds 40%. We have attempted to address this problem to the extent possible in software, using commodity hardware.

Page table look-up is the most important algorithm to optimize in software. We have presented the variable radix page table, which attempts to minimize the depth of page table look-ups. Measurements show that page table look-up time is dominated by cache misses.

Superpages present the single biggest opportunity for reducing TLB overhead by extending the coverage of the TLB and thus reducing the frequency of misses. VRPT is ideal for VM subsystems that use superpage optimizations. It provides efficient support for page size mixtures without restricting the way they are used. However, further analysis is required to determine whether sophisticated policies are required to take advantage of superpages, or whether simple policies such as increasing the page size across the board is sufficient.

Another open question is whether the hardware complexity of a superpage TLB is justified given the complexity this adds to operating system software. Clearly a configurable page size is a very desirable feature to allow future expansion or scaling to large memory configurations, but the benefit of supporting arbitrary page size mixtures must be evaluated against simpler TLB configurations. In particular, a TLB with a per-process page size and/or a sub-block TLB[24] may be attractive to compare with a superpage TLB.

References

1. Clark, D.W., Emer, J.S.: Performance of the VAX-11/780 translation buffer: Simulation and measurement. ACM Trans. Comp. Syst. **3** (1985) 31–62
2. Huck, J., Hays, J.: Architectural support for translation table management in large address space machines. In: Proc. 20th ISCA, ACM (1993) 39–50
3. Romer, T.H., Ohllrich, W.H., Karlin, A.R., Bershad, B.N.: Reducing TLB and memory overhead using online superpage promotion. In: Proc. 22nd ISCA, Santa Margherita Ligure, Itay, ACM (1995) 176–87
4. Subramanian, I., Mather, C., Peterson, K., Raghunath, B.: Implementation of multiple pagesize support in HP-UX. In: Proc. 1998 USENIX Techn. Conf., New Orleans, USA (1998)
5. Navarro, J., Iyer, S., Druschel, P., Cox, A.: Practical, transparent operating system support for superpages. In: Proc. 5th USENIX OSDI, Boston, MA, USA (2002)
6. Kandiraju, G.B., Sivasubramaniam, A.: Going the distance for TLB prefetching: An application-driven study. In: Proc. 29th ISCA, Anchorage, USA (2002)
7. Ganapathy, N., Schimmel, C.: General purpose operating system support for multiple page sizes. In: Proc. 1998 USENIX Techn. Conf., New Orleans, USA (1998)
8. Swanson, M., Stoller, L., Carter, J.: Increasing TLB reach using superpages backed by shadow memory. In: Proc. 25th ISCA, ACM (1998) 204–213

9. Chapman, M., Wienand, I., Heiser, G.: Itanium page tables and TLB. Technical Report UNSW-CSE-TR-0307, School Comp. Sci. & Engin., University NSW, Sydney 2052, Australia (2003)

10. Wiggins, A., Tuch, H., Uhlig, V., Heiser, G.: Implementation of fast address-space switching and TLB sharing on the StrongARM processor. In: 8th ACSAC, Aizu-Wakamatsu City, Japan, Springer Verlag (2003)

11. Khalidi, Y.A., Talluri, M.: Improving the address translation performance of widely shared pages. Technical Report TR-95-38, Sun Microsystems Laboratories, Mountain View CA (1995)

12. Talluri, M., Hill, M.D., Khalid, Y.A.: A new page table for 64-bit address spaces. In: Proc. 15th ACM SOSP, Copper Mountain Resort, Co, USA (1995) 184–200

13. Morrison, D.R.: Patricia: Practical algorithm to retrieve information coded in alphanumeric. Journal of the ACM **15** (1968) 514–534

14. Liedtke, J.: Improving IPC by kernel design. In: Proc. 14th ACM SOSP, Asheville, NC, USA (1993) 175–88

15. Elphinstone, K.: Virtual Memory in a 64-bit Microkernel. PhD thesis, School Comp. Sci. & Engin., University NSW, Sydney 2052, Australia (1999) http://www.cse.unsw.edu.au/~disy/papers.

16. Andersson, A., Nilsson, S.: Improved behavior of tries by adaptive branching. Information Processing Letters **46** (1993) 295–300

17. Nilsson, S., Tikkanen, M.: Implementing a dynamic compressed trie. In Mehlhorn, K., ed.: 2nd WS. Alorithmic Engin. (1998) URL http://www.nada.kth.se/~snilsson/public/papers/dyntrie.

18. Corbet, J.: Kernel development. Linux Weekly News (2002) http://lwn.net/2002/0207/kernel.php3.

19. Dillon, M.: Design elements of the FreeBSD VM system. Daemon News (2000) http://www.daemonnews.org/200001/freebsd_vm.html.

20. Chen, J.B., Borg, A., Jouppi, N.P.: A simulation based study of TLB performance. In: Proc. 19th ISCA, ACM (1992)

21. Elphinstone, K., Heiser, G., Liedtke, J.: L4 Reference Manual: MIPS R4x00. School Comp. Sci. & Engin., University NSW, Sydney 2052, Australia. (1997) UNSW-CSE-TR-9709.

22. Liedtke, J., Elphinstone, K.: Guarded page tables on MIPS R4600 or an exercise in architecture-dependent micro optimization. Technical Report UNSW-CSE-TR-9503, School Comp. Sci. & Engin., University NSW, Sydney 2052, Australia (1995)

23. Bala, K., Kaashoek, M.F., Weihl, W.E.: Software prefetching and caching for translation lookaside buffers. In: Proc. 1st USENIX OSDI, Monterey, CA, USA, USENIX/ACM/IEEE (1994) 243–253

24. Talluri, M., Hill, M.D.: Surpassing the TLB performance of superpages with less operating system support. In: Proc. 6th ASPLOS. (1994) 171–182

L1 Cache and TLB Enhancements
to the RAMpage Memory Hierarchy

Philip Machanick[1] and Zunaid Patel[2]

[1] School of ITEE, University of Queensland,
Brisbane, Qld 4072, Australia,
philip@itee.uq.edu.au
[2] School of Computer Science, University of the Witwatersrand,
Johannesburg, Private Bag 3, 2050 Wits, South Africa,
zunaid@cs.wits.ac.za

Abstract. The RAMpage hierarchy moves main memory up a level to replace the lowest-level cache by an equivalent-sized SRAM main memory, with a TLB caching page translations for that main memory. This paper illustrates how more aggressive components higher in the hierarchy increase the fraction of total execution time spent waiting for DRAM. For an instruction issue rate of 1 GHz, the simulated standard hierarchy waited for DRAM 10% of the time, increasing to 40% at an instruction issue rate of 8 GHz. For a larger L1 cache, the fraction of time waiting for DRAM was even higher. RAMpage with context switches on misses was able to hide almost all DRAM latency. A larger TLB was shown to increase the viable range of RAMpage SRAM page sizes.

1 Introduction

The RAMpage memory hierarchy moves main memory up a level to replace the lowest-level cache with an SRAM main memory, while DRAM becomes a first-level paging device. Previous work has shown that RAMpage represents an alternative, viable design in terms of hardware-software trade-offs [22] and that it scales better as the CPU-DRAM speed gap grows, particularly by virtue of being able to take context switches on misses [21].

In previous work, it was hypothesized that RAMpage would be more competitive across a wider range of SRAM page sizes (equivalent to line size of the lowest-level cache) with a more aggressive TLB. Secondly, it was hypothesized that a more aggressive L1 cache would emphasize differences in lower levels of the hierarchy. In this paper, we report on investigation of both hypotheses as separate issues. Improving the TLB and L1 has different effects on performance. The intent in presenting both in the same paper is to add several data points to our case for RAMpage.

In some studies, TLB misses have accounted for as much as 40% of run time [13], with figures in the region of 20–30% common [6, 23]. RAMpage has the potential to reduce the significance of the TLB on performance for two reasons. Firstly, unless the reference which causes a TLB miss would also miss in the

A. Omondi and S. Sedukhin (Eds.): ACSAC 2003, LNCS 2823, pp. 305–319, 2003.

SRAM main memory, no reference to update the TLB needs go to DRAM, with the page table organization used for RAMpage. Secondly, there is no mismatch between the size of page mapped by the TLB and the "line size" of the "lowest-level cache", as would be the case with a conventional hierarchy. Consequently, the TLB can more easily be designed to map a specific fraction of the SRAM main memory, than is the case for a conventional cache.

The role of increasingly aggressive on-chip caches also needs to be evaluated, against the view that such caches address the memory wall problem. Quadrupling the size of a cache may halve the number of misses [28], but such expansion may not always be practical. Increasing the size of caches in any case makes it harder to scale up their speed [11].

The approach in this paper is to compare RAMpage with a conventional 2-level cache hierarchy as the size of the TLB scales up, across different SRAM main memory page sizes, as well as a variety of L1 cache sizes, in separate experiments. The simulated L2 cache of 4Mbytes runs at a third of the issue rate excluding misses. The intent is to emphasize that even a very fast, large on-chip cache results in a large fraction of run-time being spent waiting for DRAM. Even so, given that DRAM references are the dominant effect being measured, a fast cache should not invalidate the general trends being studied.

TLB measurements show that both models see a reduction in TLB miss rates as the TLB size increases, but RAMpage becomes more viable with smaller SRAM main memory page sizes. Cache measurements show that as L1 size increases, the fraction of time spent waiting for DRAM increases (even if overall run time decreases), which makes the option in the RAMpage hierarchy of taking a context switch on a miss more attractive.

The remainder of this paper is structured as follows. Section 2 presents more detail of the RAMpage hierarchy and related research. Section 3 explains the experimental approach, while Section 4 presents experimental results. In conclusion, Section 5, summarizes the findings and outlines future work.

2   Background

The RAMpage model was proposed [20] in response to the memory wall [16, 30]. The key idea of the RAMpage model is to minimize hardware complexity, while moving more of the memory management intelligence into software. A RAMpage machine therefore looks very like a conventional model, except the lowest-level cache is replaced by a conventionally-addressed physical memory, though implemented in SRAM rather than DRAM.

A number of other approaches to addressing the memory wall have been proposed. This section summarizes the memory wall issue, followed by more detail of RAMpage. After presenting other alternatives, the options are discussed.

2.1   Memory Wall

The memory wall is the situation where the effect of CPU improvements becomes insignificant as the speed improvement of DRAM becomes a limiting factor. Since the mid-1980s, CPU speeds have improved at a rate of 50-100% per year, while DRAM latency has only improved at around 7% per year [12]. If predictions of the memory wall [30] are correct, DRAM latency will become a serious limiting factor in performance improvement. Attempts at working around the memory wall are becoming increasingly common [9], but the fundamental underlying DRAM and CPU latency trends continue [27].

2.2 The RAMpage Approach

RAMpage is based on the notion that DRAM, while still orders of magnitude faster than disk, is increasingly starting to display one attribute of a peripheral: there is time to do other work while waiting for it [24], particularly if relatively large units are moved between DRAM and SRAM level. In RAMpage, the lowest-level cache is managed as the main memory (i.e., as a paged virtually-addressed memory), with disk a secondary paging device. The RAMpage main memory page table is inverted, to minimize its size. An inverted page table has another benefit: no TLB miss can result in a DRAM reference, unless the reference causing the TLB lookup is not in any of the SRAM layers [22].

RAMpage is intended to have the following advantages:

- *fast hits* – a hit physically addresses an SRAM memory
- *full associativity* – full associativity through paging avoids the slower hits of hardware full associativity
- *software-managed paging* – replacement can be as sophisticated as needed
- *TLB missess to DRAM minimized* – as explained above
- *pinning in SRAM* – critical OS data and code can be pinned in SRAM
- *hardware simplicity* – the complexity of a cache controller is removed from the lowest level of SRAM
- *context switches on misses to DRAM* – the CPU can be kept busy

These advantages come at the cost of slower misses because of software miss-handling, and the need to make operating system changes. However, the latter problem could be avoided by adding hardware support for the model.

The RAMpage approach has in the past been shown to scale well in the face of the grown CPU-DRAM speed gap, particularly with context switches on misses. The effect of context switches on misses is that, provided there is work available for the CPU, waiting for DRAM can effectively be eliminated [21]. Context switches on misses have the most significant effect.

2.3 Alternatives

Approaches to addressing the memory wall can loosely (with some overlaps) be grouped into latency tolerance and miss reduction. Some approaches to latency tolerance include prefetch, critical word first, memory compression, write buffering, non-blocking caches, and simultaneous multithreading (SMT).

Prefetch requires loading a cache block before it is requested, either by hardware [5] or with compiler support [25]; predictive prefetch attempts to improve accuracy of prefetch for relatively varied memory access patterns [1]. In critical word first, the word containing the reference which caused the miss is fetched first, followed by the rest of the block [11]. Memory compression in effect reduces latency because a smaller amount of information must be moved on a miss. The overhead must be less than the time saved [18]. There are many variations on write miss strategy, but the most effective generally include write buffering [17]. A non-blocking cache (lockup-free) cache can allow an aggressive pipeline to continue with other instructions while waiting for a miss [4].

SMT is aimed at masking DRAM latency as well as other causes of pipeline stalls, by hardware support for more than one active thread [19]. SMT aims to solve a wider range of CPU performance problems than RAMpage.

These ideas have costs (e.g., prefetching can displace needed content, causing unnecessary misses). The biggest problem is that most of these approaches do not scale with the growing CPU-DRAM speed gap. Critical word first is less helpful as latency for one reference grows in relation to total time for a big DRAM transaction. Prefetch, memory compression and nonblocking caches have limits as to how much they can reduce effective latency. Write buffering can scale provided buffer size can be scaled, and references to buffered writes can be handled before they are written back. SMT could mask much of the time spent waiting for DRAM, but at the cost of a more complex CPU.

Reducing misses has been addressed by increasing cache size, associativity, or both. There are limits on how large a cache can be at a given speed, so the number of levels has increased. Full associativity can be achieved in hardware with less overhead for hits than a conventional fully-associative cache, in an indirect index cache (IIC), by what amounts to a hardware implementation of RAMpage's page table lookup [10]. A drawback of IIC is that all references incur overhead of an extra level of indirection. Earlier work on software-based cache management has not focused on replacement policy [7, 14].

The advantages of RAMpage over SMT and other hardware-based multi-threading approaches are that the CPU can be kept simple, and software implementation of support for multiple processes is more flexible (the balance between multitasking and multithreading can be dynamically adjusted, according to workload). An advantage of IIC is that the OS need not be invoked to handle the equivalent of a TLB miss in RAMpage. As compared with RAMpage, an IIC has more overhead for a hit, and less for a miss.

2.4 Summary

RAMpage masks time which would otherwise be spent waiting for DRAM by taking context switches on misses. Other approachs either do not aim to mask time spent waiting for DRAM, but to reduce it, or require more complex hardware. RAMpage can potentially be combined with some of the other approaches (such as SMT), so it is not necessarily in conflict with other ideas.

3   Experimental Approach

This section outlines the approach to the reported experiments. The simulation strategy is explained, followed by some detail of simulation parameters; in conclusion, expected findings are discussed.

3.1   Simulation Strategy

A range of variations on a standard 2-level hierarchy is compared to similar variations on RAMpage, with and without context switches on misses. RAMpage without context switches on misses to conveys the effects of adding associativity (with an operating system-style replacement strategy). Adding context switches on misses shows the value of alternative work on a miss to DRAM. Simulations are trace-driven, and do not model the pipeline. Processor speed is in GHz, representing instruction issue rate without misses, not clock speed.

Ignoring the pipeline level neglects effects like branches and the potential for other improvements like non-blocking caches. However, the results being looked for here are relatively large improvements, so inaccuracies of this kind are unlikely to be significant. What is important is the effect as the CPU-DRAM speed gap increases, and the simulation is of sufficient accuracy to capture such effects, as has been demonstrated in previous work.

3.2   Simulation Parameters

Parameters are similar to previous published work to make results comparable. The following parameters are common across RAMpage and the conventional hierarchy. This represents the baseline before new L1 and TLB variations:

- L1 cache – 16Kbytes each of data and instruction cache, physically tagged and indexed, direct-mapped, 32-byte block size, 1-cycle read hit, 12-cycle penalty for misses to L2 (or RAMpage SRAM main memory); for data cache: perfect write buffering (zero effective hit time), writeback (12-cycle penalty; 9 cycles for RAMpage: no L2 tag to update), write allocate on miss
- TLB – 64 entries, fully associative, random replacement
- DRAM level – Direct Rambus [8] without pipelining: $50ns$ before first reference started, thereafter 2 bytes every $1.25ns$
- paging of DRAM – inverted page table: same organization as RAMpage main memory for simplicity, infinite DRAM with no misses to disk
- TLB and L1 data hits fully pipelined – only time for L1d or TLB replacements or maintaining inclusion costed as "hits"

The same memory timing is used as in earlier simulations. Although faster DRAM has since become available, the timing can be seen as relative to a particular CPU-DRAM speed gap, and the figures can accordingly be rescaled.

Context switches are modelled by interleaving a trace of text-book code. A context switch is taken every 500,000 references, though RAMpage with context switches on misses also takes a context switch on a miss to DRAM. TLB misses are handled by a trace of page table lookup code, with variations on time for a lookup based on probable variations in probes into an inverted page table [22].

Specific to Conventional Hierarchy

The "conventional" system has a 2-way associative 4Mbyte L2. The L2 cache and its bus to the CPU the are clocked at one third of the CPU issue rate (the cycle time is intended to represent a superscalar issue rate). The L2 cache-CPU bus is 128 bits wide and runs Hits on the L2 cache take 4 cycles including the tag check and transfer to L1. Inclusion between L1 and L2 is maintained [12]. The TLB caches virtual page translations to DRAM physical frames.

Specific to RAMpage Hierarchy

In RAMpage simulations, most parameters remain the same, except that the TLB maps the SRAM main memory, and full associativity is implemented in software, through a software miss handler. The OS keeps 6 pages pinned in the SRAM main memory when simulating a 4 Kbyte-SRAM page, i.e., 24 Kbytes, which increases to to 5336 pages for a 128 byte block size, a total of 667 Kbytes.

Inputs and Variations

Traces are from the Tracebase trace archive at New Mexico State University[1]. 1.1-billion references are used, with traces interleaved to create the effect of a multiprogramming workload.

To measure variations on L1 caches, the size of each of the instruction and data caches was varied from the original size of 16 KB to 32 KB, 64 KB, 128 KB and 256 KB. To explore more of the design space, L1 block size was measured at sizes of 32, 64 and 128 bytes. We did not vary L2 block sizes when varying L1: an optimum size was determined in previous work [21, 22]. However, while varying the TLB, we did vary L2 block size in the conventional hiearchy, for comparison with varying the RAMpage SRAM main memory page size. To measure the effect of increasing the TLB size, we varied it from the original 64 entries to 128, 256 and 512. Even larger TLBs exist (e.g., Power4 has a 1024-entry TLB [29]), but this range is sufficient to capture variations of interest.

3.3   Expected Findings

As L1 becomes larger, RAMpage without context switches on misses should see less of a gain. While improving L1 should not affect time spent in DRAM, RAMpage's extra overheads in managing DRAM may have a more significant effect on overall run time. However, as the fraction of references in upper levels increases without a decrease in references to DRAM, context switches on misses should become more favourable.

As the TLB size increases, we expect to see smaller SRAM page sizes become viable. If the TLB has 64 entries and the page size is 4 KB with a 4 MB SRAM

---

[1] From   ftp://tracebase.nmsu.edu/pub/traces/uni/r2000/utilities/   and ftp://tracebase.nmsu.edu/pub/traces/uni/r2000/SPEC92/.

main memory, 6.25% of the memory is mapped by the TLB. If the TLB has 512 entries, the TLB maps 50% of the memory. By comparison, with a 128 B page, a 64-entry TLB only maps about 0.2% of the memory, and a big increase in the size of the TLB is likely to have a significant effect.

The effect on a conventional architecture of increasing TLB size is not as significant because it maps DRAM pages (fixed at 4 KB), not SRAM pages. Further, variation across L2 block sizes should not be related to TLB size.

4   Results

This section presents results of simulations, with some discussion. The main focus is on differences introduced by changes over previous simulations, but some advantages of RAMpage, as previously described, should be evident again from these new results. Presentation of results is broken down into effects of increasing L1 cache size, and effects of increasing TLB size, since these improvements have very different effects on the hierarchies modelled. Results are presented for 3 cases: the conventional 2-level cache with a DRAM main memory, and RAMpage with and without context switches on misses.

The remainder of this section presents the effects of L1 changes, then the effects of TLB changes, followed by a summary.

4.1   Increasing L1 Size

Figure 1 shows how miss rates of the L1 instruction and data caches vary as their size increases for both RAMpage with context switches on misses and the standard hierarchy. (RAMpage without switches on misses follows the same trend as the standard hierarchy.) As cache sizes increase, the miss rate decreases, initially fairly rapidly. The trend is similar for all models.

Execution times are plotted in Fig. 2, normalised to the best execution time at each CPU speed. As expected, larger caches decrease execution times by reducing capacity misses, as evident from the reduced miss rates – with limits to the benefits as L1 scales up. The best overall effect is from the combination of RAMpage with context switches on misses and increasing the size of L1. The execution time of the fastest variation speeds up 10.7 over the slowest configuration, as compared with the clock speedup of 8. Comparing a given hierarchy's slowest (1GHz, 32 KB L1) and fastest case (8GHz, 256 KB total L1) results in a speedup of 6.12 for the conventional hierarchy, 6.5 for RAMpage without switches on misses and 9.9 for switches on misses. For slowest CPU and smallest L1, RAMpage with switches on misses has a speedup of 1.08 over the conventional hierarchy, rising to 1.74 with the fastest CPU and biggest L1. For RAMpage without switches on misses, the scaling up of improvement over the conventional hierarchy is not as strong: for the slowest CPU with least aggressive L1, RAMpage has a speedup of 1.03, as opposed to 1.11 for the fastest CPU with largest L1. So, whether by comparison with a conventional architecture or by comparison with a slower version of itself, RAMpage scales up well with more aggressive hardware, but more so with context switches on misses.

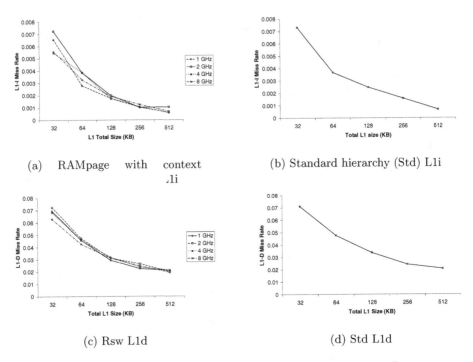

(a) RAMpage with context L1i

(b) Standard hierarchy (Std) L1i

(c) Rsw L1d

(d) Std L1d

Fig. 1. L1 miss rate *vs.* L1 size for varying issue rates. *L1d size = L1i size.*

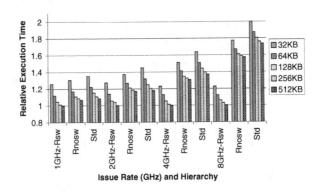

Fig. 2. Relative execution times (normalised: best at each issue rate = 1) as cache sizes vary with instruction issue rates.

Figure 3 shows relative times each variation of the slowest and fastest CPU spend waiting for each level of the various hierarchies, as L1 size increases. The 8 GHz issue rate for the conventional hierarchy spends over 40% of total execution time waiting for DRAM for the largest L1 cache – in line with measurements of the Pentium 4, which spends 35% of its time waiting for DRAM running SPECint2k on average at 2 GHz [28]. This Pentium 4 configuration corresponds

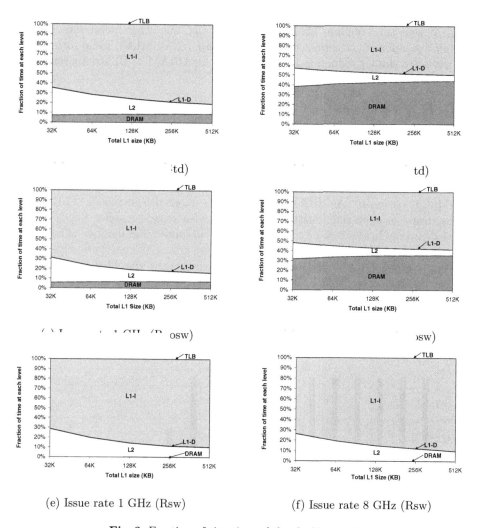

(e) Issue rate 1 GHz (Rsw)   (f) Issue rate 8 GHz (Rsw)

Fig. 3. Fraction of time in each level of hierarchy.

roughly to a 6 GHz issue rate in this paper. The similarity of the time waiting for DRAM lends some credibility to our view that our results are reasonably in line with real systems.

While cache size increases boost performance significantly, as CPU speed increases, a large L1 cannot save a conventional hierarchy from the high penalty of waiting for DRAM. In Fig. 3(d), it can be seen that RAMpage only improves the situation marginally without context switches on misses.

With RAMpage with context switches on misses, time waiting for DRAM remains negligible as the CPU-DRAM speed gap increases by a factor of 8 (Fig. 3(f)). The largest L1 (combined L1i and L1d size 512KB) results in only about 10% of execution time being spent waiting for SRAM main memory, while DRAM wait time remains negligible. By contrast, the other hierarchies, while seeing a significant reduction in time waiting for L2 (or SRAM main memory), do not see a similar reduction in time waiting for DRAM as L1 size increases.

4.2   TLB Variations

All TLB variations are measured with the L1 parameters fixed at the original RAMpage measurements – 16 KB each of instruction and data cache.

The TLB miss rate (Fig. 4), even with increased TLB sizes, is significantly higher in all RAMpage cases than for the standard hierarchy, except for a 4 KB RAMpage page size. As SRAM main memory page size increases, TLB miss rates drop, as expected. Further, as TLB size increases, smaller pages' miss rates decrease. In the case of context switches on misses, the number of context switches increases as the CPU-DRAM speed gap grows, since the effective time waiting for one DRAM reference g rows. Consequently, the TLB miss rate is higher for a faster clock speed in this case (Fig. 4(c)), whereas it does not change significantly for the other variations measured. Note also that L2 block size has little effect on TLB miss rate in the standard hierarchy (Fig. 4(a)).

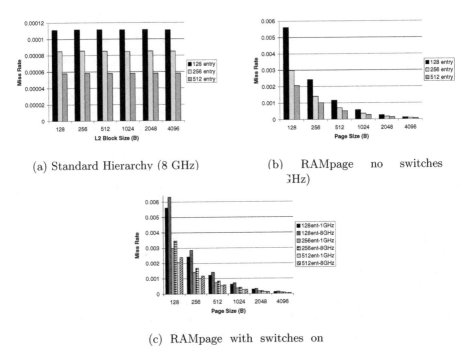

(a) Standard Hierarchy (8 GHz)

(b)   RAMpage   no   switches
ȝHz)

(c) RAMpage with switches on misses

Fig. 4. TLB miss rate vs L2 block/SRAM page size.

Figure 5 shows how TLB miss and page fault handling overhead varies with page and TLB size for all hierarchies with an 8 GHz processor issue rate. Overhead here is measured as extra references generated, which is conservative, as the actual cost can be up to double, once memory hierarchy effects are taken into account [15]. From 1024 B pages upwards percentage differences in overhead between 256 and 512 entry TLBs are minor. Although overheads of TLB and page fault handling are still relatively high for small pages, with a 4 KB page, RAMpage without context switches on misses is within 50% of the overhead of the standard hierarchy. RAMpage TLB misses do not result in references to DRAM, unless there is a page fault, so the additional references should not result in a similarly substantial performance hit.

Figure 6 illustrates execution times for the hierarchies at 1 and 8 GHz, the speed gap which shows off differences most clearly. There are two competing effects: as L2 block (SRAM page size) increases, miss penalty to DRAM increases. In RAMpage, reduced TLB misses compensate for the higher DRAM miss penalty, but the performance of the standard hierarchy becomes worse as

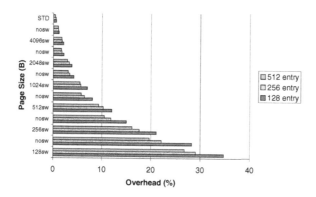

Fig. 5. TLB miss, page fault overhead (fraction of all references, 8GHz)

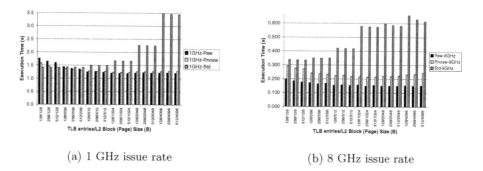

(a) 1 GHz issue rate   (b) 8 GHz issue rate

Fig. 6. Comparison of execution times for each hierarchy with different TLB and page or L2 cache block sizes.

block size increases. TLB size variation makes little difference to performance of the standard hierarchy with the simulated workload. Performance of RAMpage with switches on misses does not vary much for pages of 512 B and greater even with TLB variations, while RAMpage without switches is best with 1024 B pages.

The performance-optimal TLB and page size combination for RAMpage without context switches on misses, with a 512 entry TLB, is a 1024 B page for all issue rates. In previous work, with a 64-entry TLB, the optimal page size at 1 GHz was 2048 B, while other issue rates performed best with 1024 B pages. Thus, a larger TLB results in a smaller page size being optimal for the 1 GHz speed. While other page sizes are still slower than the 1024 B page size, for all cases with pages of 512 B and greater RAMpage without context switches on misses is faster than the standard hierarchy.

For RAMpage with context switches on misses, the performance-optimal page size has shifted to 1024 B with a larger TLB. Previously the best page size was 4096 B for 1, 2 and 4 GHz and 2048 B for 8 GHz. A TLB of 256 or even 128 entries combined with the 1024 B page will yield optimum or almost optimum performance. With a 1024 B page and 256 entries, a total of 256 KB, or 6.25% of the RAMpage main memory is mapped by the TLB, which appears to be sufficient for this workload (a 4 KB page with a 512-entry TLB maps half the SRAM main memory, overkill for any workload with reasonable locality of reference). Nonetheless, TLB performance is highly dependent on application code, so results presented here need to be considered in that light.

Contrasting the 1 Ghz and 8 GHz cases in Fig. 6 makes it clear again how the differences between RAMpage and a conventional hierarchy scale as the CPU-DRAM speed gap increases. At 1 GHz, all variations are reasonably comparable across a range of parameters. At 8 GHz, RAMpage is clearly better in all variations, but even more so with context switches on misses. A larger TLB broadens the range of useful RAMpage configurations, without significantly altering the standard hierarchy's competitiveness.

4.3   Summary

In summary, the RAMpage model with context switches on misses gains most from L1 cache improvements, though the other hierarchies also reduce execution time. However, without taking context switches on misses, increasing the size of L1 has the effect of increasing the fraction of time spent waiting for DRAM, since the number of DRAM references is not reduced, nor is their latency hidden. As was shown by scaling up the CPU-DRAM speed gap, only RAMpage with context switches on misses, of the variations presen ted here, is able to hide the increasing effective latency of DRAM. Increasing the size of the TLB, as predicted, increased the range of SRAM main memory page sizes over which RAMpage is viable, widening the range of choices for a designer.

5   Conclusion

This paper has examined enhancements to RAMpage, which measure its potential for further improvement, as opposed to similar improvements to a conventional hierarchy. As in previous work, RAMpage has been shown to scale better as the CPU-DRAM speed gap grows. In addition, it has been shown that context switches on misses can take advantage of a more aggressive core including a bigger L1 cache, and a bigger TLB. The remainder of this section summarizes results, outlines future work and sums up overall findings.

5.1   Summary of Results

Introducing significantly larger L1 caches – even if this could be done without problems with meeting clock cycle targets – has limited benefits. Scaling the clock speed up by a factor of 8 achieves only about 77% of this speedup in a conventional hierarchy measured here. RAMpage with context switches on misses is able to make effective use of a larger L1 cache, and achieves superlinear speedup with respect to a slower clock speed and smaller L1 cache. While this effect can only be expected in RAMpage with an unrealistically large L1, this result shows that increasingly aggressive L1 caches are no t as important a solution to the memory wall problem as finding alternative work on a miss to DRAM.

That results for RAMpage without context switches on misses are an improvement but not as significant as results with context switches on misses suggests that attempts at improving associativity and replacement strategy will not be sufficient to bridge the growing CPU-DRAM speed gap.

Larger TLBs, as expected, increase the range of useful RAMpage SRAM main memory page sizes, though the performance benefit on the workload measured was not significant versus larger page sizes and a more modest-sized TLB.

5.2   Future Work

It would be interesting to match RAMpage with models for supporting more than one instruction stream. SMT, while adding hardware complexity, is an established approach [19], with existing implementations [3]. Another thing to explore is alternative interconnect architectures, so multiple requests for DRAM could be overlapped [24]. HyperTransport [2] is a candidate. A more detailed simulation modelling operating system effects accurately would be useful. SimOS [26], for example, could be used. Further variations to explore include virtually-addressed L1 and hardware TLB miss handling. Finally, it would be interesting to build a RAMpage machine.

5.3   Overall Conclusion

RAMpage has been simulated in a variety of forms. In this latest study, enhancing L1 and the TLB have shown that it gains significantly more from such improvements than a conventional architecture in some cases. The most important finding generally from RAMpage work is that finding other work on a miss to DRAM is becoming increasingly viable. While RAMpage is not the only approach to finding such alternative work, it is a potential solution. As compared with hardware multithreading approaches, its main adva ntage is the flexibility of a software solution, though this needs to be compared to hardware solutions to establish the performance cost of extra flexibility.

Acknowledgements

Financial support for this work has been received from Universities of Queensland and Witwatersrand, and South African National Research Foundation. We would like to thank the referees for helpful suggestions.

References

1. Thomas Alexander and Gershon Kedem. Distributed prefetch-buffer/cache design for high-performance memory systems. In *Proc. 2nd IEEE Symp. on High-Performance Computer Architecture*, pages 254–263, San Jose, CA, February 1996.
2. AMD. HyperTransport technology: Simplifying system design [online]. October 2002. http://www.hypertransport.org/docs/26635A_HT_System_Design.pdf.
3. J. M. Borkenhagen, R. J. Eickemeyer, R. N. Kalla, and S. R. Kunkel. A multi-threaded PowerPC processor for commercial servers. *IBM J. Research and Development*, 44(6):885–898, November 2000.
4. T. Chen and J. Baer. Reducing memory latency via non-blocking and prefetching caches. In *Proc. 5th Int. Conf. on Architectural Support for Programming Languages and Operating Systems (ASPLOS-5)*, pages 51–61, September 1992.
5. T-F. Chen. An effective programmable prefetch engine for on-chip caches. In *Proc. 28th Int. Symp. on Microarchitecture (MICRO-28)*, pages 237–242, Ann Arbor, MI, 29 November – 1 December 1995.
6. D.R. Cheriton, H.A. Goosen, H. Holbrook, and P. Machanick. Restructuring a parallel simulation to improve cache behavior in a shared-memory multiprocessor: The value of distributed synchronization. In *Proc. 7th Workshop on Parallel and Distributed Simulation*, pages 159–162, San Diego, May 1993.
7. D.R. Cheriton, G. Slavenburg, and P. Boyle. Software-controlled caches in the VMP multiprocessor. In *Proc. 13th Int. Symp. on Computer Architecture (ISCA '86)*, pages 366–374, Tokyo, June 1986.
8. R. Crisp. Direct Rambus technology: The new main memory standard. *IEEE Micro*, 17(6):18–28, November/December 1997.
9. B. Davis, T. Mudge, B. Jacob, and V. Cuppu. DDR2 and low latency variants. In *Solving the Memory Wall Problem Workshop*, Vancouver, Canada, June 2000. In conjunction with 26th Annual Int. Symp. on Computer Architecture.
10. Erik G. Hallnor and Steven K. Reinhardt. A fully associative software-managed cache design. In *Proc. 27th Annual Int. Symp. on Computer Architecture*, pages 107–116, Vancouver, BC, 2000.
11. J. Handy. *The Cache Memory Book*. Academic Press, San Diego, CA, 2 ed., 1998.
12. J.L. Hennessy and D.A. Patterson. *Computer Architecture: A Quantitative Approach*. Morgan Kauffmann, San Francisco, CA, 2 ed., 1996.

13. J. Huck and J. Hays. Architectural support for translation table management in large address space machines. In *Proc. 20th Int. Symp. on Computer Architecture (ISCA '93)*, pages 39–50, San Diego, CA, May 1993.

14. B. Jacob and T. Mudge. Software-managed address translation. In *Proc. Third Int. Symp. on High-Performance Computer Architecture*, pages 156–167, San Antonio, TX, February 1997.

15. Bruce L. Jacob and Trevor N. Mudge. A look at several memory management units, TLB-refill mechanisms, and page table organizations. In *Proc. 8th Int. Conf. on Architectural Support for Programming Languages and Operating Systems (ASPLOS-VIII)*, pages 295–306, San Jose, CA, 1998.

16. E.E. Johnson. Graffiti on the memory wall. *Computer Architecture News*, 23(4):7–8, September 1995.

17. Norman P. Jouppi. Cache write policies and performance. In *Proc. 20th annual Int. Symp. on Computer Architecture*, pages 191–201, San Diego, CA, 1993.

18. Jang-Soo Lee, Won-Kee Hong, and Shin-Dug Kim. Design and evaluation of a selective compressed memory system. In *Proc. IEEE Int. Conf. on Computer Design*, pages 184–191, Austin, TX, 10–13 October 1999.

19. J.L. Lo, J.S. Emer, H.M. Levy, R.L. Stamm, and D.M. Tullsen. Converting thread-level parallelism to instruction-level parallelism via simultaneous multithreading. *ACM Trans. on Computer Systems*, 15(3):322–354, August 1997.

20. P. Machanick. The case for SRAM main memory. *Computer Architecture News*, 24(5):23–30, December 1996.

21. P. Machanick. Scalability of the RAMpage memory hierarchy. *South African Computer Journal*, (25):68–73, August 2000.

22. P. Machanick, P. Salverda, and L. Pompe. Hardware-software trade-offs in a Direct Rambus implementation of the RAMpage memory hierarchy. In *Proc. 8th Int. Conf. on Architectural Support for Programming Languages and Operating Systems (ASPLOS-VIII)*, pages 105–114, San Jose, CA, October 1998.

23. Philip Machanick. *An Object-Oriented Library for Shared-Memory Parallel Simulations*. PhD Thesis, Dept. of Computer Science, University of Cape Town, 1996.

24. Philip Machanick. What if DRAM is a slow peripheral? *Computer Architecture News*, 30(6):16–19 December 2002.

25. T.C. Mowry, M.S. Lam, and A. Gupta. Design and evaluation of a compiler algorithm for prefetching. In *Proc. 5th Int. Conf. on Architectural Support for Programming Languages and Operating Systems*, pages 62–73, September 1992.

26. M. Rosenblum, S.A. Herrod, E. Witchel, and A. Gupta. Complete computer system simulation: The SimOS approach. *IEEE Parallel and Distributed Technology*, 3(4):34–43, Winter 1995.

27. Ashley Saulsbury, Fong Pong, and Andreas Nowatzyk. Missing the memory wall: the case for processor/memory integration. In *Proc. 23rd annual Int. Symp. on Computer architecture*, pages 90–101, Philadelphia, PA, 1996.

28. Eric Sprangle and Doug Carmean. Increasing processor performance by implementing deeper pipelines. In *Proc. 29th Annual Int. Symp. on Computer architecture*, pages 25–34, Anchorage, Alaska, 2002.

29. J. M. Tendler, J. S. Dodson, Jr. J. S. Fields, H. Le, and B. Sinharoy. POWER4 system microarchitecture. *IBM J. Research and Development*, 46(1):5–25, 2002.

30. W.A. Wulf and S.A. McKee. Hitting the memory wall: Implications of the obvious. *Computer Architecture News*, 23(1):20–24, March 1995.

Legba: Fast Hardware Support
for Fine-Grained Protection

Adam Wiggins[1], Simon Winwood[1], Harvey Tuch[1], and Gernot Heiser[1,2]

[1] University of New South Wales, Sydney 2052, Australia
[2] National ICT Australia, Sydney, Australia
{awiggins,sjw,htuch,gernot}@cse.unsw.edu.au

Abstract. Fine-grained hardware protection, if it can be done without slowing down the processor, could deliver significant benefits to software, enabling the implementation of strongly encapsulated light-weight objects. In this paper we introduce Legba, a new caching architecture that aims at supporting fine-grained memory protection and protected procedure calls without slowing down the processor's clock speed.

This is achieved by separating translation from protection, which allows the use of virtually-addressed caches and moving the TLB off-core. Protection is implemented in two stages. We add protection information in the form of an object ID to each cache line. This object ID is combined with a per-protection context identifier, and the result is used to index into a protection cache, which delivers the access rights. As no range check is required on the protection cache, it can be set-associative, allowing it to be made large, fast and low-power, compared to a fully associative TLB. On a cache miss, the object ID is retrieved in parallel to the cache line fetch, performing the protection range check off-core.

A new switch permission enables Legba to implement protected procedure calls, where the new context identifier is taken from the instruction cache line's object ID. This mechanism is similar to call gates but more flexible. The paper compares Legba with approaches based on the idea of a protection look-aside buffer, in particular with respect to coverage.

1 Introduction

Mobile code is becoming increasingly widespread, and thus secure execution of untrusted code is presents a significant challenge to modern computer systems[1]. As well, dynamic extensibility has long been promoted as a way to manage the complexity, and improve maintainability and reliability of operating systems[2–5]. Recently, the low reliability of some system components, particularly device drivers, has triggered renewed efforts to isolate such components[6, 7].

The common problem here is the need to isolate untrusted (buggy or potentially malicious) code. In addition, component technology[8–10], which is an attractive way of constructing extensions, is leading to a reduced granularity of the units of code and data that require protection or isolation[11].

While a memory-management unit (MMU) provides mechanisms for implementing protection and isolation, attempts to use these for mobile code or OS extensions has

A. Omondi and S. Sedukhin (Eds.): ACSAC 2003, LNCS 2823, pp. 320–336, 2003.

in the past generally lead to poor performance[1], mostly resulting from the high cost of protection domain crossings (i.e. context switches). This has lead to a widespread employment of pure software techniques for protection and isolation of extensions[3, 12–15]. These approaches are generally justified with the high cost and coarse granularity of hardware-based protection.

This high cost is not unavoidable. Even on present hardware, careful design and implementation of OS primitives can reduce the cross-domain invocation cost to within a single order of magnitude of that of a normal function call[16, 17]. While this still constitutes significant overhead on primitive operations, in terms of overall system execution times this is often reduced to a few percent[18, 19]. Still, the overheads may be too high for component software with high invocation frequencies.

However, software-only protection has its cost too: run-time checks cannot be avoided unless restrictive programming models are imposed, and the size of the *trusted computing base* (TCB) dramatically increases due to the inclusion of compilers and language runtime systems. Perhaps most critically, a single security flaw in a system employing software-only protection will generally provide an attacker with the full privileges of the underlying virtual machine[11].

Hardware mechanisms would be the preferred means of providing protection or isolation, if they provided finer granularity and if the cost of context switches could be reduced compared to present processors.

This paper presents *Legba*, a new protection cache architecture, which is designed to reduce the granularity of protection, without limiting the processor's clock rate. Legba furthermore supports a *protected procedure call*[20, 21] mechanism which allows a program to change its protection domain in a controlled manner without the need to enter the operating system (OS) kernel. This enables fast protected component invocation.

The reminder of this paper is organised as follows. Section 2 presents related work, Section 3 introduces our proposed Legba architecture. Section 4 describes the experimental setup we used, and Section 5 presents the results, followed by conclusions and future work in Sections 6 & 7.

2   Related Work

2.1   Translation Look-Aside Buffer

Current processors employ a *translation look-aside buffer* (TLB), which caches page translations as well as access rights. In order to allow sharing of the TLB between different processes, and thus reduce context switching costs, the TLB is usually tagged with an *address-space identifier* (ASID). The ASID of the currently active process is stored in a processor register and concatenated with the virtual address on a TLB lookup.

Making protection more fine-grained in such a system would mean reducing the page size. Small page sizes, however, imply more memory-management overhead in the OS, and reduced I/O performance when paging. The trend in modern operating systems is towards *larger* rather than smaller page sizes. As a single page size is anyway unlikely to provide good performance under all circumstances, TLBs of modern architectures support a range of page sizes. Multiple page sizes, however, are in general implemented via a fully-associative TLB[22]. Since large fully-associative caches are slow and energy hungry, and since the TLB is on the processor core, TLB capacity is generally limited to, at most, a few hundred entries. Consequently, TLB coverage is inherently limited, and would be further degraded by smaller page sizes.

The inadequate coverage of modern TLBs has been highlighted by several studies[23–26]. Several attempts have been made to address this, including *super-pages*[22], *sub-blocking*[27], *in-memory translation*[28], *virtually-addressed memory hierarchies*[29, 30], *in-cache translation*[31], and even *software-managed address translation*[32]. However, all these studies focused on improving translation coverage, while protection issues have at best been a secondary consideration.

2.2   De-coupling Protection from Translation

Given the conflicting requirements on the granularity of translation (which should be large in order to maximise translation coverage) and protection (which should be small), it makes sense to consider separating the hardware mechanisms for protection and translation.

One such approach is that used in the PA-RISC[33] and Itanium[34] processors. These tag TLB entries with a *protection-key*, which is used to look up additional access information in a separate protection cache. On the Itanium this cache is a small (16 on the first generation processor) fully-associative set of *protection-key registers* (PKRs) without context-specific tags.

The small size of the PKR file is probably a result of the lookup being on the critical path and the lack of a context tag, which means that the PKRs must be invalidated or reloaded on a context switch. However, there is no obvious inherent limitation on the size of the PKR file, as it could be made set-associative and tagged with a context ID.

The main advantage of protection keys is that they allow sharing TLB entries of shared pages, even if different context have different rights to the page, thus somewhat increasing TLB coverage in the presence of sharing[35]. However, protection keys do not support protection at sub-page granularity and only partially decouple protection from translation. Furthermore, they require an additional cache (the PKRs) on the processor core (although the lookup latency can be hidden in the pipeline) and the TLB remains on the processor core.

An alternative approach, the *protection look-aside buffer* (PLB), completely decouples protection and translation[36]. In this scheme, all protection data is removed from the TLB, which can then be moved off-core if a virtually-addressed L1 cache is used. The PLB is essentially a TLB with no translation information (making it smaller), and thus has essentially the same drawbacks as a classical TLB: it is in the processor's critical path, and the need to support a range of protection granularities implies that it is fully associative. Hence, its speed and capacity (and thus coverage) are limited in the same way as a TLB.

The recently proposed *Mondrian memory protection* (MMP)[37] addresses some of these shortcomings. It assumes a single, shared (virtual or physical) address space with access rights defined by per-context *permissions tables*. A PLB is used to cache these rights. In order to move the PLB off the critical path, Witchel et al. introduce the concept of *sidecar registers*, which are associated with each of the processor's registers able to hold addresses. These sidecars cache the base, limit and access rights of the last memory reference via those registers, utilising locality of pointer references. The sidecars reduce the frequency of PLB accesses and have the advantage that the segment information they hold does not need to be aligned to any particular block size. Unlike PLB entries, the sidecars are not tagged with a protection-domain ID, and thus need to be flushed on a context switch.

2.3 Protected Procedure Calls

The idea of protected procedure entry points goes back to Multics *call gates*[20], which were a transparent, secure mechanism for increasing a process's privileges. Similar mechanisms exist on the x86[38] and Itanium[34] architectures. These are tied to the hierarchical privilege model supported by these architectures. The hierarchical model has proven to be inflexible, and, with one recent exception[39], no operating system on x86 uses more than two privilege levels.

The IBM System/38 generalised call gates into a mechanism, called *profile adaptation*[40], for executing encapsulated (but not necessarily privileged) code. This mechanism is highly dependent on System/38's capability-based protection model. Recently, a protection domain *switch* mechanism was proposed for the Sombrero single-address-space architecture[41]. The design uses a PLB generalisation, called the *range protection look-aside buffer* (RPLB), in order to cache access rights, including for protection-domain switches. The Sombrero design requires an RPLB entry for each caller-entry-point combination, which uses up the RPLB very quickly. Furthermore, the RPLB is unlikely to scale to high clock speeds.

3   The Legba Architecture

3.1   Principle of Operation

What really limits performance, and thus the ability to apply protection at a fine granularity, in schemes designed around some form of TLB or PLB is the need to perform an associative lookup of an address *without knowing the base address* of the object whose attributes are cached. Essentially, a TLB or PLB is limited by the need to mask the page size in order to obtain the base address.

Any effective solution must avoid a cache lookup for an unknown base address (a range check). This can be achieved by *associating the protection information with each I/D-cache line*.

Placing the actual protection bits in each cache line has been proposed before[42]. However this approach makes the protection bits global (i.e., independent of the protection context) which can only be avoided by either flushing the caches on a context switch, or adding a PDID tag to them. In addition, protection updates require that each cache line's permissions be updated in a sequential manner.

The main idea behind Legba is to eliminate the range-check problem by adding a level of indirection. While this has the potential to increase costs, we will show that it will, in fact, make fine-grained protection feasible, by trading transistors for clock speed.

Fig. 1 shows the main features of the architecture. We tag cache lines with an *object identifier* (OID). On a cache hit, the OID is concatenated with the *protection-domain*

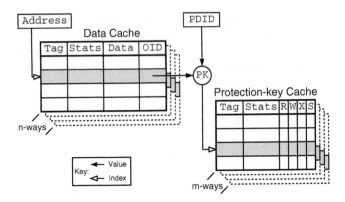

Fig. 1. Legba cache architecture.

identifier (PDID) of the presently executing process. The result is used to look up a *protection-key cache* (PKC) which holds the protection bits. Neither cache lookup requires a range check, and there is no need for the PKC to be fully associative, allowing it to be large with less limitations on its speed.

3.2   Protection-Key Caching

The PKC index should be generated from the OID only, in order to support inexpensive flushing of object accesses. This creates a potential for high collision rates where objects are heavily shared between many protection domains, suggesting that the PKC's associativity should be reasonably high.

As the object name space is completely separate from the address space, it is possible to re-tag objects dynamically (i.e. change their OID). Generating the PKC indexing solely from the OID supports dynamic re-tagging, which can then be used by the operating system to "re-colour" objects if a high rate of PKC collisions is detected.

On a miss, the PKC must be reloaded from a *protection-key table* (PKT). This is organised as a two-level hash table, where the OID is used to index the first table, the *object hash table*. This contains a pointer to the second table, the *protection-domain hash table*, which is indexed by the PDID. This lookup can be done by a fast hardware walker; on a miss in either table, a software exception is raised.

These tables are themselves memory objects, and can be cached like any data, similar to hardware-walked page tables on some architectures. Since they are memory objects, these hash tables themselves are protected by Legba memory protection. Among others, this means that object "ownership" can be given to user code by giving it write access to the protection-domain hash table of the object. The owner can then update the access control list of the object by modifying its protection-domain hash table.

3.3   Instruction and Data Cache Misses

Storing the object ID in the cache line slightly complicates cache miss handling. The hardware not only must fetch the cache line, but also the OID. However, since the cache data and the OID lookup utilise the same address, they can be done in parallel, potentially allowing the OID lookup latency to be hidden by the cache line fetch.

This relaxation of time constraints allows the use of a large fully-associative cache to implement (*address* $\rightarrow$ *OID*) mappings. This cache is called the *object look-aside buffer* (OLB). It can support multiple page sizes, or even a more expensive (*base*, *limit*) form of segmentation.

The design space contains further alternatives. For example, the OID mapping could be held in lower-level caches, with software miss handling similar to *software-managed address translation*[32].

3.4 Protected Procedure Calls

In addition to the familiar (R)ead, (W)rite and e(X)ecute rights, Legba also supports a (S)witch permission, similar to that proposed for Sombrero[41], which guards protected procedure call objects.

A protection-domain crossing in Legba requires two interlocked instructions, which can be viewed as a replacement for the syscall or trap instructions supplied by most architectures. The first is a **branch-linked-locked** instruction, which differs from a normal branch-linked by additionally setting a condition flag. That flag requires the branch target to contain a **switch-load** instruction, otherwise an exception is raised. Execution of a **branch-linked-locked** instruction, like any other instruction, requires X permission to the code object containing the instruction.

The **switch-load** instruction marks an entry point into a protection-domain. Unlike other instructions, its execution requires the S permission to the code object it resides in. The instruction performs a normal load of a general-purpose CPU register (GR), but at the same time loads the OID of the code object into the PDID register. Thus, the execution of the **branch-linked-locked/switch-load** pair changes the protection context of the executing thread. The GR load can be used to set up the stack pointer for the execution of the protected procedure.

3.5 Pipeline Implementation

Since a protection-key cache lookup depends on the OID (obtained from the instruction or data cache) it should be located in the pipeline after the respective cache. Fig. 2 shows an example Legba pipeline. Here, a single-issue 5-stage in-order pipeline is employed with split instruction and data caches (ICache, DCache) as well as split instruction and data protection-key caches (IPKC, DPKC). The IPKC handles the execution-type access rights of X and S, while the DPKC handles the data-access rights of R and W. The IPKC also controls the loading of the current PDID register via the switch operation.

Because the protection-key caches reside in the pipeline stages after the cache references, access permission faults will incur a single cycle delay penalty in addition to the exception handling overheads.

For out-of-order pipelines, protection cache (either PLB or PKC) lookups do not have to complete until instruction retirement, effectively removing them from the processor's critical path. However, the lower access time of the PKC should enable higher instruction retirement rates, compared to a PLB-based design.

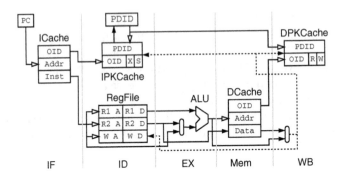

Fig. 2. Example Legba pipeline.

3.6 Sidecar Implementation

To reduce the number of PKC accesses, Legba supports a sidecar optimisation similar to that proposed in Witchel et. al.[37]. During a memory reference, the OID stored in the sidecar is compared to the one stored in the cache line. On a match the permission bits from the sidecar are used, avoiding a PKC access.

As opposed to the range check required by MMP, Legba's sidecars require a simple comparison of the OID. This implies that Legba's register file with sidecars is at most half of the size the Mondrian model. This size difference should lead to a lower access energy, which is significant considering the sidecars are accessed on every instruction, potentially multiple times.

3.7 Summary

Legba can be regarded as a two-stage PLB. The first stage associates an address range with an object. Because this stage is off-core and only invoked on a data cache miss, the cost of its range-check can be shielded by the expense of the cache miss[1]. The second stage associates the object and current protection-domain context with an access permission. This stage is on-core and accessed on every cache reference, to validate the access rights of the reference. The key consequence of the architecture is that the range check is removed from the core, facilitating the use of protection caches with increased coverage at lower energy consumption and higher access speeds.

Legba works equally well for virtually-addressed as for physically-addressed caches. However, it is most powerful when used with virtually-addressed caches, as this completely removes the TLB (and thus any range check) from the processor's core. This is unlike traditional architectures, where (even with virtual caches) a TLB lookup is still required to obtain the protection information.

The cost of Legba is an increase in first-level I/D-cache size to accommodate OIDs, a similar increase in bandwidth requirements for cache line fetches, and the addition of an off-core OLB. The benefits are increased coverage of the protection-key cache over TLB- or PLB-based approaches.

---

[1] The cost of the OLB range-check is only shielded by a cache miss if the access hits in the OLB.

4   Experimental Evaluation

The performance evaluation of Legba was done in three stages. Firstly, we generated memory reference traces for the MediaBench[43] benchmark suite running on a simulated ARM[44] processor.

One of the motivations for this work was fine-grained protection on high-performance embedded systems, where processors such as the ARM are common.

Secondly, these traces were fed into a cache-level simulator for a number of cache architectures: a hypothetical ARM system for the baseline, a Legba system, and a PLB-based system. Each configuration was run for a range of protection granularities and protection-cache sizes.

Finally, a cache modeller was used to generate timing and energy profiles for each architecture and configuration.

The remainder of this section is organised as follows: Section 4.1 introduces the simulation environment in more detail, while Section 4.2 describes the different cache architectures. Section 4.3 outlines the benchmarks used and their protection characteristics, and Section 4.4 discusses the anticipated differences between the simulation environment and a real implementation.

4.1   Simulation Environment

We used the SimpleScalar[45] ISA simulator to generate a set of memory traces. SimpleScalar simulates the user-level portion of a system, forwarding all system calls to an OS emulation layer inside the simulator, emulating Linux in this case. This results in traces which do not include any OS interference, especially cache pollution.

To simulate the various cache architectures, we separated SimpleScalar's cache functionality into a separate cache simulator called *tracesim*. This simulator takes in a memory trace, a set of cache parameters, and a set of object descriptors, and generates cache statistics for each combination of cache parameters. The simulation output (number of hits and misses for each cache) was then processed by the CACTI[46] cache modeller and combined with the time and energy characteristics of SDRAM to produce a total energy consumption and runtime. The time and energy characteristics of the register file and sidecar registers, as well other parts of the processor, were not modelled.

The granularity of objects and protection domains was varied to examine the behaviour of these systems under different protection scenarios. Accordingly, PDIDs and OIDs were generated as follows: for the finest grain of protection domains, each function was assigned a separate PDID. For the coarse grain protection domains, the application code was assigned one PDID, while any libraries — primarily libc — were assigned another. Finally, to provide fine-grained OIDs each program variable, whether dynamic or static, was assigned a unique OID.

4.2   Simulation Configuration

Each cache configuration was based on a hypothetical ARM processor modelled after Intel's XScale processor, with characteristics as in Table 1.

Table 1. Baseline configuration

Parameter	Value
Clock speed	600MHz
I-TLB	32-entry, fully assoc.
D-TLB	32-entry, fully assoc.
I-Cache	32k, 32-way, 32byte line size
D-Cache	32k, 32-way, 32byte line size
Pagesize	4kB
TLB-reload	hardware; 2-level page table
Memory	100MHz SDRAM

Table 2. Legba and PLB configurations

Architecture	Parameter	Value
Legba	I-PKC	128-, 256-, 512-, and 1024-entry, 32-way
	D-PKC	128-, 256-, 512-, and 1024-entry, 32-way
	OLB	128-entry, fully-assoc.
PLB	I-PLB	32-, 64-, and 128-entry, fully-assoc.
	D-PLB	32-, 64-, and 128-entry, fully-assoc.
	S-PLB	32-, 64-, and 128-entry, fully-assoc.

To simplify the simulation, system data structures, such as page tables, were simulated as being loaded directly from memory. We also assume that a cache write-back will require another translation to obtain the physical address.

In the Legba and PLB configurations, a protection table lookup was assumed to use the minimum number of memory accesses required by the destination object's size.

For the baseline configuration, the TLB is accessed in parallel to the cache in order to check permissions.

The Legba configuration is shown in Table 2. As Legba provides an alternate protection mechanism, the TLB is not required on a cache access, and so was moved off-core. Sidecar registers were consulted on every memory access (whenever an instruction was fetched, the PC's sidecar was consulted), and the respective protection key cache was only accessed on a sidecar miss. On a cache miss, the OLB was consulted. To model protection granularity down to that of a single word, an OID was stored per word in the cache line, as a result the OLB could be consulted multiple times per cache miss if the OLB entry did not map the entire cache line. This form of word-level granularity is not particularly compact, leaving room for improvement.

In order to model a protection domain-switch, the I-PKC was accessed and the sidecars were flushed each time the current protection domain changed (via executing an instruction tagged with a different PDID).

The PLB configuration is also shown in Table 2. As with Legba, the TLB was also moved off-core. Sidecar registers were consulted on every memory reference, with a miss going to the respective PLB. If the result was a PLB hit, the PLB's super-page entry was copied into the sidecar. On a PLB miss, the segment's base and limit were copied into the sidecar and the largest power of two page of the access region loaded into the PLB.

To provide an equivalent to Legba's switch instruction for the PLB case, a Switch-PLB (S-PLB) was simulated. This caches the destination PDID and permissions, and is tagged with the entrypoint and current PDID. The S-PLB is accessed whenever the PDID changes. While the S-PLB can be set associative, preliminary benchmarks suggested that the only practical implementation would be fully associative, as lower associativities resulted in significantly reduced performance due to *conflict misses*.

On an S-PLB miss, a 3-level protection table lookup was assumed. As with Legba, the sidecars were flushed on a PDID change.

4.3   Benchmarks

The MediaBench[43] suite was chosen as representative of embedded applications with a relatively short run time — a desirable characteristic given the simulation overhead. Table 3 shows the number of protection domains, object IDs, and protection domain switches for each benchmark. The benchmarks presented in Section 5 were chosen as those exhibiting interesting, representative, or significant behaviour.

Table 3. Properties of benchmarks

Benchmark	No. Protection Domains & Context Switches				
	Coarse	context switches	Fine	context switches	OIDs
jpeg	2	13070	866	350681	449
g721	2	6922258	639	25457220	442
mpeg2	2	5813793	746	23286653	652
pegwit	2	1835251	719	4507475	476
pgp	2	1122637	1087	11526264	782
rasta	2	6663146	1000	15959160	1366
adpcm	2	665126	626	679288	433
mesa	2	12885420	1635	37622046	604
gsm	2	281158	732	17631406	489
epic	2	194591	657	965314	575

4.4   Simulation Accuracy

Although our simulation attempts to mirror a real system, time and complexity constraints meant that some aspects of the system had to be simplified.

The primary simplification was that all tables would be loaded from main memory. We expect a real system to reload the protection caches (the PKCs and PLBs) from in-cache tables, with the TLB and OLB being loaded from main memory.

We believe, however, that our results are still significant; the trends discussed in Section 5 are inherent characteristics of the two models, and the loading of protection entries from memory will not significantly effect our results.

5   Results

The results for run time and run energy are presented, normalised to the baseline configuration. Fig. 3 shows the time and energy performance for coarse-grained PDIDs and fine-grained OIDs, when no sidecar registers are employed. While Legba's time and energy results improve with increased PKC size, the PLB exhibits a tradeoff between time and energy. In most cases the 32-entry PLBs have insufficient coverage, requiring at least 64-entry and sometimes even 128-entry PLBs to match Legba's performance, The energy results show the inverse with the larger PLBs using more power; the 128-entry PLB being generally about 25% more power-hungry than a Legba configuration.

In nearly all cases the 32-entry PLB uses less energy than all the Legba configurations. This is due to the energy overheads of reading out the OIDs from the I/D caches on each cache reference[2]. The 64-entry PLBs then lose this advantage, levelling out with the Legba configurations while the 128-entry PLBs use more energy in every case.

Fig. 4 shows the same results with sidecars added. While on average performance increases only marginally, energy shows a significant decrease. The shielding of the protection caches (PLB or PKC) by the sidecars causes the core's energy to be dominated by the cost of I/D cache references for most benchmarks. Exceptions are benchmarks,

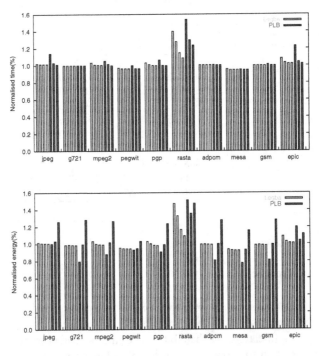

Fig. 3. Coarse-grained PDIDs and fine-grained OIDs (left to right: 128-, 256-, 512-, 1024-entry PKCs, 32-, 64-, 128-entry PLBs) without sidecars (top: execution time, bottom: energy).

---

[2] We believe the energy overheads of reading the OIDs from the caches were overstated due to limitation of simulating them in CACTI.

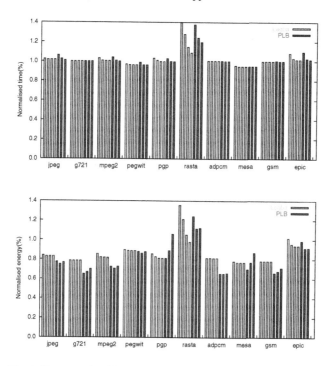

Fig. 4. Coarse-grained PDIDs and fine-grained OIDs, with sidecars.

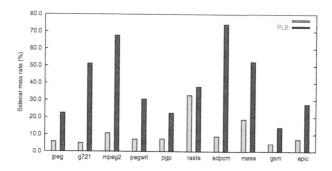

Fig. 5. Sidecar miss rates for largest PKC and PLB, coarse-grained PDIDs and fine-grained OIDs.

like Rasta, where a larger number of objects are referenced, and a large number of protection table lookups are pushing up the energy costs.

As expected, Legba shows consistent improvements in energy consumption with increasing PKC sizes, as the energy consumption of the PKC itself is quite insignificant. The PLB results, while generally showing a decrease in energy consumption with increasing PLB size, show several cases where the opposite is true. This shows that the optimal PLB size, with respect to energy, is quite application dependent.

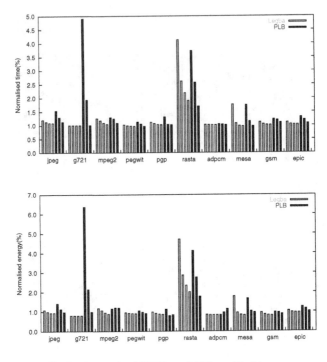

Fig. 6. Fine-grained PDIDs and OIDs, with sidecars.

Fig. 5 shows the sidecar miss rates for the largest PKC/PLB configurations. Legba's sidecars clearly exhibit much higher hit rates. This is a result of how sidecars are loaded on a miss: as PLB entries are aligned power-of-two ranges, in many cases several PLB entries are required for a single segment, leading to sidecars not covering the complete segment after a reload form the PLB. Only on a PLB miss are full (*base, limit*) entries loaded into the sidecar.

Fig. 6 shows the results for both fine-grained objects and protection-domains. On average Legba's increased coverage manages fine-grained protection more effectively. Out of the PLB configurations, only the 128-entry one consistently approaches Legba's performance, however it nearly always fares worse in terms of energy. The exception is the Rasta benchmark, where Legba's increased table accesses cause it to be both slower and use more energy.

Fig. 7 shows, once again, that the Legba's sidecar miss rate is much lower than the PLB setup.

To try and get a feel for the how 64-bit addressing would impact performance we reran the time and energy simulations using a 5-level protection table to reload both Legba's OLB and the PLBs. The results showed little variation to the 3-level table. Besides fairly consistent degradation in time and energy for both Legba and the PLB, the only notable result was that for fine-grained PDIDs and OIDs, Legba's time and energy for the Rasta benchmark out-performed that of the PLB.

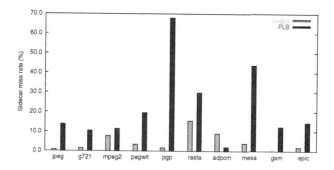

Fig. 7. Sidecar miss rates for largest PKC and PLB, fine-grained PDIDs and OIDs.

6   Conclusions

In this study we have introduced the Legba cache architecture for fine-grained protection and evaluated its time and energy performance to that of the PLB. The results show that Legba's protection caches scale more effectively than the PLB organisation. In particular while increases in the size (and hence coverage) of the PKC show modest increases in energy and time costs. Similar increases in PLB coverage need to be weighted against the significant energy and time impact of their fully-associative nature.

One of the most significant result of the study has been to show that with the use of MMP's sidecar registers, Legba or PLB based protection combined with an off-core TLB makes fine-grained protection cheaper in both energy and time (for the majority of the benchmarks evaluated) than a on-core TLB with only page-based protection.

We also show that Legba's sidecars are simpler and have lower miss rates than MMP's range-based sidecars. However, one drawback of the Legba approach that has limited its performance in this evaluation environment has been the cost of additional memory accesses over the PLB. Because both the OLB and PLB were loaded from hardware walked tables, the overhead of a PLB miss is negligible compared to that of a PKC miss, as both require on average two memory references. A major focus of future work will be to reduce this overhead through more intelligent OID mapping tables and protection-key tables.

7   Future Work

While the results of this evaluation have shown Legba to an attractive architecture for fine-grained protection environments, a number of limitations in the both the evaluation and architecture still need to be addressed.

A major limitation of the evaluation was the lack of any OS modelling, and that the protection and translation tables were loaded from main memory and not the caches. This leaves significant uncertainty about the overheads that both the Legba and PLB architectures will incur in a real system. In addition, any future studies will need to look at the effects of 64-bit architectures and software loaded tables.

Adam Wiggins et al.

Further work is required to investigate the ability of the Legba architecture to provide effective support for word- and even byte-grained protection. We are currently exploring a number of approaches resulting in small, constant increase in the size of the L1 caches. A related issue is that of OLB organisation. The segmented (*base*, *limit*) nature of protection attributes suggest that OLBs with some form of support for segmentation in the OLB would improve its hit rate, particularly if multiple segments could be mapped per OLB entry. Again we are currently exploring a number of designs that provide just this.

References

1. Drew Dean and Edward W. Felten. Secure mobile code: Where do we go from here? In *DARPA Workshop on Foundations for Secure Mobile Code*, Monterey, CA, USA, Mar 1997.
2. W. Wulf, E. Cohen, W. Corwin, A. Jones, R. Levin, C. Pierson, and F. Pollack. HYDRA: The kernel of a multiprocessor operating system. *Comm. ACM*, 17:337–345, 1974.
3. Brian N. Bershad, Stefan Savage, Przemyslaw Pardyak, Emin Gün Sirer, Marc E. Fiuczynski, David Becker, Craig Chambers, and Susan Eggers. Extensibility, safety and performance in the SPIN operating system. In *Proc. 15th ACM SOSP*, pages 267–284, Copper Mountain, CO, USA, Dec 1995.
4. M.I. Seltzer, Y. Endo, C. Small, and K.A. Smith. Dealing with disaster: Surviving misbehaved kernel extensions. In *Proc. 2nd USENIX OSDI*, pages 213–228, Nov 1996.
5. Dawson R. Engler, M. Frans Kaashoek, and James O'Toole, Jr. Exokernel: An operating system architecture for application-level resource management. In *Proc. 15th ACM SOSP*, pages 251–266, Copper Mountain, CO, USA, Dec 1995.
6. George Candea and Armando Fox. Recursive restartability: Turning the reboot sledgehammer into a scalpel. In *Proc. 8th HotOS*, pages 125–130, 2001.
7. Michael M. Swift, Steven Marting, Henry M. Levy, and Susan G. Eggers. Nooks: An architecture for reliable device drivers. In *Proc. 10th SIGOPS European WS.*, pages 101–107, St Emilion, France, Sep 2002.
8. Clemens Szyperski. *Component Software: Beyond Object-Oriented Programming*. Addison-Wesley/ACM Press, Essex, England, 1997.
9. The component object model specification. Technical report, Microsoft Corporation and Digital Equipment Corporation, 1995. http://www.microsoft.com.
10. Corba components. TC Document orbos/99-02-05, Object Management Group, Mar 1999. ftp://ftp.omg.org/pub/docs/orbos/99-02-05.pdf.
11. Trent Jaeger, Jochen Liedtke, and Nayeem Islam. Operating system protection for fine-grained programs. In *Proc. 7th USENIX Security Symp.*, pages 143–157, San Antonio, Tx, USA, Jan 1998.
12. Chris Hawblitzel, Chi-Chao Chang, Grzegorz Czajkowski, Deyu Hu, and Thorsten von Eicken. Implementing multiple protection domains in Java. In *Proc. 1998 USENIX Techn. Conf.*, pages 259–270, New Orleans, USA, Jun 1998.
13. Michael Golm, Jürgen Kleinöder, and Frank Bellosa. Beyond address spaces: Flexibility, performance, protection, and resource management in the type-safe JX operating system. In *Proc. 8th HotOS*, pages 3–8, Schloß Elmau, Germany, May 2001.
14. Brian N. Bershad, Stefan Savage, Przemyslaw Pardak, David Becker, Marc Fiuczynski, and Emin Gün Sirer. Protection is a software issue. In *Proc. 5th HotOS*, Orkas Island, WA, USA, May 1995.
15. Laurent Daynès and Grzegorz Czajkowski. Lightweight flexible isolation for language-based extensible systems. In *Proc. 28nd VLDB Conf.*, Hong Kong, China, 2002.

16. Jochen Liedtke, Kevin Elphinstone, Sebastian Schönberg, Herrman Härtig, Gernot Heiser, Nayeem Islam, and Trent Jaeger. Achieved IPC performance (still the foundation for extensibility). In *Proc. 6th HotOS*, pages 28–31, Cape Cod, MA, USA, May 1997.

17. Takahiro Shinagawa, Kenji Kono, and Takashi Masuda. Exploiting segmentation mechanism for protecting against malicious mobile code. Technical Report 00-02, Dept. of Information Science, University of Tokyo, May 2000.

18. Hermann Härtig, Michael Hohmuth, Jochen Liedtke, Sebastian Schönberg, and Jean Wolter. The performance of μ-kernel-based systems. In *Proc. 16th ACM SOSP*, pages 66–77, St. Malo, France, Oct 1997.

19. Andrew Whitaker, Marianne Shaw, and Steven D. Gribble. Scale and performance in the Denali isolation kernel. In *Proc. 5th USENIX OSDI*, Boston, MA, USA, Dec 2002.

20. Jerome H. Saltzer. Protection and the control of information sharing in Multics. *Comm. ACM*, 17:388–402, 1974.

21. Brian N. Bershad, Thomas E. Anderson, Edward D. Lazowska, and Henry M. Levy. Lightweight remote procedure call. In *Proc. 12th ACM SOSP*, pages 102–113, Dec 1989.

22. Madhusudhan Talluri, Shing Kong, Mark D. Hill, and David A. Patterson. Tradeoffs in supporting two page sizes. In *Proc. 19th ISCA*. ACM, 1992.

23. J. Bradley Chen, Anita Borg, and Norman P. Jouppi. A simulation based study of TLB performance. In *Proc. 19th ISCA*. ACM, 1992.

24. Jerry Huck and Jim Hays. Architectural support for translation table management in large address space machines. In *Proc. 20th ISCA*, pages 39–50. ACM, 1993.

25. Madhusudhan Talluri. *Use of Superpages and Subblocking in the Address Translation Hierarchy*. Phd thesis, University of Wisconsin-Madison Computer Sciences, 1995. Technical Report #1277.

26. Gokul B. Kandiraju and Anand Sivasubramaniam. Characterizing the d-TLB behavior of SPEC CPU2000 benchmarks. In *Proc. ACM SIGMETRICS*, 2002.

27. Madhusudhan Talluri and Mark D. Hill. Surpassing the TLB performance of superpages with less operating system support. In *Proc. 6th ASPLOS*, pages 171–182, San Jose, CA, USA 1994.

28. Patricia J. Teller. Translation-lookaside buffer consistency. *Trans. Computers*, 23:26–36, 1990.

29. Xiaogang Qiu and Michel Dubois. Options for dynamic address translation in COMAs. In *Proc. 25th ISCA*, pages 214–225, 1998.

30. Xiaogang Qiu and Michel Dubois. Towards virtually-addressed memory hierarchies. In *HPCA*, pages 51–62, Jan 2001.

31. David A. Wood, Susan J. Eggers, Garth Gibson, Mark D. Hill, Joan M. Pendleton, Scott A. Ritchie, George S. Taylor, Randy H. Katz, and David A. Patterson. An in-cache address translation mechanism. In *Proc. 13th ISCA*, pages 358–365, 1986.

32. Bruce Jacob and Trevor Mudge. Uniprocessor virtual memory without TLBs. *Trans. Computers*, 50:482–499, 2001.

33. Ruby B. Lee. Precision architecture. *IEEE Comp.*, 22(1):78–91, Jan 1989.

34. Intel Corp. *Itanium Architecture Software Developer's Manual*, Feb 2000. URL http://developer.intel.com/design/itanium/family.

35. Matthew Chapman, Ian Wienand, and Gernot Heiser. Itanium page tables and TLB. Technical Report UNSW-CSE-TR-0307, School Comp. Sci. & Engin., University NSW, Sydney 2052, Australia, May 2003.

36. Eric J. Koldinger, Jeffrey S. Chase, and Susan J. Eggers. Architectural support for single-address-space operating systems. In *Proc. 5th ASPLOS*, pages 175–86, 1992.

37. Emmett Witchel, Josh Cates, and Krste Asanović. Mondrian memory protection. In *Proc. 10th ASPLOS*, Oct 2002.

38. Intel Corp. *IA-32 Architecture Software Developer's Manual*, 2002.   URL http://developer.intel.com/design/pentium4/manuals.

39. Tzi-cher Chiueh, Ganesh Venkitachalam, and Prashant Pradhan. Integrating segmentation and paging protection for safe, efficient and transparent software extensions. In *Proc. 17th ACM SOSP*, pages 140–153, Kiawah Island, SC, USA, Dec 1999.

40. Viktors Berstis. Security and protection in the IBM System/38. In *Proc. 7th Symp. Comp. Arch.*, pages 245–250. ACM/IEEE, May 1980.

41. Alan C. Skousen and Donald Miller. Resource access and protection in the Sombrero protection model, software protection data structures and hardware range protection lookaside buffer. Technical Report TR-95-013, Computer Science and Engineering Department, Arizona State University, May 1996.

42. Bruce Jacob and Trevor Mudge. Software-managed address translation. In *Proc. 3rd HPCA*, pages 156–167, 1997.

43. Chunho Lee, Miodrag Potkonjak, and William H. Mangione-Smith. Mediabench: a tool for evaluating and synthesizing multimedia and commu nicatons systems. In *Proceedings of the thirtieth annual IEEE/ACM international symposi um on Microarchitecture*, pages 330–335. IEEE Computer Society Press, 1997.

44. Dave Jagger, editor. *Advanced RISC Machines Architecture Reference Manual*. Prentice Hall, Jul 1995.

45. T. Austin, E. Larson, and D. Ernst. SimpleScalar: an infrastructure for computer system modeling. *IEEE Computer*, 35(2):59–67, Feb 2002.

46. Steven J. E. Wilton and Norman P. Jouppi. CACTI: An enhanced cache access and cycle time model. *IEEE Journal of Solid-State Circuits*, 31(5):677–688, May 1996.

Live-Cache: Exploiting Data Redundancy to Reduce Leakage Energy in a Cache Subsystem

Mohan G Kabadi[1] and Ranjani Parthasarathi[2]

[1] Department of Computer Science and Engineering, S.J.C. Institute of Technology,
Chickaballapur – 562 101, India,
mohan_kabdi@cs.annauniv.edu
[2] School of Computer Science and Engineering, Anna University,
Chennai – 600 025, India,
rp@cs.annauniv.edu

Abstract. Large on-chip caches can significantly improve the processor performance. But, they also increase the on-chip energy spent. With the increase in transistor density and decrease in feature sizes, the dominant component of the energy spent is the leakage energy. Since, on-chip caches consume a major portion of the chip's transistor budget, they are good candidates for the control of leakage energy. In the cache hierarchy, most of the time, the data present at the first level also exists in the lower levels, and hence expends the leakage energy in all the levels that it is present. This paper proposes a mechanism to reduce this leakage energy by exposing the redundancy. In this mechnism, sub-blocks of the L1-data cache are turned off, when the data also exists in the register file. Also, a control mechanism is proposed to turn-off the blocks of L2-cache (in both instruction cache and data cache portions) when the data also exists in L1-cache. An architectural technique is also proposed, to effectively turn-off the portions of the L1 and L2-caches, which are never used for data storage by keeping the cache circuitry initially in low-leakage mode. The effectiveness of the proposed schemes has been demonstrated through cycle accurate simulation using a set of media and SPEC CPU 2000 benchamrks. This mechanism yields an average of about 33% to 36% reduction in the leakage energy for 16 KB to 32 KB dll-cache and an average of 79% and 86% for 128 KB of dL2 and iL2 caches respectively, albeit with a little performance degradation.

1 Introduction

The fabrication technology of VLSI circuit is steadily improving and the chip structures are being scaled down. But, the number of transistors on a chip is increasing at a higher ratio. Also, the drive towards increasing levels of performance has pushed the operating clock frequencies higher and higher, which has resulted in increased level of power consumption. Power has thus become an important parameter, not only for wireless and mobile electronics, but also for high performance microprocessors. In these processors, on-chip caches constitute a significant portion of the transistor budget and the leakage energy of such

A. Omondi and S. Sedukhin (Eds.): ACSAC 2003, LNCS 2823, pp. 337–351, 2003.

caches plays a vital role in the process of processor design. It has been estimated that leakage energy accounts for 30% of L1-cache energy and 70% of L2-cache energy for a 0.13 micron process [1].

Several techniques have been proposed to reduce the power dissipated by on-chip caches [2], [3], [4], [5]. These techniques do little to minimize the leakage energy of the memory cells as long as the power supply is maintained to them, irrespective of whether they are used or not. Various circuit level techniques [6], [7] have been proposed to reduce leakage power of the idle cache blocks. These techniques, either completely turn-off circuits by creating a high impedance path to ground or trade-off increased execution time for reduced static power consumption. Gated-Vdd [6] is a circuit level technique to control the supply voltage and is used to dynamically shutdown the portion of I-cache [8] to reduce the leakage energy in the cache's unused section. Gated-Vdd mechanism has been applied at cache block level granularity in [9], [10] and used in conjunction with a compiler-assisted technique to eliminate the dead-blocks in i-cache [11].

This paper examines the option of exploiting the redundancy of information present in the cache hierarchy for reducing leakage energy in dL1-cache, dL2-cache and the iL2-cache. It is to be noted that when a line is copied from L2 to L1 cache, the L2 cache line information is redundant, but continues to occupy the cache, thus leaking power. Hence such blocks of L2-cache may be forced to the low leakage mode. Similarly, when a sub block of dL1-cache is copied to register file, the corresponding sub block of dL1-cache is redundant. Hence it is proposed that such sub blocks be invalidated and moved to a low leakage mode there by saving leakage power. The details of this approach are explained here.

The next section presents the proposed method, called the "Live-cache". The experimental methodology and the results of the simulation experiments conducted to validate the proposed method are given in section 3. In section 4, an overview of related work relevant to the proposed approach is presented and section 5 concludes the paper.

2   Live Cache

The crucial idea of the Live-cache approach is that, maintaining only one copy of 'Live-data/information' can save power. That is, if the same information is available in two levels of the memory / cache hierarchy, only the information present at the higher level needs to be retained, and the lower level redundant information can be discarded, if possible. This saves power since only the information block in the higher level cache needs to be powered on, and the corresponding lower level cache block can be turned-off.

This simple idea works for both instruction and data caches, provided a suitable mechanism to identify the redundancy of data could be devised. The overall strategy is that, whenever a miss occurs in the higher-level cache, a block of information is copied from a lower-level cache to higher-level cache. Such a transition can be traced on the fly and the corresponding block of lower-level cache can be put to a low-leakage mode using a mechanism such as the gated supply [6]. However, the blocks of lower-level cache, which are put into low-leakage mode, may be accessed in future when (i) the corresponding block is evicted from the higher-level cache or (ii) against a miss in the lower-level cache that maps to the same block. At such time, the line needs to be brought back to the active state.

It can be seen that this concept can be readily applied to the L2-cache to save leakage energy. That is, when the data / instruction is moved from the dL2 / iL2 cache in to the dL1 / iL1 cache, the dL2 / iL2 block can be put into low-leakage mode. These blocks are activated when they are to be actually used again. In case of the reactivation due to a cache miss that maps to the same block, both dL2 and iL2 cache can be handled in the same way. However, when the reactivation is due to a L1-cache miss that requires a write-back, there is a difference in the way the dL2 and iL2 caches are to be handled. While dL1 to dL2 cache write-back is a standard feature in all cache systems, iL2 cache is normally not written back to. Hence, this needs to be handled carefully. A simple architectural modification to support this operation with minimal overhead is proposed in section 2.3.

As for the L1-caches, moving to a higher level from L1 cache implies the loading of data into registers in the case of dL1 cache, and fetching of instructions into the instruction buffer for an iL1 cache. And, there is a clear distinction in the applicability of this scheme to the data and instruction caches. Intuitively, it can be seen that while this scheme will work well for dL1 cache when the data is moved from L1 cache to the processor register file, without performance degradation, the same cannot be said about the iL1 cache (when the instructions are moved to the instruction buffer). There could be a performance degradation because of the penalty paid in terms of increased latency in bringing back the low-leakage cache lines to active state, when they are accessed again. While the data that has been accessed from dL1 cache is unlikely to be accessed again and again before a write-back (store to dL1), instructions typically would be (due to temporal locality), resulting in performance degradation. Hence, it has been decided to apply this mechanism to the dL1-cache alone.

Also, speaking of performance penalty, the effect of awakening the cache blocks needs to be examined for both L1 and L2 caches. Typically, L1 cache access time is 1 cycle and L2 cache access time is about 6 cycles (for 0.07 micron process technology, 0.5 nS cycle time). Hence the reactivation latency should not add significantly to these values. Hence, it is suggested that two different low leakage modes 'sleep-mode' and 'drowsy-mode' with different reactivation latencies, be used for the two levels. The sleep-mode (state-destroying mode) typically has a reactivation time of 30 cycles, while the drowsy-mode (state-preserving mode) has a reactivation time of 1 cycle [7]. However, the leakage power in sleep-mode is 0%, whereas in drowsy-mode it is 10% of normal leakage power. Hence it is suggested that the drowsy-mode be used for the L1 cache and the sleep-mode be used for the L2 cache. Since L1 to L2 cache transfer is a secondary process, the additional latency can be hidden so that the processor's performance is not affected.

Hence the proposal is to apply the 'live-cache' technique to iL2, dL1 and dL2 caches, with the L1 cache using drowsy-mode as the low-leakage mode and L2 cache using sleep-mode as the low-leakage mode. The details of the design for each of these cases are presented below.

2.1 Strategy for Invalidating dL1-Cache Lines

Against each load instruction executed, the content of one or multiple sub blocks are copied from dL1-cache to the register file. A copy of the data, which is loaded in to the register is available in dL1-cache also. Hence, during the execution of the load instruction, such sub-blocks, which are copied from the dl1-cache to the register file, are put into drowsy-mode. Similarly, against each store instruction issued, the content of a register is to be transferred back to a sub-block of dL1-cache. At this time it is reactivated. Thus, this leakage control mechanism does not require any architectural changes, except for the drowsy-cache mechanism for each of the 'sub-blocks' in the dL1-cache. As mentioned earlier, the reactivation of the sub-blocks from 'drowsy-mode' to 'active mode' takes one cycle and hence this will increase the store latency. However, since store latencies are hidden by mechanisms such as load-store queue, this should not cause any noticeable degradation in performance.

2.2 Strategy for Invalidating dL2-Cache Lines

When a line from dL2-cache is copied to dL1-cache, the corresponding line of dL2-cache can be invalidated. Such an invalidated line is put in to 'sleep-mode'. Thus a line that is copied into dL2-cache from memory, effectively stays in dL2-cache till it is copied to dL1-cache. Then it is destroyed when the line is put into 'sleep mode'. That line is 'woken-up' from the 'sleep mode' when it needs to be used again.

There are two cases when the line would need to be used again. One is on a dL2 miss that maps to that line, and the other is when the corresponding dL1-cache line is evicted from the dL1-cache. While the former case is that of regular functioning of any cache, the latter is specific to the proposed modification. In a general L1-L2 data-cache hierarchy, the replacement of a line from dL1-cache causes a write back only when the line is dirty. If the line is clean, it is not written back and a subsequent access to the same line will hit in the L2 cache provided some other line has not replaced it. However, in 'Live-cache' when the line in the dL2-cache is turned-off for the sake of reducing leakage energy, the data present in the line will be lost. Hence a subsequent access to the same line will cause an L2 cache miss necessitating a memory access cycle. Thus, to avoid this overhead, and not to lose out on performance, on the eviction of the corresponding dL1-cache line, it is necessary to write it back to dL2-cache irrespective of the line being dirty or clean. Obviously, copying it from memory takes more time than the time for writing it back. Hence it is preferable to write back to L2 on eviction from L1 even when the line is clean. Thus after the information of a line is brought to L2-level, it physically transit from dL2-cache to dL1-cache and from dL1-cache back to dL2-cache, until it is replaced in the dL2-cache.

2.3 Strategy for Invalidating iL2-Cache

The strategy for invalidating iL2-cache blocks is similar to the one adopted for dL2-cache blocks, but for a small architectural modification to support iL1 to iL2 write-backs. As mentioned earlier, while there exists a dL1 to dL2 write-back mechanism in all cache subsystems, iL1 to iL2 write-back is not supported. This is due to the fact that an iL1 line is never going to be dirty and the iL2 line would any way be present for subsequent access.

However, using the same argument as in dL2, since the iL2 line would have been turned-off in the 'Live-cache' mechanism, the information would be lost. Hence to save on access time during subsequent access, iL1 to iL2 write-back becomes necessary. Thus, as in the case of dL2 cache, the instructions of a line, after being brought to iL2-cache from memory, physically transit from iL2-cache to iL1-cache and from iL1-cache back to iL2-cache, until they are replaced in the iL2-cache.

The provision of a write-back mechanism is the addition required to the normal cache subsystem to provide low-leakage. The proposed architecture for this mechanism is shown in Figure 1. It consists of a small write-back buffer (16 words buffer is chosen) between iL1 and iL2. When a line is evicted from the iL1-cache, it is stored in a write-back buffer temporarily, and the requested line that caused the iL1-cache miss is brought and stored in iL1-cache. After the reactivation of iL2-cache line, the content of the write-back buffer is transferred to iL2-cache. This arrangement hides the reactivation latency of iL2-cache write-backs. Also, one additional bit called 'mode bit' is used along with each line to indicate the state (active or sleep) in which the current line is. These bits are always powered on. The mode-bit is placed along with the tag array and is accessed in parallel with the tag-array against an iL1-miss (i.e., during an iL2-access). The mode-bit is initially set to zero indicating that the line is in 'sleep-mode' and this bit will be set to one when the line is turned-on.

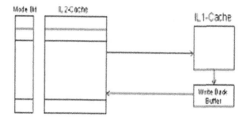

Fig. 1. Hardware Modification

2.4   L2-Cache Initial State

Using the strategy mentioned above, only those lines that transit from level 2 to level 1 cache (i.e., iL2 to iL1 or dL2 to dL1) are traced and turned-off. In effect, as and when the content of the cache line is copied from L2 level to L1 level, the corresponding L2 cache line is *turned-off*. But, the lines that have not been occupied at all continue to be in the on-state thus leaking power. Hence it is suggested that all lines initially be kept in off state there by conserving power. in effect, the cache lines of level 2 are turned on as and when the informtion is copied from the memory to level 2 cache. This does not cause any performance degradation as explained below.

Against a miss in L2-cache, the process of target line activation and initiation of memory read are done concurrently. The latency of memory read is typically 100 cycles and the delay for turning-on a line is about 30 cycles [12]. As the latency for memory read is more than thrice the time for reactivation of the line, the turning-on latency is completely hidden by memory access latency and no performance degradation would be caused.

3   Experimental Methodology and Results

The Simplescalar 3.0 toolkit [14] has been used to implement the proposed scheme. A set of benchmark programs from the SPEC CPU 2000 benchmark suite [15] and the Media benchmark suite [16] has been used to evaluate the performance.

3.1   Experimental Setup

The sim-outorder, a cycle accurate Superscalar out-of-order issue simulator from Simplescalar-3.0 tool suite [14] is used. The simulator is modified to switch-off blocks of iL2- and dL2-caches and also the sub-blocks of dL1 cache based on the invalidation strategy chosen (as explained in section 2). Benchmarks from SPEC CPU 2000 [15] and Mediabench [16] suite have been chosen to show the effectiveness of the 'Live-cache' mechanism. The benchmarks are chosen in such a way that the selected set represents a good mix of applications. Programs depicting real time applications are selected from the Media benchmarks and the programs representing integer and floating point intensive data applications are selected from the SPEC benchmarks. The simulator parameters are shown in Table 1. The benchmarks chosen from Media-bench are run to completion, whereas, each of the benchmark chosen from SPEC 2000 CPU are run for 2 billion instructions after fast forwarding sufficient number of instructions initially [17].

3.2   Simulation Results

The main metrics considered in the evaluation of the effectiveness of Live-cache are reduction in leakage energy and Instructions executed Per Cycle (IPC). While the former measures energy saving, the latter is an indication of performance.

Table 1. Parameters used in the simulation

Simulation Parameter	Value
Fetch width	4 instructions per cycle
Decode width	4 instructions per cycle
Issue width	4 instructions per cycle
Commit width	4 instructions per cycle
LSQ size	8
L1 Instruction cache	512 sets, 32 bytes, 1-way
L1 Data cache	128/256 sets, 32 bytes, 4-way
L1 Data cache sub-block size	4 bytes
L1 I-cache/D-cache latency	1 cycle
L2 Instruction cache	1024/2048 sets, 32 bytes, 4-way
L2 Data cache	512/1024/2048/4096 sets, 32 bytes, 4-way
L2 I-cache/D-cache latency	6 cycles
Dl1 state transition latency (from drowsy mode)	1cycle
Dl2/Il2 state transition latency (from sleep mode)	30 cycle
Integer/Floating point registers	32 each
Memory latency	100 cycles
cycle time	0.5 nS
technology	0.07 micron

The leakage energy of the live cache is normalized with respect to the leakage energy in a conventional cache (base model) and expressed as a percentage. The leakage energy spent is proportional to the number of lines that are active [9] and the laekage energy saved is computed using equation (1).

$$\% \ Energy \ Saved \ = \left(1 - \frac{\sum(No. \ of \ active \ lines \times Duration \ of \ Activity)}{Total \ number \ of \ lines \times Total \ duration}\right) \times 100$$

With respect to performance, the 'wake-up' latencies should not have a negative effect on performance. Further, any increase in cache access latency translates directly into increased execution time. To study the impact of 'wake-up' latencies, the number of instructions executed per cycle (IPC) is chosen as reference and the IPC obtained during simulation of "Live-cache", for all the benchmarks chosen are compared with the IPC of the corresponding base model. The base model cache is a conventional cache with no leakage energy saving mechanism, or in other words, the leakage energy saved in such caches is zero.

Figure 2 shows the leakage energy saved for two different sizes of dL1-cache and Figure 3 compares the IPC with 'Live-cache' implemented in dL1 ("dL1 Live cache") with that of the base model. Also, Table 2 shows the comparison of miss-rates of 'dL1 Live-cache' and the base model cache. From the results obtained, it is observed that as the cache size is increased from 16 KB to 32 KB, there is a variation in the leakage energy saved. In some benchmark programs, namely *art*, *mcf*, *gcc*, *ammp*, *rawcaudio* and *rawdaudio*, the leakage energy saved decreases as the cache size increases, whereas in the remaining programs that

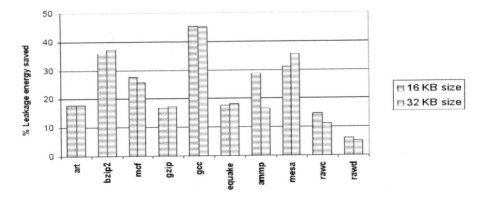

Fig. 2. Normalised leakage energy saved in DL1_Live cache

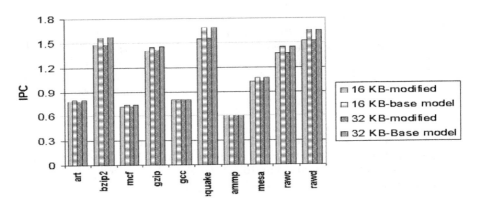

Fig. 3. Comparison of IPC (for 'dL1_Live cache' and base model)

have been run, the leakage power saving increases as the cache size increases. This is due to the following reasons. In the former case, the change in IPC is either zero (as in the case of *art, gcc, ammp, rawcaudio* and *rawdaudio*) or negligible (as in the case of *mcf*) with respect to increase in the cache size of the respective models. Hence, the additional cache used has not reduced the miss rates. In other words, the additional augmented portion due to increase in cache is not utilized in storing the data. Since, in the dL1 cache, only such of the sub-blocks which transit from dL1 to register file are traced and turned off, the portion of the cache which is not used for storing the data remains in on state and continues to spend the leakage energy. Because of this reason, as the cache size increases the leakage energy saving is found to decrease in these programs. Whereas, in the latter case, (namely in *bzip2, gzip, mesa* and *equake* programs) the dL1-miss rate decreases when the cache size is increased (refer Table 2). Thus, a portion of the augmented cache has been utilized for the data storage, which is also controlled by the 'Live-cache' mechanism. This leads to increase in the leakage energy saving as the cache size is increased.

Table 2. Comparison of the miss rates of DL1 Live cache and the corresponding base model cache

Program	16 KB Live	16 KB Base	32 KB Live	32 KB Base
art	0.0881	0.0881	0.0881	0.0881
ammp	0.1319	0.1320	0.1319	0.1320
bzip2	0.0116	0.0116	0.0101	0.0100
equake	0.0061	0.0049	0.0047	0.0047
gcc	0.1158	0.1158	0.1157	0.1157
gzip	0.0405	0.0375	0.0364	0.0332
mcf	0.1077	0.1099	0.1056	0.1067
mesa	0.0031	0.0031	0.0027	0.0027
rawcaudio	0.0001	0.0001	0.0001	0.0001
rawdaudio	0.0001	0.0001	0.0001	0.0001

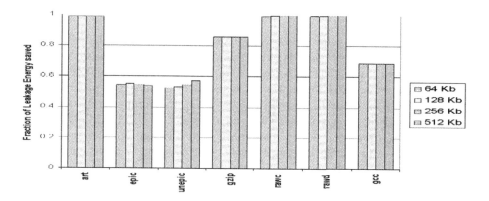

Fig. 4. Normalised leakage energy saved in dL2_Live cache

Figure 3 shows that, the decrease in IPC due to the Live-cache mechanism is very small compared to the base model. Except for two programs namely *rawdaudio* and *equake*, the decrease in IPC is less than 5% when compared to the base model. In *rawdaudio* and *equake*, the decrease in IPC is about 7.5%. However, the average decrease in IPC is only 3.63% and 3.79% for the 16 Kb and 32 Kb caches respectively.

Figure 4 shows the leakage energy saved for different sizes of dL2-cache and Figure 5 compares the IPC with 'Live cache' implemented in dL2 with that of the base model. From Figure 4, it can be seen that in some of the programs namely *art*, *rawcaudio* and *rawdaudio* programs, the power saved is about 99%. In the remaining programs also, the fraction of leakage energy saved is greater than 54%. From the results obtained, it is clear that the fraction of leakage energy saved is high in dL2-Live cache compared to the dL1-Live cache (Figure 2). This can be explained by two reasons. One is that the activity of the dL2-cache will be less compared to the dL1-cache. The data will move between the dL2 and dL1 less frequently. Or in other words the duration for which the data will reside in the dL2 is always less compared to dL1-cache. Secondly, all the blocks of dL2-

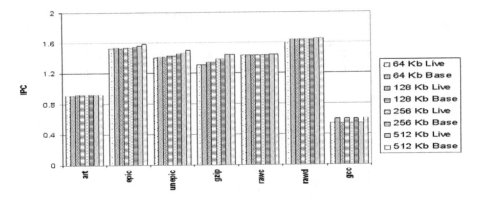

Fig. 5. Comparison of IPC (for 'dL2-Live cache' and base model)

Live-cache are initially kept in low-leakage mode, because of which, the portion of the cache that is never used for data storage will effectively remain in sleep-mode. The high leakage energy savings found in the *rawcaudio* and *rawdaudio* programs, can be explained using the same argument. In these two programs, for 512 Kb cache (i.e., when dL2 contains 16384 lines), the number of dL2 accesses is only 544 and 1059 respectively. Thus, use of 'dL2-Live' mechanism, will keep a minimum of 15840 and 15325 lines in off state through out the simulation period, for these two programs respectively. Thus, yielding a very high leakage energy savings in the above two programs.

Another factor to be considered is the overhead caused by the 'Live-cache' mechanism. Overheads occur because of the additional write backs required in the 'Live-cache' mechanism. In the case of dL2 Live cache mechanism, in the event of dL1 replacements, the repalced line is written back to dL2 cache irrespective of whether the line is dirty or clean. Such a mechanism may increase the dL1 write-back rates and there by may also decrease the performance. This may also induce the consumption of additional dynamic energy. To study the effect of this, the percentage of additional write-backs has been studied. Figure 6 shows the dL1 write backs for both dL2-Live-cache and conventional cache. From the Figure 6, it is observed that, the dL1 write-back rate of the dL2-Live-cache is same as the write-back rate of the conventional cache for the three programs (namely, *art*, *gcc* and *gzip*). For the remaining four programs that are considered, the dL1 write-back rate increases by a small amount when compared to the corresponding conventional cache. Any way, the average increase in dL1 write-back rate is less than 5% of the corresponding size of the conventional cache.

Table 3 shows the percentage of the energy spent in additional write-backs induced due to the 'dL2-Live-cache' mechanism for the four programs in which the write-back rates are different from the corresponding convevntional caches. Column 2 shows the size of the cache in Kbytes. Column 3 indicates the number of dL1 write-backs occuring against dL1 replacements. Column 6 shows the energy overhead due to additional write-backs incurred by 'dL2-Live-cache' mechanism. Column 7 shows the leakage energy saved by the 'dL2-Live-cache'.

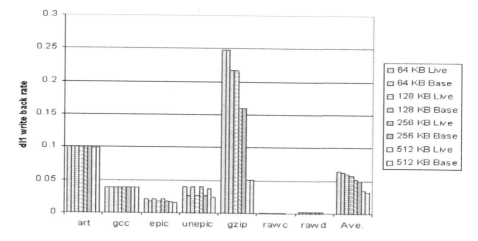

Fig. 6. Comparison of dL1 write-back rates for various programs.

Table 3. Energy overhead due to write-backs induced by "dL2 Live cache" mechanism.

Program	cache size	#dL1_wb 'dL1-Live '	#dL1_wb Base cache	Additional writeback	Wb_overhead (mJ)	Energy saved(mJ)	Overhead (%)
rawc	64	10316	4671	5645	0.0164	12.932	0.127
rawc	128	10316	4671	5645	0.0164	31.845	0.0514
rawc	256	10316	4671	5645	0.0164	51.942	0.032
rawc	512	183	86	97	0.00028	103.65	0.0003
rawd	64	10314	10234	80	0.00023	8.465	0.0027
rawd	128	10314	10234	80	0.00023	17.392	0.001
rawd	256	10314	10234	80	0.00023	34.832	0.0007
rawd	512	181	133	48	0.00014	69.45	0.0002
epic	64	531064	194892	336172	0.9749	38.198	2.55
epic	128	531068	194892	336176	0.97491	77.556	1.26
epic	256	531580	194892	336176	0.97491	152.53	0.639
epic	512	418926	157745	261181	0.7574	298.68	0.254
unepic	64	228673	148805	79868	0.232	7.15	3.24
unepic	128	228671	148805	79866	0.232	14.38	1.61
unepic	256	228667	148805	79862	0.232	29.18	0.794
unepic	512	214713	141181	73532	0.213	59.91	0.36

The last column shows the percentage of the energy saved spent to overcome the dynamic energy induced by 'dL2-Live-cache' mechanism. It can be seen that the percentage overhead is negligible and ranges from 0.0003% to a maximum of 3.24%.

Figure 7 shows the percentage leakage energy saved in 'iL2-Live cache' and Figure 8 shows comparison of IPC with 'iL2-Live-cache' implemented to that of the base model. In 'iL2-Live-cache' also, the results obtained are more or less similar to that of the 'dL2-Live-cache'. From the Figure 7, it is clear that, in some of the benchmark programs (namely *art, rawcaudio* and *rawdaudio*)the

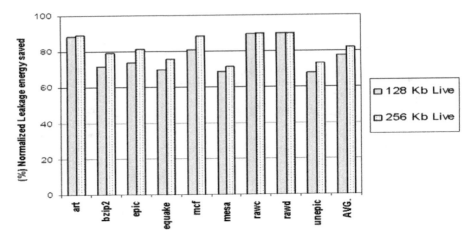

Fig. 7. Normalised leakage energy saved in iL2_Live cache

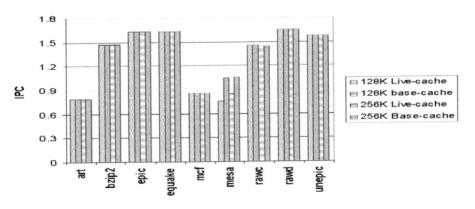

Fig. 8. Comparison of IPC (for 'iL2_Live cache' and base model)

percentage leakage energy saved is around 99% and for the remaining programs it is greater than 75.45%. The average percentage power saved is 86.54% and 91.13% for the iL2 Live-cache of 128 KB and 256 KB sizes respectively. Figure 8 shows that for the 'iL2 Live-cache' the performance degradation is negligible compared to the base model for all the benchmarks except for *mesa* program. In this program, the iL1-write-back rate is very high compared to all the remaining programs. Hence, the performance degradation is high in this program.

4   Related Work

To place the proposed idea in perspective, this section explains some of the related work, for saving leakage power in cache. The effectiveness of any approach used for controlling the cache leakage power mainly depends on the ability to identify the idle lines or evictable lines (i.e., which line to turn-off) and the time at which these lines are to be turned-off (i.e., when to turn-off). In the Cache-Line Decay mechanism [9], [10], a cache line that is not accessed within a fixed time interval called 'decay-interval' is turned-off using gated-Vdd technique [6]. For identifying the lines that are idle, a global counter as well as cache line counters are used. These counters help to identify the lines that are idle over a period and when the count value reaches saturation, the line is turned off.

In the mechanism suggested by Powell et.al., [8], the cache size is modified dynamically to optimize the utility of the cache. In Adaptive Mode Control cache [13], the hardware tracks the performance using miss rates (hypothetical and real misses) and adaptively changes the size of the cache. The turn-off interval can be dynamically adjusted based on such information.

The work by Li et.al.,[12], is very close to the idea proposed here. There again, the data duplication present across the cache hierarchy is exploited. State preserving as well as state destroying leakage optimization mechanisms are used for a level-2 unified cache. Five different strategies are given for the leakage energy optimization of which speculative-IV strategy is close to our work. This strategy reactivates a sub block of the L2-cache, which is in low-leakage mode against L1 eviction. But, it is to be noted that, such a strategy will be able to handle the eviction of dL1 lines without main memory access, without any architectural modification, where as, the eviction of lines from iL1 will cause memory access in the absence of proper architectural modification. In live-cache mechanism, iL1 cache write back is handled as a special case using a simple architectural modification, to avoid such memory access. Such mechanism provides a better power performance. To make a comparison, the results obtained by live-cache are compared with the results obtained in [12]. For example, the leakage energy savings for *rawcaudio* and *rawdaudio* programs are more or less similar in both these methods (~92% for 1 Mb unified L2 cache [12] and 99% for 512 KB split Live-cache), neglecting the size differences .

Further, it is to be noted that, from energy saving point of view, a smaller cache array is always preferred [4]. Thus, a split cache at level 2 (for example 512 KB split) is more power efficient when compared to the unified cache of similar size (1MB unified cachce). But, in the programs epic and unepic a difference is found in the results obtained by these two methods, especially in unepic. For epic and unepic the leakage energy saved is approximately 30% and -5% respectively (as per [12]). Whereas, for the same two programs, the leakage energy saved is higher in Live-cache. The leakage energy saved is about 50% in dL2 live-cache and about 80% in iL2 live-cache, for both epic and unepic programs. Thus, live-cache gives an improved power savings.

5   Conclusion

In this paper, the Live-cache mechanism that keeps the 'used-up' as well as 'never-used' blocks of L2 caches in the low leakage mode has been proposed. The main focus here is, exploitation of the data redundancy present across the

L2, L1 and processor levels. While the L2-L1 data redundancy is obvious, the identification of the L1-processor data redundancy is a significant contribution of this work. The promise of this scheme is well supported by the simulation results that have been obtained, giving a power saving of over 30% to 99% for various levels. This idea has also opened up a few more possibilities, which can be explored. One possibility is to study the effect of the initial state of the cache lines. For instance, in dL1-cache, all the blocks are assumed to be initially in active state. It is possible to keep them initially in low leakage state. The live cache has not been applied to iL1 cache. That can also be studied. Studying the combined effect of the live cache at all levels is another topic to be explored. However, there is one drawback of this scheme that needs to be addressed. Turning off the data in a lower level cache implies that the inclusion property normally supported in multi-level cache is being violated. This could cause a problem in multi-processor scenarios. This needs to be studied and handled appropriately.

References

1. M.D.Powell, S.Yang, B.Falsafi, K.Roy and T.N.Vijayakumar: "Reducing Leakage Energy in a High-Performance Deep-Submicron Instruction Cache" IEEE Transaction on VLSI, Vol. 9, No.1, Feb.2001.

2. Kanad Ghose and Milind B Kamble: "Reducing Power in Superscalar Processor Caches Using Subbanking, Multiple Line Buffers and Bit- Line Segmentation" ISLPED, ACM Press, New York, USA, pp 70-75,1999.

3. D.H.Albonesi: "Selective Cache Ways: On Demand Cache Resource Allocation" Proc. MICRO-32, pp 248-259, November 1999.

4. J.Kin, M.Gupta and W.Mangione-Smith: "The Filter Cache: An Energy Efficient Memory Structure" Proc. IEEE Int'l Symp. Microarchitecture, IEEE CS Press, pp 184-193, 1997.

5. Hongbo Yang, Guang R Gao, Andres Marquez, George Cai and Ziang Hu: "Power and Energy Impact by Loop Transformations" http://research.ac.upc.es/-pact01/colp/paper12.pdf

6. Michael D Powell, Se-Hyun Yang Babak Falsafi, Kaushik Roy and T N Vijayakumar: "Gated-Vdd: A circuit Technique to Reduce Leakage in Deep-Submicron Cache Memories" Proc.lSLPED'00, pp 90-95, 2000.

7. Krisztian Flautner, Nam Sung Kim, Steve Martin, David Blauw and Trevor Mudge: "Drowsy-Caches: Techniques for Reducing Leakage Power" Proc. Int'l Symp. Computer Architecture, ISCA-29, May-2002.

8. Se-Hyun Yang, Michael D Powell, Babak Falsafi, Kaushik Roy and T N Vijayakumar: "An Integrated Circuit/Architectural Approach to Reducing Leakage in Deep-Submicron High-Performance I-Caches" Proc. Int'l Symposium on High Performance Computer Architecture (HPCA'01), January 2001.

9. Stefanos Kaxiras, Zhigang Hu, Girija Narlikar and Rae McLellan: "Cache-Line Decay: A Mechanism to Reduce Cache Leakage Power" IEEE workshop on Power Aware Computer Systems, 2000.

10. Stefanos Kaxiras, Zhigang Hu and Margaret Martonosi: "Cache Decay: Exploiting Generational Behavior to Reduce Cache Leakage Power" Proc. of Int'l Symp. Computer Architecture, ISCA-28,pp 240-251, June 2001.

11. Mohan G Kabadi, Natarajan Kannan, Palanidaran Chidamabaram, Suriya Narayanan M S, and Ranjani Parthasarathi: "Dead Block Elimination in Cache: A mecahanism to Reduce I-Cache Power Consumption in High Performance Microprocessors" Proc. HiPC'02, pp 79-88, December 2002.

12. L.Li, I.Kadayif, Y-F. Tsai, N.Vijayakrishnan, M.Kandemir, M.J.Irwin and A.Sivasubramanian: "Leakage Energy Management in Cache Hierarchies" Proc. 11th Int'l Conf. on Parallel Architecture and Compilation Techniques (PACT'02), September 2002.

13. Huiyang Zhou, Mark C Toburen, Eric Rottenberg and Thomas M Conte: "Adaptive Mode-Control: A Low-Leakage, Power-Efficient Cache Design" TR, Dept. of Electrical & computer engg. North Carolina State University, Raleigh, NC, 27695-7914, Nov 2000.

14. D Burger, Todd M Austin: "The Simplescalar Tool Set, version 2.0 :" CSD Technical Report #1342. University of Wisconsin-Madison, June 1997.

15. "SPEC CPU 2000 benchmark suite" www.spec.org

16. C.Lee, M.Potkonjak and W.H.Mangione Smith: "MediaBench: A Tool for Evaluating Multimedia and Communication Systems" Proc. of MICRO-30, pp 330-335, December1997.

17. Suleyman Sair and Mark Charney: "Memory Behavior of the SPEC2000 Benchmark Suite" Technical Report, IBM, 2000.

Implementation of Fast Address-Space Switching and TLB Sharing on the StrongARM Processor

Adam Wiggins[1], Harvey Tuch[1], Volkmar Uhlig[2], and Gernot Heiser[1,3]

[1] University of New South Wales, Sydney 2052, Australia
[2] University of Karlsruhe, Germany
[3] National ICT Australia, Sydney, Australia,
{awiggins,htuch,gernot}@cse.unsw.edu.au

Abstract. The StrongARM processor features virtually-addressed caches and a TLB without address-space tags. A naive implementation therefore requires flushing of all CPU caches and the TLB on each context switch, which is very costly. We present an implementation of fast context switches on the architecture in both Linux and the L4 microkernel. It is based on using domain tags as address-space identifiers and delaying cache flushes until a clash of mappings is detected. We observe a reduction of the context-switching overheads by about an order of magnitude compared to the naive scheme presently implemented in Linux. We also implemented sharing of TLB entries for shared pages, a natural extension of the fast-context-switch approach. Even though the TLBs of the StrongARM are quite small and a potential bottleneck, we found that benefits from sharing TLB entries are generally marginal, and can only be expected to be significant under very restrictive conditions.

1 Introduction

A *context switch* occurs in a multi-tasking operating system (OS) whenever execution switches between different processes (i.e. threads of execution in different addressing/protection contexts). Such a switch requires the operating system to save the present execution context (processor registers) as well as the addressing context (virtual memory translation data, such as page tables). This generally requires a few dozen (or at worst a few hundred) instructions to be executed by the operating system, and the cost could therefore be of the order of 100 clock cycles[1].

Some architectures, however, make context switches inherently more expensive, as changing the addressing context can costs hundreds or thousands of cycles, even though it may take less than a dozen instructions. One such architecture is the ARM[2], which is especially targeted to embedded applications. High context switching costs are not an issue for many embedded systems, which may only consist of a single application with no protection between subsystems. Even if the system features several processes, context switching rates are often low enough so that the cost of individual context switches is not critical.

However, embedded systems are becoming increasingly networked, and increasingly have to execute downloaded code, which may not be trusted, or is

A. Omondi and S. Sedukhin (Eds.): ACSAC 2003, LNCS 2823, pp. 352–364, 2003.
© Springer-Verlag Berlin Heidelberg 2003

possibly buggy and should not easily be able to crash the whole system. This leads to an increased use of protection contexts, and increases the relevance of context-switching costs.

Furthermore, there is a trend towards the use of microkernels, such as μITRON[3], L4[4] or Symbian OS[5], as the lowest level of software in embedded systems. A microkernel provides a minimal hardware abstraction layer, upon which it is possible to implement highly modular/componentised systems that can be tailored to the specific environment, an important consideration for embedded systems which are often very limited in resources.

In a microkernel-based system, most system services are not provided by the kernel, and therefore cannot be obtained simply by the application performing an appropriate system call. Instead, the application sends a message to a *server* process which provides the service, and returns the result via another message back to the client. Hence, accessing system services requires the use of message-based inter-process communication (IPC). Each such IPC implies a context switch. Therefore, the performance of microkernel-based systems are extremely sensitive to context-switching overheads.

An approach for dramatically reducing context-switching overheads in L4 on the StrongARM processor has recently been proposed and analysed[6]. In this paper we present an implementation of this approach on two systems: Linux, a monolithic OS and L4KA::Pistachio[7], a new and portable implementation of the L4 microkernel under development at the University of Karlsruhe.

2   StrongARM Addressing and Caching

The ARM architecture features virtually-indexed and virtually-tagged L1 instruction and data caches. This ties cache contents to the present addressing context. Furthermore, and unlike most modern architectures, entries in the ARM's translation-lookaside buffer (TLB) are not tagged with an address-space identifier (ASID). As a consequence, multitasking systems like Linux flush the TLB and CPU caches on each context switch, an expensive operation. The direct cost for flushing the caches is 1,000–18,000 cycles. In addition there is the indirect cost of the new context starting off with cold caches, resulting in a number of cache misses ($\approx$ 70 cycles per line) and TLB misses ($\approx$ 45 cycles per entry). Worst case this can add up to around 75,000 cycles, or $\approx 350\mu$sec on a 200MHz processor.

These costs can be avoided by making systematic use of other MMU features provided: *domains* and *PID relocation*[6].

2.1   ARM Domains

The ARM architecture uses a two-level hardware-walked page table. Each TLB entry is tagged with a four-bit *domain ID*. A *domain access control register* (DACR) modifies, for each of the 16 domains, the TLB-specified access rights for pages tagged with that domain. The domain register can specify that access is as specified in the TLB entry, that there is no access at all, or that the page is fully accessible (irrespective of the TLB protection bits).

Domains allow mappings of several processes to co-exist in the TLB (and data and instructions to co-exist in the caches[1]), provided that the mapped parts of the address spaces do not overlap. In order to achieve this, a domain is allocated to each process, and the domain identifier is essentially used as an ASID. On a context switch, instead of flushing TLBs and caches, the DACR is simply reloaded with a mask enabling the new process's domain and disabling all others. Shared pages can also be supported (provided they are mapped at the same address in all processes using them), by allocating one or more domains to shared pages.

Obviously, this scheme is much more restrictive than a classical ASID, due to the small number of domains. In a sense, however, it is also more powerful than an ASID: if TLB entries of shared pages are tagged with the same domain, the TLB entries themselves can be shared between the contexts, reducing the pressure on the relatively small number of TLB entries (32 data-TLB and 32 instruction-TLB entries). Such sharing of TLB entries is particularly attractive for shared libraries, which are very widely shared and tend to use up a fair number of instruction TLB entries.

2.2   StrongARM PID Relocation

The requirement of non-overlapping address spaces, while natural in a single-address-space operating system[8, 9], is in practice difficult to meet in traditional systems such as Linux, and would severely limit the applicability of domains. At the least it requires using position-independent code not only for libraries but also for main program text, which implies a different approach to compiling and linking than in most other systems. For that reason, the StrongARM implementation[10] of ARM supports an address-space relocation mechanism that does not require position-independent code: Addresses less than 32MB can be transparently relocated into another 32MB partition. The actual partition, of which there are 64, is selected by the processor's *PID register*. This allows the operating system to allocate up to 64 processes at non-overlapping addresses, provided their text and data sections fit into 32MB of address space. Stacks and shared libraries can be allocated in the remaining 2GB of address space, although, in practice, the stack will also be allocated below 32MB.

2.3   Fast Context Switching on StrongARM

Using domains IDs as an ASID substitute and PID relocation of small address spaces, context switches can be performed without having to flush caches and TLBs. The limited number of domains, however, imposes severe restrictions on

---

[1] The caches do not have any protection bits, so a TLB lookup is performed even on a cache hit, in order to validate access rights.

this scheme (which is probably the reason Windows CE[11] does not use domains, and therefore does not provide protection between processes).

PID relocation, by itself, does not lead to sharing of TLB entries. In order to share TLB entries, memory must be shared (with unique addresses). This can be achieved by allocating shared regions (everything that is mmap()-ed, including shared library code) in a shared address-space region outside the 32MB area. In order to avoid collisions with the PID relocation slots, this shared area should be the upper 2GB of the address space.

The 32-bit address space is too small to prevent collisions outright. Hence, address space must be allocated so that collisions are minimised, but if they occur, protection and transparency are maintained (at the expense of performance). This can be done via an optimistic scheme that will try to allocate mmap()-ed memory without overlap as far as possible, uses domains to detect collisions, and only flushes caches if there is an actual collision[6].

The approach is based on making use of the ARM's two-level page table. Normally, the *translation table base register* is changed during a context switch to point to the new process's *page directory* (top-level page table). In order to detect address-space collisions, we never change that pointer. Instead we have it point to a data structure, called the *caching page directory* (CPD), which contains pointers to several processes' *leaf page tables* (LPTs). As page directory entries are also tagged with a region ID, it is possible to identify the process to which a particular LPT belongs.

Fig. 1 illustrates this. The CPD is a cache of PD entries of various processes, tagged with their domain IDs. If two address spaces overlap, then after a context switch an access might be attempted which is mapped via a CPD entry that belongs to another process (as indicated by the domain tag). As the DACR only enables access to the present process' domain, such an access will trigger a fault. The kernel handles this by flushing TLB and caches, reloading the CPD entry from the currently running process' PD, and restarting execution. Flushes will then only be required under one of the following circumstances:

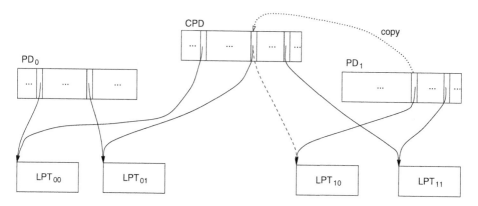

Fig. 1. Caching page directory (CPD) and per-address-space page tables

1. a process maps anything (e.g. using the MAP_FIXED flag to the Linux mmap() system call) into the PID-relocation region between 32MB and 2GB, and the corresponding PID(s) are presently in use;
2. a process maps anything (using MAP_FIXED) into the shared region above 2GB and it collides with a mapping of another process;
3. there is no more space in the shared region for all mappings (which need to be aligned to 1MB);
4. the kernel is running out of domains to uniquely tag all processes and shared memory regions.

Given the small number of available domains (16), and the fact that the use of MAP_FIXED is discouraged, the last option is the most likely, except when very large processes are running.

3   Implementation

3.1   Fast Address-Space Switching

With the approach described in Section 2.3, the TLB, caches and page tables do not normally get touched on a context switch. All that needs to be done is to reload the DACR with a mask enabling access to the domain associated with the newly scheduled process, as well as any shared domains used by that process. The DACR value becomes part of the process context.

Flushes are required at context switch time if the new process does not have an associated domain, and no free domain is available, or when a shared mapping is touched that has no domain allocated. In that case, a domain ID must be preempted, and all CPD entries tagged with that domain need to be invalidated. With a total of 16 domains, and some domains being required for shared regions, this is not an infrequent event.

Cache and TLB flushes are also required if an address collision is detected. This is the case when a process accesses a page which is tagged in the CPD with a domain the process has no access to. In order to minimise the occurrence of collisions, the following steps are taken in Linux:

– The data and bss segments as well as the stack are allocated in the 32MB region. This does not limit the size of the heap, as malloc() will mmap() more space if brk() fails.
– mmap()-ed areas are, where possible, grouped (by process) into non-overlapping 1MB blocks allocated in the top 2GB of the address space.

In L4, all such mappings are under full control of the user-level code, hence no specific steps are required in the L4 kernel in order to minimise collisions.

Whenever caches are flushed, all domains are marked *clean*. A domain is marked dirty if a process with writable mappings in that domain is scheduled. Clean domains can be revoked without flushing caches.

3.2   TLB Sharing

On Linux we also implemented sharing of TLB entries for pages shared between processes. The implementation will transparently share TLB entries for memory shared via `mmap()`, provided the pages are mapped at the same address in both processes. The approach will not share TLB entries for program executables (as opposed to library code), as it is unlikely to produce any benefit on the StrongARM. In order to share the executable between processes, the two processes would have to be located in the same 32MB slot. This would cause maximum collisions on their stacks and data segments, unless those were staggered within the 32MB region. The programs could no longer be linked with their data segment at a fixed address (which introduces run-time overhead for addressing data). Furthermore, the need to share a single 32MB region between several processes would be too limiting to make the scheme worthwhile.

The present implementation allocates a separate domain for each shared region. The domain ID is kept in the VMA data structure linked to the in-memory inode.

Dynamically linked libraries account for a large amount of executed code in the system. In particular the standard C library consumes multiple megabytes of code and data. This code is relocated and linked at run time whereby code and data is relocated for the respective application. Shared libraries are commonly divided into one read-only part containing code and constant data, which is directly followed by a writable part.

In order to support sharing of library code, we modified the dynamic linker to separate the library's text and data segments. The data segments are allocated within the lower 32MB region, while the code is mapped into the shared area above 2GB.

Each library is given a preferred link address which is, at present, stored globally in the system. The first application using the library creates a copy of the binary image and, instead of performing a relocation of a privately mapped view, the copied image is relocated and saved. Afterwards, other processes can use the same image and map it into their address spaces. For security reasons we have two copies, one which can only be written with root privileges and a private per-user copy. When the pre-allocated link address is not available (e.g., it is already in use by another library), the linker falls back to the private linking scheme.

The separation of code and data has certain drawbacks. Relocation information is based on the fixed layout of the library in the address space. The ARM architecture has a very restrictive set of immediate operations. Hence, most immediate values are generated by storing offsets or absolute values interleaved with the code and using PC-relative addressing.

To separate code and data, and, in particular, share the code over multiple address spaces, we had to replace the mechanism to reference the global offset table (GOT) storing references to functions and global data. Instead of calculating the GOT address via a PC-relative constant (per function!), we divided the address space into slots of 1MB and maintain a table of GOT addresses for each slot of shared library code; larger libraries allocate multiple slots. At link time the code is rewritten from PC-relative references into PC-relative references within the GOT slot. ARM's complex addressing scheme allows inlining this address computation, which therefore results in no extra overhead. Finally, we eliminated the constant reference in the procedure linkage table (PLT).

TLB entry sharing was not implemented in L4.

4 Evaluation

4.1 Benchmarks

Linux

lmbench. We use the following benchmarks from lmbench[12]: lat_ctx, hot_potato and proc_create. These are the subset of lmbench which can be expected to be sensitive to MMU performance.

lat_ctx measures the latency of context switches. It forks n processes, each of which touches k kilobytes of private data and then uses a pipe to pass a token round-robin to the next process.

hot_potato consists of two processes sending a token for and back. The *latency* test uses file locks, a FIFO, a pipe or UNIX sockets for synchronisation.

proc_create tests the latency of process creation. It consists of the following: the *fork test* tests the latency of fork() followed by an immediate exit() in the child. In the *exec test* the child performs an exec() to a program which immediately exits. The *shell test* times the latency of the system() service.

extreme. We use a synthetic benchmark, which we call extreme, designed to establish the maximum performance gain from TLB entry sharing. It forks n child processes all running the same executable. Each child mmap()-s the same p pages, either private or shared. The child then executes a loop where it reads a byte from each page and then performs a yield(). The benchmark is designed to stress the data TLB.

When using private mappings the benchmark will not benefit from sharing TLB entries; it will thrash the TLBs as much as possible. With shared mappings it will share as many DTLB entries as possible (up to the lesser of p and the TLB capacity).

L4. The L4 benchmarks measure IPC times similarly to the Linux hot potato benchmark. A server process fires up a number of client processes, each of which IPCs back to the server (for synchronisation) and waits. The server process then IPCs random client processes, which immediately reply. The average latency of a large number (100,000) of such ping-pong IPCs measured. This benchmark concentrates on the property most critical to a microkernel-based system — the IPC cost. The benchmark is run for a varying number of client processes.

Table 1. Lmbench performance of original Linux vs. fast address-space switch ("fast") kernel. Numbers in parentheses indicate standard deviations of repeated runs. The last column shows the performance of the FASS kernel relative to the original kernel.

Benchmark	original	fast	ratio
lmbench hot potato latency [μs]			
fcntl	39 (50)	25 (3)	1.56
fifo	263 (1)	15.6 (0.1)	17
pipe	257 (3)	15.4 (0.1)	17
unix	511 (10)	30.7 (0.1)	16
lmbench hot potato bandwidth [MB/s]			
pipe	8.77 (0.02)	14.76 (0.03)	1.7
unix	12.31 (0.02)	12.94 (0.00)	1.05
lmbench process creation latency [μs]			
fork	4061 (4)	3650 (4)	1.1
exec	4321 (12)	3980 (10)	1.08
shell	54533 (40)	51726 (27)	1.05

4.2   Results

StrongARM results were taken from a system with 32MB of RAM, a 200MHz SA-1100 CPU and no FPU. The StrongARM has a 32-entry ITLB and a 32-entry DTLB, both fully associative. It has a 16kB instruction and an 8kB data cache, both fully virtual and 32-way associative, and no L2 cache.

lmbench hot potato and process creation results for Linux are shown in Table 1. Latencies of basic Linux IPC mechanisms (FIFOs, pipes and Unix sockets) in the original kernel are between 35% and 75% of the worst-case value of $2 \times 350\mu sec$ quoted in Section 2. File locking is faster, as the test code touches very few pages and cache lines, which reduces the indirect costs of flushing.

The table shows the dramatic effect the fast-context-switching approach has on basic IPC times, with FIFO, pipe and socket latency reduced by more than an order of magnitude. Pipe bandwidth is also significantly improved (by 70%), while the improvement of the socket bandwidth is marginal. Even process creation latencies are improved by 5-10%. This is a result of lazy flushing of caches, which in many cases can defer the cleanup of a process's address space and cache contents until the next time caches are flushed anyway, hence reducing the number of flushes.

Fig. 2 shows lmbench context switch latencies. For the case of zero data accessed (i.e. pure IPC performance) the improvement due to fast context switching is dramatic, between almost two orders of magnitude (factor of 57) for two processes and a factor of four for 13 processes. After that, domain recycling kicks in (three domains are reserved for kernel use in ARM Linux), and the relative improvement is reduced. However, IPC costs in the fast kernel remain below 60% of the cost in the original kernel.

The runs where actual work is performed between the IPCs (in the form of accessing memory) show that the absolute difference between the IPC times remain similar, at least for smaller number of processes. This is a reflection of the

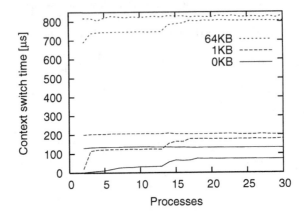

Fig. 2. Lmbench context switching latency (lat_ctx) as a function of the number of processes for different amount of memory accessed. Higher lines are for the original kernel, lower lines for the kernel with fast context switching.

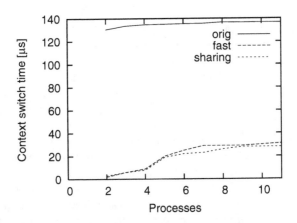

Fig. 3. Lmbench context switching latency over the number of processes with (zero accessed memory), comparing original kernel, fast kernel, and fast kernel with TLB entry sharing enabled.

actual IPC overhead being almost unaffected by the amount of memory accessed between IPCs.

Fig. 3 shows a magnified view of the zero-memory case of Fig. 2, with an additional set of data points corresponding to TLB entry sharing turned on. It is clear from this graph that the TLB is not a bottleneck in these benchmarks. Consequently, the improvement of IPC performance is not dramatic, varying between zero and 23%.

We used the extreme benchmark in order to determine the best-case effect of TLB entry sharing. Results are shown in Fig. 4, which compares the fast kernel

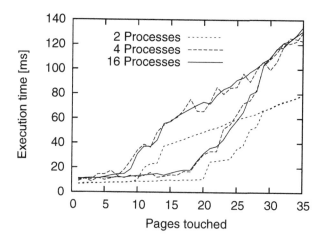

Fig. 4. Execution time over number of pages accessed for the extreme DTLB benchmark for 2, 4 and 16 processes. Higher lines are for the private mappings, lower lines for the shared mappings.

with private mappings (and hence no TLB entry sharing) and with shared mappings (and TLB entry sharing). With private mappings execution slows markedly as soon as more than about ten pages are touched. With shared mapping, performance remains essentially constant until about 20 pages are touched. Performance is the same once the number of pages reaches 32, which is the capacity of the ARM's data TLB. Execution times differ by factors of up to 9 (two processes) or 3.7 (16 processes). The effect is less pronounced with larger number of processes, as library code is not shared in this benchmark, and for larger process numbers the instruction TLB coverage is insufficient.

In practical cases the performance benefits from TLB entry sharing will be somewhere in between those of Figures 3 and 4, but most likely closer to the former. The reason is that the window for significant benefits from TLB entry sharing is small. The following conditions must hold:

– high context switching rates
– large amount of data shared between processes
– page working set no larger than the TLB size.

This combination is rare in present day applications. We made similar observations when examining the effect of TLB entry sharing on the Itanium architecture[13].

The effect of fast context switching in the L4 microkernel is shown in Fig. 5. In the standard kernel the cost of a round-trip IPC is around 135μsec (67.5μsec per context switch or about 1/5 of the worst-case figure of 350μs), quite independent of the number of processes. Fast context switching reduces the round-trip IPC cost to a minimum of 10μsec, a more than thirteen-fold improvement, rising slowly with the number of processes to 12μsec with 14 client processes (total of

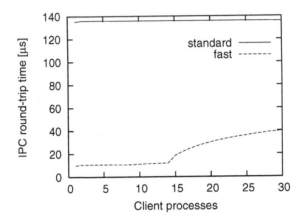

Fig. 5. L4 IPC times with standard and fast context switching implementation.

15 processes), still a more than eleven-fold improvement. The increase of the IPC cost with larger number of processes is probably a result of increased competition for TLB entries and cache lines, an effect that is invisible in the standard kernel, as all caches are flushed on each context switch.

From 15 client processes the IPC cost rises faster. This is the point where the number of active processes (16) exceeds the number of domains available (15, as one is reserved for kernel use).

With a further increase of the number of processes, the IPC cost increase slows down. This may surprise at first, as the probability of the client thread having a domain allocated decreases. However, when a domain is recycled, all caches are flushed, making all allocated domains "clean" and therefore cheap to preempt. Hence, the direct and indirect cost of flushing caches is amortised over several IPCs. The IPC cost in the fast kernel stays well below that of the standard kernel.

These results have been obtained on a mostly unoptimised kernel. For example, 10μsec (2000 cycles) per round-trip IPC is actually very high for L4. Even with the generic IPC code in L4Ka::Pistachio we would expect to see a figure of less than 5μsec. We suspect that the kernel still has some performance bug, possibly an excessive cache footprint. Furthermore, coding the critical IPC path in assembler is known from other architectures to reduce the cost of simple IPC operations by another factor of 2–4. An optimised round-trip IPC should be around 2μsec. Such improvements would be essentially independent of the number of processes, and thus have the effect of shifting the lower line in Fig. 5 by a constant amount (significantly increasing the relative benefit of fast address-space switching).

5   Conclusion

Our results show that fast context switching, based on using domain IDs as address-space tags, is a clear winner on the StrongARM processor, in spite of the small number of available domains. We found no case where the overheads associated with maintaining domains outweighed their benefits. For basic IPC operations the gain was at least an order of magnitude, but even process creation times benefited.

There seems to be no reason not to use this approach in a system like Linux. In a microkernel, however, where the performance of systems built on top is critically dependent on the IPC costs, fast context switching is essential.

In contrast, the benefits of sharing TLB entries are marginal. It seems that this will only show significant benefits in a scenario characterised by high context-switching rates, significant sharing, and the TLB big enough to cover all pages if entries are shared, but too small of entries are not shared. The combination of high context-switching rates and intensive sharing of pages is rare in today's computer systems.

Acknowledgements

The Linux implementation of this work was carried out while Adam Wiggins was an intern at Delft University of Technology, Netherlands. We would like to thank all the members of the Delft's UbiCom project, in particular Jan-Derk Bakker, Koen Langendoen and Erik Mouw, for making this work possible.

Availability

Patches for fast-context switching support in Linux are available from http://www.cse.unsw.edu.au/~disy/Linux/, L4Ka::Pistachio for StrongARM, including support for fast-context switching, is available from http://l4ka.org.

References

1. Liedtke, J., Elphinstone, K., Schönberg, S., Härtig, H., Heiser, G., Islam, N., Jaeger, T.: Achieved IPC performance (still the foundation for extensibility). In: Proceedings of the 6th Workshop on Hot Topics in Operating Systems (HotOS), Cape Cod, MA, USA (1997) 28–31
2. Jagger, D., ed.: Advanced RISC Machines Architecture Reference Manual. Prentice Hall (1995)
3. ITRON Committee, TRON Association: μITRON4.0 Specification. (1999) http://www.ertl.jp/ITRON/SPEC/mitron4-e.html.
4. Liedtke, J.: On μ-kernel construction. In: Proceedings of the 15th ACM Symposium on OS Principles (SOSP), Copper Mountain, CO, USA (1995) 237–250
5. Mery, D.: Symbian OSversion 7.0 functional description. White paper, Symbian Ltd (2003) http://www.symbian.com/technology/whitepapers.html.

6. Wiggins, A., Heiser, G.: Fast address-space switching on the StrongARM SA-1100 processor. In: Proceedings of the 5th Australasian Computer Architecture Conference (ACAC), Canberra, Australia, IEEE CS Press (2000) 97–104
7. L4Ka Team: L4Ka — Pistachio kernel. http://l4ka.org/projects/pistachio/ (2003)
8. Chase, J.S., Levy, H.M., Feeley, M.J., Lazowska, E.D.: Sharing and protection in a single-address-space operating system. ACM Transactions on Computer Systems **12** (1994) 271–307
9. Heiser, G., Elphinstone, K., Vochteloo, J., Russell, S., Liedtke, J.: The Mungi single-address-space operating system. Software: Practice and Experience **28** (1998) 901–928
10. Intel Corp.: Intel StrongARM SA-1100 Microprocessor Developer's Manual. (1999)
11. Murray, J.: Inside Microsoft Windows CE. Microsoft Press (1998)
12. McVoy, L., Staelin, C.: lmbench: Portable tools for performance analysis. In: Proceedings of the 1996 USENIX Technical Conference, San Diego, CA, USA (2996)
13. Chapman, M., Wienand, I., Heiser, G.: Itanium page tables and TLB. Technical Report UNSW-CSE-TR-0307, School of Computer Science and Engineering, University of NSW, Sydney 2052, Australia (2003)

Performance of the Achilles Router

Sonny Tham and John Morris

School of Electrical, Electronic and Computer Engineering,
The University of Western Australia,
WA 6009, Australia,
stham@amristar.com.au, morris@ee.uwa.edu.au

Abstract. The Achilles Router provides low latency, high bandwidth connections between processors, enabling a network of low-cost processors to perform as a high-performance parallel processor. It is also economical, being constructed from low cost Field Programmable Gate Arrays (FPGAs). These programmable devices allow it to be re-programmed for use in a variety of network topologies; they also permit 'tuning' the router for optimum performance in different applications. A key factor in its simplicity and performance is the 3-D structure: this allows us to build a full cross-bar switch with a wide, high-bandwidth datapath. The simple cross-bar circuit also has very low latency: we measured latencies of $\sim 800ns$ in the hardware and $2.5\mu s$ when software overheads were included. We measured the basic performance of an inter-processor link using Achilles, and then, using a range of benchmarks with different characteristics, showed that Achilles clearly outperforms Fast Ethernet.

Keywords: Parallel processor interconnection, networks of workstations, cross-bar switching.

1 Introduction

Inter-processor communication bandwidth is often the limiting factor in a parallel processor's performance: inadequate bandwidth can make it impossible to obtain any speed-up using multiple processors to solve certain problems. In particular, this lack of bandwidth constrains our ability to effectively use cheap, readily available commodity processors in 'network of workstations' (NoW) systems to solve problems with even moderate communication:computation ratios. Clock frequencies in state-of-the-art commodity processors now exceed 2GHz whereas the commonest type of interconnection, Fast Ethernet, limits the interprocessor data rate to ~ 10 Mbytes/s with latencies of tens of microseconds. Various research and commercial projects have attacked the problem of providing more bandwidth and lower latencies[1–7], but some target general 'messaging' applications where the key requirements differ from those for high performance parallel processing applications. For example, ATM was originally designed for telephony (requiring quality of service guarantees), but its small packets suit the many commercial and information processing applications which use large numbers of small messages. On the other hand, large scientific and engineering

A. Omondi and S. Sedukhin (Eds.): ACSAC 2003, LNCS 2823, pp. 365–379, 2003.

Fig. 1. An assembled Achilles router 'stack'. Ten PCBs are installed in a bus backplane.

applications often require the exchange of large blocks of data: the use of small packets in such applications introduces overheads which use significant fractions of available 'raw' bandwidth in communications links.

Routers can be divided into two broad classes: circuit-switched, in which a real circuit or physical link is effectively created between end-points, and packet-switched, in which (generally small) packets of data work their way through a network, possibly being queued or buffered at many points along the way. Packet-switched routers, although more complex because they must provide buffers in addition to switching elements, have generally been favoured for interprocessor connections because they will typically show better overall utilisation of resources: most of the resources (switches and buffers) are shared and thus used by packets traversing many different source/destination paths. However packet switching affects the latency as each small packet passes through multiple buffers, each one adding to the total latency.

Increasing device densities lead to abundant cheap, circuit resources (even in the relatively small programmable devices used here), and thus we can afford to build circuits which may show relatively low utilization factors if there is an overall gain in performance. Thus Achilles uses circuit switching rather than packet switching and has effectively no limit on message size[1], therefore we expect to lose a smaller fraction of the raw bandwidth to overheads and have significantly lower latencies.

1.1   Network Topologies

The topology of a network determines factors such as the message latency and the bandwidth available for data transmission between any pair of hosts on it.

---

[1] Achilles' reconfigurability allows simple changes to message headers to accommodate larger messages.

An ideal network topology would allow simultaneous bi-directional data transfer at the maximum bandwidth permitted by the physical links between any pair of hosts attached to it. In pratical terms, a cross-bar switch is close to the ideal: it offers simultaneous links between up to $n/2$ pairs of hosts in an n processor network: it only blocks when two hosts attempt to connect to a common destination at the same time. This limitation can be alleviated by providing buffers in output ports[8] or - at considerable cost in complexity - input ports which can be inspected for messages which can be transmitted without blocking at the current time. At the other end of the spectrum, a bus topology provides a single physical link to which all hosts are connected: the single physical link means that only one pair of hosts can communicate at any one time² but it is much simpler, cheaper and easier to realize than a cross-bar.

A single Achilles router is a full cross-bar switch, with no buffers or other resource constraints which can lead to blocking. This contrasts it with topologies used in other interconnection architectures. Bus topologies like Ethernet are the least efficient: all packets use a common physical connection and thus only one packet can be 'in flight' at any time. Other architectures provide multiple paths, but less than the one per processor provided by the full cross-bar architecture implemented in Achilles. This implies that other interconnection architectures will block when the network becomes congested with packets destined for random processors: a full cross-bar blocks only when two packets try to reach the same destination at the same time.

1.2   Cilk

Cilk is a language implementing a dataflow programming model[9]: it is a dialect of C augmented with a small number of additional keywords, such as the `thread` or `cilk` qualifier which causes a function to be compiled for execution as a thread. The Cilk pre-processor converts a Cilk program into C which is compiled and linked with the Cilk run-time library. The run-time system uses a 'work-stealing' strategy in which idle processors 'steal' work (represented by Cilk 'closures') from busy processors. Work can also be explicitly distributed to specific processors, but the work-stealing load-balancing strategy has been shown to be efficient in its progress towards completion of a program.

Cilk's dataflow model is well suited to NoW parallel processing because each closure or parcel of work consists of a description of the computation to be performed, along with the actual data on which the work will be performed, so that each parcel can be sent to and then executed on any host in a NoW. Threads can easily be programmed to perform relatively large amounts of computation, achieving efficient use of a NoW system, even when the communication bandwidth is relatively low. Since it generally tolerates slower links better than

---

² Modern Ethernet switches provide some buffering which may provide the illusion that multiple hosts are communicating at the same time, but there will often be a single internal bus, possibly operating at much higher bandwidth than the processor-router links, but nevertheless providing a communication bottle-neck.

MPI[10], it is slightly harder for the benefit of Achilles' additional bandwidth to show itself in benchmarks.

1.3   MPI

Many parallel programming systems are based on the Message-Passing Interface (MPI)[11]. In a set of separate experiments, Tham has measured the performamce of Cilk and MPI implementations of the problems used here. In general, Cilk performed slightly better than MPI, but the differences between them is the subject of a separate study[10]. The results reported here are generally those obtained from the Cilk implementations.

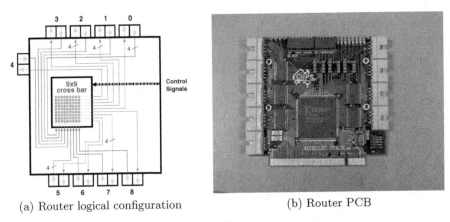

(a) Router logical configuration   (b) Router PCB

Fig. 2. Achilles router PCB: nine are programmed as routers and a tenth as the controller - installed in a backplane (Fig. 3) to form a 'stack' (Fig. 1)

Fig. 3. An Achilles router backplane

2   Achilles Structure

The Achilles interconnection architecture consists of a high speed cross-bar circuit switching router and PCI compliant network interface adaptors that allow host workstations to gain access to the Achilles network. The aim of the hardware design of Achilles was to minimise router circuit complexity to keep hardware latency low for channel establishment. This section describes the design of the Achilles hardware architecture.

The Achilles architecture was developed using Xilinx 4000 series Field Programmable Gate Arrays (FPGAs)[12]. Use of FPGAs enabled fast *in situ* testing of various strategies for both the router and the PCI interface adaptor with very short turnaround times between development and testing. In addition to providing fast development time, minor changes to the FPGA 'programs' allow the routers to be elements of various network topologies. It also gives the PCI interface adaptor (which has one FPGA also, see Fig. 4) additional flexibility to perform custom functions based on application or parallel execution environment. In the current implementation, this FPGA calculates and checks 32-bit CRC words which are appended to each message. This reduces host software overheads by several cycles for each word transmitted.

The Achilles router is a 9 × 9, 32-bit wide cross-bar circuit switch. Up to nine host workstations (nodes) can be connected to a single Achilles router. Cross-bar routing allows any node to communicate directly to any other node without data passing through any intermediate nodes (see Fig. 2). In circuit switching, a dedicated channel is established between the two communicating nodes and held open until communication between nodes has been completed, similar to a traditional telephone exchange, which connects two parties with a dedicated channel until their conversation has been completed. In contrast, a packet switching device breaks the data to be sent between nodes up into small

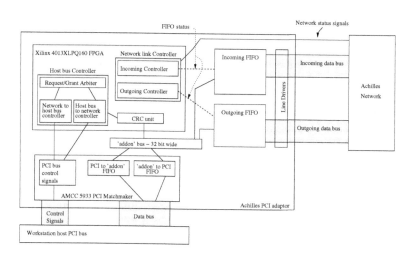

Fig. 4. Logical structure of the Achilles PCI network interface adaptor.

packets or chunks: each packet received by the router is queued in a buffer and then handled separately for forwarding to its destination.

The logic in the router is very simple. Achilles is able to set up and close connections quickly compared to the time taken for the data to be transferred once the connection is open. This makes it possible to use the system as a packet switch[13]. This is known as 'short hold mode' and this principle has been used for many years to perform packet switching in low speed circuit switched X.21 networks[14]. Short hold mode packet switching has also been demonstrated to be effective in the IBM Enterprise Systems Connection (ESCON) architecture and in experimental RAINBOW all-optical networks[13]. Thus Achilles can be used like a packet switch when necessary and has the added advantage of being able to transfer long bursts of data across the network much more efficiently than a conventional packet switching system.

A unique feature of the Achilles router is the 3-D arrangement of the router PCBs: this enables us to achieve a very high overall bandwidth by using a very wide (32 data bits + 4 control signals) datapath. Each router PCB (see Fig. 2) handles 4 bits of the data path, thus we are able to implement a full 9×9 crossbar switch without requiring an excessive number of pins on any device. Ten of these router boards are built into a stack (see Fig. 1): nine of these are routers and the tenth interprets routing information from message headers and controls the configuration of the other nine by passing signals along the bus backplane.

The state machine which controls the router was clocked at 20MHz. This is relatively slow, but it only affects the channel establishment time: once the channel is open, it is essentially an end-to-end physical link and signal transmission along it is controlled by the sender and receiver circuitry. Current FPGAs will operate with much higher clock frequencies - leaving open the possibility to reduce wiring in the physical links by multiplexing.

2.1   Network Interface Adapter

Hosts are connected to an Achilles router using a standard PCI card equipped with a commercial PCI interface chip (AMCC Matchmaker), an FPGA and two sets of 32-bit 512-word FIFOs. Logic in the FPGA performs routine control operations - driving the PCI interface chip, the FIFOs and handshaking with the Achilles router. It also calculates a 32-bit CRC word which is appended to outgoing messages and checks it on incoming ones. The FIFOs have two important functions: for outgoing messages: they ensure that short messages do not block the PCI bus by buffering messages which the network of routers may not be able to accept and they provide limited protection against the blocking that would occur if several messages were simultaneously destined for a common destination[8]. For example, in several problems, multiple 'slave' processors are assigned similar tasks which complete at the same time and attempt to send a short result to a master would block a cross-bar until the master can process interrupts. The incoming message FIFOs allow a slave message to be accepted immediately and the network freed so that other slaves are not blocked from sending their results to the master.

Table 1. Characteristics of network interconnection architectures

Architecture	Max throughput		Min total latency μs	Max packet or message size	Technology
	(per host) Mbytes/s	(per router) Mbytes/s			
Achilles	128^a	~ 1152	2.5	reconfigurable	cross-bar circuit switching
Myrinet	128^a	~ 1900	4.8	> 4 Mbytes	cross-bar packet switching
Dolphin SCI	400^b	400	~ 4	256 bytes	cross-bar packet switching
ATOLL	500^b	N/A	~ 4	64 bytes	cross-bar packet switching
ARCTIC	60^a	400	5.6	96 bytes	cross-bar packet switching
ATM^c	Varies	~ 62	45	48 bytes	packet switching
Fast Ethernet	~ 9.5	~ 9.5	29	~ 1500 bytes	CSMA/CD (packet)
Gigabit Ethernet	~ 95	~ 95	29	~ 1500 bytes	CSMA/CD (packet)

[a] 32 bit 33MHz PCI
[b] 64 bit 66MHz PCI
[c] Typical commercially available switch in 2000/2001

2.2   The Myrmidons

Experiments were performed on a network, *the Myrmidons*[3], consisting of up to nine 150MHz Pentium processors with 16Mbytes of memory and either an Achilles PCI interface or a Fast Ethernet interface. An ethernet hub completed the Fast Ethernet network.

3   Performance

3.1   Link Performance

The ribbon cable used to connect hosts and routers can support data rates up to ~ 150 Mbits/s: the Xilinx FPGA I/O buffers will operate at 60 MHz. With a 32-bit data path, this implies that the physical links can transfer data at up to 240Mbytes/s. This is in excess of obtainable transfer rates across the PCI bus (~ 128 Mbytes/s for 33MHz 32-bit PCI), so the PCI bus becomes the limiting factor.

We measured the hardware latency (time delay from receipt of a message in the Achilles interface from the PCI bus on one host to the PCI bus of the another) at ~ 800ns. Total latency, including driver overheads on 150MHz systems, was 2.5μs (see Table 1). Note that the hosts used were relatively slow in 2003 so that we would expect this to reduce even further with faster hosts and faster PCI buses.

---

[3] Achilles led an army of Myrmidons in the siege of Troy.

3.2   Linux Device Driver Performance

Paull measured the 'raw' performance of the link *including software overheads* using a small set of simple C programs[15]. Figure 5 shows the measured bandwidth for several variants of the driver (polled, using interrupts, zero-copy, *etc.*): with the exception of the software-polled variant, effective bandwidths of > 25Mbytes/s were achieved for packet sizes over 1Kbytes with nearly 30Mbytes/s being achieved for the 'user-space' driver (which avoids copying by moving data directly from the user's address space to the device). Although a 32-bit 33MHz PCI interface is theoretically capable of ~ 132 Mbytes/s, bus overheads and contention mean that transfer rates will generally be lower. The experiments reported here were carried out with Paull's drivers and thus do not reflect the maximum rate achievable with Achilles: we have subsequently overcome some problems with setting up the AMCC PCI chip used and measured transfer rates of ~ 120 Mbytes/s, *i.e.* close to that maximum expected on an 'active' system with other transactions contending for the bus. Thus the performance improvements for Achilles over Fast Ethernet reported here are actually smaller than we believe we could now achieve.

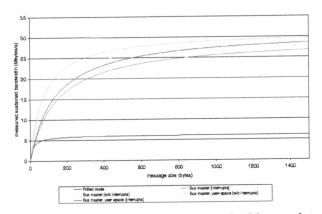

Fig. 5. Linux device driver performance: bandwidth *vs* packet size

3.3   Network Performance

We chose a number of benchmark problems with varying communications demands to measure the improvement in overall performance gained by using Achilles: their characteristics are listed in Table 2. The remainder of this section describes each problem and the results obtained with it.

Matrix multiplication. A simple problem with parallelism that is easily realized, but only at the expense of communication overhead, with $\mathcal{O}(n^2)$ communication cost in a $\mathcal{O}(n^3)$ algorithm, matrix multiplication only shows significant speed-up for large matrices: Figure 6, shows the higher speed-ups measured with Achilles for a range of problem sizes.

Table 2. Benchmark problem summary

Problem	Parameters	Complexity	No. of Messages	Message Size	Regular?	Synchronisation
Matrix	matrix size n	$\mathcal{O}(n^3)$	$\mathcal{O}(p)$	$\mathcal{O}(n^2)$	Yes	Computation end
TSP	# cities n, seq threshold s	$\mathcal{O}(n!)$	$\mathcal{O}(P_s^n)$	$\mathcal{O}(n)$	No	Every iteration
Quick sort	list length n, seq threshold s	$\mathcal{O}(n \log n)$	$\mathcal{O}(\log_s n)$	$\mathcal{O}(n)$	No	Every iteration
Gauss	matrix size n	$\mathcal{O}(n^3)$	$\mathcal{O}(n)$	$\mathcal{O}(n^2)$	Yes	Every iteration
FFT	vector length n	$\mathcal{O}(n \log n)$	$\mathcal{O}(n)$	$\mathcal{O}(n)$	Yes	Last $n - p$ iters
Fin Diff (per iter)	matrix size n	$\mathcal{O}(n^2)$	$\mathcal{O}(p)$	$\mathcal{O}(n)$	Yes	Every iteration

- p denotes the number of processors participating in the computation.
- P_y^x denotes the number of permutations of y items which can be generated from a list of x items.
- Full details, code listings *etc.* may be found in Tham[10].

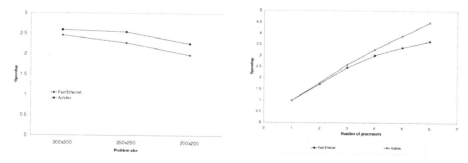

Fig. 6. Matrix multiplication: Achilles *vs* Fast Ethernet (left) as a function of matrix size with 3 processors; (right) as a function of number of processors (300×300 matrix)

On the right of Fig. 6, we see that as the number of processors increases, network congestion causes the speed-up curve to start to level off with Fast Ethernet, whereas it continues to rise with Achilles - although the slope is decreasing slightly. This is a direct consequence of the increased bandwidth in Achilles: data is transferred from the 'master' processor to the workers at more than three times the rate than Fast Ethernet can provide.

Travelling salesman. The travelling salesman problem is a classic hard problem: its complexity is $\mathcal{O}(n!)$. The data set is very small; it has only n integers and thus the data transmission demands are relatively small. Almost perfect speed-ups are therefore easily obtained with large problems in which n processors are set to work on problems of size $n - 1$. For our experiments, the problem was set up so that work was distributed to slave processors until a threshhold number of cities, s, remained to be evaluated. At this point, the algorithm completed

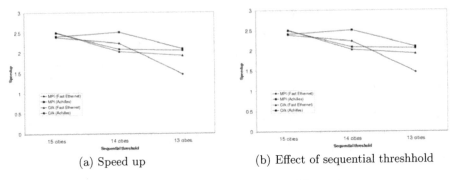

(a) Speed up   (b) Effect of sequential threshhold

Fig. 7. Travelling salesman problem

the evaluation of the best tour for these s cities on a single processor. Thus the communication:computation ratio could be adjusted with small values of the threshhold, s, generating large numbers of communications events and stressing the network. An optimization which reduced computation times and added more network load was introduced: evaluation of a sub-tour was abandoned if its cost exceeded the minimum total tour distance already found. With 16 cities and a sequential treshhold of 15, Fig. 7(a) shows very little dependence on the network capability with Achilles and Fast Ethernet showing similar speed-ups for both Cilk and MPI implementations, although there is a significant difference between Cilk and MPI. (This difference is analyzed in separate work[10].)

However, if the amount of communication is increased by lowering the sequential threshhold, then Fig. 7(b) shows that speed-ups are maintained better with the Achilles router: its much lower latency handles large numbers of small messages better.

3.4   Quick Sort

A quick sort has a computational complexity of $\mathcal{O}(n \log n)$. A problem size of 2,097,152 floating point elements (8Mbytes of data or half the RAM available on each workstation) was chosen. The benchmark implementation recursively partitions the full list into pairs of sub-lists which may be distributed to other processors which continue to partition the data until a threshhold is reached at which the sort is completed sequentially on the current processor. The threshold for reversion to sequential computation was set at 131,072 elements (512kbytes) to allow approximately 16 sequential tasks to be generated for parallel sorting.

Each of the sublists must be sent to a processing unit and then returned once it has been sorted: a total of $2n$ data points are transferred. There are $\mathcal{O}(\log n)$ computations per data point transferred. This is much lower than for the travelling salesman problem that also uses recursion for problem decomposition. Even with a large sequential threshold, the performance of the parallel quick sort algorithm will depend heavily on the performance of the underlying interconnections.

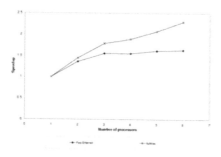

Fig. 8. Quick sort: Speed up for Achilles and Fast Ethernet as a function of number of processors

Figure 8 shows the less than ideal speed-ups expected for quick sort: with 6 processors, we see only 2.3 for Achilles *vs* 1.6 for Fast Ethernet. However Achilles' higher effective bandwidth allows higher speed-ups to be obtained.

3.5 Fast Fourier Transform

The FFT implemented here uses the Cooley-Tukey decimation in time algorithm [16], which recursively subdivides the problem into its even and odd components until the length of the input is 2. This base case is a 2-point discrete Fourier transform (DFT), whose output is a linear combination of its inputs. The Cooley-Tukey method requires a vector whose length is a power of 2.

For a vector of n points, $\log_2 n$ passes are required: the first pass performs $n/2$ 2-point DFTs and in each subsequent iteration the number of 2-point DFTs is halved. The total complexity is $\mathcal{O}(n \log n)$ - $\log_2 n$ passes with $\mathcal{O}(n)$ arithmetic operations per pass.

A simple parallel decomposition for p processors $(p = 2^k)$ allows the first $\log_2 n - \log_2 p$ passes to proceed without interprocessor communication. Before the beginning of the last $\log_2 p$ passes each processor exchanges the previous iteration's results with one other processor. The first $\log_2 n - \log_2 p$ passes require no interprocessor communication except the transmission of the initial vector, so a communication cost of $\mathcal{O}(n)$ is amortized over $\mathcal{O}(n) \times \log n$ computations, assuming $n \gg p$. For each of the final $\log_2 p$ passes, a total of n points must be transferred on which $\mathcal{O}(n)$ arithmetic operations are performed. Overall, there are $\mathcal{O}(\log n)$ computations per data point communicated: this is lower than, for example matrix multiplication, but the computations are considerably more complex, allowing reasonable speed-ups to be achieved.

The speed-ups shown in Fig. 9 were measured with a vector of 2^{18} (262,144) points. Achilles ability to transfer large blocks of data efficiently is reflected in speed-ups which approach the ideal values[4] whereas they drop off with a Fast Ethernet based system.

---

[4] At least for the small system used here: a failure of several processors prevented us from obtaining further data.

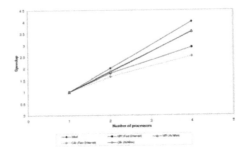

Fig. 9. Speed up for FFT algorithm.

3.6   Gaussian Elimination

This algorithm solves a system of n linear equations on n variables. The result is
a square matrix decomposed into upper and lower triangular submatrices. The
computation for an $n \times n$ matrix requires $\mathcal{O}(n^3)$ time. The algorithm repeatedly
eliminates elements of the matrix beneath successive diagonal elements. The the
number of rows and columns to be processed begins at n and falls by one on
each successive pass. The pseudo-code for the sequential algorithm is:

```
for i := 1 to n do
  for j := i+1 to n do
    for k:= n+1 downto i do
      a[j][k] := a[j][k] - a[i][k]*a[j][i]/a[i][i];
```

'Partial pivoting' is usually employed to improve numerical stability. Before
the beginning of the 'j' loop, the row with the largest absolute value in the
currently active column is swapped with the row currently containing the active
diagonal element. The aim is to make the active diagonal element as large as
possible.

In the parallel version, stripes of columns are assigned to different processors.
Each processor performs a part of the 'j' loop in each iteration. For each iteration
of the 'i' loop, the processor that is responsible for the ith column performs a
local pivoting operation, then sends the index of the pivot row and the data
in the pivot column to all other processors. The other processors then use this
index to perform their own local pivoting operations and the pivot column data
to compute the 'k' loop.

As the computation progresses, columns on the left side of the matrix are
progressively completed and take no further part in the computation. Thus,
if a simple striping technique is used, processors progressively drop out of the
computation. A further optimization allocates narrow stripes to processors in a
round-robin fashion to ensure that none become idle.

For p processors, each processor works on n/p stripes. In iteration i, $\mathcal{O}(n)$
data points are transferred to p processors each of which does $\mathcal{O}(n^2)$ work in
that iteration. This is similar to matrix multiplication but the computation requires approximately twice as long for the same size matrix - leading to slightly

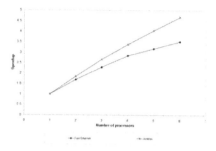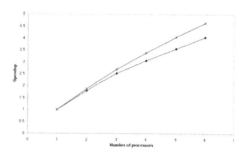

Fig. 10. Achilles vs. Fast Ethernet as number of processors is increased: (left) Gaussian elimination; (right) finite differencing

better speed-ups, with Achilles' higher bandwidth leading to a 30% reduction in execution time for a 400×400 matrix (19.8s for Cilk on Achilles *vs* 29.3s on Fast Ethernet, for a speed-up of 3.8 on 5 processors, see Fig. 10).

3.7   Finite Differencing

Finite differencing is an iterative algorithm where, in each iteration, each element in a matrix is replaced by the average of its four nearest neighbours (above, below, left and right). Iteration continues until convergence is reached.

Our Jacobi algorithm[17] uses two stages for each iteration. In the first, 'new' values computed from 'old' values are stored in a copy of the matrix. Then 'new' values are copied over the 'old' values and used in the next iteration. (The alternative Gauss-Seidel method updates elements[18] in one pass.)

For an initial matrix of size $n \times n$ and p processors: stripes of n^2/p elements are sent to each processor. In each iteration, $\mathcal{O}(n^2)$ work is done and $\mathcal{O}(n)$ elements from the boundaries of each stripe are interchanged between processors. The initial $\mathcal{O}(n^2)$ cost of distributing work to each processor is amortized over many iterations needed to reach convergence and has little effect on the results. The computation per 'cell' is simple and fast (compared to, say, matrix multiplication which has the same computation:communication ratio) and communication is needed in each iteration (whereas matrix multiplication communicates only final results) therefore large problems of this type are needed for speed-ups to be measured: a matrix size of 900×900 elements was chosen here.

The Cilk version of this algorithm does not use a strict dataflow decomposition of the computation. The master thread spawns p processing threads and assigns a stripe to each of them. It then waits for all the processing threads to terminate before exiting. Explicit active messages are used the for per iteration interprocessor communication needed for boundary updates.

Data blocks of 900 elements fit into a small number of physical Ethernet packets (~ 1500 bytes) and so message latency will tend to be as important as raw bandwidth and is a significant contributor to Achilles' better performance, see Fig. 10 (right).

4   Conclusion

Our experiments show that the increased bandwidth of Achilles provided the expected benefits for applications which required significant communication between processors. It is notable that when communication requirements were high, as in the matrix multiplication example, Achilles was able to demonstrate speed-up s for smaller problem sizes than Fast Ethernet. This has important ramifications for more complex problems, which may be composed of many non-trivial sub-problems, for example, large numbers of multiplications of matrices with varying sizes. All the processors in a network may be used effectively for more of the time in such cases. The benefits of low latency are evident also in the travelling salesman problem: it requires relatively small amounts of data transfer and thus does not benefit to such a high degree from increased bandwidth, but speed-ups are observed at lower granularity - as demonstrated by the ability to see speed-up at lower sequential threshholds. The simple, fast logic which results in the low latency, also allows Achilles to perform like a packet switching system - allowing Achilles to exhibit the advantages of a packet switcher while also handling large messages efficiently. It should be noted that, due to some setup problems with the commercial PCI interface we used, the experiments reported here did not use the maximum host to network bandwidth achievable and that, with the raw data rates that we have subsequently been able to achieve, Achilles' relative performance should improve even further: neither the FPGAs nor the physical network links were operating at full capacity in these experiments.

The 3-D structure of the Achilles stack is the key to achieving the performance gains we have observed in a low cost, effective design: it allows a very high effective bandwidth with readily obtainable components. We believe that this project only starts to demonstrate the potential of the 3-D switch design: we have achieved impressive results with relatively low internal clock frequencies (~ 20 MHz) in the switch elements. State-of-the-art devices are capable of much higher clock speeds. Wire signalling speeds are similarly low: cheap, readily available ribbon cable can be driven at nearly $10\times$ the rate we used. This allows us to consider replacing multiple signal cables with multiplexed cables to reduce the cable clutter. We could also use higher capability electrical protocols, *e.g.* LVDS, which is supported by state-of-the-art FPGAs, or optical fibre. The present design is inherently limited by the bandwidth of the 32-bit 33MHz PCI bus which we chose because it is found in a systems from many manufacturers. Since we are not driving either the physical interconnects or the FPGA logic at their full capacity, it should be possible to use the current design with the 64-bit 66MHz PCI bus systems that are starting to appear by multiplexing signals onto the existing wires. This would allow us to retain one of the prime advantages of the Achilles router design: it uses readily available, popular components, ensuring a low-cost solution.

Acknowledgements

Richard Gregg (University of Tasmania) designed the Achilles prototype[19, 20].

References

1. Ang, B., Chiou, D.: StarT-Voyager. In: Proceedings of the MIT student workshop for scalable computing, Massachusetts: Cambridge, USA (1996)
2. Boughton, G.: Arctic switch fabric. In: Proceedings of the 1997 Parallel Computing, Routing and Communication Workshop, GA: Atlanta, USA (1997)
3. Dolphin Interconnect Solutions Inc.: The Dolphin SCI interconnect. Technical report, Dolphin Interconnect Solutions Inc., California: Westlake Village, USA (1996)
4. Gillet, R., Kaufmann, R.: Using the Memory Channel network. IEEE Micro (1997) 19–25
5. Kluge, J., Bruning, U., Fischer, M., Rzymianowicz, L.: The ATOLL approach for a fast and reliable System Area Network. In: PDPTA'99, Nevada (1999)
6. Myricom: Myrinet performance measurements. http://www.myri.com (1997)
7. von Eicken, T., Culler, D., Goldstein, S., Schauser, K.: Active messages: a mechanism for integrated communication and computation. In: 19th International Symposium on Computer Architecture, Gold Coast, Australia (1992)
8. Peterson, L.L., Davie, B.S.: Computer networks: a systems approach. Morgan Kauffman, San Francisco (2000)
9. Blumofe, R., Joerg, C., Kuszmaul, B., Leiserson, C., Randall, K., Zhou, Y.: Cilk: an efficient multithreaded runtime system. In: PPoPP'95, Santa Barbara (1995)
10. Tham, C.K.: Achilles: A high bandwidth, low latency, low overhead network interconnect for high performance parallel processing using a network of workstations. PhD thesis, The University of Western Australia (2003)
11. Snir, M.: MPI: The complete reference. MIT Press, MA: Cambridge, USA (1996)
12. Xilinx Inc.: Xilinx component data sheets. http://www.xilinx.com (2000)
13. Elliott, J., Sachs, M.: Enterprise systems connection (ESCON) architecture. IBM journal of Research and Development **36** (1992)
14. Dutton, H., Lenhard, P.: High-speed networking technology: an introductory survey. 3rd edn. Prentice Hall, Inc, New Jersey: Upper Saddle River, USA (1995)
15. Paull, D.: The Need for speed. B.E.(Hons) thesis. Electrical and Electronic Engineering, University of Western Australia (1998)
16. Press, W.H., Flannery, B.P., Teukolsky, S.A., Vetterling, W.T.: Numerical Recipes: The Art of Scientific Computing. Cambridge University Press, Cambridge (1986)
17. Young, D.: Iterative solution of large linear systems. Academic Press, New York (1971)
18. Hageman, L., Young, D.: Applied Iterative Methods. Academic Press, New York (1981)
19. Gregg, R.R., Herbert, D., McCoull, J., Morris, J.: Thetis: A Parallel Processor Leveraging Commercial Technology. In: Proc Australian Computer Science Conference, Adelaide. (1995)
20. Tham, S., Morris, J., Gregg, R.: Achilles: High bandwidth, low latency, low overhead communication. In: Australasian Computer Architecture Conference, Auckland, New Zealand, Springer-Verlag, Singapore (1999) 173–184

Latency Improvement in Virtual Multicasting

Philip Machanick[1] and Brynn Andrew[2]

[1] School of ITEE, University of Queensland,
Brisbane, Qld 4072, Australia,
philip@itee.uq.edu.au
[2] School of Computer Science, University of the Witwatersrand,
Johannesburg, Private Bag 3, 2050 Wits, South Africa,
brynn@cs.wits.ac.za

Abstract. Virtual multicasting (VMC) combines some of the benefits of caching (transparency, dynamic adaptation to workload) and multicasting (reducing duplicated traffic). Virtual multicasting is intended to save bandwidth in cases of high load, resulting from unpredictable but high demands for similar traffic. However, even in cases where relatively low fractions of traffic are similar (hence offering few opportunities for VMC), introducing VMC can have a disproportionate effect on latency reduction because of the generally beneficial effect of reduction in traffic, including reduced contention. This paper presents results of a study of latency reduction across a range of workloads, illustrating the potential for VMC even in situations where the extent of overlapped traffic is light.

1   Introduction

Information Mass Transit (IMT) is a general design philosophy aimed at exploiting commonality of data on a medium to reduce bandwidth demands and improve latency [14]. The name derives from an analogy with mass transit, where apparently-slower modes of transport like buses and large passenger aircraft are faster for moving large numbers of people with common destinations than apparently faster alternatives (cars, executive jets). Sharing a common form of transport reduces congestion, and makes better use of common media.

Internet congestion is a growing problem: as capacity increases, so does demand. Given that there could be significant common traffic at peak times, it seems reasonable to investigate sharing common data as far as possible. By analogy with the mass transit idea for moving people, if much traffic at the same time is similar, grouping this similar traffic could have significant advantages.

Virtual Multicasting (VMC), a specific instance of IMT, finds common streams which have started at similar times, and combines them. The general model can vary in different implementations. For example, grouping FTP streams may not introduce significant latency or real-time concerns, provided the streams are large enough that saving transmission time dominates any cost of grouping similar traffic. Where streams can be combined, latency can be reduced, since the server is in effect moved closer. Reduction of congestion (queueing delays, lost or corrupted packets, retransmits because of timeouts, etc.) can also reduce latency.

A. Omondi and S. Sedukhin (Eds.): ACSAC 2003, LNCS 2823, pp. 380–394, 2003.

In this paper, the main focus of the investigation is the effect of VMC on Internet traffic with no special opportunities for VMC. The intent is to show that VMC can offer a significant advantage in reducing congestion, even when the opportunities for reducing overlap are limited.

1.1   Information Mass Transit

A number of applications of the IMT idea have been proposed [14]. The general model is one of sharing a stream; actual realization may vary considerably.

One example is the Scalable Architecture for Video on Demand (SAVoD), which aims to implement a video on demand system which scales up to an unlimited number of users [13]. SAVoD streams multiple instances of a movie continuously, so that a virtual VCR can be implemented by finding a suitable point in any given stream, to perform operations such as fast forward, rewind, or start a new movie. The principle is to invest in a large amount of bandwidth, with the goal of removing all requests to the server. Consequently, the biggest latency problems in scaling up to unlimited users are removed.

VMC is the next attempt at realizing the broader IMT idea.

1.2   Virtual Multicasting

Virtual Multicasting (VMC) aims to exploit short-term similarities in Internet traffic, particularly higher up the bandwidth hierarchy. A high volume of similar traffic may periodically occur as new software is downloaded, a large number of clients join the same audio or video stream, or visit a new web site.

Such traffic cannot easily be cached for two reasons:

- the repeated traffic may be transient, and the demand may no longer exist by the time it is cached
- the users may be widely spaced around the Internet, and only the higher-bandwidth links at the top of the hierarchy may see duplicated traffic, i.e., endpoints are not the right place to cache this kind of traffic

The transient nature of this kind of similar traffic also makes multicasting an inadequate approach to reducing wastage of bandwidth. Setting up a multicast route requires prior knowledge that it is required, which may not be easy to predict, since demand for similar content may be hard to predict in advance.

1.3   Remainder of Paper

The remainder of this paper is structured as follows.

Section 2 provides an overview of the VMC concept and related approaches, as related to the general IMT model. The basis for experiments is described in Section 3, followed by results in Section 4. Finally, conclusions, including possible future work, are presented in Section 5.

2   Background and Related Solutions

Virtual Multicasting attempts to reduce or control Internet congestion. It does this by moving away from the traditional model of content delivery (unicast) to one that makes more effective use of the available bandwidth. Instead of having data distributed from a single point, VMC aims to distribute the dissemination of data, reducing the congestion of servers and interconnected networks, freeing bandwidth and as a result, reducing latency from a user's point of view.

VMC is intended to be implemented as an extension of IP routing, in which common TCP streams are identified, and combined. As opposed to standard multicasting [6], there is no explicit setup, and if a client joins a stream late, it will receive earlier traffic out of sequence, sent as a separate stream.

VMC works by maintaining a record of data travelling on the router. If a new client requests data that the VMC router is transmitting already, the request is not passed to the server. Instead, the router creates a response for the previously-transmitted portion of the data, and copies the current stream to the new client. If the router has previously seen multiple requests for the same content, a new client is simply added to an existing VMC session, and the router can send the missed content to the client from its buffer. The first time a duplication is detected, the router starts buffering content, and has to request the missing initial part of the stream from the original server.

The router ends up with two or more clients receiving the same data from a single source, once the VMC setup is complete.

Once the download is complete for the first client, the clients which joined the VMC session later issue a request for data they missed.

For playing a movie, VMC has potential to reduce latency for viewers by bringing content closer to all but the first recipient. More significantly, reducing congestion will likely reduce latency for all network users, not just participants in the VMC session, given the bandwidth required for a movie. Unlike typical file downloads, a movie can run for more than an hour (2 to 3 hours, if it is a full feature), and relieving load even by finding a single extra viewer could have a significant effect on the network. A movie, however, presents a problem: if the client has missed some initial content, significant buffering would be required at the client side to receive the VMC stream as well as the missing initial content.

Real-time traffic (e.g., Internet radio or TV) should be easier for VMC than other examples, because patching in previous missed content is unnecessary.

VMC can be contrasted not only with multicasting, but also with proxy caches, which save recent content to avoid repeated delivery. VMC differs from caching in that it occurs in the highest-traffic segments and routers, rather than at the endpoints. Further, VMC happens on the fly, whereas caching stores a stream for future use. VMC therefore exploits very short-term locality, and locality across a different part of the Internet.

Ideally, VMC should be completely transparent. However, in our initial work, we are prepared to make simple modifications to standard protocols to demonstrate feasibility.

The remainder of this section provides a brief overview of conventional multicasting, proxy caches and an experimental VMC implementation.

2.1   Multicasting

IP multicasting is the transmission of a packet to a subset of hosts in a network [7]. It provides packet delivery to these hosts at a lower network and host cost than broadcasting to all hosts or unicasting to each host in the group.

Hosts to whom a multicast is destined share a Class D group address (a class reserved for multicast groups [6]). Routers need to know which hosts are in a group: this can be determined by a router polling hosts, or by hosts informing routers [19]. Multicasting has a high setup overhead: a router needs to construct a spanning tree, pruned to exclude hosts not in a multicast group [4].

Another problem is that many routers on the Internet are not configured to allow the transmission of multicast packets. These routers have to be bypassed by IP tunneling [20], a non-trivial task – as a result multicasting is not widely supported by Internet Service Providers (ISPs).

Multicasting suffers several problems in scaling up, such as the acknowledgement implosion problem, resulting from the fact that many more acknowledgements will be routed back to the sender than the original number of multicast packets [15]. There have been various attempts at addressing the scalability problems of multicasting, including Protocol Independent Multicasting (PIM) [5]. However, PIM introduces yet another standard, which increases the difficulty of providing multicasting capabilities across the Internet.

While there has been some work on using multicasting to support video on demand, the proposed solutions are complex, and still need work [12].

Finally, the "best-effort" attempt at data delivery that multicast operates with, is not good enough for many applications which need data to be reliably transferred. Reliable multicast protocols have been developed, but they are inefficient in the delivery of data and have a propensity to cause packet storms [11].

2.2   Proxy Caching

A proxy cache (often simply called a "cache") is a service between web servers and clients. Generally, a proxy cache is close to users, and aims to exploit similarities in local demand. It watches requests for web objects (e.g., HTML pages, images and files) and saves a copy of objects locally. Subsequent requests for the same object can then be served from the cache.

A cache is implemented transparently, in that once it is set up, a client need not specifically request content from a cache. The cache intercepts traffic and serves requests it can meet, and passes others on. A browser may be configured to point to a specific cache, but caching can be completely transparent (a client is not configured specifically to use the cache). Caches can reduce latency as seen by clients and reduce the bandwidth used by the clients. Caches can be seen as a congestion avoidance mechanism, since they reduce Intenet traffic by storing data locally.

Some incoming data cannot be cached. This is due to factors such as dynamic content and rapidly changing web pages. Studies have shown that the amount of Web traffic that cannot be cached is as high as 20% [18]. Furthermore, even with an infinite cache size, the upper bound for the hit rate is 30-50% [1, 18].

It is not always useful to have a cache hit, because the cache server may be overloaded and unable to serve the object efficiently [17]. Furthermore, the time taken to check the validity of the object might be longer than retrieving the object itself. Caches may also be slower on misses than an uncached connection, since the time taken searching a hierarchy for the object may be longer than retrieving the data from the origin server [18]. Every slowdown in the cache adds to the latency experienced by the user.

Finally, caches are often large, and based on expensive hardware and software which have to be configured and constantly maintained. If there is a problem with the cache server, an entire network may be deprived of Internet connectivity, which may be unacceptable for many applications (e.g. Internet banking).

2.3   Comparison to VMC

The common basis of multicasting and caching is that they are bandwidth saving and congestion reduction mechanisms. VMC uses the single data stream idea of multicasting and the transparent nature of caching to produce a mechanism with the benefits of both, while attempting to limit the costs and problems of multicasting and caching.

Unlike caching, VMC occurs near the top of the hierarchy, so the cost would only be incurred at high-throughput routers, whereas caching occurs at endpoints, and is therefore a highly replicated cost. Caching at endpoints could still catch traffic widely spaced in time, which VMC would miss. Multicasting requires prior knowledge that a stream will be shared, and has a high setup cost. VMC, by focusing on traffic through the highest-traffic routers, reduces the setup cost. Further, the VMC approach of transparently initiating sharing when a need is detected means that it is not necessary to predict the need for sharing in advance. However, where it is known in advance that a multicast session is required, it would still be a viable option where it was supported, since routing could be carried out without the requirement of VMC-aware routers.

Finally, VMC routing is intended to occur only through selected routers near the top of the hierarchy, which means that it is not necessary that a large part of the Internet be aware of VMC routing.

3   Experimental Framework

The main goal of this research is to provide a feasibility study of VMC. It is thus necessary to focus on potential obstacles to VMC's implementation rather than on a complete solution.

While FTP should benefit from VMC, the FTP protocol does not lend itself to simple modification to evaluate our ideas. HTTP has the option of requesting a range – a feature used by caches [2]. While FTP does have a "restart" option, it is not supported in most file transfer modes [16], which would make sending a missed range of a file more complex than with HTTP. HTTP encapsulates all the file transfer mechanisms of FTP and is widely used as a substitute for FTP. Furthermore, the protocol itself is cleaner and better defined – particularly for our purposes. Our approach therefore was to base our investigation on changes to HTTP to support VMC.

This section presents a brief summary of preliminary results which further justified the research, then outlines an experimental version of VMC. The approach used in experiment described in this paper is described, and, finally, our expectations for results are summarized.

3.1   Preliminary Results

A preliminary study of FTP logs from a commercial Internet service provider showed that there was significant overlap of FTP traffic from their site. The overlap of traffic could be eliminated by VMC, since streams would be sharing this data. We did very rudimentary calculations (not taking congestion and latency issues into account), over 11 consecutive days of logged traffic, of the potential bandwidth savings.

The total number of bytes transferred normally over the log days examined was 5.67×10^{10}. The number of bytes eliminating all overlaps was 2.99×10^{10}, 52% less than the normal mode of transfer. The biggest saving through eliminating overlaps was 71% and the smallest was 19%. This initial study [3] showed that VMC had considerable promise, and was worth further investigation. Clearly, a more realistic experiment was the next step. However, these logs represented a relatively high degree of overlap, so we chose to find other logs where the overlap was much lower, to illustrate the potential for gains across a range of traffic conditions.

Accordingly, our more realistic experiment used logs from another source, with much less overlap.

3.2   Experimental VMC Implementation

Establishing the feasibility of the VMC approach takes a number of forms. First, the actual mechanics of VMC have to be developed and demonstrated. Second, it will be no good if the method exists in a vacuum, so good interaction with the current Internet protocols must be demonstrated. Finally, VMC is likely to add latency. This additional latency must be measured and weighed against latency gains, to decide the effectiveness of the method.

In order to evaluate these feasibility issues, an experimental VMC system has been built. The strategy was to start with a simple implementation, to minimise complexity of understanding the results. Accordingly, a simple network topology was implemented, to abstract the main features of the design. This simplified network implemented a VMC router on a computer with a single web server playing the role of multiple servers. While a real VMC route would be

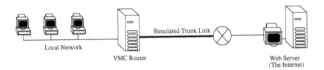

Fig. 1. Experimental Setup

several layers away from the servers and client machines, intermediate links were removed to simplify measurement.

The Virtual Multicasting router software was implemented as a simple test bed, designed to experiment with variations on simulated workloads, based on data from cache logs. In the absence of VMC routing, standard IP routing takes place, as a base line from which to compare overheads and advantages of VMC. Fig. 1 illustates the experimental setup.

The setup is intended to abstract the key requirements of a VMC route: servers providing potentially similar information, and clients with potentially overlapping requirements.

To simulate traffic from a large network, traffic logs from the University of the Witwatersrand cache were used to generate traffic from a single server, with a link approximating the speed of the university's link to the outside world. This traffic had much less overlap than that of our preliminary study.

The VMC router uses the same strategy as a proxy cache for identifying like traffic: it looks for TCP packets with a destination port of 80, and requests are indexed using the MD-5 hash of the universal resource indicator (URI) in the request. A VMC application on the router PC is handed any packets with a destination port of 80, using the IP_REDIRECT capabilities of netfilter [10].

Traffic is buffered in the router, and if the same request is detected (by hashing on the URI), it is directed to the buffered content. The VMC router in effect proxies connections, but disguises the fact that it does so from clients by rewriting addresses.

Clients have to be modified so that if they receive partial content, they are aware of this and are able to request the missing data. The router has to send a Partial Content response to a client specifying the range of the supplied bytes. Thereafter, the client has to issue a request for the missing range of bytes.

All of these details are contained in the specification of HTTP 1.1 [9]. The only change in usage is that range responses are usually only generated on request. The simplest way of introducing this change would be to add it in to proxy caches, so they would cooperate with VMC routers, but a better long-term change would be to modify the HTTP protocol, so clients could use VMC routers directly. The standard as currently worded does not prohibit clients from dealing with ranges. However, most do not, because a range-response is not a usual outcome of issuing a non-range request, so the proposed change would be to amend the HTTP standard to ensure that clients are implemented to understand a range-response from a non-range request.

However, in this research, we have confined ourselves to evaluating the VMC idea, rather than considering how to change standards to accommodate it.

3.3   Experimental Approach

The experiment reported on here compared a calculated latency gain, based purely on time saved resulting from overlaps in files in a simulated workload, with actual latency gain as measured on a simulated VMC environment. The intent was to evaluate the predictive value of a simplistic measurement, as well as to show the value of even relatively small bandwidth savings in terms of latency improvement. The simulated environment did not take into account latency gains from reducing traffic on multi-hop routes to a client, and therefore underestimates latency gain in a real environment.

The University of the Witwatersrand uses a Squid proxy server to service about 10,000 users. Web requests are logged, and information logged includes that which we needed: time of request, size of the request and time taken to service the request. The size and diversity of the academic community is sufficient to give an approximation to a more general scenario. The phenomenon of self-similarity [8] suggests that our traffic logs are likely to be representative of a wider sample of the real Internet – though the logs we used in our preliminary work suggest that there is a wide variety of traffic patterns.

Our approach was to clean the log files, so extraneous information was removed, as were requests which did not result in data being returned, or which were not well-formed. We then used the logs to generate random bytes up to the length of each request. Had we been exploring issues where the content was significant (e.g., compression), we would not have been able to use random data, but that was not an issue for our experiments.

The data used is selected from real data from 3 days of logs, as well as two artificial pathological cases, representing unrealistically high overlap, and no overlap. The pathological cases are intended to illustrate the extremes: a best-case and a worst-case scenario for VMC. The worst-case scenario provides a measure of the overheads introduced by VMC, since no savings are made (i.e., the only difference is the overhead of trying to find VMC opportunities).

The high-load cases are taken from 4 hours of logs, at busy times of the day, while the low-load cases are taken from 8 hours of logs during quiet times (late at night and early in the morning). The pathological case of no overlap was created by taking a log from a low-traffic period, and eliminating the overlaps. The artificial case of very high overlap with high load was created by interleaving extra requests for a 1Mbyte file as every fifth download.

The calculated latency gain was based on a simple subtraction of the time saved if overlaps identified in the files transferred were removed. The experimental scenarios and calculated latency savings are presented in Table 1. The low-traffic scenarios were generally taken from logs early in the morning on a Monday or late at night on a Friday, when usage was low. The high-traffic scenarios were taken from logs during the day time on a week day, when usage was relatively high. The degree of overlap is relative: as can be seen from the bandwidth saved in the Results section (Table 2), the degree of overlap is not very high except in the contrived case of very high overlap.

Table 1. Experimental scenarios (calculated latency gains based on examining logs).

scenario		Workload	Calculated Latency
load	overlap	files/hour	Saving (%)
low	low	3410.75	0.93
high	high	105322.00	8.12
high	low	898891.75	1.95
low	high	16583.75	2.18
pathological cases			
high	v. high	82221.5	23.05
low	none	3410.75	0.00

The experimentally-determined latency gain was measured as the difference between elapsed time for transmission of the entire workload with and without VMC. This experimentally-determined latency gain is a more realistic measure than the calculated latency gain, since it takes into account the overall effect of VMC on the network, including the extra latency of VMC and improvements resulting from the reduction in network traffic (including reduced congestion).

In our experiments, we eliminated the possibility of high load adding to latency because of limitations of our network cards, by dividing simulation runs (which varied from approximately 25,000 to 420,000 files) into runs of 5,000 files at a time. In a real scenario, this issue would not be a problem because we were simulating activity of an entire campus on a small number of machines.

3.4 Expected Results

Given that the calculated latency savings are only based on reducing the transmission time for the saved bytes, we expected that the measured latency savings would be significantly higher. Any reduction in network traffic will generally improve latency, through reducing collisions (in a network which permits collisions such as ethernet) and generally reducing contention for shared resources.

We expected that the achieved latency gain would therefore be significantly higher than that which was calculated.

Further, we expected latency gains, given the nature of the traffic, to be significantly higher than bandwidth gains. Much traffic resulting from web page access is relatively small files (e.g., an icon, or the text of a web page), which makes the probability of overlaps being significant in size and occurring close enough in time to be useful for VMC to be low. On the other hand, any such overlaps which are found have the potential to reduce congestion. Even in a lightly loaded network, overlaps can potentially lead to short-term hot spots, which VMC has the potential to alleviate.

4 Results

In this section, we present results of experimental bandwidth and latency gains, which are compared with the calculated latency gains. The aim is to highlight the difference between latency and bandwidth gains. VMC is designed to reduce congestion on the Internet, with latency reduction – the measure of most interest to the user – the goal. Accordingly, the focus in presenting the results is on presenting latency reduction as the measure of interest. Bandwidth reduction is also shown as a basis for understanding why latency has improved.

In general, bandwidth savings are modest and on their own do not make a convincing case for VMC. Latency gains, on the other hand, are significant, and do make a case for further investigation of the idea.

The remainder of this section is presented in the following order. First, plots of bandwidth gains and latency variation with and without VMC are shown, followed by a table summarizing results. Finally, the results are discussed.

4.1 Bandwidth and Latency Savings

To illustrate how latency gains can be amplified by hot spots, the latency gains are shown as cumulative plots of latency, compared with plots of bandwidth gains. Total bandwidth is not plotted, because the differences between with and without VMC do not show on any of the graphs, except on the pathological case of very high overlap on a high load.

Fig. 2 illustrates the case of low overlap with low load. As can be expected, total latency saved is relatively small (Fig. 2(b)). Bandwidth saved is only 0.02% of the total. However, the overall saving of latency is 6.88%, which compares well with the calculated saving of 0.93% (7.4 times higher). A large fraction of the overlap occurred towards the end of the workload (probably because this workload was measured up to 8am), as can be seen in Fig. 2(a).

Fig. 3 illustrates the opposite case: a relatively high load with a relatively high degree of overlap. There are several significant steps in the graph showing saving in bandwidth (Fig. 3(a)). These steps correspond roughly to increases in the bandwidth graphed for the "normal" (non-VMC) case – particularly at about the point where 250000 files have been downloaded. Another observation which is clearer in this case than the low load, low overlap case is that the VMC

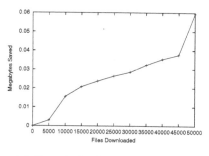

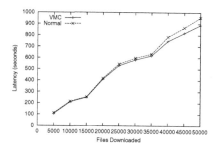

(a) Cumulative bandwidth savings   (b) Cumulative latency

Fig. 2. Low overlap, low load.

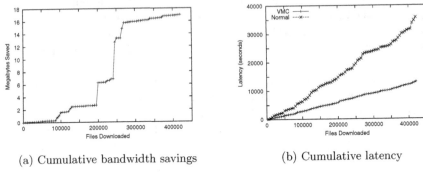

(a) Cumulative bandwidth savings   (b) Cumulative latency

Fig. 3. High overlap, high load.

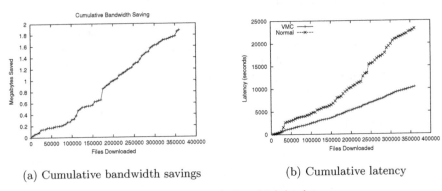

(a) Cumulative bandwidth savings   (b) Cumulative latency

Fig. 4. Low overlap, high load.

cumulative latency graph is smoother than the "normal" graph, illustrating the fact that VMC has reduced hot spots.

The case of high load with low overlap (Fig. 4) is interesting because it illustrates again how VMC is able to smooth out hot spots, even when they may be relatively uncommon. The overall effect is that, despite only saving 0.05% of the bandwidth, latency is improved by 55.36% overall (as compared with the calculated saving of 1.95%).

The final case of a workload based on a real usage pattern is that of high overlap with a low load, as shown in Fig. 5. In this case, again, the value of eliminating hot spots is illustrated. While the total bandwidth saving of 0.14% is very modest, latency overall is reduced by 52.2%. This latency saving is compared with the calculated latency saving of 2.18%. What should be noted specifically here is that the overlaps, while few, are bursty in nature, with each overlap resulting in a big step in the bandwidth savings graph (5(a)).

Finally, the artificially-constructed case of very high overlap (Fig. 6) shows how VMC could reduce latency in an extreme case (e.g., a new major software release, a popular movie available for download), In this situation, over 90% of the bandwidth is saved, and the latency improvement is 71.21%, as opposed to the calculated 23.05%. The artificial case of no overlap is not graphed; the result is obvious: graphs for the VMC and "standard" cases are almost identical, except for a small extra overhead on latency for VMC, totalling 0.74%.

Table 2 summarizes the results.

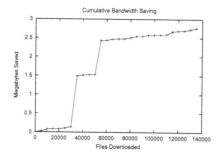
(a) Cumulative bandwidth savings

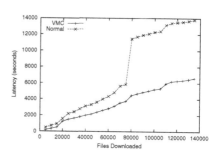
(b) Cumulative latency

Fig. 5. High overlap, low load.

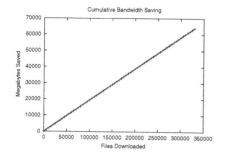
(a) Cumulative bandwidth savings

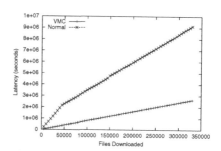
(b) Cumulative latency

Fig. 6. Artificially high overlap, high load.

Table 2. Measured bandwidth and latency gains.

scenario		Mbyte transferred		saving %	
load	overlap	Normal	VMC	bandwidth	latency
low	low	338.13	338.07	0.02	6.88
high	high	4263.82	4246.86	0.40	63.42
high	low	3528.81	3526.93	0.05	55.36
low	high	1928.13	1925.36	0.14	52.2
pathological cases					
high	v. high	68556.81	4564.23	93.34	71.21
low	none	381.33	381.33	0	-0.74

4.2   Summary of Findings

Latency gains, as calculated, varied from 0.93% to 6.69% (excluding pathological cases). These gains translated to measured gains varying from 6.88% to 63.42%. Since these are cumulative measures, they do not convey the improvement which would be seen by a user, where a hot spot in network activity would cause annoying delays. Smoothing out the cumulative latency graphs, as VMC has done in all cases, should translate to a more predictable user experience.

Modest bandwidth savings have given disproportionate latency savings. Latency gains have varied from nearly 7 times to almost 30 times the calculated gain. Such variation should not be too surprising: the calculated gain did not take into account the effect of traffic reduction on other network traffic. In particular, removal of hot spots has a disproportionate effect on reducing latency.

The overall effect, as seen by a user, could include lower annoyance with unpredictable behaviour, e.g., reduction of jitter and other artifacts of congestion. If the latency savings were to translate into a real-world scenario, VMC would be worth implementing.

5   Conclusions

VMC is a promising idea, and a potentially implementable instance of the broader information mass transit (IMT) idea. The version we have investigated here could be realised with simple changes to web applications. Clients (browsers) need to be aware that they should respond to a portion of a data-object (given in the HTTP response codes) by requesting the rest of the object. Alternatively, proxy caches could be used to hide this extra step from the clients, but the costs and benefits of the alternatives are still to be investigated.

The remainder of this section summarizes our results, and proposes further work. Finally, we conclude by considering the potential of both VMC and IMT.

5.1   Summary of Results

Our results show that even with relatively modest bandwidth reduction, VMC can achieve significant latency gains. While the most significant gains are under high load with a high degree of overlap, a large improvement in latency was also seen where there was a high degree of overlap with a light load, or a low degree of overlap with a high load. Particularly in the cases of high overlap, the gains smooth out the cumulative latency graph; this effect is clearest in the case of high overlap and low load. The likely effect as seen by users would be a reduction of artifacts of congestion, such as short-term spikes in latency.

The pathological cases illustrate that the effect on a network with no overlap is insignificant (overhead of less than 1%), while a very high overlap on a highly loaded network, as would be expected, shows VMC to best advantage.

5.2   Future Work

Further work on IMT includes investigation of implementation issues for SAVoD, and investigation of further application of the principles in other areas.

We further propose to investigate areas where VMC can be implemented transparently, and modifications to standard protocols where it cannot be implemented transparently. Specifically, it would be useful to investigate simple alterations to proxy caches to hide VMC from clients, as well as extensions to HTTP which would define behaviour for VMC-aware clients.

More detailed modeling of network traffic would also be useful, to make clearer what the sources of the latency gains are. Insights from such measurement could lead to improvements in VMC, or in other approaches to latency reduction or congestion control.

5.3   Potential of IMT and VMC

VMC has promise. Our initial implementation made it possible to measure the trade-off between benefits and extra costs of VMC. In all cases measured, except the contrived case with no overlap, benefits were significantly better than the cost. With no overlaps, VMC added under 1% to latency, significantly less than the worst gain of 6.88%. More significantly, we found that small reductions in bandwidth could result in significantly bigger gains in latency – much greater than would be predicted by simply calculating the change in transmission time for the reduction in traffic. This finding emphasizes the potential for VMC to reduce hot spots resulting from congestion.

In general, IMT is worth exploring. As Internet bandwidth scales up, traditional models of communication very quickly result in loss of the benefit of new bandwidth. Applications like video on demand are notoriously difficult to scale up, and most proposals have called for very complex hardware and software. Real-time applications, such as web-based TV or radio, are strong candidates for VMC, since they eliminate the need for patching in missed content.

We believe that a new approach is called for, and IMT (including its particular manifestations, SAVoD and VMC) attempts to address this need.

Acknowledgments

We would like to thank The Internet Solution for providing logs on which our preliminary work was based. Logs for the results reported here were provided by Computer and Network Services, University of the Witwatersrand. This work has been supported by the National Research Foundation in South Africa.

References

1. Marc Abrams, Charles R. Standridge, Ghaleb Abdulla, Stephen Williams, and Edward A. Fox. *Caching Proxies: Limitations and Potentials* [online]. December 1995. Available from `http://ei.cs.vt.edu/~succeed/WWW4/WWW4.html`.

2. B Andrew and P. Machanick. The virtual multicasting approach to bandwidth conservation. In *Proc. SATNAC 2000*, Somerset West, South Africa, September 2000. published on CD.

3. B Andrew and P. Machanick. Virtual multicasting as an example of information mass transit. *South African Computer Journal*, (26):252–255, November 2000.

4. S. Deering, D. Farinacci, V. Jacobson, C.-G. Liu, and L. Wei. An Architecture for Wide-Area Multicast Routing. In *Proc. ACM SIGCOMM Conf. on Communications, Architecture and Protocols*, pages 126–135, 1994.

5. S. Deering, D.L. Estrin, D. Farinacci, V. Jacobson, C.-G. Liu, and L. Wei. The PIM architecture for wide-area multicast routing. *IEEE/ACM Transactions on Networking*, 4(2):153–162, April 1996.

6. S. E. Deering. Host Extensions for IP Multicasting. RFC 1054 [online]. May 1988. Available from `ftp://ftp.rfc-editor.org/in-notes/rfc1054.txt`.

7. S. E. Deering and D. R. Cheriton. Multicast Routing in Datagram Internetworks and Extended LANs. *ACM Transactions on Computer Systems*, 8(2):85–110, February 1990.

8. A. Feldmann, A.C. Gilbert, P. Huang, and W. Willinger. Dynamics of ip traffic: a study of the role of variability and the impact of control. In *Proc. Conf. on Applications, Technologies, Architectures, and Protocols for Computer Communication*, pages 301–313, Cambridge, Massachusetts, United States, 1999. ACM Press.

9. R. Fielding, J. Gettys, J. Mogul, H. Frystyk, L. Masinter, P. Leach, and T. Berners-Lee. Hypertext Transfer Protocol – HTTP 1.1. RFC 2616 [online]. June 1999. Available from `ftp://ftp.rfc-editor.org/in-notes/rfc2616.txt`.

10. Jozsef Kadlecsik, Harald Welte, James Morris, Marc Boucher, and Rusty Russell. The netfilter/iptables project [online]. 2003. Available from `http://www.netfilter.org/`. last accessed February 2003.

11. Brian Neil Levine. *A Comparison of Known Classes of Reliable Multicast Protocols*. Master's thesis, University of California, Santa Cruz, 1996.

12. Huadong Ma and Kang G. Shin. Multicast video-on-demand services. *ACM SIGCOMM Computer Communication Review*, 32(1):31–43, January 2002.

13. P. Machanick. Design of a scalable video on demand architecture. In *Proc. SAICSIT '98*, pages 211–217, Gordon's Bay, South Africa, November 1998.

14. P Machanick. Streaming *vs.* latency in information mass-transit. *Computer Architecture News*, 26(5):4–6, December 1998.

15. Sridhar Pingali, Don Towsley, and James F. Kurose. A comparison of sender-initiated and receiver-initiated reliable multicast protocols. In *Proc. 1994 ACM SIGMETRICS Conf. on Measurement and Modeling of Computer Systems*, pages 221–230, Nashville, Tennessee, United States, 1994. ACM Press.

16. J. Postel and J. Reynolds. File transfer protocol (FTP). RFC 959 [online]. October 1985. Available from `ftp://ftp.rfc-editor.org/in-notes/rfc959.txt`.

17. Harrick M. Vin Renu Tewari, Michael Dahlin and Jonathon S. Kay. *Beyond Hierarchies: Design Considerations for Distributed Caching on the Internet*. Technical Report TR98-04, The University of Texas at Austin, 1998.

18. A. Rousskov and V. Solokiev. On Performance of Caching Proxies [online]. August 1998. Available from
http://www.cs.ndsu.nodak.edu/ rousskov/research/cache/squid/profiling/papers.

19. Andrew S. Tanenbaum. *Computer Networks*. Prentice-Hall, fourth edition, 2003.

20. B. Zhang, S. Jamin, and L. Zhang. Host multicast: A framework for delivering multicast to end users. In *Proc. 21st Annual Joint Conf. of IEEE Computer and Communications Societies*, volume 3, pages 1366–1375, New York, June 2002.

A Router Architecture
to Achieve Link Rate Throughput
in Suburban Ad-hoc Networks

Muhammad Mahmudul Islam, Ronald Pose, and Carlo Kopp

School of Computer Science and Software Engineering, Monash University, Australia,
{sislam,rdp,carlo}@mail.csse.monash.edu.au

Abstract. Static nodes, e.g. houses, educational institutions etc, can comprise ad-hoc networks using off-the-self wireless technologies with a view to bypass expensive telecommunication solutions. A suburban ad-hoc network (SAHN) aims to provide such an inexpensive broadband networking alternative for communities of cooperating users using wireless medium. There exists a plethora of efficient routing solutions for ad-hoc networks where nodes are mobile. However, less attention has been paid towards optimizing these protocols and developing a real routing system for ad-hoc networks where nodes are not mobile. In this paper we have made analyses of various router architectures and outlined a design framework to perform routing tasks in the SAHN efficiently. We have also presented a survey result for choosing a feasible realtime operating system for our development and deployment purposes.

1 Introduction

The ever increasing trend towards huge amounts of data transfered at high speeds through the Internet has inspired researchers to come up with many new efficient networking technologies. Unfortunately most of the new technologies offering high rates of data transfer require costly infrastructure and high service charges which are only feasible for large educational institutions, governmental organizations, companies and research groups. People in small offices, companies and homes can only enjoy similar performance at great cost. Usually these facilities are only available in close proximity to service providers. Many voluntary networking groups[1] have been formed to provide wireless internetworking facilities by connecting households, schools, community centres and local businesses together at low initial costs and almost no service charges. But these solutions are threatened by unauthorised intrusions. Moreover participants in a community have to rely on centralised routing nodes for intercommunication. This results in performance bottlenecks as well as inefficient use of aggregate network capacity. As a consequence these solutions are still less attractive than the traditional and costly solutions provided by various telecommunication service providers. It can even be argued that Nokia's wireless broadband solution (Nokia RoofTop) for residential users, which has an optimized IP protocol stack

A. Omondi and S. Sedukhin (Eds.): ACSAC 2003, LNCS 2823, pp. 395–407, 2003.

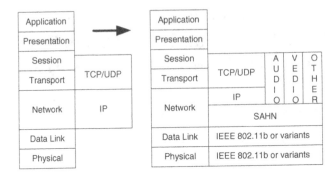

Fig. 1. The SAHN protocol stack in the OSI model [3]

with custom-built OS for routing, may result in marginal performance in ad-hoc wireless networks. To alleviate these expensive, oversubscribed, area limited and low secured solutions, a networking framework has been proposed termed the 'Suburban Ad-Hoc Network' [2] or SAHN. The SAHN is a low-maintenance, decentralized, cooperative wireless networking architecture offering low cost internetworking solutions among its users. The inherent symmetric throughput in both upstream and downstream channels at reasonably high rates allows the facility to provide traditional costly broadband throughput at low cost. The security scheme at the network layer is particularly appealing to security conscious business users. Additionally the wireless interconnecting property makes the SAHN suited to extend the Internet infrastructure to areas of inadequate wired facilities.

Each SAHN node is capable of authenticating neighboring nodes to participate in the network. Each node also acts as a dynamic router to discover and maintain routes itself. Initial investigation showed that, the SAHN routing protocol shares the properties of both ad-hoc on-demand and static table driven routing protocols. Notably, the protocol adopts the idea of keeping the neighbor information up-to-date like any of the static table driven routing protocols. On the other hand to find a route to an unknown node, as well as to maintain it, it adopts an on-demand route discovery and maintenance mechanism derived from the Dynamic Source Routing (DSR)[4] protocol. For data transmission over known routes with sufficient QoS attributes, the SAHN routing protocol exploits mixed principles of DSR and the Ad-hoc On Demand Distance Vector Routing (AODV)[5] protocol. As the SAHN does not carry source routes in each data packet, a large network overhead can be eliminated in networks with many nodes[5]. The motivation to adopt a hybrid routing protocol with certain quality of service metrics and resource access control capabilities, is to eliminate the shortcomings of any individual protocol [3][6][7].

The SAHN project aims to come up with a working solution for real ad-hoc networks. As simulation alone of the proposed routing protocol is not enough, we should design an efficient hardware architecture for it to achieve link rate throughput at each node. We should also select a suitable development and target platform, so that the software development cycle is minimized with least efforts and costs. We have addressed these issues in this paper.

We have organized our paper as follows. In Section 2, we have made some analyses of available design approaches to adopt for the SAHN router. We have also outlined the SAHN routing engine in this section. Finally in Section 3, we have done a requirements analysis as well as a survey to facilitate the choice of a suitable operating system to support our routing protocol.

2 SAHN Router Architecture

Packet processing and switching in a router is always a critical job in terms of time and memory. Without proper hardware and software design a router can be a bottleneck. Proper design means to isolate the time critical packet processing with the non-time critical ones. At the same time it is essential to employ appropriate hardware for the tasks so that they can be processed faster and if possible independent tasks in parallel. Here we will present the hardware architecture and the associated implementation framework to achieve link rate throughput in each of the SAHN nodes.

To begin our analysis, we should know what are the basic components and their related tasks of any router. These are

- Several network interface cards attached to network media to receive and transmit packets
- Some processing modules or forwarding engines to validate incoming packets, to create and maintain routing tables, to update packet header information and finally to encrypt and transmit them through appropriate outbound interface cards
- Buffering modules to hold packets, routing tables etc.
- An internal interconnecting unit like a bus or a switch fabric to enable communication among various working modules.

We can summarize that, a router consists of some tasks to perform routing, some working modules to perform these tasks and interconnecting fabrics to enable intercommunications among various modules. In the following subsections, we will discuss these in detail with respect to the SAHN.

2.1 Routing Tasks

The SAHN router follows the basic tasks of any generic router. Moreover, it has to accomplish some other tasks specific to the SAHN environment. Generally the SAHN router has to carry out the following responsibilities:

1. Receiving a packet at the interface card, the header is separated, classified, decrypted and validated. Taking only the header for the rest of the processing enables us to work faster with a small amount of memory.
2. Then a path entry is searched against the routing information available in the cache or the routing table.

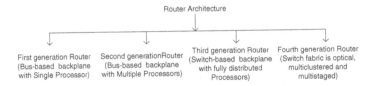

Fig. 2. Classification of router architecture [8][9][10]

3. If the destination path is not found, a route discovery takes place according to the SAHN routing algorithm.
4. If the destination is reachable, the next hop towards the destination and the interface through which the next node is reachable is determined and the packet header information is updated and the level2 header is encrypted for the next hop. Then the level2 and level1 headers are prepended with the rest of the packet.
5. At last the packet is transmitted through the interface card connected to the next node.

In order to achieve router throughput close to the data rate of the interface cards, we have to isolate the time critical tasks (directly related to packet forwarding) from the non-time critical ones and employ appropriate hardware components with an efficient interconnection or switching fabric. A close investigation into the above steps reveals that except from step 3, all other steps can be considered as directly related to forwarding a packet in the SAHN routing module. Step 3 along with some other tasks like route maintenance, providing QoS, route management and error control are not done on a per packet basis. For example route discovery is only needed if the route is not present in the route table/cache. In such case the corresponding packet can be buffered until the route is found. In the mean time all other packets received with known routes can be processed. Best router throughput can be achieved if packets are handled by multiple heterogeneous processing modules (both hardware and software) where each of them specializes in a specific task and work simultaneously where possible.

2.2   Interconnection Fabric

A well designed switch fabric is essential for non-blocking interconnection of the critical components with much higher capacity and speed. The most common switch fabrics used in routers have been discussed elaborately in [8], [11] and [9]. Here we will present an analyses of these switch fabrics before selecting one for our purpose.

A backplane interconnection fabric connects ingress ports with egress ports. Ingress and egress ports are combinations of incoming/outgoing line cards, forwarding engines etc. A well designed intercommunicating backplane switch fabric is very important as it has the effect on overall system throughput. Even though there may be fast processors and fast memories to process any incoming packet at

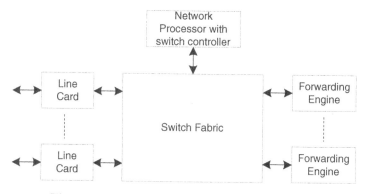

Fig. 3. General structure of high-speed router [10]

link rates, an inefficient switching fabric may not sustain the aggregate through-put of on-board processors and memories. Consequently system throughput may not be as same as the link rate.

First generation router was built around conventional computer architectures with a shared backplane bus, a CPU, shared pool of memory and some line cards connected to the media. Packets arriving at any line cards are transferred to the CPU through a shared bus. All processing and forwarding decisions are made in the CPU and buffered in a central shared memory until the outbound link becomes free. Finally the packets are transferred through the shared bus to outbound line card/s and transmitted to the media connected to the next hop. Though this design is attractive for its simplicity, it has the disadvantage of having data crossing the shared bus several times, imposing a severe system bottleneck.

Fast processors with cache memory in the line cards and in the forwarding modules can reduce some dependence on shared bus. This approach was taken in designing second generation routers. However, bus based architectures always have a traffic dependant throughput as there is always a physical limitation on bus speed. Besides only one port is given permission to use the bus at a time.

Third generation routers (Fig. 3) were designed with switch fabric architec-tures instead of a shared bus to alleviate this bottleneck. Here a switch fabric is used for non-blocking interconnection of time critical components with much higher capacity and speed than a traditional backplane bus [10]. Most common switch fabrics have been discussed elaborately in [8], [11] and [9]. These are (a) shared medium switch fabric, (b) shared memory switch fabric, (c) distributed output buffered switch fabric and (d) space division or crossbar switch fabric with input buffers.

Shared medium switch fabric is like bus based backplanes of first generation routers. Due to the physical limitation of bandwidth capacity, a shared medium switch fabric imposes a serious performance bottleneck for inter-module traffic flow.

Shared memory switch fabric connects input and output ports to a central memory pool in parallel. As a result, input and output ports can have simul-

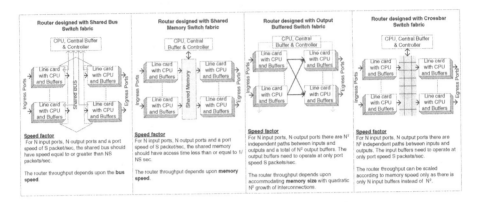

Fig. 4. Comparison among various switch fabrics

taneous read and write accesses to a shared memory. This can provide better throughput than a shared bus architecture. But this approach is limited by memory access time.

An output buffered switch fabric architecture can improve this limitation by splitting the shared memory into separate output buffers for each output port. There exists a mesh to connect all input ports to their respective output buffers. This approach creates scalability issues for backplane layout and memory size in systems with large port counts. On the other hand, an input buffered crossbar switch fabric is sometimes more attractive solution for its highly scalable, low cost and non-blocking switching solution.

A crossbar switch fabric is an alternative to alleviate aforementioned limitations. With some improvements in crossbar architecture, it can even achieve a terabit throughput rate [12]. A crossbar is formed by connecting all input and output ports in such a manner that inter-port traffic flows in unicast fashion. All input ports have their own buffer. So, the speed of memory buffer need not to be more than that of its associated port.

2.3   Working Modules

Various design approaches have been proposed by many researchers to achieve router throughput close to the link data rate. Commonly known designs are described and compared in [8], [9] and [10]. Many leading high-speed router manufactures, such as CISCO, 3Com, Lucent Technology and NetStar, have provided their routing solutions based on these basic principles. Like them, we have also decided to follow the generic router design approach (Fig. 3) for our SAHN routing module.

CISCO has its own forwarding engine called NPE (network processing engine) which combines line cards on a midplane. The backplane uses a crossbar switch fabric to interconnect the midplanes. The NetStar's GigaRouter includes the forwarding engine within the line cards [13]. The main idea is to reduce the flow of inter module traffic over the switch fabric. However in [14], a gigabit router design has been proposed with separate line cards, forwarding engines and the central controller unit, connected through a switched backplane. It has been argued to have forwarding engines distinct from the line cards for two reasons. One reason was they were not sure if they had enough board real estate to fit both the forwarding engine functionality with the line card functionality on a target card size. Another reason was to have more scalability. They found many router designs where the line cards were built with inadequate processors, throttling the performance to the processor's speed. To keep up with modern state of the art technology, they thought it was better to have separate forwarding engine which could be upgraded with the fastest processors if required. The last argument is one of our design goals too. But keeping the forwarding engine apart from the line cards may introduce a performance bottleneck in the switch throughput as the switch fabric will be allowing more inter module traffic flows.

Depending on various approaches available, the SAHN routing module follows a hybrid approach. There is a separate forwarding engine called the packet processing engine (PPE) connected to each line card and a central routing processing engine or RPE to perform the non-time critical tasks. The PPE, connected with its line card, forms the packet forwarding engine or PFE. The PFEs are connected to each other through a suitable switch fabric. Rather than using the same switch fabric, a separate switch fabric is used to connect the RPE with the PFEs. Using a distinct RPE to PFE connection is very important for the SAHN. The traditional routers are used mostly in structured infrastructure rather than a dynamic ad-hoc environment. Thus route discovery is not that frequent in ad-hoc networking infrastructure. Sharing the same switch fabric for both time critical and non-time critical tasks may lead to severe traffic congestion and poor system throughput. Whether to use a crossbar switched fabric or traditional bus based switch fabric for the non-time critical path, has to be tested in a real environment.

A question may arise whether this hybrid design framework is enough for the SAHN routing module. The answer is very straight forward. The forwarding engine in [14] used a DEC Alpha 21164 processor and achieved an overall rate of 111 Mpps. Other design approaches discussed in this section with fast crossbar switching fabrics and forwarding engines (CISCO uses MIPS processors in their NPE) are used for large routers in the multigigabit/terabit range with more than 500 Kpps packet switching rate [13]. But for the SAHN we are considering only a few network interfaces with media speed around 50 Mbps. Then we are targeting packet switching rate in the range of 25 Kpps to 50 Kpps which can be easily achieved with the derived hybrid design framework. Figure 5 shows the functional partitioning of tasks with associated hardware modules for the SAHN router. Before we give details of the modules it should be mentioned that our design approach has been influenced greatly by the solutions of CISCO, 3Com, Lucent and Linksys. Actually the basic principles followed by the major companies are almost the same. So it is reasonable that our design framework will be a variant of these available approaches.

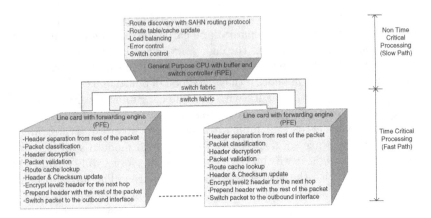

Fig. 5. Time critical and non-time critical functional modules in SAHN router

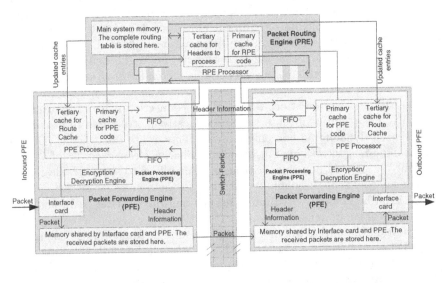

Fig. 6. A possible design outline of the SAHN routing module

The Packet Forwarding Engine (PFE). This section outlines the design of our network processing engine. Each of the packet forwarding engines has a direct link between its PPE and the corresponding network interface card (see Fig. 6). The PFE is responsible for the followings major stages: (a) packet receiving stage, (b) fast packet switching stage and (c) packet transmitting stage.

Fast packet switching is done if the next hop information to the destination is already in the PPE cache. If the route to the destination is not known or if the packet is one of the special control packets like 'Hello', 'Hello Reply', 'Route Request' (RREQ), 'Route Reply' (RREP) or 'Route Error' (RERR), the routing processing engine (RPE) is employed. We will discuss the RPE in next section.

The inbound interface card receives a packet by copying it from the link into the receive memory buffer. Soon after a packet is received, the associated NPE processor is notified by an interrupt signal. Each NPE shares the same memory buffer with its interface card so that packet is not copied from buffer to buffer. This approach saves inter buffer transfer latency. The level 1 header is checked for classification. If it is not one of the special control packets and not destined for this router, the level 2 header is separated, decrypted and validated. Considering only the header rather than the whole packet makes the processing faster with small amount of memory. Now the forwarding/switching cache is examined to determine if the next hop information for the destination exists. If the next hop information is not available in the cache, the PPE puts the header into the RPE's queue and generates an interrupt to the RPE processor to let it know a header is waiting in the input queue to be processed. Otherwise the packet header is updated with the information from the cache. Then the outbound PPE is determined to forward the packet.

The updated header is queued into the outbound PPE and notified by an interrupt signal. The outbound PPE updates some of the header fields like the next hop MAC address, the HTL (hop to live), the TT (transmission time) etc. Then the level 2 header is encrypted according to the negotiated encryption scheme with the next hop and prepended with the rest of the packet. The QoS module in the PPE takes the remaining responsibilities. The QoS module provides flow control which is a part of load balancing. Depending upon the value of RTT (round trip time), packet length and destination, the QoS module schedules the packet's flow by putting it into the appropriate position in the input queue of the outbound interface. If there is congestion in the queue, it is the responsibility of the QoS module to discard the packet. Finally the packet in the front of the queue is transmitted through the outbound interface card and an interrupt signal of successful transmission is sent to RPE processor to update some values in the routing table.

The Routing Protocol Engine (RPE). The non-time critical tasks are handled by the routing protocol engine or RPE. These mainly include tasks of (a) managing routing tables, (b) updating forwarding caches and (c) handling the control packets (Hello, Hello Reply, RREQ, RREP and RERR). Update in the forwarding caches for load balancing is also performed here periodically. The RPE consists of a general purpose processor, and its own memory modules to hold the routing table.

Once the RPE processor receives the interrupt signal from a PPE, it assumes that a header has been inserted in its input queue. If it's any of the control packets, the whole packet is also transferred from the PFE memory buffer to the RPE memory area. In all cases the header in the RPE's input queue contains a pointer to the memory location of the packet (whether it is in the PPE memory or in the RPE memory). An appropriate process is determined and scheduled to process the header in the front of the queue.

If the packet is not destined for the router itself then, after it has been processed, the appropriate outbound PFE is determined by consulting the central route table. The header is updated with the relevant next hop information and passed to the input queue of the outbound PFE with an interrupt signal to its PPE.

If the header corresponds to any of the control packets, the central routing table is updated with the new route information. The RPE periodically invalidates the aged entries in the central routing table and downloads the updated next hop information into the forwarding caches. The main advantage of having separate forwarding caches and routing table is that the forwarding caches only have to indicate the next hop entries for a particular destination. For this reason, the forwarding tables are much smaller and can be maintained in the cache of the PPE processor [14]. Decoupling the processing of route and next hop updates from the fast processing of the forwarding engines make them to work independently at a higher throughput. All the fast routers at present follow almost the same technique.

3   Operating System for the Routing Module

Previous sections had presented discussions about the hardware architecture for the SAHN routing protocol. In this section we will discuss to select an appropriate realtime operating system (RTOS) as a base for implementing the routing protocol. The RTOS must be able to execute the routing protocol properly and give us the option to port the final product into an embedded system.

Before going any further we may state the reason behind using a RTOS instead of a normal OS. The SAHN routing module is a real-time system since the time critical tasks have to be performed in real time. So, it is reasonable to use an appropriate real-time operating system (RTOS) to run the routing module. The RTOS for our purpose, should have the following properties.

- The higher-priority tasks must always be executed in preference to the lower-priority tasks. There should be support for fixed-priority preemptive scheduling for all of its tasks. Interrupt latency as well as the amount of time required to perform a context switch should be as small as possible. These are important because they represent overheads across the entire system.
- It must be as cheap as possible. Sometimes the RTOS source code is necessary to resolve problems with the application code.
- It has to be highly portable to various processor families as faster processors will continue to emerge. This makes the system more scalable to upcoming technologies. So, an application code written with the present RTOS can be used as a standardized piece of code for future projects.
- It must be capable of supporting multiple processors simultaneously. This is important as there are some tasks in the PFE and the RPE modules that may require their individual processing power at the same time to achieve desired performance.
- Its image should be small enough to fit in a small ROM/Flash-disk as our end product will be embedded.

	VxWorks Wind River System www.windriver.com	ThreadX Green Hills Software www.ghs.com	C Executive JMI Software Systems, Inc.	QNX Neutrino QNX Software Systems Ltd. www.qnx.com	RTLinux FSMLabs www.fsmlabs.com	LynxOS LynxWorks www.lynx.com	Embedix Lineo www.lineo.com	RTAI DIAPM RTAI www.aero.polimi.it/~rtai/ (many supports are provided by Lineo)
Target Supported	PowerPC, Coldfire, 68K, Intel Architecture, Intel StrongARM and XScale, ARM, SuperH, MIPS	PowerPC, Coldfire, 68K, MCORE, ARM7, ARM9, ARM/Thumb, StrongARM, SH, TriCore, XScale, StarCore, ZSP, i960, V8xx, MIPS	PowerPC, 29K, 68K, ColdFire, i960, MIPS, SH, SPARC, V800, MIPS	PowerPC, x86, 175PowerPCO A, MIPS	PowerPC, x86, Alpha6, MIPS	PowerPC, PowerQUICC, PowerQUICC II, Intel Architecture, MIPS	PowerPC, ColdFire, Dragonball, ARM 7 & 9, StrongARM, SuperH, x86/IA32, MIPS	PowerPC, x86 (with and without FPU and TSC), ARM (StrongARM; ARM7: clps711x-family, Cirrus Logic EP7xxx, CS89712), MIPS
Development Host	Self-Hosted	Self-Hosted	UNIX, Solaris, Windows	Self-Hosted, Linux, Solaris, Windows, QNX4	Linux	Solaris, SunOS, RS6000, LynxOS	Linux, Self-Hosted	Linux
Languages Supported	C, C++	C, C++	C, C++, Assembly	C, C++, Assembly, Java	C, C++	C, C++, Ada, Pascal, Java, Modula-2	C, C++	C, C++, PERL
Min ROM/RAM required (KB)	15/5	2/1	5/1	64/varies	1500/4000	37/11	10/10	2000/2000
Typical context switch time/Interrupt Latency(μs)	10	1.7(40MHz ARM7)/0.5(200MHz PowerPC)	3/2 (100MHz)	1.95/4.3(Pentium 133), 2.6/4.4(Pentium 100)	<30 (Interrupt Latency on 486/33MHz PC)	4 -19/14	7/15	4/20
Multitasking Strategy	Round-Robin, Time slice, Tasks can dynamically alter priorities, Rate monotonic Scheduling	Time slice, Fixed priority, Tasks can dynamically alter priorities	Time slice, Fixed priority, Tasks can dynamically alter priorities	Round-Robin, Time slice, Fixed Priority	One-shot, Time slice, Fixed Priority	Round Robin, Time slice, Fixed priority, Tasks can dynamically alter priorities, Rate monotonic		One-shot, Periodic
Multiprocessor Support	Yes	No	No	Yes	Yes	Yes	Yes	Yes
Source Code Included	No	Yes	No	No	Yes*	No	Yes*	Yes*
Base price (USD)	$3000-$4000	$7500+ (Royalty Free)	$2500 (Royalty Free)	$3,995 (run time $50/ seat)	Free. (Royalty free).		$149. (Royalty Free)	Free*

*as per GNU Public Licensing agreement

Fig. 7. Comparison among various RTOSs

- It should have a familiar development environment, possibly POSIX compliant. Familiarity and competence with the development environment rather than struggling with a new working platform can effectively reduce the development time of any software product.

Taking the aforementioned properties as the quantitative measures, we have made comparisons among some of the well reputed RTOSs in the current market. These have been summarized in Fig. 7. Readers are referred to [15], [16], [17], [18] for more details. Some relative comparisons have been presented graphically in Fig. 8 from an analysis performed by University of Wisconsin.

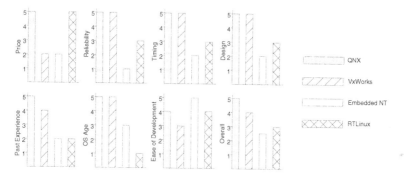

Fig. 8. Relative comparison among various RTOSs

It is apparent from these figures, the RTOSs providing more scalable properties (different types of processor support, less ROM/RAM requirements etc) tend to be far more expensive in terms of both upfront costs and recurring royalty/licensing fees. Some of them are not provided with source codes. So, initially we have decided to work with the RTOSs which are freely available like RTLinux or RTAI (They are free under GNU Public Licensing agreement). Their underlying Linux kernels can give the flexibility to develop and test our SAHN routing modules in any Linux system. Moreover there have been some real world tests and performance evaluations of ad-hoc routing protocols[19][20][21] in the Linux environment. All these experimental setups were based upon the Linux kernel for its familiarity, robustness, and more importantly, free availability. Though it is evident from Fig. 7 that the Linux solutions require more memory, memory is getting cheaper day by day.

At the end here is a simple argument for our intention to use an of-the-shelf RTOS rather than building one of our own. Our routing module is separated into simple smaller modules (RPE, PPE etc). Each of them can be implemented in a smaller embedded system. In that case we may not need the complicated scheduling, context switching of any available RTOS. Each of the small modules can have their own lower abstraction layer written by us. But initially it will be time consuming to write and test our own RTOS. A better approach is to create the application layer (the SAHN routing module) and test it with an appropriate of-the-shelf RTOS. We will make the routing module as general as possible so that it can be ported to any RTOS for performance evaluation. In future it can be integrated with our own optimized RTOS.

4   Conclusion

In this paper we have proposed a possible design outline and implementation framework for an efficient on-demand routing protocol suitable for ad-hoc community networks, such as the SAHN. At present we are developing and testing our routing protocol in the GLOMOSIM (ver2.03). We have also built a testbed with desktop PCs to test our work in real environment. Each of these PCs acts as a SAHN node. Currently a node is capable of communicating with other two nodes through wireline networking technology. Eventually this wireline network will be replaced by wireless networking and each of the PCs by individual integrated routing modules as proposed in Section 2. Though we believe that more optimizations and changes may be required during prototype implementation and testing, the proposed architecture and survey analyses can be adapted to many ad-hoc community networks.

References

1. 24/01/2003. http://www.wirelessanarchy.com.
2. R. Pose and C. Kopp. Bypassing the home computing bottleneck: The suburban area network. *3rd Australasian Comp. Architecture Conf. (ACAC)*, pages 87–100, Feb 1998.

3. E. Makalic A. Bickerstaffe and S. Garic. CS honours theses, Monash Uni, 2001. www.csse.monash.edu.au/~rdp/SAN/.
4. D.B. Johnson. Routing in ad-hoc networks of mobile hosts. Technical report, IEEE Workshop on Mobile Computing systems and Applications, Dec. 1994.
5. Royer E.M. Perkins C.E. and Das S.R. Adhoc on demand distance vector (AODV) routing. IETF Internet Draft, Nov. 2000. http://www.ietf.org/internet-drafts/draft-ietf-manet-aodv-07.txt.
6. R. Pose M. M. Islam and C. Kopp. Efficient Routing in Suburban Ad-Hoc Networks (SAHN). *The 2003 International Conference on Communications in Computing (CIC 2003)*, June 23-26 2003. In Press. Las Vegas, USA.
7. R. Pose M. M. Islam and C. Kopp. Routing In Suburban Ad-Hoc Networks. *The 2003 International Conference on Computer Science and its Applications(ICCSA 2003)*, July 1-2 2003. In Press. San Diego , California , USA.
8. Aweya James. Ip router architectures: An overview. Nortel Networks. Ottawa, Canada, K1Y 4H7, 05/01/2003. http://www.owlnet.rice.edu/~elec696/papers/-aweya99.pdf.
9. A new architecture for switch and router design, 05/01/2003. http://www.pmc-sierra.com/pressRoom/pdf/lcs_wp.pdf.
10. G. Minshall P. Newman and L. Huston. Ip switching and gigabit routers. *IEEE Comms. Magazine*, Jan. 1997.
11. Sayrafian Kamran. Overview of switch fabric architectures, July 2002. http://www.zagrosnetworks.com.
12. N. Uzan S. Papavassiliou and J. Yang. The architecture design for a terabit ip switch router. *IEEE Workshop on High Performance Switching and Routing*, pages 358–362, 2001.
13. Gigabit networking: High-speed routing and switching, 05/01/2003. http://www.cis.ohio-state.edu/~jain/cis788-97/gigabit_nets/.
14. C. Partridge et al. A 50-gb/s ip router. *IEEE/ACM Transactions on Networking*, 6:237–248, June 1998.
15. Dedicated systems encyclopedia, 12/11/2002. http://www.realtimeinfo.be/encyc/-BuyersGuide/RTOS/Dir228.html.
16. Embedded systems programming, 12/01/2003. http://www.embedded.com/story/-OEG20021212S0061.
17. SDTimes software development, 13/01/2003. http://www.sdtimes.com/news/027/-emb4.htm.
18. i Appliance Web, 13/01/2003. http://www.iapplianceweb.com/appDirectory/-IAW_OPERATING_SYSTEMS.
19. S. Desilva and S.R. Das. Experimental evaluation of a wireless ad hoc network. *9th Int. Conf. on Computer Comms. and Networks (IC3N), Las Vegas*, Oct. 2000.
20. E.M. Royer and C.E. Perkins. An implementation study of the AODV routing protocol. *EEE Wireless Comms. and Networking Conf. (WCNC)*, 3:1003–1008, 2000.
21. S.J. Lee S.H. Bae and M. Gerla. Multicast protocol implementation and validation in an ad hoc network testbed. *IEEE Intl. Conf. on Comms. (ICC)*, 10:3196–3200, 2001.

Author Index